The Postmodernism Debate in Latin America

a boundary 2 book

The Postmodernism

Debate in Latin America

Edited by John Beverley, Michael Aronna, and José Oviedo

DUKE UNIVERSITY PRESS   Durham and London 1995

© 1995 Duke University Press
All rights reserved
Printed in the United States of America on acid-free
paper ∞
Typeset in Helvetica by Tseng Information Systems, Inc.
Library of Congress Cataloging-in-Publication Data
appear on the last printed page of this book.
The text of this book was originally published as volume
20, number 3 of *boundary 2: an international journal of
literature and culture,* with the exception of the following
additional material: Neil Larsen, "Postmodernism and
Imperialism"; María Milagros López, "Postwork Society
and Postmodern Subjectivities"; Raquel Olea,
"Feminism: Modern or Postmodern?"; Roberto Schwarz,
"National by Imitation"; and The Declaration from the
Lacandon Jungle of the Zapatista National Liberation
Army. Permissions appear on last printed page.

Contents

Note to This Edition

For this edition of *The Postmodernism Debate in Latin America* we have added essays by Neil Larsen, María Milagros López, Raquel Olea, and Roberto Schwarz, and the text of the Declaration of the Zapatista National Liberation Army. We have modified our introduction somewhat to reflect these additions and have also made some minor corrections in the text.

We would like to dedicate this collection to the memory of two colleagues whose voices, raised on opposite sides of this debate, are now joined in death: Agustín Cueva of Ecuador and Francisco Lopes of Brazil.

The Postmodernism Debate in Latin America

Introduction

John Beverley and José Oviedo

There is something about the very idea of a Latin American post-modernism that makes one think of that condition of colonial or neocolonial dependency in which goods that have become shopworn or out of fashion in the metropolis are, like the marvels of the gypsies in *One Hundred Years of Solitude,* exported to the periphery, where they enjoy a profitable second life. For surely after all the articles, books, conferences, exhibitions, videos, and performances, after Lyotard and Habermas, Madonna and Baudrillard, the concept of postmodernism has itself begun to be devoured by habitu-alization and to lose the power of aesthetic *ostranenie* that recommended it to our attention in the first place. Yet, it is precisely at this point that, in the last four or five years, it has come to the top of the agenda of Latin American cultural, political, and theoretical debate.

It is the purpose of this collection to give some sense of what this engagement has involved, less to present a "regional" variant of postmod-ernism than to resituate the concept itself, which risks being colonized by Anglo-European provincialism, in a more genuinely international framework (by the year 2000, Latin America will have twice the population of the United States). More particularly, in a context in which the argument for postmod-ernism has been made mainly from anti- (or post-) Marxist positions, and in which a visceral anti-postmodernism has predominated among sectors of the traditional left, it seemed important to us to offer a vision of the Latin American discussion that not only emphasized its affinity with the project of the left but also saw it as an important means of renovating the left's exhausted or discredited political imaginary.

Postmodern seems a particularly inappropriate term for nation-states and social formations that are usually thought of as not yet having gone through the stage of modernity, in Weber's sense of the term, or, perhaps more exactly, that display an "uneven modernity" (what society does not, however?). To compound the problem, the words modernismo and posmodernismo designate in Latin American Spanish early-twentieth-century literary movements that have no direct correspondence to what are generally understood as modernism and postmodernism in English.[1] Noting the anachronism, Octavio Paz has argued that postmodernism is yet another imported grand récit (like liberalism?) that does not fit Latin America, which needs to produce its own forms of cultural periodization. He has been echoed in this claim, from the other side of the political spectrum, by Marxist critics such as Nelson Osorio.[2] There was, moreover, a clear coincidence between the appearance and spread of postmodernism in Western Europe and the United States and the political hegemony of the New Right in the 1980s, a coincidence that gives some credence to the idea that postmodernism is a new form of cultural imperialism, the "American International," as Andreas Huyssen once put it.[3] There is the related danger that—as in

1. The not quite identical Spanish equivalent of modernism is vanguardismo, not modernismo, so that by the logic of the Anglo-European narrative, postmodernism as a stylistic concept should be posvanguardismo. Posmodernismo designates, in Spanish American literary history, a short-lived and transitional movement in poetry around 1910 in reaction to the hegemony of modernista aestheticism (its manifesto was a sonnet by a Mexican poet that began with the words, "Wring the neck of the swan!"). But, as the essays gathered here indicate, posmodernismo in the Anglo-European sense is now coming into general usage in both Spain and Latin America. The situation is different in Brazil, where modernismo and posmodernismo already correspond to the English meanings, with the qualification that modernismo designates both a specific movement in Brazilian poetry and modernism as an international style or movement.

2. See Octavio Paz, "El romanticismo y la poesía contemporánea," Vuelta 11, no. 127 (1987): 26–27; Osorio's remarks are in the transcription of a debate on postmodernism at a 1988 Dartmouth symposium on Latin American literary criticism, Revista de Crítica Literaria Latinoamericana 29 (1989): 146–48.

3. It is worth recalling here that the rise of the New Right was itself prepared in part by the imposition of reactionary military dictatorships in the Southern Cone countries of Latin America in the early 1970s, and that Ronald Reagan launched himself as a national can-

the case of Baudrillard's writings on the United States—the production of a postmodernist "sublime" in relation to Latin America may involve the aesthetic fetishization of its social, cultural, and economic status quo, thereby attenuating the urgency for radical social change and displacing it into cultural dilettantism and quietism. George Yúdice, who has been perhaps the most astute commentator on the question of Latin American postmodernism in this country, notes along these lines that "to celebrate 'parasitism' (whose Latin American correlate is the problem of informal economies) or the hyperreal (which in Latin America is wrought by the hyperinflationary effects of the external debt and narcotraffic) is like cheerleading on the sidelines as neoconservatives sell out the country."[4]

These reservations, however, also seem to miss something of the nature of postmodernism itself, the way it is bound up with the dynamics of interaction between local cultures and an instantaneous and omnipresent global culture, in which the center-periphery model of the world system, dominant since the sixteenth century, has begun to break down.[5] In Fredric Jameson's influential essay "Postmodernism, or the Cultural Logic of Late Capitalism"[6]—now itself a cultural fact of global postmodernity—postmodernism, in its most general sense, is a periodizing concept whose function is to correlate the emergence of new formal features in culture with the technological, economic, and social features of the new, transnational stage of capitalism, which is now beginning to envelop even the formerly semi-autarkic space of the Communist bloc countries and the remaining "underdeveloped" (i.e., precapitalist) spaces of the Third World. It is undoubtedly true that Jameson's totalizing construction of postmodernism involves, as Aijaz Ahmad has argued, "a suppression of the multiplicity of significant difference among and within both the advanced capitalist coun-

didate in the mid-1970s around his opposition to the Panama Canal Treaty negotiated by Kissinger during the Nixon and Ford administrations.

4. See his "Postmodernity and Transnational Capitalism in Latin America," in On Edge: The Crisis of Contemporary Latin American Culture, ed. George Yúdice, Jean Franco, and Juan Flores (Minneapolis: University of Minnesota Press, 1992), 1–28. The Argentine novelist Ricardo Piglia made the same point more epigrammatically when he noted in conversation, "Postmodernism means the poor are wrong."

5. A useful, if not unproblematic, overview of this is Immanuel Wallerstein, Geopolitics and Geoculture (Cambridge: Cambridge University Press, 1992).

6. Fredric Jameson, "Postmodernism, or the Cultural Logic of Late Capitalism," New Left Review 146 (1984): 53–92. Jameson's essay was published in Portuguese in 1985 in the Brazilian journal Novos Estudos and in Spanish in 1986 in Casa de las Américas.

tries and the imperialised formations"[7]—a point Nelly Richard and Carlos Rincón echo in their critiques here of the ethnocentrism of the dominant concept of postmodernism. Globalization of capital and communications does not mean homogenization; if anything, it tends to aggravate the normal capitalist dynamics of combined and uneven development (we have come to understand that the "primitive accumulation" is not only a feature of the *origins* of capitalism), producing, as in the earlier moment of Lenin's *Imperialism,* the welter of conflicting national, ethnic, and regional particularisms that is the stuff of the international news these days. On the other hand, there is a sense in which many contemporary "Third World" cultural expressions may be seen as postmodern, even in the very heterogeneity and specificity of their aesthetic-ideological strategies: for example, Kenyan novelist Ngugi wa Thiongo's decision to abandon the novel and write mainly in Kikuyu; Rigoberta Menchú's striking testimonial narrative of Indian resistance in Guatemala, *I, Rigoberta Menchú;* the pan-American cultural politics of Cuba's Casa de las Américas; South African township jive music; Mahasweta Devi's Bengali stories (and their translation and commentary by Gayatri Spivak); contemporary Filipino film; the punk-rock culture of the Medellín slums portrayed in the extraordinary Colombian film *Rodrigo D— No Future;* John Leguiamo's performance piece on U.S. Latino culture, *Spic-O-Rama;* or Los Angeles *gangsta* rap. It follows that for Jameson, the choice is not between a metropolitan postmodernism and something that is clearly other than it but rather between different ideological "spins" that can be given to postmodernism, what Jameson likes to call an "aesthetics of cognitive mapping."

The Latin American voices included here will qualify this claim with the recognition that, rather than something that emanates from an advanced capitalist center outward toward a still dependent neocolonial periphery (conveniently leaving the power of agency in the hands of the center), what Jameson means by postmodernism might be better understood as precisely the *effect* in that center of postcoloniality. The engagement with postmodernism in Latin America does not take place around the theme of the end of modernity that is so prominent in its Anglo-European manifestations; it concerns, rather, the complexity of Latin America's own "uneven modernity" and the new developments of its hybrid (pre- and post-) modern cultures. (José Joaquín Brunner argues that postmodernism is, in effect, the specific form modernity takes in Latin America.)

7. Aijaz Ahmad, "Jameson's Rhetoric of Otherness and the 'National Allegory,'" *Social Text* 17 (1987), 3.

The character of this engagement has had to do, above all, with its relation to the crisis of the project of the Latin American left in the wake of its defeat and/or demobilization in the period from 1973 to the present.[8] The Cuban Revolution in 1959 inaugurated a new historical dynamic in Latin America—the possibility of an alternative, noncapitalist Latin American modernity—which, however, it was unable to sustain in the face of the determination of the United States to retain its hegemony over the region. A number of interrelated developments indicate the containment and eventual exhaustion of this dynamic. These include the failure, at the end of the 1960s, of both the armed struggle strategy represented by the guerrilla *foco* and the "peaceful road to socialism" represented by Salvador Allende's coalition-building electoral politics in Chile; the eventual problematization of Cuba itself as a model for an achieved socialist society in the context of the unraveling of communism in the Soviet Union and Eastern Europe as a consequence of *perestroika;* the Sandinistas' defeat in the 1990 elections in Nicaragua, which brought to an end one of the most promising experiments in finding a non-Communist form of Latin American revolutionary nationalism; the growing role of the (for the most part privately owned) mass media, particularly television, in determining the Latin American cultural imaginary, displacing previous print-based models of cultural hegemony; the stagnation or endemic corruption of the nationalized sectors of Latin American economies; the consequent attraction of neoliberal political economy for important sectors of the Latin American bourgeoisie and intelligentsia previously tied to nationalist paradigms; and the changes in the nature of the intelligentsia itself and in its relation to the state and transnational organisms brought by the combined effects of military repression and economic internationalization. As Norbert Lechner profiles in the essay included here, which has become perhaps the best-known anatomy of the postmodern turn in Latin America, all of these factors led to a pervasive climate of "disenchantment" and a demand for a new "political realism" or "depolarization," in which the nationalist and leftist ideologies that had defined the protagonism of the Latin American intelligentsia in the previous period have been either put on hold or simply abandoned.

In the context of the crisis of the traditional left and the waning of the right-wing military dictatorships imposed to contain its force in the 1970s, the theme of democratization has played the same role in the Latin American discussion of postmodernism as the shift in aesthetic-epistemological

8. The best account is perhaps Jorge Castañeda, *Utopia Unarmed: The Latin American Left after the Cold War* (New York: Alfred Knopf, 1993).

paradigms did in Anglo-European postmodernism. The impulse for the latter came mainly from the humanities and art criticism; in Latin America it has come, as the balance of our selections suggests, from the social sciences, with this proviso: that in assuming the problematic of postmodernism, the Latin American social sciences have also begun to assume an obligation to take on problems that were posed initially in the humanities, particularly in advanced literary and cultural theory.

The restructuring of the Latin American social sciences in recent years has involved, among other things, the emergence of distinct transnational organizations for theoretical work on culture and society. These include, for example, the Center for the Study of State and Society in Argentina (CEDES); Venezuela's Centro de Estudios Latinoamericanos "Rómulo Gallegos" (CELARG); the Latin American Faculty for Social Sciences in Santiago de Chile (FLACSO); the Brazilian Center for Analysis and Planning (CEBRAP) in São Paulo; the vast conglomeration of intellectuals in or around the National University of Mexico (UNAM) and the Colegio de México; and as a coordinating center for these, and other national or regional organizations of the same type, the Latin American Council of Social Sciences (CLACSO) in Buenos Aires, formerly headed by Fernando Calderón. Many of our contributors are connected with one or another of these organizations.[9]

As noted, what in general has defined the agenda of these think tanks and networks has been the problem of the long-term viability of democratic construction in Latin America, particularly in the face of the worst economic crisis it has experienced in this century. Partly because of the crisis, this concern has involved a shift away from the equation of democratization with economic modernization, which prevailed across the political spectrum in different ideological forms ranging from dependency theory to the Alliance for Progress in the 1950s and 1960s but whose main expression was probably the work of the Economic Commission on Latin America (CEPAL). By contrast, the experience of the technocratic military dictator-

9. Among the first important representations of the Latin American postmodernism discussion were the special issue of the CLACSO journal *David y Goliath* 52 (1987) and the subsequent collection, *Imágenes desconocidas: La modernidad en la encrucijada posmoderna* (Buenos Aires: CLACSO, 1988), both edited by Calderón. For a negative appraisal of the transnationalization of the Latin American intelligentsia, however, see James Petras, "The Metamorphosis of Latin America's Intellectuals," *Latin American Perspectives* 65 (Spring 1990): 102–12; and, with Michael Morley, *Latin America in the Time of Cholera* (New York: Routledge, 1992).

ships in Brazil, Chile, Argentina, and Uruguay in the 1970s demonstrated not only that democratization did not necessarily follow economic modernization but also that political modernity (democracy, formal rights, full citizenship, etc.) might, under certain conditions, actually be an *impediment* to economic modernization under neoliberal capitalist auspices.

What began to displace both modernization and dependency models, therefore, was an interrogation of the interrelation between the respective "spheres" (culture, ethics, politics, etc.) of modernity, an interrogation that required of social scientists a new concern with subjectivity and identity as well as new understandings of, and tolerance for, the cultural, religious, and ethnic heterogeneity of Latin America. In the 1970s, this led to a wide reading, or rereading, of Gramsci that institutionalized a neo-Gramscian language among many Latin American intellectuals. This was followed in the 1980s by the impact of Foucault (and, less so, Derrida), Habermas, Baudrillard, feminist theory, and a general "return to Weber" evident in many of the contributions here.

A landmark in the redefinition of the Latin American social sciences was CLACSO's conference entitled "The Social Conditions of Democracy," held in Costa Rica in 1978, which, if it did not exactly inaugurate the idea of the crisis of Latin American modernity (which is as old as the endemic crisis of Latin American liberalism itself), certainly highlighted it in the wake of the problematization of the alternative project of modernity represented by Cuba and the Left. As a follow-up, now explicitly recognizing the failure of the Left and the epistemological collapse of previous models of Latin American development, in 1987 CLACSO launched a project portentously titled "The Social Sciences, Crisis, and the Need for New Paradigms of the Relationship between State, Society, and the Economy."

As the statement of the Latin American Subaltern Studies Group evidences, this new sense of modernity as paradoxical and contradictory has led to, among other things, a self-interrogation of the intelligentsia itself, a questioning of the linkage between the state and intellectuals as designers of the future, or, what may amount to the same thing, between the cultural practices of hegemony developed by elites and the disciplinary discourses of the humanities and social sciences that seek to study these practices. This has been not only a matter of self-criticism and paradigm shifts, however. New, "horizontal" relations between intellectuals and both new and traditional social movements are emerging with the redefinition of political agency suggested by postmodernist perspectives. Xavier Albó's reworking of the parameters of national identity in Latin America, for example, is connected to his work with grass-roots indigenous peoples organizations in Bolivia, work that has included, among other things, writing radio soap opera scripts in Aymara. The idea has been to move from a politics (and epistemology) of representation to one of solidarity and participation.

Perhaps the greatest failure of our collection, in this respect, has been its inability to connect, except in passing, the postmodernist turn with the rapid and extensive spread of feminism and women's organizations in Latin America in the last ten or fifteen years.[10] We share with Nelly Richard the belief that the rise of a Latin American feminism (and the questioning of hegemonic gender identity formations generally) may be, in the long run, the most radical, and radicalizing, expression of a Latin American post-modernism. As Raquel Olea details here, it is also, however, a limitation of the postmodernist discussion in Latin America today (and by no means only there) that, while it assumes the feminist critique of phallocentrism and celebrates the "practice" of new social movements that challenge traditional divisions between the political and the experiential, the public and the private, its "theoretical" dimension is still largely articulated by male intellectuals.

This brings us to another area that could also be better represented in our collection: the relation between postmodernism and Latin American religion, particularly its intersections (and divergences) with liberation theology. The contribution here by Enrique Dussel suggests some of the issues involved in the critique of modernity being undertaken by Latin American philosophers and theologians such as himself, Gustavo Gutiérrez, and Leonardo Boff. In a contribution to the CLACSO seminar mentioned above, Franz Hinkelammert characterizes the post-Medellín reforms in the Latin American church as a reaction to the loss of subjectivity in a world dominated by economism. As in Daniel Bell's idea of the "spiritual crisis" induced by consumer society, Hinkelammert sees the "return" of religion in Latin America as, in effect, a postmodernist phenomenon that acts to contest the self-referential "scientific" rationalization of modernity by reinstating questions of meaning, identity, and belief at the center of social life.[11]

10. For overviews of this phenomenon, see *The Women's Movements in Latin America: Feminism and the Transition to Democracy,* ed. Jane Jacquette (Boston: Unwin Hyman, 1989); Nancy Saporta Sternbach, Marysa Navarro Aranguren, Patricia Chuchryk, and Sonia Alvarez, "Feminisms in Latin America," in *The Making of Social Movements in Latin America,* ed. Arturo Escobar and Sonia Alvarez (Boulder: Westview, 1992); and Jean Franco, "Going Public: Reinhabiting the Private," in *On Edge,* 65–83.
11. Franz Hinkelammert, "Frente a la cultura de la postmodernidad: Proyecto político y utopia," *David y Goliath* 52 (1987). See also his *Crítica de la razón utópica* (DEI: Costa

There is also the possibility, suggested here by Norbert Lechner, that the renewed force of religion in Latin American life marks precisely a reaction against postmodernity and its well-known penchant for hybridity, relativism, and heterogeneity, its aesthetic hedonism, its antiessentialism, and its rejection of "great narratives" (which are often precisely narratives of redemption). One form of this reaction may be seen in the articulations, imported from the United States, between right-wing politics and religious fundamentalism, which have made major inroads among poor and working-class communities in countries such as Brazil and Guatemala. Such a reaction, however, is also implicit in the call of religious figures identified with the left, such as Nicaragua's Ernesto Cardenal or Dussel himself, to reconstitute Latin America's tradition of utopian thinking. As the conclusion of Dussel's piece makes clear, the discourse of liberation theology, like the radical hermeneutic practices of the Christian base communities it is the theoretical expression of, aims to displace Eurocentric conceptions of both modernity *and* postmodernity in favor of an entirely different theoretical and historical register. As the exercise of a "preferential option for the poor," it is not only *about* otherness and subalternity; as in the "fictions" of Borges and García Márquez discussed by Carlos Rincón, or the *testimonio,* its point is also to constitute another (an Other) way of thinking and feeling, which Dussel calls the project of a "trans-" (rather than post-) modernity.

As a critique of and practical response to capitalist modernity, in other words, liberation theology is itself part of the postmodernist turn in Latin America. At the same time, liberation theology contests positions and attitudes often associated with postmodernism in the name of a narrative of historical continuity and redemption that it composes out of elements taken from traditional Marxism, Christian eschatology, and popular and indigenous cultural memory. Whereas postmodernism emphasizes new forms of secular cultural and aesthetic agency, the theological critique of modernity seeks to reassert the central place of the sacred and of organized religion in Latin American life. What is clear in either case—and it would be useful to see liberation theology as itself constituted by the tension between these alternatives—is that in Latin America, utopian impulses are not disappearing with postmodern "disenchantment"; rather, as Aníbal Quijano and Xavier Albó make explicit in their contributions here—both of which have as a point of reference the sociocultural proposals of the native peoples of

---

Rica, 1984); José Mardónes's *Postmodernidad y cristianismo: El desafío del fragmento* (Santander: Editorial Sal Terrae, 1988); and Pablo Morande's influential *Cultura y modernización en América Latina* (Santiago de Chile: Universidad Católica de Chile, 1984).

the Andes—they are being redefined in tension with the uncertainty and openness of Latin America's future.

Despite our own evident bias in favor of the postmodern turn, we have tried to build into this selection a representation of pro and con positions in the debate, with Martín Hopenhayn's essay situating itself consciously at the center and Nelly Richard's and Hernán Vidal's at the respective extremes (Richard is the editor of the journal that Vidal profiles in his piece). Even Vidal's essay, however, which is perhaps the most overtly anti-postmodernist in the collection, ends in its declaration of affective solidarity with the project it critiques and in its appeal to study cultural-political "micro-situations" on something of a postmodernist note itself, an irony the author himself is aware of. We would be remiss, then, if we did not represent the elements of the much stronger critique of postmodernism that has been prevalent in many sectors of the Latin American left. We are fortunate to have available for this purpose Neil Larsen's polemic "Postmodernism and Imperialism: Theory and Politics in Latin America" which has itself become a part of the Latin American debate.[12]

In our opinion, however, what Larsen's and similar critiques of post-modernism from the left betray (and what they share with Habermas's *The Philosophical Discourse of Modernity*) is the discomfort of the "traditional intellectual"—in Gramsci's sense of the term—in the face of the emergence of both subaltern and commodified mass cultures, and the corresponding nostalgia for a rational politics of clearly defined class parties, based on the assumption of a transparency of representation between class position, self-consciousness as a historical agent, party, and strategic line. This is surely a transparency that not only a "culturalist" emphasis on the relative autonomy of the political but even a modest appreciation of the reality of the unconscious in human life seriously puts into question. It is not to denigrate the capacity for enlightenment of the masses that a postmodernist position emphasizes subjectivity and cultural relativity; rather, it is to underline that the intellectuals and political organizers who are supposed to be the bearers of this enlightenment are also constructed as subjects in the field of desire, and that a politics that does not pass the test of this field will fail.

What is at stake in the Latin American discussion is the relation of the problem of democratization and social integration to the new sense of cultural and aesthetic agency postmodernism posits. From a postmodernist perspective, the left needs to make of aesthetic experience itself—or, more

12. A Spanish translation appeared in *Modernidad y postmodernidad en América Latina* 1, ed. Jorge Ruffinelli, a special issue of *Nuevo Texto Crítico* 6 (1990).

broadly, symbolic production and consumption—both a place of resistance to actually existing forms of domination and exploitation and an enactment of new forms of community, work, and pleasure. This is the theme of María Milagros López's essay on postwork conditions in contemporary Puerto Rico, which describes what some of the implications of the debate are for public policy. Such a shift involves, as Néstor García Canclini and Silviano Santiago (the latter, significantly, a convert from literary criticism) suggest most urgently among the contributors here, also accepting the challenge of mass culture and the mass media rather than simply dismissing these as sites for the production of false consciousness, as tends to be the case in the dominant model of Latin American media studies, constructed around a synthesis of dependency theory and Frankfurt school critique. Beatriz Sarlo's dissection of the role of electronic simulacra in the production of the Latin American political imaginary in her essay here is closer to this model, by contrast, and as such dialogues directly with Santiago's enthusiasm for television. Also close to a Frankfurt school perspective is Roberto Schwarz's careful anatomy of "cultural copying" in the formation of Brazilian national culture.

Larsen is correct to note (he is certainly not alone in this) that what is problematic in the micropolitics of the new social movements, as in the contingent aesthetic celebration of alterity, marginality, and pastiche, is the lack of any overall strategy for hegemony beyond the sometimes feverish activity of the individual groups or an ad hoc alliance politics, since, by definition, no issue or contradiction is, or can be made, central. As Nelly Richard puts it cogently in her piece here, "Celebrating difference . . . is not the same as giving the subject of this difference the right to negotiate its own conditions of discursive control, to practice its difference in the interventionist sense of rebellion and disturbance."

While it is clear that the new social movements need not be explicitly anticapitalist, nonetheless capitalism, which has a stake in maintaining conditions of subalternity and exploitation of all sorts, represents a limit-condition to their full development. José Joaquín Brunner goes perhaps the furthest of all the contributors here in suggesting that Marxism, even in the neo-Gramscian mode from which his own work comes, has become an impediment rather than a stimulus for working through the new political, economic, and cultural processes that Latin American societies are experiencing. It is worth keeping in mind, however, that the force of class struggle is not entirely suspended in postmodernist "heterologies": Some of the most powerful of the new social movements are precisely the kinds of union organizations and union-community coalitions that have sprung up in the wake of the effects of the globalization of capital, such as the Brazilian metalworkers' union or the COSATU in South Africa. Nor is a postmodernist politics necessarily only an "antipolitics" of aesthetic vanguardism or dispersed single-issue or identity-politics groups, though this is certainly its most characteristic manifestation. We differ among ourselves about the nature and validity of the Sandinista project in Nicaragua; but we agree that, even in defeat (and precisely because of their commitment to implement and to respect democratic processes in the face of massive foreign aggression and interference), the Sandinistas are exemplary of the emergence of a postmodernist, but still explicitly socialist, form of political agency in Latin America. Along similar lines, we could also point to the evolution of FMLN-FDR in El Salvador from a coalition of Leninist sects to a broad multilayered left movement embracing electoral parties, guerrilla groups, trade unions, cultural fronts, and "popular organizations"; the Brazilian Workers Party, which sponsored the candidacy of Lula (along with the South African ANC, it is one of the few movements we know of in which poststructuralist intellectuals coexist peacefully and productively with unionized auto workers); the dynamic growth of Latin American women's groups and feminism we noted earlier; the sort of labor cum ecological activism that Chico Mendes represented in the Amazon region before his assassination; Rigoberta Menchú's Committee of Campesino Unity in Guatemala and other established or emerging organizations of indigenous peoples; the left electoral coalition that developed around Cuauhtemoc Cárdenas in Mexico, now formalized as the Democratic Revolutionary Party (PRD), that García Canclini mentions in his interview here; the Movement toward Socialism (MAS) and the more grass roots–based Causa R in Venezuela; and now the dramatic possibilities opened up by the sudden explosion of the Zapatista National Liberation Army, whose First Declaration we include here, onto the scene of Latin American politics.

Unlike traditional Communist or Socialist parties, such formations need to retain within themselves a heterogeneity of new social movements and even class components (this requirement is also the source of their internal problems and contradictions, since they have to appease groups whose interests may be structurally incompatible—as the very distinct cases of Solidarity in Poland and the Sandinistas in Nicaragua illustrate). As Fernando Calderón explains here, these formations explicitly seek to distance themselves from the "vertical" mobilization of the masses from above and from the corresponding politics of "representation" that were the mainstays of Latin America leftism and populism in the early and middle decades of this century. Yet, like populism, they also seek to raise majority support for a political project built on a more or less coherent social vision and policy guidelines, and on a set of values to give these legitimacy— a project that ultimately touches on the question of state power itself (not only who has it but also what the state is). They are, in our view, parties or political formations of a new type, which hold the promise of the possible reconstruction of the Latin American left under the conditions of postmodernity.

At the same time, we need to recognize that, because by virtue of postmodernism's very critique of essentialism there is no *necessary* connection between it and the left, a postmodernism of the right (on the model of what Stuart Hall has called Thatcher's "authoritarian populism" in Great Britain) is also flourishing in Latin America, represented, among other things, by the presidential campaigns of both Mario Vargas Llosa and Fujimori in Peru; the media populism of Menem in Argentina and Collor in Brazil (whose impeachment adds a happy and unexpected twist to the story); Hernando de Soto's neoliberal economic manifesto *The Other Path;* the complex politics and economics of narcoterrorism; the current transformation of Mexico in response to the North American Free Trade Agreement; or (to name the capital of this postmodernism of the Right) Miami. And to indicate that the left should learn to operate on new terrain in new ways does not, of course, guarantee that it can or will; witness its current impasse in the Southern Cone countries from which many of our contributors come, despite its intimate and courageous participation in the process of redemocratization there.

It may also be the case that the terrible ravages inflicted on the social fabric of Latin America by neoliberal economic policies in the last decade are producing the possibility of the revival of an overtly revolutionary politics. If that is true, and if the problems of the Latin American left are seen from the perspective (which in one form would be that of Shining Path in Peru) that there already exists a model of party building and political struggle that simply has not been implemented effectively, or that the failure of this or that leftist strategy was due mainly to the force of U.S. destabilization rather than to problems internal to it, then the effort to relate postmodernism and the project of the left in Latin America should be seen not only as "culturalist" but also as potentially demoralizing and divisive—something like an attempt to yuppify left cultural politics. The lesson of Chiapas on this score has been ambiguous: is it a "return" to the *foco* model of the sixties or a new, postmodernist form of political mobilization?

What is clear to everyone involved in the Latin America debate, however, is that if socialism failed in the form it took in the Soviet Union and Eastern Europe, by the same token "actually existing" capitalism continues to fail the majority of Latin Americans, whose standards of living, never high in the first place, have deteriorated spectacularly in the last decade or so. The question remains, then (and if it has a vaguely *mode rétro* ring, that is because the circumstances are similar), What is to be done?

Meanwhile, the judgment of Latin America on *its* other (and since this collection is intended mainly for a North American audience, it is useful to recognize that the Latin American other is also looking at you) is now almost a century old. Speaking in the Cuban Senate in 1904 against accepting the imposition of the Platt Amendment, which was to distort and cripple the Republic of Cuba in its moment of origin, Salvador Cisneros Betancourt noted of the United States: "They should remember that there is no such thing as a small enemy, and that the twentieth century will end with their decadence, and they will figure no more among the leading nations of the world" (our thanks to Roberto Fernández Retamar for this quotation).

But there is another way to read Betancourt's prophecy, a way that reminds us that the traditional polarization between the United States and Latin America has served elite interests in both regions and that recognizes, at the same time, the partial unraveling of the hegemony of economic neoliberalism with the appearance of new political and social possibilities in the Americas. The United States itself, with a Spanish-surnamed population of some twenty-five million, has now become the fifth-largest nation of the Hispanic world (out of twenty) and by the millennium will be the third or fourth. If, as we have argued here, the postmodernism debate in Latin America has been closely linked to the process of democratization (cultural, economic, political, etc.) in that region, then surely it is significant that by the year 2076, the tricentennial of the American Revolution, a majority of the population of the United States will be of African, Native American, Asian, or Latino descent. If postmodernist theory has focused on the "microphysics" of power and has been up to now limited in its consequences to the university, the art world, and avant-garde social movements, there is, in the light of this demographic mutation, the possibility (suggested most strongly here in the essays of Martín Hopenhayn and María Milagros López) of its

intersection with macroinstitutional policies and reforms at the level of state
and transnational organisms. The margin is becoming the center.

There is now a fairly extensive bibliography on the question of postmodernism and Latin America, including several major collections in Spanish and Portuguese. That this was not the case five years ago, when we
originally conceived the idea for this collection, is some measure of the importance the topic has acquired. The purpose of a collection such as this,
directed mainly to a North American audience, is to open up possibilities of
dialogue between intellectuals across the North-South divide. The problem
of postmodernism itself is not only to "inscribe" otherness in the text but
also to shift the existing international distribution of knowledge and power;
not only to *speak about* the other but also to *engage with* other voices.
Accordingly, we have emphasized in our selections here contributions that
come from Latin America. The main exceptions are the statement of the
Latin American Subaltern Studies Group, which consciously sees itself as a
transnational formation, and Neil Larsen's essay "Postmodernism and Imperialism," which we include because it is both a description and a critique
of the idea of a Latin American "left" postmodernism.

This emphasis has led us to exclude the important work of George
Yúdice, which we mention in this introduction, as well as others working on
or around this topic in the United States or Europe, such as Greg Dawes,
who has written on the relation of postmodernism and Nicaraguan revolutionary culture in *Aesthetics and Revolution;* Santiago Colas, author of
a study of postmodernism and Argentine narrative; Doris Sommer; Emily
Hicks; and William Rowe and Vivian Schelling, whose *Memory and Modernity* may be the first manual of the emerging field of Latin American cultural
studies. But even with this limitation, we could have easily produced a collection twice this size. Missing here are such important figures in the Latin
American debate as, to name just a few, Ernesto Laclau (who had to remind an audience at a conference on "Identity" organized by *October* in
New York not so long ago that he was a Latin American, not a European);
the Brazilians Luiz Costa Lima, Renato Ortiz, and Heloisa Buarque de
Holanda; our friend and sometime collaborator Hugo Achugar in Uruguay;
Benjamín Arditi, whose essay "Una gramática social para pensar lo post-
moderno" is one of the finest Latin American essays on the logic of new
social movements; the distinguished Marxist aesthetician Adolfo Sánchez
Vázquez in Mexico; the late Agustín Cueva, one of the most acerbic critics

of the postmodern turn from the left; Jesús Martín-Barbero in Colombia, the dean of Latin American communications theory; Claudia Ferman from Argentina; Arturo Escobar; the Venezuelans Celeste Olalquiaga and Luis Britto García, pro and con postmodernism, respectively; Ticio Escobar in Paraguay; the Cuban writer Antonio Benítez Rojo, whose *The Repeating Island: The Caribbean in a Postmodernist Perspective* we have significant disagreements with but recognize as an ambitious application of postmodernist theory to the question of regional identity; the brilliant Cuban art critic Gerardo Mosquera—not to speak of the hundreds of writers and artists in Latin America who have assumed a postmodernist posture more or less explicitly, such as the performance artist Guillermo Goméz Peña or the generation of painters and sculptors incubated by the Cuban Revolution in the 1980s that Mosquera has profiled in his book with Rachel Weiss, *The Nearest Edge of the World: Art and Cuba Now.*

Because of our own concern, noted above, to deconstruct the traditional opposition between Latin America and the United States, perhaps less justifiable is our decision not to include a representation of the developing discussion of postmodernism in the United States' Latino community. With the exceptions noted, however, this is a book about the postmodernism debate *in* Latin America, and the Latino discussion has its own specificity and complexity (beginning with, among other things, the problem that Latino identity itself is heuristic). It deserves its own anthology. Some sense of what such a collection might include is suggested for us by, for example, the introduction to Marc Zimmerman's *U.S. Latino Literature;* Gloria Anzaldúa's *Borderlands/La frontera;* José David Saldivar's *The Dialectics of Our America;* or the Cuban-American journal *Apuntes Postmodernos/Postmodern Notes,* edited in Miami by José Solís Silva and Ramón Santos. Because of our links with the CLACSO and FLACSO groups in Buenos Aires and Santiago, our selection is also biased towards the Southern Cone and seriously underrepresents Mexico (the absence of those rival minor gods of the Mexican pantheon, Carlos Monsiváis and Octavio Paz, is particularly notable), as well as the extensive postmodernist discussion in Brazil, which makes up in both population and size more than one third of what we call Latin America.

Because of the space limitations imposed by the publisher, we have edited all the contributions, and in some cases cut them quite drastically. We apologize to the authors for any loss in the force of their argument this may have caused; it was done with the intention of allowing a greater number of voices to be heard here. We need to thank Paul Bové, the editorial collective of *boundary 2,* and Reynolds Smith of Duke University Press for supporting the idea of this collection. Meg Sachse of *boundary 2* did a heroic job copyediting the original manuscript. John Beverley would also like to acknowledge the stimulus afforded to this project by his coparticipants in the study group on postmodernism sponsored by the Latin American Studies Association's Cuba–North America Scholars Exchange Program (from Cuba: Roberto Fernández Retamar, Cintio Vitier, Luisa Campuzano, Desiderio Navarro, and Margarita Mateo; from the United States: Mary Louise Pratt, Jean Franco, George Yúdice, and Evelyn Picón Garfield).

Michael Aronna took time out from his own important research on the national essay in turn-of-the-century Spain and Latin America to translate the bulk of the materials included here. Carlos Rincón provided us with his own translation of a much longer essay originally written in German, which we adapted, not without some difficulty. Roberto Schwarz's "National by Imitation" first appeared under a different title in *New Left Review* 167 (1988) in a translation by Linda Briggs that we have modified slightly. The essays by María Milagros López and Neil Larsen, and the "Founding Statement" of the Latin American Subaltern Studies Group, were written originally in English. The translation of the Declaration from the Lacandon Jungle of the Zapatista National Liberation Army is taken from the Internet. John Beverley is responsible for the translations of the essays by Enrique Dussel, Raquel Olea, and Silviano Santiago, and for the final editing of the manuscript as a whole.

Our Identity Starting from Pluralism in the Base

Xavier Albó

Borrowed Identities

Our very name *America* proves to be an error of historical proportions, as had been the case of the West Indies before it. In turn, it has been the object of new misunderstandings; for many, the name refers above all to the United States, and, as the joke has it, "the bad thing about South America is that it comes from the North." Compounds such as *Hispanic* or *Ibero-America*, so cherished in the mother countries, or *Latin America*, promoted in the United States and more accepted among ourselves, do not prove to be completely satisfactory either, marginalizing most of the Caribbean and the Guyanas and overemphasizing the "Latin" in our identity, as if it were simply a matter of the transfer of the Mediterranean world to these latitudes, which is a half-truth at best.

Perhaps we could arrive at a more positive definition if we start, instead, with the identity and proposals of those who have suffered and continue to suffer the history these borrowed identities designate. In their diversity, it may be possible for us to find roads that lead us to a common project, which at the same time would be the basis of a "national" culture, in the widest sense of that term, with which it would be worth identifying.

The typology elaborated years ago by Darcy Ribeiro offers an excellent point of departure. Ribeiro distinguishes, for Latin America and the world, four great "historical-cultural configurations": *testimonial peoples*, who in some way are "the modern representatives of old, original civilizations which European expansion demolished"; *new peoples*, "arisen from the conjunction, deculturation, and fusion of ethnic African, European, and Indigenous matrixes," with or without a plantation economy; *transplanted peoples*, or "modern nations created by the migration of European populations to the new global spaces." The fourth configuration, *emerging peoples*, appears, for example, in some of the new African nations, but not in our continent.[1]

Although Ribeiro speaks of "peoples," he applies his typologies mainly to existing nation-states. But the logic of this fabric of complex design that is our "Latin American" identity is perhaps better understood when we see it as a set of peoples and societies articulated not only by the present state structures but also by other ties, old and new, that cross or challenge borders. Perhaps all of our peoples are, in some sense, new peoples in transformation, but with different, specific doses and weights of the original testimonial and transplanted elements, and in different stages of the crystallization of this newness. In some cases, the outcome of the process seems more clear, for example in Argentina; in others, we still do not know in what direction it will evolve, for example in Bolivia, which has been called a case of "nationalism without a nation." Or, perhaps everything that is called "Latin America" could be seen as a great new people in gestation.

Taking the step of defining our identity from the base questions the possibility or convenience of considering as representative of the nation hegemonic groups within our countries whose fundamental role has been, or is, to be the transmission belt of foreign interests. When in the Wars of Independence, for example, the Andean Indians, who had been defeated thirty years earlier by the Hispanic-Creole alliance in the uprising of Tupac Amaru and Katari, showed themselves hesitant to accept the independence offered to them by those same Creoles, perhaps they were more lucid about our future than has been acknowledged in the official history of our continent.

1. See Darcy Ribeiro, *The Americas and Civilization* (New York: Dutton, 1971). See also Rodolfo Kush, *América profunda* (Buenos Aires: Hachette, 1962).

Our fundamental point of departure, then, is to see how the popular sectors, together with their organizations, leadership, and organic intellectuals, begin to perceive their identity and to elaborate, little by little, their own project of a future society. Those of us in the social sciences have often taken for granted that the only "scientific" way to do this was in terms of *social classes*. The other categories were too subjective, or, if their weight in past history could not be denied, they were in the context of modernity "survivals" of a prepolitical age. We felt exonerated from the equally scientific and necessary task of seeing whether our social facts really corresponded to this premise. Perhaps it has been the force of these social facts, rather than theoretical considerations, that has modified our perspective, particularly in the last decade.

We do not doubt the importance and necessity of continuing to do analysis based on the social classes and their interaction; it is essential from every point of view. But we should also seriously question ourselves about the exclusivity of such analysis. It is like a skeleton without flesh. To delineate our identity as a people, the silhouette is as important as the skeleton. Then, other dimensions of the popular movement come into consideration, such as ethnic, or racial, identity in the case of African Americans, as well as Indian and mixed-race groups; different cultural expressions, for example, in the area of popular religion or language; relations between the countryside and the city or between the capital and the urban periphery and regionalisms; the growing women's movements, in which all of these elements coexist; and so on.

The same thing occurs with organizations that channel these diverse dimensions. The role of unions, and their connection to political parties, has understandably been privileged. In the last fifteen years, however, organizations have sprung up that have emphasized the other dimensions—for example, the new indigenous peoples organizations in almost all countries, including those that only a few years ago would have asserted that they did not have Indians.

Although the emphasis on one or another of these different identities can lead to a dispersion of forces or even to conflicts within the popular movement, the opposite also occurs. With this variety come greater degrees of reflection, and a greater ideological exchange leads to more globalizing and coherent proposals closer to what is, and should be, the whole of "Latin American" society.

The mostly cultural nature of the focus of these new proposals should not be ignored, even though they may not have an explicitly political dimension. In 1985, for example, in the city of La Paz, we were able to record hundreds of organizations that reinforced the Aymaran identity of the capital of Bolivia in fields as diverse as language, music, art, medicine, the elaboration of textiles, agricultural and artisan technology, sports, history, cultural recovery, the press and radio, professional organizations, religions and popular festivals, cooperation with places of origin, and, of course, politics and popular mobilization.[2]

The increasingly numerous organisms for the creation and diffusion of popular culture throughout the continent have achieved a great deal in this search for a new grass-roots identity. There are hundreds, if not thousands, of institutions of popular education and feminine promotion. Also significant and relatively developed are the networks of alternative communication, which reappraise, for example, indigenous languages and popular music and art. There are also positive developments in the area of "high" and middlebrow culture (although unfortunately not yet in television), such as the New Latin American Song and the New Latin American Cinema.

Little by little, in the face of the depersonalized avalanche of international consumer society, an alternative image that is much more our own is beginning to be created. In this image, one can perceive the unity, born in good measure from a common history of at least five centuries during which similar processes of exploitation and deculturation have been counterpointed by new acculturations and transculturations, which have led to a shared language of exchange, to similar systems of beliefs and values, and to many shared institutions, such as the national holidays, the *compadrazco* systems, and the rural community. This is, however, a unity that articulates a great variety of things without imposing one as a uniform model on everyone.

Perhaps the most difficult groups to analyze and to incorporate into an alternative model are the intermediate sectors, which suffer, more than anyone else, the ambiguity of their situation. They are located somewhere between the poles of "Miami" and the possibility of a new "Latin American" identity coming from the base. The solidity of their economic and social position gives them a greater security and enables them to act with greater freedom to posit alternatives. On the other hand, their cultural position almost inevitably entails a lack of identity, which in turn leads to vacillation and an unpredictable behavior of imitation and passivity, on the one hand,

2. Geofredo Sandoval, Xavier Albó, and Tomás Greaves, "Chukiyawu, la cara aymara de La Paz," in *Nuevos lazos con el campo*, vol. 4 (La Paz: CIPCA, 1987).

and rebelliousness and aggressiveness, on the other. All of this causes, in these sectors, psychological insecurities, underlined by what we could call a kind of social schizophrenia. The bigger, and more complicated, the social conflicts and discrimination of a specific society are, the more probable it is that this internal, psychological conflict will surface as a group phenomenon.

It has often been proposed that the true identity and future of our continent is precisely in these intermediate sectors. Some speak of the decisive role of the middle class. Others have emphasized racial-cultural *mestizaje*—the idea that our future is in the growing demographic, cultural, and political weight of the racially and culturally mixed population, or, as Aníbal Quijano prefers to call it, the increasing power of the "emerging mestizo."

One might think that I was aiming in that same direction when I spoke before of "Latin America" as a *new people* in transformation. This is not the case. In reality, I have less and less confidence in the role of the intermediate sectors taken as a whole. My personal experience, especially in places where the social conflict is very intense and, therefore, the insecurity of these groups reaches its maximum expressions, has influenced my opinion. So, too, has the perennial use and abuse that the various populisms have made of the "mestizo" image, which, in the long run, is always reduced to a new mask to continue reproducing the old colonial stereotypes.

As noted, my stake goes, instead, with those projects that arise out of class, ethnic, cultural, and gender groups that most clearly suffer the history of inequality, exploitation, and discrimination upon which has been built what we designate as "Latin America." There are also contradictions and ambiguities in these projects. For example, the mining proletarians of Bolivia often consider themselves the "civilized" with regard to the "little Indians" who surround their camps. Freire reminds us, also, that the most compelling model for the oppressed is to imitate their oppressors. It is not a question, therefore, of something magic or automatic. At least in this sector, however, there are fewer interferences of foreign interests, and there is greater rooting in our own reality. The popular sector can dream more because it has less to lose.

Nation, State, and People

I want to limit myself here to outlining a problematic that is intimately tied to the search for identity and unity in diversity. I am referring to the concept of *nation*. In taking up this question, I will privilege the testimony that comes from the most discriminated, but also the most representative of us, the Indians, with the understanding, however, that their proposals have already been picked up and assumed by other sectors of the popular movement.

On the one hand, politicians have recognized for many years that the "national question" is one of the most potent mobilizing resources. On the other hand, social scientists have great difficulty when they try to give a universal definition of *nation*. In reality, they have never succeeded in doing this—a theoretical impasse that suggests the symbolic, almost magical, force of the national question.

What remains clear in all of this, however, is that nationalism involves seeking a primordial identity that the group feels to be above other loyalties and for which it is prepared to fight. For the same reason, *nation*, in and of itself, implies some kind of political project. As in the case of social classes, the concept acquires its full force when it reaches the level of *nation in itself*. Unlike social classes, however, it is extremely difficult to indicate a priori objective aspects (territory, history, language, market, etc.) that are necessary and sufficient to be able to speak of a *nation in itself*; these can vary noticeably from case to case.

To be or to constitute a *nation*, in some instances, will be the result of previous projects, already crystallized; in others, it will be the mobilizing memory of a previous reality that has been stolen from a people; it can also be something that has not yet occurred but that one hopes to realize. In this last case, it is unlikely that the entire group already will feel identified as a *nation*. Furthermore, it is possible for various conflicting national projects to exist within a nation.

For our purposes here, the principal point of friction is probably the force with which the modern state wants to monopolize for itself the concept of *nation*. In its permanent dialectic to consolidate its power with the repressive and ideological apparatuses, the state considers it fundamental that all citizens feel themselves to be, more than anything else, members of that *nation* whose limits coincide with those of its borders, laws, government, currency, and flag. But in the sense that this same state is in the hands of a particular group, which does not necessarily represent, or even understand, the interests of others, the marginalized sectors will not always accept this proposal. In some cases, the interests of "forgotten" or "emerging" regions as potential nations will prevail; in others, ethnic identity often spreads across various states; in others, perhaps international proletarian unity; in others, the common search for "the great Latin American nation."

This rapid outline shows the necessity of using the concept of *nation* with the flexibility that each case demands. Too often, our theoretical frames, copied from other climates and times, have become a rigid conceptual corset that has distorted our reality instead of helping us to interpret it. Concretely, this principle of the union of the state and the nation, which has been, since the time of Sarmiento, the apple of the eye of those who, in fact, control our states, certainly produces the corset effect, especially with regard to our continental identity and future. Let me suggest here two possible alternatives: the nation-under-the-state (or multinational state), and the nation-over-the-state (or transstate nation).

In the indigenous movements and organizations of the continent, whose size and force are increasing, there is a growing convergence toward the identification of their projects as *national*. Several of these indigenous movements and organizations are called "indigenous nations," and in some of their proposals, they seek the constitution of "multinational states." As Indians' political consciousness develops, they no longer accept being known simply as "ethnics," nor even less as "peasants," because it reduces them to an economic class or ethnographic category that takes away their identity as a "people." Many Indians feel that their most radical problems originate precisely from not being accepted as peoples.

The proposals of Indian organizations are undoubtedly a project for the reformulation of society itself, no matter how embryonic their present formulations are. They have found acceptance, as well as hesitation, in the upper strata of our societies. For example, in a recent revision of the statutes of the International Labor Organization (ILO) in Geneva, we may read:

> The right of these indigenous and tribal *peoples* to maintain reciprocal relations with the *national* society on a footing of *equality* through their own institutions should be recognized.[3]

The prudence shown by the italicized words reflects the opposing visions present at the meeting where the report was drafted between representatives of indigenous groups and "experts" coming from the ILO member governments.

In a similar way, the Nicaraguan Law of Autonomy for the Communities of the Atlantic Coast takes great care in the handling of this national question. It affirms that "imperialism, the Somoza oligarchy and dictatorship

3. International Labor Organization, "Revisión parcial del convenio sobre poblaciones indígenas y tribales," *ILO* 107 (Geneva, 1987).

changed Nicaragua into *two nations* unknown to each other," only to immediately add that the Sandinista Revolution "has permitted Nicaragua . . . to become conscious of its identity and to recognize itself as a multiethnic and culturally plural *nation*."[4] Almost no indigenous proposal accepts this premise.

Pope John Paul II, for example, did not feel the necessity of such shadings when, in his sermon to the Selvícolas Indians, a tiny minority within the vast state (or "united states") of Brazil, he asked that they be given a "vital space" that would not only be a base of economic survival but would also be "for the preservation of your identity as a human group, as a true people and *nation*" (sermon of 8/10/80, my italics). I want to draw attention to some aspects of the proposals of the indigenous organizations that differentiate them from European substate *national* proposals. In the first place, they do not take into account teleological historical models, typical of Marxist-Stalinist analysis, according to which there is a necessary historical evolution of the sort: tribe → ethnicity → nationality → nation → state. In this narrative scheme, nation, characterized by the creation of its own internal market system, would be the waiting room for the possibility of forming an independent state.

None of this interests our indigenous and peasant organizations. In their proposals, the desire to continue being themselves prevails, more than anything else, whatever their size and degree of economic development, and that is what they call a *nation*. While they posit the requirement that the states in which they live should be truly pluri*national*, they do not propose the formation of their own independent states but rather only the recognition of their territory and of certain margins of autonomy. Perhaps for this reason, they have not made their proposals more specific in the face of the very current circumstance of finding themselves divided as *nations* by the borders of two or more states, when these were drawn without their consultation.

Black (African) groups and organizations do not seem to have this same concern, but they are claiming the right to be recognized in their particular racial and cultural identity. There are, of course, local variations: Haiti, which could perhaps call itself a black state and nation in spite of its serious internal conflicts; the small, fundamentally black states of the

---

4. Nicaraguan Autonomy Commission, *Rescate de la unidad nacional: Anteproyecto de la ley sobre las regiones autónomas de la Costa Atlántica* (Managua: Comisión de Autonomía, 1987).

Caribbean, in which there are other ethnic minorities of Northern European, Latin, indigenous, and/or Asian origin; the unique case of Cuba, also in the Caribbean, where the revolution has tried to produce a strong state-nation in which ethnic differences are as small as possible; and the dominant case in the rest of the countries of Spanish origin and in Brazil, all of which manifest, often hypocritically, unacknowledged forms of racial discrimination. Particularly in Brazil, there is a strong movement to designate a state that accepts and even foments its pluricultural base, but, in general, the African American populations do not speak of a *nation*. Undoubtedly, their character as a transplanted people brought to the continent as a subordinated labor force substantially modifies their identifying terms. For example, they do not have their own "territory"; their cultural roots and languages remain, to some extent, in Africa (as in the case of the Jamaican Rastafari or Brazilian *candomble*, for example); under near-genocidal conditions during the period of slavery, the manifestations of their cultural diversity were reduced to cultural and ceremonial forms, and their racial unity prevailed over other differences. An African Brazilian leader once expressed this particularity best when he noted that for African Caribbean and African American peoples, unlike the Indo-Americans, the land is not their "mother" but rather their "step-mother."

A third possibility, different, in turn, from both the indigenous and African American proposals, is the regionalism that is so prevalent in our continent. Regionalism can be a product of either decadence or boom. In the first case, it is usually the result of marginalization suffered in some peripheral regions, especially if they had a more central role in the past: for example, Cuzco in Peru, Sucre in Bolivia, and Bahía in Brazil. In the second, by contrast, regionalism occurs precisely in regions that are just beginning to play an economic role superior to the one acknowledged by previous state policy, regions that begin by fighting for greater local autonomy precisely to minimize the control of a state that does not allow them to grow more. In some cases, if these regions are successful, they may end up being the new capital; in others, they may manage to separate from the state that previously sheltered them. Many of the states emerging from the wars of independence have sprung from these mechanisms: for example, Bolivia, Ecuador, and the Central American nations, which did not want to be simple appendages of their ancient viceroyalties; or Panama and Uruguay, both pushed by interests in the United States and England to constitute themselves as small puppet states.

These processes have a fundamental difference with the ethnic nationalisms. They almost always involve conflicts of economic interests between the centralist elites, who control the state, and local elites. The latter doubtlessly appeal to the regional feeling of the local populations and, in this sense, are able to create a feeling of "little nation" comparable to the substate spirit of an ethnic nation. But this continues to be a top-down process of identity formation. Such economic interests do not usually exist in ethnic nationalism, which is more a nationalism-regionalism from below. For this reason, the central point of conflict in the case of regionalism is not the *nation* per se but rather the state itself.

Those Latin American countries that, copying the North American system, call their internal jurisdictions the "state" already posit the possibility of differentiating from above the *nation* and the state. The maximum aspiration in this direction goes very far. It is expressed in that half-real, half-poetic phrase, "the great Latin American *nation*," which has been proposed mainly by those who strongly identify with the "Latin" heritage of our continent. It is, therefore, a project of those who come from the sectors that have traditionally dominated our countries but that, at the same time, feel deeply the necessity of taking up again the dreams of the liberators and breaking new dependencies. The difference between this proposal, tied to progressive sectors of the hegemonic groups, and those originating from indigenous and subaltern groups that have been condemned to a marginal role since 1492 is clear. The contrast, however, is not as total as it seems. In reality, both positions can be simultaneously defended (although the term *nation*, which motivates both positions, perhaps proves to be so flexible in this case that it ceases to be a sufficient instrument of analysis).

The theme of "the great Latin American nation" immediately evokes the theme of a possible great state or "united Latin American states." As noted, many of the nation-states that emerged from independence, contrary to the project of the liberators, were the result not only of regionalisms carried to the extreme but also of the premeditated designs of the great powers. As we know, the Roman motto Divide and Conquer also applies to the fragmentation into small and conflicting states of the former colonies. In more recent years, the same principle reappears in the constant efforts of the hegemonic powers to avoid the formation of "common markets," "debtor clubs," and other similar alliances.

If this analysis is correct, it may well be that the formation of the "united Latin American states," or something comparable, is an appropriate step toward our strengthening and greater independence. Of course, the convenience of such a step for an alternative project of identity formation from below depends on which interests and forces control this macrostate. If this fundamental point is sufficiently resolved, however, an adequate synthesis may be achieved between the necessity of being globally strong, the overriding concern of each *national* group (which often surpasses the artificial divisions imposed by existing borders), and the gradual construction of "the great Latin American nation."

When our present states were born during Independence, the national identity of the new citizens was not clear. In the colonial period, being from Puno, Potosí, or Tucumán was a secondary distinction, since all these places were in the same "Andean" administrative space. Once independence was achieved, however, the person from Puno had to accept that his identity was now Peruvian; the person from Potosí, Bolivian, a name never heard before; and the person from Tucumán, Argentine. Furthermore, if the first two were Aymara Indians, until then an ethnic "caste" separated from others in the same political-administrative space, they discovered that, in spite of their common identity as Aymaras, they were now separated by an international frontier.

The process of creating these new identities was slow, especially in those states that did not imitate colonial unities and jurisdictions and, within them, in the subaltern classes and castes that had not participated in the negotiation of the new model. In some sense, this process continues to be in effect, as we recognize when we lament the lack of genuine national unity or consciousness in our countries. Nevertheless, it would be closing our eyes to history to think that two centuries have not managed to shape new "national" identities through the daily practice of laws, the different local politics and histories, the ideology transmitted by schools, the means of communication, the military, and national symbols. Except for very isolated, remote, or fanatic groups, or groups in conflicting frontier situations (like the Central American Miskitos), any citizen from any of our countries has a clear consciousness of his country and citizenship. Moreover, the percentage of the population for whom this consciousness is the most fundamental group identity is growing more and more, especially in the vast urban areas and in the intermediate sectors that no longer recognize their ancient roots. There is no doubt, then, that the project of the nation-state has basically achieved its objective, even if there continue to be problems of regionalism/centralism or uneven integration.

This national-state consciousness is also present in the great majority of rural and indigenous groups. Military service in some areas has become the rite of passage preceding marriage, whose culmination is communally celebrated. Many of the land seizures, protests, and blockades are accompanied by the national flag. During the fifties, the Aymara on the Bolivian side laughed at the Peruvian Aymara, because the latter had not undergone agrarian reform and continued under a patronal system. On both sides, some of them actually took advantage of the border situation, which gave them opportunities for contraband, in some cases even sacrificing llamas to the respective national flags to guarantee their enterprise. On the other hand, these Bolivian and Peruvian Aymara continue to move with great facility from one side to the other in order to share celebrations, sports, et cetera, as members of the same Aymaran family that contrasts them with what they call the *Q'ara* of both countries. To feel like Bolivians or Peruvians is no obstacle to feeling very Aymaran at the same time.

What this shows us is that we should perhaps rethink the supposition that a *national* identity, in situations like ours, should imply exclusivity, a maximum loyalty above all others. This game of loyalties looks like those Russian dolls that fit one into the other. Something can occur with the same individual in his or her local, ethnic, regional, "national," or even "Latin American" identity. We should remember that the ancient *ayllu*, and, later, the colonial or present-day *comunidad*, have the same multiplicity and logic as the Russian dolls. All identities are accepted, but each one at its level. So, in cases of conflict, the question of loyalty will often be decided more by joint convenience than by visceral alternatives.

In other words, if a sufficiently tolerant and pluralist social environment is achieved, there is no problem of loyalty. Conflict arises when any one of the identities wants to proclaim its exclusivity at the expense of the others because of centralism, regionalism, or factionalism. The national question and the concept itself of *nation* acquire very different contours in an intolerant, centralist society than in another that is pluralist and receptive. The first only has room for the nation-state. The second is not afraid of the idea of a plurinational state, and in accepting and encouraging this idea is, in some sense, also constructing the possibility of simultaneously forming a new collective consciousness of the nation-state.

This pluralist and open attitude seems easier at the minimum and maximum levels; between differentiated, but equally oppressed, groups; and between groups of states that do not fight among themselves for hegemony. On the other hand, this attitude encounters more difficulty at the intermediate level of the existing states or from the emerging regionalisms, because, without a doubt, the struggle for power and control predominates in them. Is this struggle an inevitable law or something that can be overcome?

The Nation and Production

I need to mention briefly one more aspect of the problem of *nation*. Xavier Gorostiaga et al. remind us in a suggestive essay of the primordial relationship of culture with cultivation, that is to say with the socially organized production of human life.[5] In other words, no matter how much influence other elements, such as a territory, a history, a language, an education, or shared customs, have, a national identity, at any of the levels analyzed here, will only be solid and able to defend itself to the extent that it is supported by an equally solid productive base, if possible sufficiently independent (perhaps through diversification and emphasis on nutritional self-sufficiency) of the opposing interests of the great powers. From this premise stems the concern we have noted of those Marxists who tie the emergence of the *nation*, in the strict sense, first to the development of its own market system and then to the possibility of generating its own state. Likewise, "the great Latin American nation," beyond its shared identity and culture, will really be a great project only if it is economically viable. We all agree on this.

I am more interested in applying here, however, this same logic to that multitude of small substate *nations* that claim their own existence within these "united Latin American states" we are dreaming of. Their existence is equally dependent on their economic base, adapted as it is to their demographic size. For this reason, these nations give the utmost priority to their claims to have their own *territory* (not just parcels of cultivation), with preferential rights to the soil, subsoil, water, wood, et cetera. This is more than a legal question, in spite of the undoubted legitimacy of these claims; the land is also the fundamental base of their cultural identity.

At the same time, inasmuch as the growing social and productive interrelation between human groups is an irreversible process, this solidity of the productive base also implies drastic adaptations of traditional productive forms. No living culture is static, especially in its forms of controlling nature. This is not where its group identity lies. The case of the Shuar

5. Xavier Gorostiaga, ed., *Para entender América Latina: Aporte colectivo de los científicos sociales en Puebla* (San José, Costa Rica: EDUCA, 1979).

of Ecuadorian Amazonia is illustrative. Despite their small size, and their reputation as "headhunters," they have become one of the most conscious and influential *nations* in the Ecuadorian popular movement. To do this, the group has had the necessary agility to reorganize its base of subsistence and to form its own communal ranching enterprises, in addition to introducing other important innovations in the areas of organization and education.

This strategy does not involve the transformation of the productive base at any cost, however. If their objective is to strengthen the group, the forms of adaptation should not lead to the very destruction of the group. They should maintain specific rhythms and styles, which I cannot elaborate on here. Perhaps the most fundamental point is that, in contrast to the dominant capitalist models, there persists a collective and self-generating development of the productive forces concerned with maintaining the communal base to a greater or lesser degree in the majority of the indigenous *nations* we are referring to.

For many, this is a regressive utopia that goes against history. We should remember, however, that Marx himself, when he was consulted on this point apropos of the Russian *mir*, answered that

> This commune is the point of support of social regeneration in Russia. . . . [I]t can renew itself without beginning through suicide; it can take possession of the fruits with which capitalist production has enriched humanity without passing through the capitalist regime.[6]

The problem is not in going with or against history but rather in whether a favorable correlation of forces for putting together an alternative project can be successfully assembled, that is, if rowing against the current of history is necessary precisely in order to make history. This is a task in which the entire popular movement, the parties, the state, and the nongovernmental organizations have much to say and do.

In agreement with this line of argument, those small indigenous *nations*, or *testimonial peoples*, that dot our jungles and mountains, should not only manage to survive but may also constitute the basic cell of the social regeneration of the continent. Reviving the embers currently covered with ashes, they could become the embryo of that new "genuine" society we aspire to build.

6. Marx, letter of 8 Mar. 1881, cited in Rodrigo Montoya, *La comunidad indígena* (Cuzco, Perú: Centro Bartolomé de las Casas, 1980), 30, 36.

Basically, this is the proposal that a Guatemalan Indian guerrilla leader, exiled after having lost several family members under military repression, tried to transmit to us when he passionately told us that his Maya nation was also fighting for a socialist society, but a different one from that explained to them by the guerrillas from the city. His Mayan utopia was, in addition to being communist, *communal*.

A New Name?

Five hundred years ago, when the bearded peoples arrived on this continent, it began to fill up with new names, some of which merely corrupted the former names but most of which almost always replaced them with references to the world the invaders came from and to the beliefs and dreams that animated them. Some three centuries later, when their great-grandchildren, recognized or not, broke their ties with the mother country and attempted to begin a new and more independent project, they once again baptized countries, regions, towns, and squares. The new names sought to erase the colonial world; but they did not take up the original names that were there before the conquest. New heroes were evoked and a new dream of the future was projected. The name *Indies* was erased, and the name *America* consolidated in its place; La Plata became Argentina; New Granada, Colombia; Charcas, Bolivia; the city of Valladolid, Morelia; and so on.

Years later, small adjustments continue to be made, such as the name "Latin America," often enclosed in quotation marks here, considering that it continues to reflect more foreign than indigenous interests. Every country and people has also made constant adjustments in the names of their streets, squares, or neighborhoods, reflecting the permanent accumulation of collective memory, new levels of consciousness or alienation, new projects, or simply the vanity of those who govern. The underlying reality is not magically transformed with a simple change of name, but these changes also remind us of the symbolic power that names have to forge a collective consciousness and dream.

Now, five hundred years after those first changes, and almost two hundred years after the second round, we once again feel the need of designing and implementing another kind of unifying project for all of us, not only for that portion of us which, for lack of a better name, we continue to call "Latin America." Even though we will not manage to radically change anything by this, would it not be worth the effort to begin thinking of a new name for this great nation we have dreamed of, a nation that would know how to respect all of the small and varied nations that hope to take shelter within it?

In reality, these small nations have already made their proposal: *Abya-Yala*. The name comes from the language of the Cunas, a small, but dynamic, nation within the Panamanian state that knew how to defend its territory and identity, even blocking a multimillion-dollar hotel project that would have destroyed their own paradise. The choice of this name (which means "land in complete maturity") was suggested by the Aymaran leader Takir Mamani, who proposes that all of the indigenous peoples use it in their oral documents and declarations. To name our cities, towns, and con-tinents with a foreign name, Mamani argues, is equivalent to submitting our identity to the will of our invaders and their heirs. Perhaps this proposal of a testimonial people can help all of us in our rebirth as a new people.

Notes on Modernity and Postmodernity in Latin American Culture

José Joaquín Brunner

Starting from the vantage point of the contemporary debate about modernity, I want to discuss here some problems of Latin American culture in relation to its future.

The Ambiguous Status of Cultural Questions

I first need to explain, however, why one should be interested in such a discussion anyway. Seized as we are by the great themes of the moment—the foreign debt and the economic crisis, unemployment and the difficulties of industrialization, the Central American conflict, and the processes of redemocratization—what capacity of attraction can cultural problems have, especially if these, as is frequently the case, tend to overflow the usual categories at hand? To meaningfully speak of culture requires that we refer to collective representations, beliefs, cognitive styles, the communication of symbols, language games, the sedimentation of traditions, and so on, and not only to the quantifiable aspects of culture: namely, to the movements of the market of cultural goods.

The Latin American social sciences have only marginally preoccupied themselves with these cultural problems, perhaps because their study does not fall high enough on the ladder of academic prestige or because they do not lend themselves easily to the prevailing methodologies. Culture, as such, still appears to us as a supplement, identified, according to an old aristocratic conception, with the fine arts, with the Sunday editions of the great urban newspapers, and with the conspicuous consumption of art works and symbols invested with an aura of prestige.

This "cultured" vision of culture, otherwise absurd in an age of the primacy of the forms and contents of mass culture, of the media and the culture industry, is also sometimes a symptom of denial produced by a deeper, and typically modern, tendency: the predominance of the interests, including cognitive, of instrumental reason over the values of communicative rationality; the separation of a technical sphere of progress that includes the economy, science, and material conditions of daily life from the sphere of intersubjectively elaborated and communicated meanings, those found indissolubly anchored in a life-world where traditions, desires, beliefs, ideals, and values coexist and are expressed precisely in culture.

This reactive negation leads easily to the extreme of affirming that culture, as a symbolic domain, is incomprehensible for analytic reason and that only an empathetic approach suits it—an affirmation that leaves a considerable part of the social sciences out of the game and encloses the debate about the cultural universe in a new esotericism, this time made up of intuitions, mysteries, and, in the best of circumstances, poetry.

The attempt to conduct our own exploration within a relatively known, and shared, frame of reference, such as modernity, has as its purpose to avoid the double danger of, on the one hand, a purely functionalist vision of culture—obstacle or promoter of modernity?—and, on the other, an esoteric vision of culture, one that resists thought and cannot be thought.

The Problems of Modern Rationality

As a point of departure, I will begin with the report of the Economic Commission for Latin America (CEPAL), "Crisis and Development: The Present and Future of Latin America and the Caribbean."[1] In this document, the cultural dimension of our problems, of crisis as well as of development,

1. See CEPAL, *Crisis y desarrollo: Presente y futuro de América Latina y el Caribe*, vols. 1–3 (Santiago, Chile: CEPAL, 1985).

and of our time, present and future, is barely touched on. The most profound and vital issues of culture are not mentioned; nor are the more directly sociological, economic, and political issues that make up the organization of culture.

Instead, the report adopts the traditional Behaviorist idea that culture needs to adapt itself to modernity and to produce the motivations and attitudes required for the optimum performance of modern systems of production, reproduction, and social rule. All this, moreover, in the context of a relatively ingenuous concept of modernity and modernization that precisely ignores the contemporary debate over these topics. Thus, the report declares:

> The process of modernization is a contemporary mode of social change, of general validity, that is extended to the entire planet. It supposes a self-sustained economic growth, the total availability of social resources, the diffusion of the rational and secular norms of culture, the freedom and growth of social mobility, and the corresponding attitudinal transformations.[2]

Later, the report adds, in a similarly Behaviorist vein:

> In order to have modernization it is necessary that there come into play mechanisms of empathy that incorporate values, models of behavior, and aspirations originating from the most dynamic centers of civilization and that can shape demands. Nevertheless, institutions cannot be moved, they must be transformed; lifestyles cannot be changed by the free functioning of the "demonstration effect"; they must be creatively adapted so that they do not cause disturbances. The capacity of adaptation is perhaps the distinctive feature of modern societies. If modernization, because of its empathetic essence, responds to exogenous influences, our societies need to internalize it with regard to their specific histories, indigenous resources, and possibilities, through the development and free exercise of creativity. It is clear, on the other hand, that adaptive and self-sustained technological development constitutes a central component of modernization, even though the latter goes beyond it as a total social process.[3]

2. CEPAL, *Crisis*, vol. 3, 5.
3. CEPAL, *Crisis*, vol. 3, 6.

CEPAL's formulation is typically eclectic and limits itself to glossing over the problems of cultural adaptation that it poses. Nevertheless, it allows us to make out the questions it avoids: for example, the conflict between *formal rationality* (based on the calculability provided by the market) and *substantive rationality* (directed by values and goals). Thus, the report sustains that modernization supposes the "internalization of rational norms" but immediately adds that in order for such an internalized rationality to constitute an "integrating and stabilizing force," not destructive of those minimal prescriptive nuclei required by integration, it should "incorporate the criteria which permit it to elaborate the conflicts between growth and equity, present affluence and accumulation, social demands and the limits of expansion of supply, present and future comparative advantages." Where do these criteria come from and how are they made compatible with other criteria (of formal rationality) that are imposed by the functioning of the market? Because the rationality that the CEPAL document speaks about is not the same as the one, according to Weber, that is at the foundation of the processes of modernization, but rather is one that "makes implicit a comprehensive concept of efficiency in the administration of resources and opportunities," according to the CEPAL report.

Creativity, not as a function of the market or as the incessant revolutionizing of the means of production and all social relations that Marx attributed to the bourgeoisie, but as an individually or socially acquired attribute, becomes the centerpiece of this model. The CEPAL report goes so far as to speak of *creative modernization* as "the stylization of a *political process* of the search for social efficiency," especially necessary in the conditions of crisis and profound transformations that affect the region. It is important, therefore, to ask about the sociological conditions of this creativity.

In modernity, one of the principles of creativity, the liberation of energies that transformed culture, was, as Habermas demonstrates,[4] the separation of the spheres of science, morality, and art from the field of religious and metaphysical justifications and their conversion to esoteric domains of experts, a process that resulted in the penetration of these spheres by economic and administrative rationality, a rationality completely distinct from that which rules the transmission and reproduction of values and norms. Does the path of modernization in Latin America pass through these same forms of the rationalization of culture that have already proven to be efficient

4. Jürgen Habermas, "Modernity, an Incomplete Project," in Hal Foster, ed., *The Anti-Aesthetic: Essays on Postmodern Culture* (Port Townsend: Bay Press, 1983), 3–15.

in the liberation of creativity? If it does, how can such a strategy be made compatible with the declared objective of maintaining the sought-after rationalism within a frame of values and goals that point to integration, "social efficiency," justice, and solidarity? And what does it mean, in the Latin American context, to "adapt" models of behavior and aspirations capable of shaping demands from the most advanced capitalist centers, and, at the same time, to do this "creatively," according to our "specific histories, indigenous resources, and possibilities"? If demand is not culturally autonomous—how could it be in a universe of an international market of messages and goods—can the supply of creativity and products be managed locally, and, furthermore, can it be anchored in the traditions and beliefs of the internal culture?

At heart, the CEPAL document assumes a noncontradictory conception of modernity in its supposition of an uncomplicated and "creative" access to what it calls the "rational and secular norms of culture." Of what culture? We know that neoconservatives stigmatize "irrationalist" tendencies in Western culture, inasmuch as these can no longer provide the values and motivations required by the economy; and that progressives, in the fashion of Habermas, denounce the contradictions between a technical-instrumental rationality, which permeates all of social life, and a communicative rationality, which is seen as interrupted by the first in a way that provokes a replacement of meanings by consumer goods. To whom do we appeal, then, to obtain the cultural rationalism that is made to appear as a presupposition of the advance of modernization? Or, is this proposal, in its cultural implications, nothing more than an ideological "bargain," another of the many that Latin American intellectuals and technocrats have produced in recent years in their eagerness to appropriate a modernity that does not adapt itself to their models and forecasts?

The question at hand involves, perhaps, a double misunderstanding. First, about the nature of rationality itself. What, exactly, does the CEPAL report mean when it stipulates a rational and secular culture as the foundation of the processes of modernization? The rationality of the market, for example, is very different from the rationality of politics, and both differ, in turn, from technobureaucratic rationality. In each case it is a matter of personified rationalities, institutionally mediated, tied to interests that habitually interact in a conflictive manner. In culture, these rationalities imprint cognitive styles, define values, introduce habits, and stimulate varied personality structures. Therefore, there are no "rational norms" that can be so outside of their context: the laboratory, the competitive market, the noncompetitive market, the state, the parties, et cetera. A complex culture accepts, out of necessity, these various types and forms of rationality that, according to one's adopted point of view, can also be stigmatized as irrational.

The second misunderstanding has to do with the acquisition of these rationalities. The CEPAL document emphasizes an adaptation and internalization of norms that would come initially "from outside" but, once appropriated, would form rationally oriented values, motivations, and behaviors. How will this process of transference and acquisition of rationality happen? It is easiest to imagine the process as taking place through modes of collective learning based on life experiences that condition this learning: the market, education, the multiple bureaucratic or quasi-bureaucratic structures of civil society, corporations and unions, et cetera. But it is precisely these situations of learning, of existing, that will socialize individuals and groups in contextually conditioned and, therefore, by necessity, diversely situated "rationalisms."

In other words, there does not seem to be anything like a *homogeneously* rationalized culture.

Cultural Heterogeneity

As we understand it, Octavio Paz's critique of modernity points precisely to this *voluntarism of the ideologies* of modernism and modernization in Latin America.[5] And Paz is not the only one who has made this point; its antecedents can be traced far back in the history of Latin American thought. What, then, is expressed by the relative malaise with modernity that recurs in the region with almost the same frequency and force with which new modernizing projects are launched? We can answer this in the following way: What produces the malaise is the periodic conflict of those forms of modernization whose supposition is invariably the adoption and extension of rational models of conduct with what, for lack of a better term, we may call the *cultural heterogeneity* of Latin America.

This is not the same thing as supposing that our societies are formed by a superimposition of historical, cultural entities in the manner of geological layers that slide on top of each other, every once in a while producing breaks and great telluric upheavals. It may be that some compelling images in Latin American literature still function within this logic, habitually depart-

5. See Octavio Paz, *Children of the Mire* (Cambridge, Mass.: Harvard University Press, 1974), 148–64.

ing from the even more basic opposition between nature and culture. In this sense, the whole cycle of Pablo Neruda's poetry represents better than any analysis the drama of a culture that seeks to entreat nature on its own behalf, making it participate in the loves and sorrows of individuals and peoples at the same time that it reflects as culture a superimposition of histories that have not arrived at a complete synthesis.

The notion of cultural heterogeneity refers us instead to a kind of regional postmodernism *avant la lettre* that, nevertheless, is fully constitutive of our modernity. Carlos Monsiváis, in a prose collage, has insightfully captured this:

> Cable television. Superhero comics. Quick and poorly translated humor. An infinity of products which satiate, invent, and modify necessities. Television programs whose weekly apotheosis is nourished by the victories of the North American system of justice. Books (best-sellers) where the mechanics of success program the imagination and writing. Extremely refined technologies. Videocassettes. Satellite communication. The ideology of MacLuhan's global village. Videodiscs. Strategies of consumption whose implacable logistics destroy all artisanal perspective. The "philosophy" of the biggest seller in the world. Movies which have globally imposed the rhythm, themes, and point of view of North American industry. Software and hardware. International news agencies. Contempt for the history of each nation. Homogenization of "desirable" lifestyles. The imposition of a global language. A circuit of ideological transmission which goes from publicity to pedagogy. Control of the "computer revolution." Magazines which distribute "femininity." The periodic reordering of the life-styles adjustable to technological changes.[6]

The cultural heterogeneity reflected in this collage, in the "postmodernist" grafts and allegories of our modernity, is, like this modernity itself, a product of the international market. To paraphrase Raymond Williams, our identities no longer appear as such but rather as sectors of the international market, especially in the area of culture. There subsist infinite local cultural exchanges that form the framework of our daily life, that mass of more or less direct interactions in which customs, use values, images, and

6. Carlos Monsiváis: "Penetración cultural y nacionalismo," in Pablo González Casanova, ed., *No intervención, autodeterminación y democracia en América Latina* (Mexico: Siglo XXI, 1983), 75.

beliefs accumulate. But through and above this framework—can we still call it national?—flow and are articulated messages and institutions and circuits fully incorporated into a modernity whose heart is far from the heart of "our" culture.

Cultural heterogeneity, therefore, refers to a double phenomenon: (1) of segmentation and segmented participation in this global market of messages and symbols whose underlying grammar is North American hegemony over the imaginary of a great part of humanity (I will return to this point); (2) of differential participation according to *local codes of reception*, group and individual, in the incessant movement of the circuits of transmission that extend from advertising to pedagogy. What results from this double and explosive, segmented and differential participation is something similar to what is proclaimed by certain representatives of postmodernism: a de-centering, a deconstruction, of Western culture as it is represented by the manuals; of its rationalism, its secularism, its key institutions; of the cognitive habits and styles it supposedly imposes in a uniform way—something that resembles Monsiváis's collage; something that "generates meaning," but a meaning out of place, taken out of context, a graft onto another culture.

Cultural heterogeneity thus means something very different than diverse cultures (subcultures) of ethnicities, classes, groups, or regions, or than the mere superimposition of cultures, whether or not these cultures have found a way of synthesizing themselves. It means, specifically, a segmented and differential participation in an international market of messages that "penetrates" the local framework of culture on all sides and in unexpected ways, leading to an implosion of the consumed/produced/ reproduced meanings and subsequent deficiencies of identity, yearnings for identification, confusion of temporal horizons, paralysis of the creative imagination, loss of utopias, atomization of local memory, and obsolescence of traditions. Thus, Monsiváis concludes, "its values substituted . . . by others which basically modernize appearances and take advantage (for the market) of the innovations of the age, a collectivity can no longer manage to confront its experiences or verify its legitimate goals."[7]

A Multiplicity of Logics

What precise, specific meaning can the invocation of rationalism in culture and society have, then, in this "postmodernism" that characterizes

---

7. Monsiváis, "Penetración," 76.

Latin American modernity? Modernity cannot be read, in the fashion of Marshall Berman, as a singular collective experience of the modern, nor as variations of that same experience that in the long run tend to converge. If we were to proceed that way, we would have done no more than to transpose the conception of modernization through stages to the conception of our modernity.

What seems more reasonable is to imagine modernity as a trunk from which numerous branches and sub-branches extend in the most varied directions. In the case of Latin America, as we noted, the motor of modernity, the international market, provokes and then reinforces an incessant movement of heterogenization of culture, employing, stimulating, and reproducing a plurality of *logics* that act simultaneously, becoming interwoven. Logics that, from a Eurocentric and Enlightenment point of view, we could properly call modern, such as those of secularization, formal rationality, bureaucratization, individualization, futurism, alienation, et cetera. Logics of the collective imaginary, at the same time shaped by a local historical memory (which is itself sometimes varied and contradictory) and by the seductions of the mass media, as occurs with the telenovela. Logics of identification based on economic, social, and cultural positions; social logics of differentiation in a world where consumption distributes, at the same time, signs of status; sacrificial logics of giving, expenditure, and fiestas, which, by themselves, do not manage to resist the commercializing force of the market; political logics of articulation and mobilization, which are not immune to the internationalization of militancies; renewable modern logics of terror and fear in a universe of the disappeared, torture, state and private terrorism, and of the marks left on society by repression.

For this reason, proposals for modernization, whether traditional or new, that do not assume as a central fact of their "efficient" operation this cultural heterogeneity in which they are called upon to materialize themselves condemn themselves to remain on the terrain of ideological voluntarism.

Endogenous Creativity

We consider it a sign of the times that global proposals, in the manner of great laboratory tests that claim to design, on the basis of totalizing rationality, the modernization of this or that society, are not in favor, at the moment, in Latin America. On the other hand, more modest proposals for the local or partial rationalization of society are being introduced into the debate, such as CEPAL's strategy for the formation of "endogenous nuclei of technological dynamization." The CEPAL report notes apropos the future of Latin America:

> One starts from the premise that creativity is a complex process in which a wide range of agents and motivations participate: large industrial plants tied to small and medium ones, institutes of technology, institutes of basic science, the organisms which prepare qualified personnel at the different levels, the mass media, and the central state ministries and organisms which define policies and norms. . . . The interaction between these agents and their motivations is decisive for the process of creativity.[8]

This is a strategy of local rationalization that contains elements of the state and the market, of endogenous creativity, and of the appropriation of external dynamics; that supposes complex interactions between the economy, politics, the administration, and culture; that valorizes, by overlapping them, both instrumental efficiency and communicative rationality. More than the design of a modern society, or even of its economy, it is the outline of a system of relations wherein creativity encounters sociological conditions of operation.

It remains to be seen, however, whether the institutions of culture, the means of communication, institutes of training and centers of formation, research laboratories, universities, and so on, are in a condition to be incorporated into an enterprise of this sort (with an "inward" orientation, so to speak), when for a long time they have danced to the rhythm of the requirements of their differential integration into international markets. For example, universities in Latin America have been, more than anything else, enterprises of intellectual criticism, of professional certification and social mobility, leaving their participation in *enterprises of accumulation* to the mediation of complex international circuits. Their function has consisted of growing, in a sense, *against* the market, preserving at the same time, where possible, their independence from the state, under the supposition that only as such could they aspire to be the "conscience of the nation." Their politicization, not at all surprising under these circumstances, reflects a typically antimodern feature of Latin American modernity: a low level of autonomy,

8. CEPAL, *Crisis*, vol. 3, 72.

in general, of culture and of its institutional sphere, and, in particular, of the sciences, which runs parallel to a high degree of autonomy of politics and ideological creation.

The "new" proposals of development, which attempt to escape the globalism of certain previous designs and which insist on local rationalizations of "nuclei" that combine institutional segments of the economy, the administration, and culture, seem to better understand the fragmentary conditions of regional modernity; but at the same time, they can find themselves involved in the heterogeneity of culture and in the sometimes perverse effects that this provokes in the development of local cultural institutions.

The Social Uses of Religion

In a very different register, we know that some authors have posited a supposed tension between modernization and the "Catholic substratum" of Latin American culture. In reality, the problem proves to be more complex.

In the midst of the cultural heterogeneity that is the salient feature of our regional modernity, this religious "substratum" fulfills a variety of functions, only one of which corresponds to the supposed delegitimization of a modern work ethic. Moreover, it has already been shown that in very few parts of the developed world does the (puritan) work ethic play a key role any longer in individual motivation and performance. Everywhere, even in socialist regimes, there is an *uncoupling* of ethics and performance, and the market itself increasingly conditions directly economic behavior and performance.

On the other hand, the "Catholic substratum" continues to operate, in many parts of Latin America, as a symbolic foundation for popular religious practices and, what is more interesting, renews the exhausted deposit of symbols and desires capable of mobilizing radical (revolutionary) behaviors on the social and political plane. In many societies of the continent, a prophetic, testimonial, and revolutionary current is nourished by religion, around which are continually renewed ties of solidarity, seeds of communal life, and the principle of rebellion against the established order. The struggle in Nicaragua between the Catholic hierarchy and the "popular church" over the control of this deposit of revolutionary/counter-revolutionary legitimizations, for example, precisely emphasizes the discussion of the "uses" of this "Catholic substratum," whose importance is increasingly political, ideological, and cultural more than economic or (work) ethical.

The proposal of Puebla to evangelize Latin American culture partially recognizes this situation, but it supposes, at the same time, that the cultural heterogeneity of the region can be overcome through the elaboration of a new synthesis, wherein the dimensions of the modern could recuperate a sense of the sacred and the transcendental via a recoupling with a Christian ethic capable of interrupting the process of functionalization and "degradation" of secularized values. The proposal of Puebla imagines the "gestation of a new civilization" that, beyond modernity, "integrates the values which it has contributed but in the frame of (this) new civilization."[9]

Seen from the perspective of the question of modernity and modernization on the continent by the year 2000, what progress, new opening, or "solution" does this attempt to "rebaptize" Latin American culture in Catholic religious terms offer? Neoconservative proposals, following Daniel Bell's argument in *The Cultural Contradictions of Capitalism*, situate the religious question in the center of developed societies in terms of a diagnosis of the contradictions that have arisen between economy and culture in late capitalism, whereas Latin American neo-Catholic proposals, such as Morandé's,[10] still seem to reflect the classic struggle between traditionalism and modernism, secularism and religion, positivism and Catholicism. Is there not entailed here, perhaps, under the educated guise of civil tolerance, a total rejection of modernity, of its inherent dynamics and values? Is there not the risk of a new "totalizing" proposal that, precisely by ignoring the radical fact of Latin American cultural heterogeneity, seeks to base itself on religion in order to establish a cultural continuity torn to pieces long ago? And what can this proposal imply in the area of development, the economy, the new political system, the emancipation of private life, the generation of a mass culture based on the cultural industry, and the currently accepted principles of social integration and control?

Societies without Consensus

Nevertheless, as we have had the opportunity to see, the question of modern secularism is not an issue that only concerns the church or a few Catholic intellectuals. It is internationally related to various currents of neoconservatism and, in Latin America, to the not at all marginal concerns

9. CELAM, Document of Consultation to the Episcopal Conferences, III *Conferencia General del Episcopado Latinoamericano* (1978).
10. See Pedro Morandé, *Cultura y modernización en América Latina* (Santiago de Chile: Universidad Católica de Chile, 1984).

of sociologists such as Gino Germani. Even among figures originating from Marxism, such as Leszek Kolakowsky, the modern "disenchantment" of the world and the subsequent "demolition" of taboos constitute the neurological point of any critical philosophy of modernity.

We find ourselves confronted here with a reactive sensibility to modernity that is widely disseminated and that, in different forms, gives rise to a critique of cultural modernism involving a range of issues, from the loss of values, the renunciation of ethics in social relations, and the erosion of national identities to the destruction of artistic canons.

As Habermas has pointed out, however, this critique is surely misguided, since it is not possible to impute to culture, and to the professionalized agents of culture, intellectuals, the effects of a secularism that has resulted from the more or less successful development of capitalism in the economy and society. The problem, in reality, is better formulated by Germani when he wonders whether, on the basis of the new conditions created in the economy and society, once their repercussions in the cultural sphere are known (i.e., secularism), it is still possible to guarantee the minimum of consensus and integration required by the functioning of democratic governments. The alternative, according to Germani, are the modern authoritarianisms, namely, regimes that impose through force a total resocialization of the population, integrating each individual into a militarized culture.

Clearly, the underlying hypothesis is that societies cannot function, indeed run the risk of disappearing altogether, without this minimum of consensus, "an agreement over foundations," as Laski put it in a phrase Germani likes to quote. Thus:

> It is not surprising that the philosophy of history usually locates the beginning of the decadence of the great civilizations precisely in the phases of acute secularization, even if the latter is limited to the elite. Toynbee, Spengler, Sorokin and others give clear examples of this theoretical orientation.[11]

It is not our interest to explore the philosophical-historical implications of this thesis but rather to take up its sociological nucleus in the light of what we have said. In this sense, Germani's thesis is clear: Modernity generates serious problems of normative integration that weaken or make

11. Gino Germani, "Democracia y autoritarismo en la sociedad moderna," in Germani et al., *Los límites de la democracia* (Buenos Aires: CLACSO, 1985), 31.

impossible democratic governments, leading to catastrophic solutions in the guise of authoritarian regimes of total resocialization. Modernization reduces the validity of certain traditional forms of social integration and, by pushing toward an ever-increasing secularization of culture, reduces the bases of the traditional "prescriptive nucleus," weakening the old forms of legitimization based on religious beliefs. This does not mean, however, that modernization does not generate its own forms of integration, over a full range of positions from "moral" to "organic" solidarity.

The question, especially in Latin America, is whether the cultural heterogeneity constitutive of its own specific modernity, in which a motley collection of traditional and new forms of normative prescription are mixed, still makes possible the functioning of social systems in an increasingly secularized world. This question refers us in turn, at a higher level of abstraction, to the question of the necessary degree of consensus and normative integration social systems need in order to function. If one were to go by the specialist literature on this issue, it would appear no system of society should be able to function in Latin America, so scarce are the principles of integration and agreement over foundations in the region. One could argue that precisely because of this, these societies resort with relative frequency to authoritarian regimes in order to secure their government, although not their integration.

On the other hand, it would seem possible, indeed almost obligatory, to argue that, in spite of everything, the kind of societies we have characterized by a high degree of cultural heterogeneity actually do maintain and reproduce a sufficient degree of integration, but on the basis of local and partial forms of consensus that involve only limited and differentiated areas of society. Authoritarianism would, in this perspective, be a form of "governing," of controlling this plurality of forms of consensus whenever they tend to align themselves in a catastrophic manner, polarizing society.

Such a perspective might allow us to consider our societies as societies without the need for a basic consensus, without an agreement over foundations, with scarce possibility (and necessity) of conceiving themselves as "totalities"; as societies that, more than consensus, need to organize conflict and give rise to agreements of interests; as societies that, more than recuperating a political system legitimized by a nucleus of values, need to construct and live with a necessarily unstable one, which reflects agreements over the rules of government capable of inspiring mutual respect and of avoiding the war of each against all.

Political Disenchantment

The other aspect of Germani's thesis, according to which a constant erosion of the minimum prescriptive nucleus required for social integration makes democracies vulnerable, also needs to be discussed in relation to the political future of Latin America. As Norbert Lechner has recently stated,[12] the threat of the dissolution and atomization of the social order brought on by modernization (secularism and marginalization) caused and exacerbated an "ideological inflation" in the Latin America of the sixties, favoring revolution as the means of national liberation, social integration, and economic development, as opposed to what was seen as capitalist "development of underdevelopment." The revolutionary proposal implied, as Lechner demonstrates, a messianic and fundamentalist style of doing politics, which carried within itself a germ of antisecularism in culture. By contrast, in the present climate of democratic recovery, the opposite tendency finds itself reinforced, namely, the reappraisal of secularism in culture. In opposition to what Germani sustains, Lechner suggests that secularism can be beneficial for democratic recovery in the region, relieving politics of ethical-religious compromises, disseminating values of civil tolerance, and producing a certain spirit of negotiation, a "cooling-off" of values, motivations, and affects. A new kind of realism, one that values, in Lechner's words, "the institutions and procedures, or in other words, . . . the forms of doing politics over its material contents," would point in this same direction.

What is suggested here is the possibility of a profane, "disenchanted" notion of politics that restricts it to specific areas, taking away its omnipotence and freeing it from its anchorage in absolute principles in order to make it more flexible and adjustable to immediate challenges. Such a concept resonates with certain tendencies, themes, and attitudes of postmodernism, as Lechner makes clear: In both, there is a criticism of the idea of complete subjects, an abandonment of the "master narratives," a conversion of time into a continuous present, a reduction of politics to an exchange of material and symbolic goods. The risk involved for Lechner, however, is that this postmodern movement of contemporary politics in Latin America may abandon the notion that society can construct itself in a deliberate manner and that the reduction of politics to a "political market" may exclude interests and goods that cannot be exchanged in the market: human rights,

12. Norbert Lechner, "Problemas de la democratización en el contexto de una cultura posmoderna" (FLACSO manuscript).

roots, the sense of belonging, the desire for certainty, the need for transcendental referents. Secularism then presents itself ambiguously: It reinforces
tendencies that seem necessary, or at least inevitable, in the present phase
of the recuperation and consolidation of democracies; but, at the same time,
it generates a *deficit* of meaning, motivations, and collective construction of
the social order that would impede the elaboration of a democratic culture.

These postmodern features of political culture in Latin America
should be included, as I noted before, less in the context of a critique of
modernity than as a consequence of the regional form of our modernity,
which has tended precisely in the direction of a secularization of the area
of power. The "disenchantment" *of* and *with* power in Latin America necessarily passes through a dis-dramatization of power: a reduction of its
symbolic-expressive aspects and an increase in the instrumental capacities
of its gestation; a loss of ideological aura in favor of the practical interests
of actors, which are lost and found in the political market; in short, a greater
autonomy of politics because of its differentiation and specialization. This
means, of course, that politics no longer aspires to construct social identities, reserving for itself the colder terrain of changing political loyalties; that
it loses its character as a "movement" in order to be reduced to "parties"
that are "organization and program" but not an existential community nor an
ideological-transcendental vanguard of society; that it no longer provides
references of certainty nor commitments to principles, limiting itself to processing the uncertainties within a game of stipulated rules; that it retreats
from the commanding heights of revolution or restoration in order to assume, in a disenchanted world and in a reality without too many illusions,
the sphere of the administration of scarce means, of the negotiation between forces in conflict, of the persuasion of a public of citizens who do or
do not vote.

The National as a Revolutionary Force

There is, logically and historically, an alternative to Germani's thesis
about the catastrophic and authoritarian outcomes of the states of disintegration caused by the process of secularization: that of a "national-
popular" revolutionary articulation tied to divergent projects of socialization
and integration capable of being politically and institutionally expressed. In
situations of extensive cultural heterogeneity, the very notion of *national
collectivity* finds itself questioned and permanently put into tension, since
there exists a latent conflict between diverse proposals of national integra-

tion. Each of these proposals resorts, for its legitimization, to a different interpretation of the national past; each mobilizes a distinct constellation of national symbols; each imagines the international insertion of the country in a different way; and each is based, in the last instance, on insufficiently secularized principles of the construction of the nation. These proposals can be mobilized indiscriminately by political parties, the armed forces, intellectual elites, leadership groups in civil society, armed revolutionary groups, charismatic leaders, and churches or sects. In each case, it is a matter of barely secularized, exclusive, and totalizing proposals. Each contains, for that very reason, a project for the socialization and resocialization of the population, under the hegemonic control of a class, group, leader, or belief.

Faced with the reality of a "disintegrated" nation, devoid of a basic or minimal consensus, permeated by the contradictions, tensions, and conflicts caused by its heterogeneity, this kind of nonsecular, quasi-religious proposal, which appeals to total commitment and mobilizes around transcendental values and goals, or around a leader who embodies these, can prove to be very powerful. These proposals habitually offer the project of a *national* modernization tied to a nucleus of values (the nation, the class, past splendor, liberation) that offers the minimum prescriptive nucleus around which to organize the processes of resocialization and the ceremonies and rites of integration.

As in the case we looked at earlier of the neo-Catholic proposal for Latin America's future, these are antisecular projects in the field of culture that take advantage of the diffuse, but at times extensive, criticism of modernity, of its overrationalism, its ethical pluralism, its individualism, its alienation and cultural imperialism, et cetera. Perhaps for this reason, revolutions in Latin America routinely happen in a national context: They are national-popular—national-liberation, national-security, or national-development—movements. Symbols of *the national* cover a wide range of political and strategic options, but in the end, they all seek the same thing: to overcome the cultural heterogeneity constitutive of society and its "internationalist" dynamic; to curb the effects of secularism; to cancel the forms, formalities, and "games" of democracy, and to reestablish a governing principle of integration through which the majority can be resocialized.

A Peripheral Modernity

One of the threads that runs through the debates about modernity and postmodernity in Latin America (but not only there, as we will see), is that of the changing poles of the modernization of the world, and of the differentiated modes of participation in modernity. Braudel studied this matter, starting from the dynamics of capitalism in the production of the modern world-system, what he called the development of a "world-economy." He found that since the fourteenth century, a continuous "partition of the world" into concentric zones, "increasingly disfavored inasmuch as one moves away from their triumphant center," can be observed. The "long durations" are precisely processes of the centering, de-centering, and re-centering of the world-economy:

> The splendor, the wealth, and happiness of life are united in the center of the world-economy, in its very nucleus. That is where the sun of history gives brilliance to the most vivid colors; that is where are manifested high prices, high salaries, banking, "royal" manufactures, profitable industries and capitalist agriculture; that is where the point of departure and arrival of the extensive foreign trade is situated, along with a super-abundance of precious metals, of solid coins, and of titles of credit. All advanced economic modernity is concentrated in this nucleus: the traveler realizes this when he contemplates Venice in the fifteenth century, or Amsterdam in the seventeenth, or London in the eighteenth, or New York in the present.[13]

Farther out, in the circle of intermediate countries, which are "neighbors, competitors, or emulators of the center," this modernity, this level of life, decreases, and the dynamics are no longer the same as those of the center. Finally, in the marginal and dependent zones, geographically far removed from the center, "the life of men evokes purgatory, when not hell." Their subordinated integration into the division of labor and their segmented participation in the international market drags them in the wake of a modernity that only benefits them contradictorily, that penetrates them from all sides, causing unexpected, and sometimes perverse, effects, creating and multiplying the heterogeneity that ends up being their characteristic condition of life and the barely perceptible sign of their identity. Recall Monsiváis's collage.

In the world-economy of contemporary capitalism, "North Americanization" appears as a feature inseparable from modernity. From there come the impulses of modernism; there will end up the modernists and modern-

---

13. Fernand Braudel, *La dinámica del capitalismo* (Madrid: Alianza Editorial, 1985), 102–3.

isms that happen to originate in the periphery. To oppose this reality with a nationalism tied to traditions and values from the past, to a notion of national identity prior to any cultural contamination is, to say it in Monsiváis's own words, to declare that the resistance to cultural penetration finds itself defeated in advance.[14]

The question is, however, whether it is still meaningful to speak of *cultural penetration* in any case, since there is no doubt that in the present configuration of the capitalist world-economy, the center retains, in addition to the control over economic and military dynamics, a conclusive cultural hegemony. The "intermediate" countries, according to Braudel's nomenclature, see it this way. Baudrillard, referring to the relation of Europe to America, has said: "It is not only a question of a disjuncture, it is an abyss of modernity which separates us." Or again: "The United States is a realized utopia."[15]

We have been accustomed to think the cultural problem in Latin America within the parameters of dependency theory. Cultural penetration? Dependent culture? What we observe, rather, is that modernity, as a differentiated experience in the capitalist world, has a center, which radiates a zone of marginal and dependent peripheries where this same modernity creates and re-creates a cultural heterogeneity, which, in turn, in all of its fragments, breaks, folds, collages, and displacements continues to be tied to the hegemonic center. The very identity of these peripheral zones is partially constructed with the image of this other, in the same way that its culture is elaborated with fragments of this other culture. In all fields of culture—science, technology, art, utopias—the important modern cultural syntheses are first produced in the North and descend later to us, via a process in which they are "received" and appropriated according to local codes of reception. This is how it has happened with sociology, pop art, rock music, film, data processing, models of the university, neoliberalism, the most recent medicines, armaments, and, in the long run, with our very incorporation into modernity.

14. Monsiváis, "Penetración," 76.
15. Jean Baudrillard, "La utopia realizada" (Paper delivered at the Congress on the European Cultural Space, Madrid, October 17–19, 1985).

Conclusions

It should be clear that these notes have no way of concluding. It is rather a question of initiating a reflection whose larger coordinates are the ongoing debate about modernity, modernism, and modernization. At a time when a confusing fog of "posts"—postmodernism, postpolitics, posthistory, postvanguard—hovers over modernity, it becomes necessary to recover the specific character of modernization in Latin America. Here, among ourselves, the malaise in culture does not, could not, spring from the exhaustion of modernity. On the contrary, it arises from an exasperation with modernity, with its infinitely ambiguous effects, with its inevitable intentionalism, with its distortions, and with the problems that it bequeaths for the future of the region, some of which I have briefly discussed.

Condemned to live in a world where all the images of modernity and modernism come to us from the outside and become obsolete before we are able to materialize them, we find ourselves trapped in a world where not all solid things but rather all symbols melt into air. Latin America: the project of echoes and fragments, of past utopias whose present we can only perceive as a continuous crisis. This sensation of the permanent crisis of everything, of the economy, institutions, political regimes, universities, art, public services, private enterprise, the armed forces, poorly and barely hides the fact that we live and think in the middle of a modernity in the process of construction, whose dynamic is increasing the heterogeneities of our very perceptions, knowledges, and information.

What happens to us is exactly the opposite of what happens in that postmodernity in which, according to Baudrillard, "things have found a way of avoiding a dialectics of meaning that was beginning to bore them: by proliferating indefinitely, increasing their potential, outbidding themselves in an ascension to the limit, an obscenity that henceforth becomes their immanent finality and senseless reason." [16] For us, it would at times seem that it is the meaning, words, and experiences that have found a way to escape a dialectic of things that bored them: infinitely proliferating, self-empowering, self-essentializing in a game of extremes and mirrors, carried along by a senseless reason . . .

But neither is it useful to exaggerate. Here, between words and things, ideology and society, symbols and instruments, there still tend to

16. Jean Baudrillard, *Fatal Strategies* (New York: Semiotext(e), 1982), 7.

be fragile connections that permit a "coming and going" behind this dream of modernity that, only half accepted, has nevertheless already permeated the society and culture of this part of America.

The future of Latin America will not be, for this reason, very different from its present: one of a peripheral modernity, de-centered, subject to conflicts, whose destiny will depend, to some degree, on what these societies manage to do with this modernity in the process of producing it through their own complex and changing heterogeneity.

Latin American Identity and Mixed Temporalities; or, How to Be Postmodern and Indian at the Same Time

Fernando Calderón

Why, in Latin America, do millions of peasants and artisans coexist with factories, computers and electronic equipment of all sorts, and now even a few nuclear power plants? Why do almost all Latin Americans watch North American television programs, which, most of the time, implant in us the new values of the market and atomic violence? And why does the new programmed, postindustrial culture threaten to fragment us even more and to condemn us, like the rest of the world, to be numbers? Or, to ask the question another way, why does the revolutionary Gabriel García Márquez write with a hygienic, electronic computer about the magic world of Mauricio Babilona and his yellow butterflies?

Maybe because we live in incomplete and mixed times of premodernity, modernity, and postmodernity, each of these linked historically in turn with corresponding cultures that are, or were, epicenters of power. That is why our cultural temporalities are, in addition to incomplete and mixed, dependent.

Maybe this coexistence also explains why the Latin American cultural personality is ambiguous as well as multiple, metamorphic as well as dynamic, and why our identity, in its many spaces and times, is many identities, so that it is possible for us to find in ourselves many "I's." Maybe this is what the Peruvian César Vallejo wanted to teach us when he said from Paris, "Today I have spoken about myself with myself."

The times of colonial Christianity are not dead facts of the past, they are socioculturally reconstituted times. How else can we explain the presence of strong feudal and patrimonial traits or the persistence of political and military elites of such long standing in almost all the countries of our continent? Even more, how can we explain why a small group of families, independent of class connotations (landowners, industrialists, bureaucrats, bankers) or specific ideologies (conservative, republican, liberal, socialist), had, and has, an important presence in the cultural system of political decision-making in our countries? How do we explain that more than 90 percent of the parliamentary representatives of the Andean countries do not speak the vernacular languages of their constituents? How do we explain why a Brazilian peasant, when asked by North American pollsters who the president of Brazil was, answered Pedro Cabral?

Colonial culture, by the intrinsic fact of its constitution, was incomplete. The colony could not develop or confront itself or the world in order to grow toward modernity, not only because it imported Christian gods, who, unable to replace our old gods, only adapted themselves to the polytheism of our indigenous cultures, but even more because the colony defined its fundamental ethos around the cultivation of land: *pachamama* (mother earth) for some, *encomienda* for others. The cultural dispute was over the land and opposing values connected to it, and it was as difficult for the great landowners, ecclesiastics, generals, politicians, and colonial agents, as much as for Indian peasants, to fully undertake the difficult and audacious task of modernity.

In reality, modernity came to us from the outside in various ways. The first was by ship: It was called The Social Contract, and it was loaded with African slaves. Then came the revolutionaries and the liberators, influenced by the American Revolution and by French liberalism. Later, a deformed nineteenth-century modernity was introduced to the continent by the old colonial elites, now republicans. Two faces, two identities: one modern, white, and liberal, turned to the exterior in order to legitimize their relationship with the world; the other black, plagued by religious hyprocrisy, uncivil, racist, feudal, and brutally repressive, turned inward, in order to organize domination.

A review of the congressional records of these republics in the second half of the nineteenth century shows that all of our parliamentarians cited Rousseau, Voltaire, Montesquieu, and even Hobbes; but if one also examines the laws they passed that declared, for example, the "freeing from mortmain of land," their anti-Enlightenment character will be evident as well. Thought itself was, in general, very poor, trapped in a foreign, pragmatic modernity that did not arise from its own exercise of reason, the basic condition of Enlightenment. Even art was limited and impossible to compare with the expressive richness of the Brazilian, Mexican, or Andean baroque. Many colonial cities changed their physiognomy, but often for the worse, as their architecture found itself invaded by French-inspired, and in general poorly imitated, "modern," pastry-cake buildings.

In reality, modern European thought of the late nineteenth century spread in Latin America only in the twentieth century. By the same token, we have absorbed only partially the modernist production of the twentieth century, although no one can deny that in making ourselves part of it, we have also enriched it. (It is enough to mention Rubén Darío in this respect.) While Freud was not extensively read until the sixties, Weber was translated into Spanish in Mexico before he was in the United States. Nietzsche (I do not know whether for good or evil or beyond them) is still not read, but Sartre is.

Industrialization and Marxism would also arrive from the outside but would spread with much vigor on the continent. Capitalist industrialization did not come through the "Junker" path of the self-transformation of a traditional elite into a bourgeoisie, nor through a religious reformation, but rather through the penetration of international monopoly capital. Latin America was incorporated into the industrial world via interimperialist conflicts that sought raw materials, markets, and cultural domination. Marxism (a classic modernist production of the nineteenth century) similarly arrived already transformed into Leninism, a phenomenon that can be appreciated with greater clarity in the constitution of the first Latin American Communist parties and in the rich polemics that broke out among intellectuals who jumped on its bandwagon.

Perhaps the most genuinely Latin American contribution to this "modernist" impulse was the intellectual elaboration of revolutionary nationalism and of national popular, or populist, movements, particularly by Victor Raúl Haya de la Torre, but also by Lombardo Toledano and others, who invoked specifically Leninist concepts and goals to be attained through the instrument of the vanguard party and its leadership: anti-imperialism, national self-determination, class alliances, and so on. The exception was

Mariátegui, who, like Gramsci in Italy, conceived of Marxism from a less Leninist and more cultural and nationally specific perspective.

But the actual historical processes and cultural changes we lived through were as important as the ideas that populism depended on. Because of this, even with all its incoherencies, populism was the most genuine social and cultural creation of Latin America in the twentieth century. Populism changed even those who were opposed to it. It modified the culture of our peoples, their sexuality, their ways of loving, of thinking, and even of dancing and walking: in short, all of daily life. Only under populism, with the integration of the masses into the market, import substitution, urbanization, and other social changes of different degrees of intensity and rhythm, was modernity finally imposed in Latin America, with a Latin American style. Thus, from the Mexican and Bolivian Revolutions to the timid, but tragic and parodic, experience of Vargasism in Brazil, populism was the instrument of our fuller integration into the universal and paradoxical experience of modernity. Universal, as Marshall Berman would say, because it united us (culturally) with all of humanity, and paradoxical because it brought us nearer to the uncertainty of reason in the face of the absolute dangers of life and death, to the most wonderful utopian projects and dreams of equality and freedom, as well as to the Nazi extermination camps and nuclear war. To put it in Weberian terms, we were incorporated by populism into the modern game of living between bureaucratic rationalism and existential freedom. As the Mexican joke says: "If Kafka were Latin American, he would be a realist."

From the twenties to the sixties, in a thousand forms, populism reigned in the streets of Latin America, attempting to integrate processes of democratization and industrialization with an autonomous national state on the basis of relations of patronage. It did not achieve this, but it did something new that could not be destroyed by the subsequent brutal dictatorships nor by the confused maneuvers of the populist leaders themselves.

Social scientists, with all their hesitations, hairsplitting, and regrets, were also part of the ambience of this movement, and some of the most innovative were responsible for introducing modern sociology and economics and university reform to the continent. They sought to give a rational basis for the self-understanding of the age through evolutionary schemes, such as the one that describes the "stages" of modernization. They proclaimed the necessity of scientific analysis and understanding, and also of planning and state action. But history itself, at least political and economic history, was regressive and irrational, not only because of the problem of authoritarianism but also because of the strange directions that Latin America and the international system took in the course of the pursuit of modernity. As Latin Americans, we learned that it was possible to change for the better, but also for the worse.

Later, populism broke up into little pieces or became mechanical, in Durkheim's sense, and its axiological, totalizing, Latin Americanist orientations lost the social impulse that sustained them. The sixties gave rise to new modernist, and even postmodernist, impulses. For someone from the sixties to write about the sixties, is, however, to write about nothing and about alchemy, trapezes, and infinite and immeasurable utopian horizons. They were years of a tragic and lucid schizophrenia. Despite our adherence to what were essentially Enlightenment or neo-Enlightenment ideologies of progress (even Marcuse's), the idea was to believe in nothing except the present, and to make this last through time. At least this is what happened with students and revolutionaries, while society, with some exceptions, was left orphaned and isolated. Could it be that in its excessive cult of the present, the radical vanguardism of the sixties was, in effect, conservative? The problem, the big problem, is that in Latin America, the vanguardism of the sixties cannot be seen in isolation from other coexisting times and cultures. Admitting this, we would see how the sixties also gave rise to something like Allende and the Chile of the Popular Unity, a project that, with a syncretism peculiar to Latin America, achieved with great effort a totalizing identity between the vanguardism of the sixties, classical Latin American populism, and the nineteenth-century modernism of Marx. It was defeated by the other face of Latin American modernity, the technocratic authoritarianism of Pinochet.

Beginning in the seventies, with the military dictatorships and the consequent reappraisal of private life and then of democracy, it becomes possible to think that various processes and systems of thought coexist in Latin America, some complementing modernity, others developing a confused postmodernity, and others maintaining premodernity, but all in a mixed and subordinate manner. Vargas Llosa's magnificent novel *The War at the End of the World* is a good example of this. It narrates a curious nineteenth-century peasant rebellion in the Brazilian *sertão*, or backlands, led by Antonio Conselheiro, part bandit, part magician. But in my opinion, what the novelist really speaks to us about is contemporary Peru and himself: of a Peru that is falling apart and changing shape, and of the frustrations that this creates and re-creates in Vargas Llosa; in short, of the coexistence of faded or residual identities with strong emergent ones.

The Lion of Natuba in the novel is calculation or reason, dirty but effective, deformed but human, ugly but beautiful, something like Nietzsche's superman: a synthesis of many men who love danger and the infinite. It dies but also wins many battles. Conselheiro, sustained by the premodern saints who surround him, is clearly messianism, which criticizes and fights against the injustice of the traditional Brazilian oligarchy of the northeast (Baron Canabaras is the decadent oligarchy of Lima) by proposing a return to the past, to a millenarian Christianity, a utopian project that finds an echo in popular faith, but, and this is the brilliant twist of the author, that is also a form of instrumental rationality, seeking to achieve military victory in confrontation with the Brazilian state and to communicate with the world through a journalist. Isn't this rebellion a phantasmagorical mirror of Shining Path? And isn't the confused journalist Varguitas the same "little" Vargas who, having lost his glasses, or more precisely his paradigms, cannot understand what is decisive in the situation of Peru today? Isn't he perhaps one more intellectual detached from his reality who, while worrying about his fallen glasses on the ground, does not see what is growing in that very ground?

All of Latin America is experiencing a difficult time of the redefinition of its identities in the midst not only of democratic reappraisal but also of brutal and strange transformations that tie it to a new (the old) postindustrial and programmed world, to a modern world in decline and perhaps to another emerging postmodern world: that is, to a world that simultaneously tends to a greater production of wealth and to a growing social marginalization and terrifying cultural homogeneity, a world of increasing noncommunication between races, of cages, more legal than legitimate, of pastiche and of schizophrenia, which tends to completely negate the search for liberating identities. The foreign debt, the declining Latin American economic participation in the world market, the greater concentration of power in transnational elites and corporations, the loss of influence and capacity of the nation-state, the technological revolution and the interstitial, binary role of data processing, the subjugation of everything to the market, the internationalization of national conflicts (such as the conflict in Nicaragua, which was turned into an East-West confrontation), the enormous growth of the informal sector, the emergence of political actions void of social meaning, the fragmentation of social actors and the loss of centrality of the working class, the anomalous urban violence, and the perverse economic logic of drugs: Phenomena such as these make one confront the limitations to the creative reproduction of Latin American and international society and thought. The great challenge to Latin America today consists in finding ways of adapting these unignorable phenomena to the construction of democracy and of a new social order that would enable the creative expansion and mutation of our social identities without abandoning the need for economic development and equity. More apocalyptic authors, such as Gino Germani, see intrinsically totalitarian features in the very process of modernization. Others, such as Alain Touraine, point to the possibility of a new Enlightenment; and there are also those who visualize the possibility of a communal reconstruction of our societies from the base up.

The phenomenon of cocaine and the new social movements are perhaps extreme and opposite cultural facts in Latin America; nevertheless, in their crudeness and nakedness of their difference, they may demonstrate the limits and possibilities of this new order. The report of the Select Committee on Narcotics of the United States House of Representatives estimated that the illicit narcotics industry did an annual business of approximately $110 billion, which indicated an annual growth rate of 10 percent. Of these $110 billion, $40 billion, approximately, corresponded to the cocaine industry; for every dollar invested in coca leaves in the regions of production, $300 are earned in the streets of the United States. Only $1 of the $300 remained in the hands of the growers. Cocaine production is a large-scale industry that affects highly industrialized societies as well as a considerable number of Latin Americans living in rural poverty. Cocaine is not only a new and transcendental economic fact; it is, above all, a new cultural fact that involves a breakdown of significant social relations, and a loss of notions of time and space, and of personal and social identity.

State or private programs for confronting the problems caused by cocaine have remained mostly at the level of police actions, interdiction, individual or small-scale psychological therapy: that is, the effects of the problem are confronted, but not its causes. Cocaine perversely unites the humble peasant of tropical Chapare with the sophisticated atomic physicist of the Silicon Valley. Why are drugs being consumed now as never before? Because among the youth of the industrialized societies and in the middle classes of our own countries, there is an ever-decreasing possibility of constructing an autonomous personality, as Bettelheim defines this concept. This is because of, among other things, the new social roles of men and women, the breakdown of the classical model of the patriarchal, nuclear family, decreased familial or collective communication and socialization, the growth of aggressive behaviors without outlets, solitude controlled by self-aggression, the predominance of feelings of death, a pedagogy that no longer inculcates Enlightenment values but rather teaches by rote technology and uncritical competency: in short, a society that demands greater maturity of its youth while at the same time providing fewer means of acquiring it. Paradoxically, the very virtues of productivity, competency, and thrift characteristic of the Protestant ethic and the capitalist spirit contain their own condemnation, among other reasons because of the progressively more restricted and selective channels of upward social mobility. It is possible to imagine that many young people in the process of integration into market society consume drugs in order to achieve greater productivity and efficiency, which, in fact, they do; but in the process, they lose, in the long run, their vitality and identity. In this sense, the sociocultural reproduction of the fabled American Way of Life has become problematic; it is a way of life that needs to commit suicide in order to live. Some take drugs because they are brutally excluded from this way of life, others because they are perversely included in it.

And upon this cultural demand of drug consumption is built a hidden world of mafias and gangs that feed on and become wealthy from their own carrion and that have ever-more real and formal power, including functions in the new transnational consumer capitalism. Such is their power in the empire of the North as well as in, for example, the villages in the south of my own country, Bolivia, which cannot be understood apart from this phenomenon not only because of the decadence of the mining economy and the uncertain future of its workers but also because of the erosion of its socioeconomic fabric and its ethical standards by the effects of narcotraffic. But, how can one ask a group of poor peasants who cultivate coca and who, for the first time in history, have favorably modified the terms of trade to comprehend that they are harming North American youth, when one cannot make even a nuclear scientist comprehend that the elaboration of certain models of atomic decomposition is helping to create bombs that will destroy humanity? In any case, what is certain is that the peasants would prefer to plant oranges and live in legality.

This is, perhaps, a postmodern phenomenon, but one that also underlines the inability of states to confront the problem of drugs, permitting unconscious suicide: an alarming and pathological symptom of a society incapable of facing itself. It is the new and perverse logic of capitalism stripped of its historical sense.

I cannot think of a better way of mapping the current Latin American scene than astronomy. Seen from the point of view of modernity, social movements have lost their vital impulse, and their former order has been replaced by a kind of big bang; those subjects and actors who constructed history are today fragmented and dispersed, and the new social practices and actors are more expressive and symbolic than political. The social universe is like a great galaxy in formation, incandescent and embryonic, but also spastic, with restricted identities, but also with great ethical cohesion. It is like a joining around a black hole of dispersed energies, which perhaps will be stars tomorrow.

Sociologically, however, this state of things need not imply a dramatic change in the real content of the system of historical action but rather the resignification and restructuring of previously given forms of behavior. It is true that there existed tendencies of social fragmentation before, that many of the social or cultural movements such as populism had strong monist tendencies, that in many cases identities were presented in a restricted way; but this is not really the point. Historically, we should be experiencing a kind of "uneven" disturbance of identity, stronger in some places and groups and weaker in others. But something different is taking place, and the course of this movement is uncertain.

The social movements seek to reconstitute their past identities in a new way and with other actors; however, it is impossible to understand them with the Cartesian eyeglasses of little Vargas (that is, of modernism), methodologically organizing Picasso's paintings, with eyes looking up on the right, hands perpendicular to each other on the left, and a horse at bottom center. Instead, it is a question of finding the signifiers of the multiplicity of figures and symbols and perhaps of a new historicity; for example, to say in Latin American: behind those two little eyes, there is a vision; or a horse that falls down but also gets up again; or better yet, Latin America stands up falling down, but it stands up; or the dead child dreams. And in this way, we can try to identify something common to all these figures, not something that homogenizes or classifies them, but something that permits them to coexist and to oppose that which oppresses them, something constructive in them. Because no one can deny that the figures of *Guernica* are somehow confined, that there is something that oppresses and affects them, something that is alive and can be imagined even though it cannot be seen, that is there with its pressure and immense power. How do we reaffirm our identities if we are no longer what we wanted to be? How do we coexist respecting and alternating with others, at the same time fighting against what oppresses us, if not by accepting ourselves as we are, but without ceasing to dream?

Some texts of recent artistic creation in Latin America perceive or describe aspects of this new universe in formation. For example, Rubén Blades, who sings while people dance to his *salsa* "Buscando America": "I'm looking for America, and sometimes I'm afraid I won't find her, and if I find her, I'm afraid I won't know her"; or the Aymara group WARA, which plays ancestral Indian flutes to the accompaniment of electric guitars and which sings, "To your roots you must go, leaf by leaf, with sweet and sad lucidity"; or the poet Hugo Mujica, who tells us,

> There is a god looking at itself,
> in the blindness of every human being.

Eurocentrism and Modernity (Introduction to the Frankfurt Lectures)

Enrique Dussel

Modernity is, for many (for Jürgen Habermas or Charles Taylor, for example),[1] an essentially or exclusively European phenomenon. In these lectures, I will argue that modernity is, in fact, a European phenomenon, but one constituted in a dialectical relation with a non-European alterity that is its ultimate content. Modernity appears when Europe affirms itself as the "center" of a *World* History that it inaugurates; the "periphery" that surrounds this center is consequently part of its self-definition. The occlusion of this periphery (and of the role of Spain and Portugal in the formation of the modern world system from the late fifteenth to the mid-seventeenth centuries) leads the major contemporary thinkers of the "center" into a Eurocentric fallacy in their understanding of modernity. If their understanding of the genealogy of modernity is thus partial and provincial, their attempts at a critique or defense of it are likewise unilateral and, in part, false.

It is a question of uncovering the origin of what I call "the myth of

---

1. Jürgen Habermas, *Der philosophische Diskurs der Moderne* (Frankfurt: Suhrkamp, 1988); Charles Taylor, *Sources of the Self: The Making of Modern Identity* (Cambridge: Harvard University Press, 1989).

modernity" itself. Modernity includes a rational "concept" of emancipation that we affirm and subsume. But, at the same time, it develops an irrational myth, a justification for genocidal violence. The postmodernists criticize modern reason as a reason of terror; we criticize modern reason because of the irrational myth that it conceals. The theme of these lectures will be the need for the "negation" and "transcendence" of modernity understood in this second sense.

According to my central thesis, 1492 is the date of the "birth" of modernity, although its gestation involves a preceding "intrauterine" process of growth. The possibility of modernity originated in the free cities of medieval Europe, which were centers of enormous creativity. But modernity as such was "born" when Europe was in a position to pose itself against an other, when, in other words, Europe could constitute itself as a unified ego exploring, conquering, colonizing an alterity that gave back its image of itself. This other, in other words, was not "dis-covered" (*descubierto*), or admitted, as such, but concealed, or "covered-up" (*encubierto*), as the same as what Europe assumed it had always been. So, if 1492 is the moment of the "birth" of modernity as a concept, the moment of origin of a very particular myth of sacrificial violence, it also marks the origin of a process of concealment or misrecognition of the non-European.

Since I am delivering these lectures in Frankfurt, at the invitation of the Johann Wolfgang Goethe University, I will discuss some of the great thinkers associated with this city, from Hegel, who spent part of his early career here, to Habermas and the famous school that bears the city's name. I should mention in passing that it was a Jew from my country involved in the export trade in agricultural commodities between Argentina and Great Britain, who provided the initial subsidy for the Institute that Horkheimer and others founded in this city. That is, it was the value produced by the labor of the gauchos and peons of the pampa, objectivized in wheat or beef and appropriated by the great landowning and merchant families of Argentina, that, transferred to Germany, gave birth to the Frankfurt school. It is in the name, then, of those semi-Indians, peons, and gauchos of my country, demanding, in a way, an accounting of the uses to which the fruit of their lives and labor were put, that I undertake to deliver these lectures here and now. I need to add one more detail: In 1870, a poor carpenter, a socialist and Lutheran from the town of Schweinfurt am Main only a few kilometers from here, arrived in Buenos Aires looking for work, freedom from persecution, and peace. His name was Johannes Kaspar Dussel. He was welcomed in Argentina, given opportunities to make good, and he raised a family and died in those lands. He was my great grandfather. Today, when so many foreigners come to Germany looking for the same things, by contrast, they are repudiated, expelled, treated . . . like Turks! Germany has forgotten the hospitality that was extended to *its* poor by other countries in the nineteenth century.

I have said that the concept of modernity occludes the role of Europe's own Iberian periphery, and in particular Spain, in its formation. At the end of the fifteenth century, Spain was the only European power with the capacity of external territorial conquest, as it demonstrated in the conquest of the Kingdom of Granada from Islamic rule in 1492, the last phase in the centuries-long "reconquest" and colonization of Andalusia. Until that moment, Europe had been itself the periphery of a more powerful and "developed" Islamic world (just as, until Columbus, the Atlantic was a secondary ocean). The Iberian Reconquest, with the extreme sectarian violence it unleashed in its final stages (broken treaties, elimination of local elites, endless massacres and tortures, the demand that the conquered betray their religion and culture under pain of death or expulsion, the confiscation and repartition in feudal form of lands, towns, and their inhabitants to the officers of the conquering army), was, in turn, the model for the colonization of the New World.

Understanding this, I believe, allows Latin America to also rediscover its "place" in the history of modernity. We were the *first periphery* of modern Europe; that is, we suffered globally from our moment of origin on a constitutive process of modernization (although the term as such wouldn't have been in use at the time) that afterward would be applied in Africa and Asia. Although our continent was already known to Europe—as the 1489 world map of Henricus Martellus in Rome demonstrates—only Spain, thanks to the political ability of the Catholic kings and the daring of Columbus, attempted formally and openly, with the corresponding assumption of rights and privileges (and in open competition with Portugal), to launch itself toward the Atlantic in search of a route to India. This process of discovery and conquest, whose quincentenary is commemorated this year, is not simply of anecdotal or historical interest: It is part of the process of the constitution of modern subjectivity itself.

The myth of origin that is hidden in the emancipatory "concept" of modernity, and that continues to underlie philosophical reflection and many other theoretical positions in European and North American thought, has to do above all with the connection of Eurocentrism with the concomitant "fallacy of developmentalism." The fallacy of developmentalism consists

in thinking that the path of Europe's modern development must be followed unilaterally by every other culture. Development is taken here as an
ontological, and not simply a sociological or economic, category. It is the
"necessary movement" of Being for Hegel, its inevitable "development."[2]

Kant's answer to the question posed by the title of his essay "What
is Enlightenment?" is now more than two centuries old. "Enlightenment is
the exodus of humanity by its own effort from the state of guilty immaturity,"
he wrote. "Laziness and cowardice are the reasons why the greater part
of humanity remains pleasurably in this state of immaturity." For Kant, immaturity, or adolescence, is a culpable state, laziness and cowardice its
existential ethos: the *unmündig*. Today, we would ask him: An African in
Africa or as a slave in the United States in the eighteenth century; an Indian
in Mexico or a Latin American *mestizo*: Should all of these subjects be
considered to reside in a state of guilty immaturity?

Hegel answered this question in the following way. In his *Lectures
on the Philosophy of History*, he showed how World History is the self-
realization of God (a *theodicy*), Reason, and Freedom. It is the process
toward enlightenment:

> Universal History represents . . . the *development* of the conscious-
> ness that the Spirit has of its freedom and also the evolution of the
> understanding that the Spirit obtains through such consciousness.
> This *development* implies a *series of stages*, a series of determina-
> tions of freedom, which are born from its self-concept, that is, from
> the nature of freedom to become conscious of itself. . . . This neces-
> sity and the necessary series of the pure abstract determinations of
> the concept are the province of Logic.[3]

In Hegelian ontology, "development" (*Entwicklung*) is what determines the
very movement of the "concept" (*Begriff*) until its culmination in the "Idea"
(from indeterminate Being to the Absolute Knowledge of the *Logic*). De-

2. From Hegel, the category of "development" passed to Marx, and from there to its
usage in current sociology and economic theory. If I insist here on its original "philosophic"
content, it is to recall that an "underdeveloped" country is, for Hegel, "not-modern," pre-
Aufklärung.

3. I use here the text of the *Lectures* in G. W. F. Hegel, *Sämtliche Werke*, ed. J. Hoffmeister
(Hamburg: F. Meiner, 1955), 167, my italics. This work is hereafter cited as *Lectures*. I am
indebted to Martin Bernal's discussion of Hegel's philosophy of Universal History in *Black
Athena: The Afroasiatic Roots of Classical Civilization*, vol. 2 (New Brunswick: Rutgers
University Press, 1991).

velopment is dialectically linear: It is a primordially ontological category, particularly in the case of World History. It has, moreover, a direction in space: "The movement of Universal History goes from the East to the West. Europe is the absolute end of Universal History. Asia is its beginning" (*Lectures*, 243).

This idea of a "necessary" movement of history from East to West, one can readily appreciate, must first have had to eliminate Latin America and Africa from the movement of World History, situating them like Asia in a state of "immaturity" or "childhood" (*Kindheit*). In effect,

> The world is divided into the Old World and the New World. The name of the New World comes from the fact that America . . . has only recently come to be known by Europeans. But it should not be thought for that reason that the distinction is purely external. It is essential. This world is new not only relatively but also absolutely; it is so in all of its aspects, physical and political. . . . The sea of islands that extends between Latin America and Asia reveals also a certain immaturity with respect to its origin. . . . No less so New Holland offers the characteristics of a young geography, for if, departing from the English colonies, we enter into its territory we discover enormous rivers that have not yet found their course. . . . We have evidence of the development of America and its level of civilization, especially in Mexico and Peru, but as an entirely particular culture, which expires the moment in which the Absolute Spirit approaches it. . . . The inferiority of these individuals in all respects is manifest. (*Lectures*, 199–200)

This "immaturity" (*Unreife*) is total, physical (even the vegetation and animals are more primitive, brutal, monstrous, or simply weaker or degenerate). It is the sign of (Latin) America.[4] Hegel writes:

> In respect to the elements that compose it, America has not yet completed its formation. . . . America is, consequently, the land of the future. Only in future ages will its historical importance become evident. . . . But as a land of the future Latin America has no interest for us, because the philosopher does not make prophesies. (*Lectures*, 209–10)

4. On European and, in particular, Hegel's views of American flora and fauna, see Antonello Gerbi, *La naturaleza de las Indias Nuevas* (Mexico: Fondo de Cultura Económica, 1978).

As a land in childhood, then, Latin America remains outside World History.[5] The same happens with Africa. Hegel still shares the medieval, premodern conception of the world as a trinity composed of Europe, Asia, and Africa, but it is a trinity in which the axis of history has been displaced toward Europe. Thus:

> The three parts of the world maintain between themselves, therefore, an essential relation and constitute a totality (*Totalität*). . . . [But] The Mediterranean sea is the element of union between them, and this converts it into the *center* of all Universal History. . . . The Mediterranean is the axis of Universal History. (*Lectures*, 210)

Hegel has a number of pages on Africa that deserve to be read, although one needs to approach the task with a sense of humor, since they are a kind of fantastic apotheosis of racist ideology, full of superficial prejudices and received opinions and a seemingly infinite sense of superiority that illustrate well the European state of mind at the beginning of the nineteenth century. For example:

> Africa is in general a closed land, and this maintains its fundamental character. (*Lectures*, 212)

> Among negroes it is the case that consciousness has not attained even the intuition of any sort of objectivity, such as, for example, God or the law, in which man is in relation with his will and has the intuition of his essence. . . . [The negro] is the man as beast. (*Lectures*, 218)

> This mode of being of the Africans explains why it is extraordinarily easy to turn them into fanatics. The realm of the Absolute Spirit is so impoverished among them and the natural Spirit so intense that any representation which they are inculcated with suffices to impel them to respect nothing, to destroy everything. . . . Africa . . . does not have history as such. Consequently we abandon Africa, to never mention it again. It is not part of the historical world; it does not evidence historical movement or development. . . . What we understand properly as Africa is something isolated and without history, still mired in the

---

5. For Hegel, the child represents only the "real potential" of reason. The "immediacy" of the child's consciousness allows it to be, therefore, only the periphery (or possibility) of experience but not its center. "Only the adult has intelligence . . . and is the center of everything" (*Lectures*, 16).

natural Spirit, and therefore can only be located here at the entrance gate of Universal History. (*Lectures*, 231–34)

European racial pride—the Hegelian "immoderateness" Kierkegaard was so fond of ironizing—is nowhere more evident than in these remarks. As "South," both Latin America and Africa lie outside the East-West movement of World History. But Hegel also consigns Asia to a preparatory, introductory role:

Asia is the part of the world where one can verify origin as such. . . . But Europe is absolutely the Center and the End (*das Zentrum und das Ende*) of the ancient world and of the West as such, Asia the absolute East. (*Lectures*, 235)

Asia is the Spirit only in its infancy. Oriental despotism allows only the One (the emperor) to be free. It is thus the dawn, but in no sense the culmination of World History. The "beginning" and "end" of History is Europe.[6] But there are various Europes. There is Southern Europe: Portugal, Spain, southern France, and Italy. There the Spirit dwelt in antiquity, when the North was still "uncultivated" (*unkultiviert*). But Southern Europe "is not marked with a nucleus (*Kern*) of development in itself" (*Lectures*, 240); destiny is to be found, rather, in Northern Europe. (With this, Hegel discards, in a fashion followed by most contemporary European and North American thinkers, as I suggested earlier, the importance of Spain and Portugal in the period between the fifteenth and the eighteenth centuries—that is, the age of mercantilism—in the development of modernity.)

But there are also two distinct Northern Europes. One is Eastern Europe, consisting of Poland and Russia, which have always existed in relation to Asia. The one that needs to be spoken of, however, is Western Europe: "Germany, France, Denmark, the Scandinavian countries are the heart of Europe" (*Lectures*, 240). In relation to this idea, Hegel's writing takes on something of the sonority of Wagner's trumpets:

The Germanic Spirit is the Spirit *of the New World* (*neuen Welt*), its end is the realization of absolute truth, as the infinite self-

---

6. Francis Fukuyama's much discussed thesis—in the essay "The End of History," *The National Interest* (Summer 1989)—derives directly from this remark of Hegel's. Fukuyama maintains, to be precise, that the United States and the capitalist free market are, with the collapse of communism in the "North" after 1989, the only possible model of society and polity, with no other alternative, and thus are the "end" of history.

determination of freedom, which has as its content its own absolute form. The principle of the German Empire must be adjusted to the Christian religion. The destiny of the Germanic peoples is to provide the missionaries of the Christian Principle.[7]

Expressing a thesis that is the exact contrary of the one I want to develop in these lectures, Hegel continues:

> There arises via the reestablishment of Christian freedom the consciousness of the self-justification of the Spirit. The Christian principle has passed through the formidable discipline of culture; the Reformation gives it its exterior dimension *with the discovery of America.* . . . The principle of the free Spirit makes itself here the banner of the whole world, and from it develop the universal principles of reason. . . . Custom and tradition no longer have validity; the different forms of right need to legitimize themselves as founded on rational principles. Thus is the Spirit's freedom realized. (*Werke*, 12:413–14; my italics)

For Hegel, in other words, modern Christian Europe has nothing to learn from other worlds, other cultures. It has its principle in itself and is, at the same time, the full "realization" of that principle: "The principle has been achieved, and because of this the Last Days have arrived: the idea of Christianity has achieved its full realization" (*Werke*, 12:414).

The three stages of the "Germanic world" are the "development" of this same Spirit. They are the kingdoms of the Father, the Son, and the Holy Ghost. The Germanic Empire is "the kingdom of the Totality, in which we see a repetition of past ages" (*Werke*, 12:417). These are the First Age, the migrations of the Germanic tribes in the times of the Roman Empire, and the Second Age, the feudal Middle Ages. This Second Age comes to an end with three events: the Renaissance, the discovery of America, and the discovery of the passage to India via Cape Horn. These events signal the end of the terrible night of the Middle Ages, but they do not constitute in themselves the new, or Third, Age. This Age, the age of modernity, begins with a properly German event: the Lutheran Reformation, whose principle is, in turn, "developed" fully in the Enlightenment and the French Revolution.[8]

---

7. I cite here from G. W. F. Hegel, *Werke*, vol. 12 (Frankfurt: Suhrkamp, 1970), 413, italics mine. This work is hereafter cited as *Werke*.
8. As the passages cited above indicate, Hegel projects onto the German past—onto the Reformation, to be specific—the radical effects that the discovery of the New World pro-

This embodiment of World History in Europe endows Europe with a kind of universal right, as Hegel explains in a passage from his *Encyclopedia*:

> History is the configuration of the Spirit in the form of becoming. . . . The people that receives such an element as a natural principle . . . is the dominant people at this moment of World History. . . . Against the absolute right that such a people possesses by virtue of being the bearer of the development of the world Spirit, the spirit of other peoples *has no rights* (*rechtlos*).[9]

This people, the North, Europe (and, for Hegel, Germany and England in particular), has, in other words, an "absolute right" because it is the "bearer" (*Träger*) of the Spirit in its "moment of development" (*Entwicklungstuffe*). In the face of this, no other people can be said to have any rights proper to it, and certainly none that it could pose *against* Europe. This is one of the clearest definitions not only of Eurocentrism but of the sacralization of the imperial power of the North or the Center over the South, the Periphery, the colonial and dependent world of antiquity. Further commentary is unnecessary. The texts speak in their frightening cruelty of a limitless cynicism that masks itself as the "development" of "reason" itself, *Aufklärung*.

In addition—and this is something that has passed unnoticed by many commentators and critics of Hegel, including Marx—it is worth noting that for Hegel, the contradictory character of European "civil society" is transcended in the "state" in part thanks to the constitution of "colonies":

> Through a dialectical impulse to transcend itself that is proper to it, such a society is, in the first place, driven to seek outside itself new consumers. For this reason it seeks to find ways to move about among other peoples that are inferior to it with respect to the resources that it has in abundance, or, in general, its industry. . . .
>
> This development of relations offers also the means of colonization towards which, in either an accidental or systematic way, a completed civil society is impelled. Colonization allows a portion of its

---

duced in Europe at the end of the fifteenth and the beginning of the sixteenth centuries. If Latin America is excluded as such from World History, then North, or Anglo-Saxon, America is the West at a second level for Hegel, and thus has a place in World History.
9. G. W. F. Hegel, *Encyklopädie der philosophischen Wissenschaften: im Grundrisse*, ed. F. Nicolin and O. Pöggler (Hamburg: F. Meiner, 1969), 430, sections 346 and 347, my italics.

population to return to the principle of family property in the new territory, and, at the same time, it acquires for itself a new possibility and field of labor.[10]

Europe thus "occupies" foreign lands. Hegel does not seem to realize that this means they must be seized from other peoples. The periphery of Europe is a "free space" that allows the poor, produced by the contradictions of capitalist development, to become capitalists or property owners themselves in the colonies.[11]

Habermas is still essentially in this Hegelian mode when he writes that "the historical events that are decisive for the implantation of the principle of [modern] subjectivity are the Reformation, the Enlightenment, and the French Revolution."[12] For Habermas, as for Hegel, the discovery of America is not a constitutive fact of modernity.[13] Habermas also follows Hegel's example in discounting the role of Spain in the origins of modernity.[14] My intention in these lectures is to give an account of modernity that shows the contrary: that the experience not only of "discovery" but especially of "conquest" is essential in the constitution of the modern ego, not only as subjectivity per se but as a subjectivity that is the "center" and "end" of history. Latin America is thus the "other-face" (*teixtli*, in Aztec), the essential alterity of modernity. The immature European ego, or subject, in the Middle Ages itself peripheral to and dependent on the Islamic world, "develops" until it arrives, with Cortés and the Conquest of Mexico (the first extra-European space in which it can carry out a prototypic "development"), at the point of becoming the "master-of-the-world"—a Will to Power specific to its self-consciousness. This sense of the relation between the conquest

10. G. W. F. Hegel, *Philosophy of Right* (Oxford: The Clarendon Press, 1957), sections 246 and 248.
11. When, in Hegel's day and after, as I have noted already, Europe had a "surplus" or chronically poor population, it sent this population to the Third World. Today, Europe closes its frontiers to similar populations from the Third World.
12. Habermas, *Der philosophische Diskurs*, 27.
13. Habermas mentions the discovery, but gives it no particular importance (see *Der philosophische Diskurs*, 15).
14. Hegel writes, for example: "Now we come upon the lands of Morocco, Fez, Algeria, Tunis, Tripoli. It can be said that this region does not belong properly to Africa but to Spain, with which it forms a geographical basin. The polymath de Pradt claims on these grounds that Spain is part of Africa. . . . [Spain] is a country that has limited itself to sharing the destiny of the great nations, a destiny that is decided elsewhere; it is not called upon to acquire its own individuality [as a historical agent]" (*Lectures*, 213).

of America and the formation of modern Europe permits a new definition, a new global vision of modernity, which shows not only its emancipatory but also its destructive and genocidal side.

We are now in a position to summarize the elements of the myth of modernity. (1) Modern (European) civilization understands itself as the most developed, the superior, civilization. (2) This sense of superiority obliges it, in the form of a categorical imperative, as it were, to "develop" (civilize, uplift, educate) the more primitive, barbarous, underdeveloped civilizations. (3) The path of such development should be that followed by Europe in its own development out of antiquity and the Middle Ages. (4) Where the barbarian or the primitive opposes the civilizing process, the praxis of modernity must, in the last instance, have recourse to the violence necessary to remove the obstacles to modernization. (5) This violence, which produces, in many different ways, victims, takes on an almost ritualistic character: the civilizing hero invests his victims (the colonized, the slave, the woman, the ecological destruction of the earth, etc.) with the character of being participants in a process of redemptive sacrifice. (6) From the point of view of modernity, the barbarian or primitive is in a state of guilt (for, among other things, opposing the civilizing process). This allows modernity to present itself not only as innocent but also as a force that will emancipate or redeem its victims from their guilt. (7) Given this "civilizing" and redemptive character of modernity, the suffering and sacrifices (the costs) of modernization imposed on "immature" peoples, enslaved races, the "weaker" sex, et cetera, are inevitable and necessary.

This understanding of the myth of modernity has a different sense for us than for Horkheimer and Adorno in their *Dialectic of Enlightenment*, or for the postmodernists such as Lyotard, Rorty, and Vattimo. Unlike the postmodernists, we do not propose a critique of reason as such; but we do accept their critique of a violent, coercive, genocidal reason. We do not deny the rational kernel of the universalist rationalism of the Enlightenment, only its irrational moment as sacrificial myth. We do not negate reason, in other words, but the irrationality of the violence generated by the myth of modernity. Against postmodernist irrationalism, we affirm the "reason of the Other."[15]

15. In Tzvetan Todorov's *Nous et les autres* (Seuil: Paris, 1989), for example, the "we" are the Europeans, the "others" us, the peoples of the periphery. Similarly, when Rorty argues for the desirability of "conversation" in place of a rationalist epistemology, he does not take seriously the asymmetrical situation of the other, the concrete empirical impos-

The "realization" of modernity no longer lies in the passage from its abstract potential to its "real," European, embodiment. It lies today, rather, in a process that will transcend modernity as such, a trans-modernity, in which both modernity and its negated alterity (the victims) co-realize themselves in a process of mutual creative fertilization. Trans-modernity (as a project of political, economic, ecological, erotic, pedagogical, and religious liberation) is the co-realization of that which it is impossible for modernity to accomplish by itself: that is, of an *incorporative* solidarity, which I have called analectic, between center/periphery, man/woman, different races, different ethnic groups, different classes, civilization/nature, Western culture/Third World cultures, et cetera. For this to happen, however, the negated and victimized "other-face" of modernity—the colonial periphery, the Indian, the slave, the woman, the child, the subalternized popular cultures—must, in the first place, discover itself as innocent, as the "innocent victim" of a ritual sacrifice, who, in the process of discovering itself as innocent may now judge modernity as guilty of an originary, constitutive, and irrational violence.

---

sibility that the "excluded," "dominated," or "compelled" can intervene *effectively* in such a discussion. He takes as his starting point "we liberal Americans," not "we Aztecs in relation to Cortés," or "we Latin Americans in relation to a North American in 1992." In such cases, *not even conversation* is possible.

The Hybrid: A Conversation with Margarita Zires, Raymundo Mier, and Mabel Piccini

Néstor García Canclini

Mier: I would like to introduce the notion of the hybrid, so very important, it seems to me, in Néstor's book.[1] The notion of the hybrid suggests to me, perhaps because of my complete ignorance of biology, a frontier species, a happening, the sudden eruption of a morphology still without a well-established place in the taxonomies. The entrance of the hybrid into taxonomy necessitates the abandonment of this category in favor of another, less drastic, one, which might be the variant, species, et cetera. The hybrid designates a liminality, a material whose existence exhibits the dual affirmation of a substance and its lack of identity, that which is in the interstices, which profiles itself in a zone of shadow, which escapes, at least in appearance, repetition. The hybrid is the name of a material without identity, of an evanescent condition. The hybrid could then be a very fortunate name because of the density of its evocations of the singular, of an event. In this

This is an extract from a longer text that appeared as "Figuraciones: Las culturas y políticas de la modernidad," *Versión* 1 (October 1991): 11–42.
1. Néstor García Canclini, *Culturas híbridas: Estrategias para entrar y salir de la modernidad* (Mexico, D. F.: Grijalbo, 1990).

marginality with regard to taxonomies, the hybrid permits only an oblique analysis, a zone of effects, of detachments. It can be understood, but only through the traces of its anticipated or confirmed disappearance, through the modalities of its hardening.

To me, the idea of hybrid cultures, then, seems extraordinarily suggestive, because it permits the imagination of social morphologies, fields of singularized regularity, designations of catastrophe, but a catastrophe that is not a limiting border, a mere point of singularity, the space of a fracture. Hybrid culture does not designate a void, a fissure, in the process of transition, rather the very material of a culture, of its vitality and its force of singularized and dissipated invention. In this way, however, it confronts us with a challenge. How do we analyze this dense, interstitial "material" of a liminal culture if its meanings appear only in order to anticipate its disappearance as such, its precipitation toward more stable orderings of meaning? It seems to me that this proposal of hybrid cultures is a methodological challenge in all fields of culture. Specifically, the adjective *hybrid*, referring to culture, pushed to its extremes, seems to put the very concept of culture into interdiction.

Zires: In relation to the point you raise, Raymundo, I believe it's important to recall the notion of culture until now in effect within anthropology and sociology and that has also penetrated other fields, such as communications. This notion of culture is tied to the idea of homogeneous nuclei of more or less coherent beliefs, products, or social behaviors pertaining to a community, group, or nation. Homogeneity is emphasized, coherence is emphasized, and with them the possibility of classification.

Now, in your book, Néstor, you speak about hybrid cultures, which leads us to think about a different notion of culture. According to this notion, culture would not have the coherence that has been attributed to it, nor would it refer to a static body of products or specific cultural elements, but rather to processes of the interrelation of discursive elements that have multiple forms, genres, or formats and that are in permanent transformation. This interrelation, I believe, would always be fragmentary. It would put into question the homogeneous character of the operative conception of culture and its implicit notion of identity as an immovable nucleus.

On the other hand, the hybrid refers us to something that belongs to different areas at the same time, and, in this sense, I believe that what is hybrid cannot have a permanent identity. I think it's important to point out that the processes of hybridization are not a new phenomenon—they have always existed and are always going to exist in societies in general, although they have been called other names. For example, in Mexico, much has been said about how the Aztecs assimilated the religion and culture of the peoples they came to dominate in the pre-Hispanic age. Many have documented the process of religious and cultural syncretism that was produced later during the time of colonization. Some authors who have studied the processes of syncretism as forms of hybridization have pointed out the way in which cultural and political identities are put in jeopardy in these processes.

But these examples shouldn't lead us to think that it's only during periods of the domination of one people over another that processes of hybridization exist, especially if we consider this phenomenon from the perspective of intertextuality. In this sense, we would have to ask whether all culture is not simply a hybrid amalgam and, in that case, we would have to argue that there are no cultures that are not hybrid.

What we can point out with regard to the present situation, which you allude to in your book, Néstor, is that we are witnessing a particular process of hybridization in contemporary societies in which communication technologies play a very important role.

Canclini: I detect two different movements in what Raymundo and Margarita are saying. If I understand Raymundo's concern, it would follow that the hybrid is the indeterminate, something that is constantly changing, while Margarita spoke of processes of hybridization, in which the hybrid becomes formalized. For me, the hybrid is almost never indeterminate, it does not present itself, even in contemporary societies, by degrees of indeterminacy, although cultural crossings have become much more intense recently, and I find in this intensification one of the explanations for the collapse of paradigms and the difficulty of grasping meaning. The hybrid is almost never something indeterminate because there are different historical forms of hybridization.

I tried to work out the following problem in the book: How have combinations of pre-Columbian and colonial traditions with the processes of modernization historically arisen in Latin America? I find historical logics that organize the successive hybridizations. Even the artistic avant-gardes, which were accused of being disintegrative, can be read as searches for modernization; they involve ways of assuming local traditions, of understanding the folklore of a country, of asking oneself what can be done with the heterogeneity of Latin American societies. In a similar way, the principal cultural configurations identified in modernity—high, popular, and mass culture—are the result, as are their crossings, of processes of hybridization that occur in conditions partially predetermined by social systems. For example, modern art can incorporate both artisanal objects and television, but these objects, which until recently were seen as strange and which many criticized when they appeared in museums of modern art, are received by a certain logic, a grammar. The museum gives them a defined space that subordinates them to a history of art and perception, that organizes intercultural hybridizations.

The same occurs when our record collection combines salsa, rock, classical music, ranchera, et cetera—all that we habitually do, in fact, combine in a personal collection. But this doesn't mean it is entirely random. Even though we may want to buy this variety of records, we know that not all of them are sold in the same place, that there are classifications for these goods, that some are for listening with some friends and others with different ones in different social situations. There are no entirely arbitrary crossings, and often we ourselves construct the system that contains them. There are artists who deliberately choose to belong at once to high, popular, and mass culture circuits. In the structure and composition of the messages, a type or style is especially underlined or marked. It's possible to mix salsa and baroque music, but at the same time to mark the predominance of a category, that of rock, jazz, or classical music, at times according to the venue in which the music is going to be played: in the Palace of Fine Arts or at a rock concert, for example.

I agree with what you were saying, Margarita, that objects belong to different fields; I would also say that as subjects, we belong to different areas and we enjoy cultural and artistic goods in different spaces—we can relate them fluidly with different genres. To be a resident in a big city at the end of the century implies being able to relate oneself to varied fields, simultaneously to high, popular, and mass cultural levels. It implies listening to Zabludova on television, going to the folk concerts of the Nezahuacóyotl, going to a rock concert, and dancing to salsa in California: All of these fragmentary experiences coexist in an urban resident, but they are not totally arbitrary. This fragmentation is regulated in part by objective social systems and in part by rituals established by subjects themselves. The rituals serve to classify the real, to establish a before and after, to establish procedures of passage from one situation to another. In the middle of the crossings and hybridization, they establish separate fields that can be connected but that are not totally mixed up. We need rituals because we do not tolerate excessive hybridization.

Certain antiauthoritarian philosophical positions tend to see rituals only as forms of discipline and repression, but the persistence of rituals in contemporary societies can also be interpreted to mean that as subjects we can't live in permanent indetermination and transgression. In order to perceive the complexity of the real and to accept it as people do in fact experience it, we should take into account that people live a great deal of time in the midst of rituals, that they need forms of classification of the real. That is why we don't understand the hybrid if we only look at it as complete dissemination, rather than as something that is also ordered, that is experienced as classified or as in need of classification in order to contain the dissolution of the signifieds.

Zires: Yes, Néstor, but rituals are tied not only to systems of ordering but also to forms of breaking such systems, to the transformation of classifications.

Canclini: Yes, but insofar as they are ordering rituals, they also incorporate the possibility of social transgression. Bourdieu says that there are rituals that involve the simple reproduction of the social, that are tied to the most natural activities of life (birth, marriage, death), and that there are rituals that have to do with the institutionalization of transgression: Through these, it is accepted that transgression exists. Rituals institutionalizing transgression tend to occur in a marginal context, for example, carnival, but although it is possible to cross-dress in carnival (so that men may be women, or women men, or the poor rich), all of this has limits; they are restricted transgressions that have a defined period in which symbolic efficacy can be exercised. When they seek to reach a real efficacy, then repression appears.

Mier: I would like to turn to the question of the incidence of this reflection on the hybrid in the political field. In fact, to me, the notion of hybrid culture poses the problem of how political strategies arise as moments of signification, as precarious regimes of confrontation between systems of discourse. The very notion of power, of strategy, would appear intimately tied to this appearance of hybrid regularities in the construction of signification. And this, I believe, also leads, perhaps, to another problem that is very evident in everyday discourse: the perception of cultural, social, and political processes as being in crisis. The notion of crisis seems to offer another matrix, to unfold an analogous, but divergent, face of the notion of the hybrid and its resonances with political strategies and discursive tensions. Perhaps it would be interesting to introduce an element of differentiation: Crisis appears as a "scene" in different senses of that word. In this scenic dimension, the notion of crisis would have its support in an "effect of meaning" caused by certain conditions of culture in the perception of a subject. This has to do with the perception of a vacuum, of a substantial fracture in the order of experience and of the imminence of the dissolution of that order, of its collapse. This notion of crisis refers me to crucial question, in spite of its apparent distance from Latin American political conditions. What is the condition—the political, strategic condition—of the subject? What are the resources for the re-creation of the meaning of a subject in a liminal culture whose orderings, processes of exchange, and regimes of reciprocities and solidarities find themselves submitted to mobile tensions and incessant transitions, and that therefore also offer mobile and varied "scenographies" in permanent abandon?

I would like to expand a little more on this question of the subject and its experience of dissolution of solidarities in societies in disintegration, in contrast, if there is one, to the subject and its experience of cultural hybridization. If crisis and hybridization are two moments with antagonistic political polarities, is there a fragile tension in this dualism that prevents the catastrophic passage from one to the other? Do hybrid cultures construct the order of their own scenification, the scenification of their provisional stability, of changing modalities of life under other forms of representation, of "perceptible" deployment? This dualism between crisis and hybridization, to me, seems to be at the center of a relevant political question. It is said that in conditions of the collective perception of crisis, there is an exacerbation of conservatism. The uncertainty and the anxiety experienced by the political classes and subjects in tension, faced with the vacuum of the dissolution of the networks of solidarity and symbolic exchange, provoke a return, a relapse to the most rigid and authoritarian regimes, including despotic and fascist ones, which preceded the crisis or which lie buried as potential regimes in weakened institutions. The dualism of crisis and hybridization would seem to suggest, as I pointed out before, two divergent outcomes for diverse collective subjects: a tension between the restoration of disciplinary fields or a relapse to more harshly instituted systems that encourage ultraradical movements that are inevitably conservative, on the one hand, and the invention of new fields marked as mobile, destined for greater flexibility, on the other. This second outcome is perhaps impossible, but the image of hybridization appears at least to suggest it.

Piccini: Radicals are conservative of what? Could you please explain this a bit more?

Mier: Conservative in the sense that radical movements tend to resolve the perceived tensions by struggling for regimes of maximum stability.

Piccini: I would like to add something to the already complex panorama of hybrid cultures in the present reorganization of cultural spaces. Now, Raymundo introduces the idea that there might be hybrid subjects located in certain planes of interstitial character. I wonder whether these figures arise on the contemporary scene as the result of the philosophies called postmodern—that is, do they become visible just because of a particular theoretical focus, or are they also constitutive features of the cultural scene at the end of the millennium? I have the impression that these hybridizations are characteristic of any cultural process in any historical period and that it is, above all, a theoretical perspective that permits us to distinguish the mixtures of cultures, of symbolic forms, or the processes of intertextuality. I agree, of course, that there is another factor that facilitates the full visibility of these new anthropological landscapes; I believe that the new audiovisual techniques intensify these processes—they confer upon them a new certainty at the same time that they permit us to distinguish, in a different way, the recomposition, articulation, and disarticulation of the cultural fields, the migration of symbolic meanings and forms from one field to another, from one message to another, in the signifying chains.

Now, in the particular, I'm interested in taking up the characteristically political aspects of the modern reorganization of cultural spaces, the new ties that are established between political systems and symbolic processes. In Néstor's book, there is an attempt at explaining the particular efficacy that neoconservative policies have acquired in our countries, an efficacy that has a special relevance to the topic of hybrid cultures and the new subjects of hybridization. I'm interested in a discussion about these things, especially because it's recently become intellectually fashionable to emphasize the so-called forms of resistance of the popular sectors in the face of mass media messages, or the variety of "readings" social groups can make of something, or the need to de-center the idea of a "verticality of power" in relation to new cultural technologies and political practices. No doubt these positions opened new paths for understanding the cultural life of groups and classes in our countries and also for reposing the problem of social conflicts and domination. But I feel it's necessary to remember, just in case we forgot, that along with the new utopias of democracy, we are witnessing new forms of domination, and that domination is central in order to understand the behavior of our political systems and the exercise of cultural power. With respect to this, Néstor introduces an idea that is of great interest to me: the idea of "oblique powers" as a notion that serves to analyze the new exercise of social controls coming from the hybridization of cultures.

If the new rituals reorganize chaos by establishing certain kinds of social pacts between the members of a group or community; if they seek to establish new relations of complicity between the citizens and the government (which are now called, as in early sociology, relations of solidarity) just at the very moment when our societies are making possible, with the new projects of economic and political modernization, the ideal of an informed community, I wonder: What is the basis for the success of neoconservative politics? What relation do these policies have to the reorganization of the cultural field? What are the "oblique powers"? What are the new techniques for recruiting wide sectors of society?

There is much talk in current social theory of the appearance of a new individualism in modern democracies. The rhetoric of the individual at the end of the twentieth century is certainly not the one we inherited from the nineteenth century. We have to recognize that the new forms of retreat into private life and the consequent defense of "individual liberties" and the "consumer society" manifest a cultural transformation of major proportions and a substantive reorganization of rituals, symbolic forms, and social and political disciplines. In these changes, I believe that the development of communication technologies, and the power that these networks have to diagram new forms of daily life, occupies a central place: In the majority of cases, they involve domestic "terminals," networks that define the space of the family as the place of encounter with the new symbolic forms of modernity.

I'm interested in reconsidering all these things, situating the emergence of hybrid cultures, the generalized syncretisms, the technologies of domestic seclusion, the simultaneity of information and of cultural contacts in the frame of the new systems of control and domination in our societies.

Canclini: For me, what has given up the ghost is much clearer than the kind of society we are entering. In order to understand what has happened, I believe that we have to address centrally the transformations of symbolic markets or cultural structures. Lamentably, this is still almost always absent in analyses. For example, when one speaks about the loss of the credibility of political parties and of the low representativity of politicians, one alludes to matters like corruption and verticalism. No doubt, these must be taken into account, but it seems to me that there are changes in the sociocultural structure of society that explain why certain forms of the development of domination or hegemony have entered into crisis and are being replaced by others.

I see one of the symptoms of this senility in the loss of pertinence of the traditional versus the modern distinction, or of the divisions among the institutional apparatuses dedicated to high, popular, and mass culture. In Mexico, there is the INBA [National Institute of Fine Arts], which concerns itself with the fine arts; then there are the organisms of popular culture, dedicated to indigenous education or the cultural promotion of ethnic and popular groups; and finally, there is a communicational apparatus, generally in the hands of private companies, but that still occupies a certain place in the political system. These three scenarios, or these three kinds of apparatuses, have been moving in different directions since the forties in Mexico.

In the postrevolutionary period, cultural policies aimed at some kind of integration of high culture, popular culture, and mass culture: This is what occurred with the *Vasconcelist* or *Cardenist* policies for the appropriation of popular culture. On the one hand, they incorporated popular culture in education, the murals, and the great monuments; on the other hand, they promoted the popularization of elite international culture in the schools and in popular and worker collectives. These attempts at integration, or reconciliation, under a national patrimony of the learned and the popular, began to weaken with *Alemanismo*. In 1947 and 1948, the National Indigenist Institute and the Institute of Fine Arts were created, along with a series of institutions that fragmented and segmented cultural development. This segmentation in Mexico resembled what happens in nearly all nations where high, popular, and mass cultural levels are separated. Through various processes, which I analyze in the book, however, this tri-partition of the cultural sphere practically does not exist anymore. It was always artificial, but now, due to crossings in which each of the systems appropriates elements of others, there is a fluid interconnection. This is recognized by the cultural organisms themselves when their most innovative leaders talk about how fine arts should appear on television or how popular culture benefits from the development of fine arts. Nevertheless, there are no institutional structures capable of grasping the hybridism of this intercultural reality. These kinds of phenomena demonstrate the confinement, the exhaustion, of a style of compartmentalization of state apparatuses and political conceptions with regard to culture.

Perhaps there is another newer, and more radical, issue here, though. I'm referring to the decline of the communicative strategies of traditional politics that have been centered in the written culture. Even those who seek to represent the popular sectors, such as the parties of the Left, still have a Gutenbergian conception: lots of books, lots of pamphlets, but an almost unanimous inability to intervene in the cultural industries. Neither the state nor the opposition parties have developed alternative policies appropriate to the rapid development of the cultural industries. What has happened is that the most imaginative private companies, with a high dependence on models from the United States, have expanded radio, television, and other cultural industries. They have occupied a communicative space that is now clearly hegemonic, as much for the number of people it reaches as for the kinds of effects it has on communication structures and social organization. It seems to me that we're barely beginning to take account of the displacement of the state as well as the opposition parties and other traditional forms of doing politics, such as unions, by this cultural reorganization. A key to this loss of credibility, of influence, of the summoning capacity of traditional political actors, is found in their inability to insert themselves into the present structures of communication. To promote leftist, progressive, or popular politics this late in the twentieth century requires the elaboration of absolutely different communicative strategies. I see only small and beginning steps in this direction in some experiences of the Brazilian PT [Workers Party], which has done interesting work on radio and television, or the Vote-NO campaign against Pinochet in Chile, where the opposition used advertising and mass-marketing techniques with very good results. Aside from this, I find that what almost always happens when the intellectuals or "progressives" try to use the cultural industries is, as Fatima Fernández said not long ago, that instead of making cultural television, we make televised culture; instead of making political communication, we transfer structures of political thought and communication that were formed in print culture to the mass media. Thus, from the start, we place ourselves in a situation of ineffectiveness, of inability to intervene in those systems.

There is another, more complicated issue. I'm thinking about the new kinds of mechanisms that these communicative restructurings have created. A little while ago, I read a book by Paul Virilio that speaks about different stages in the development of war. It refers to modern war as a basically communicative war, where performance takes place at long-distance and where there is practically no intervention through land attacks. In the Gulf War, there was performance at a distance by the bombardiers, guided by computer systems, and there were practically no body-to-body conflicts as in traditional wars. This performance at a distance, through communicative exchanges and the consequent concealment of what is taking place in these very concentrated communicative spaces, represents a new contemporary development with a high concentration of communicative powers in the hands of specialists with a very high technological background, who in turn accompany their *performance* (I deliberately say performance instead of *action*) with mechanisms of simulation of informational democratization and the possibilities of participation. When we read the newspaper or watch television, which, to a great degree, involves operations of simulacra, we are confronted with this tension between the most radical concentration of information and communication that has existed in history and the simulation that the new technologies permit the realization of an amply extended participation by the public. This is the reorganization we are asking ourselves about.

Zires: I believe that what you're saying, Néstor, also yields a new perspective on the political problematic of culture in the present situation. You began by speaking about some initiatives of political parties of the Left to insert themselves in the contemporary political-cultural processes, and you mentioned the problems that they have had relocating themselves in a new cultural context. I would like to connect this with something you point out in your book that seems very interesting to me. You say there that we are witnessing a reordering of the public and the private spheres, the creation of a new urban culture that, we could say, is expanding rapidly in contemporary societies in Latin America, and a new role within these societies for communications technologies. All of this modifies the political-cultural order so that the parties don't know how to insert themselves in it anymore, which is due, I believe, to a too-narrow conception of power politics, as well as of the field of communication and culture.

On the other hand, it seems to me that we can learn from what is going on now: the war in the Persian Gulf. Here is something that calls our attention to cultural politics, or, better yet, the present communicative politics. Until now, the media has tried to represent the defeat of socialism or the breakup of the socialist bloc as the victory of democracy and implicitly as the victory of the North American system. Recently, we witnessed an apparent act of spectacular information democracy, which could be better classified as an invasion of images by CNN, the company that has most concentrated the power of information in this communicative war, as you were pointing out. Now then, this invasion of images that has been so overwhelming leads me to wonder whether it has not also provoked people to begin to doubt precisely the simulacrum of information democracy and participation in current communication. For me, the protests against the war suggest this last possibility.

Mier: I wonder if the idea of credibility isn't itself at a crossroads, if we aren't seeing a transformation in the modalities of the construction of truth. I'm going to venture what may seem like a peculiar hypothesis: I wonder if the contemporary systems for the institutional production of knowledge, instead of improving the relation between knowledge and ethics or, in Habermas's words, between conditions of truth and truthfulness, which previously seemed more clear, have produced, rather, a separation of these. The ethical force of truth has completely dissipated, as has the cognitive capacity of ethics. The knowledge produced by specialized institutions has ceased to be an ethical problem in itself. There is only a problem with regard to its instrumentality, its practical dimension. This unarticulated duality of the dimensions of truth and truthfulness seems to project itself into the political sphere, particularly if we consider the contemporary modalities of the political representativity that is at the base of the terrible bureaucratization of the machinery of government. The problem of political representativity used to constitute, we could say, a modality of articulation between the collective regimes of the social construction of truth and those of truthfulness. In our enormous government bureaucracies, this no longer has any meaning.

The basis of political strategy seems to be drastically modified. If I know that the representative of my district not only does not represent me but that he or she absolutely ignores my existence, and that this condition is irreversible, which is as true for public administration as for cultural politics, there is no ethical reflexivity in the conditions of representation. A phenomenon pointed out in much current social thought is accentuated and disseminated: the political efficacy of specularity—politics as spectacle, life as spectacle, including the paradox of privacy as spectacle, the publicity of the private, the secrecy of the residues of the public in the private. The exploitation of visibility as a rhetoric that influences the patterns of cultural production seems to be becoming more frequent, a rhetorical primacy of visibility supported by the artificiality of the dualism between truth and truthfulness. Artistic production is completely inscribed in this logic, sometimes in order to sustain it, sometimes in order to degrade its efficacy. Aesthetics gets mixed up with this process that compromises ethics and truth in order to dissolve, it seems to me, its own equivocal position in our societies.

Piccini: I'd like to add something with respect to the emergence of a new aesthetic of war and the weight of the audiovisual cultures and information on aesthetics and ethics in our societies. There is no doubt that we are witnessing the maximum concentration of cultural powers, understanding by this the concentration of electronic circuits and effects; with this, we are witnessing, at the same time, the maximum expansion of the visible real or of the visibility of the real. I believe that this is a problem of some importance and that it opens the way to other problems in the fields of culture and cultural politics. As we all know, the forces of the Left in different countries of the continent, those represented by movements or parties as well as those active in intellectual work, engaged in a prolonged battle for what was then called, under the aegis of the United Nations, a New International Information Order. (I hesitate to recall here that Bush anticipates with the end of the Persian Gulf War the appearance of a New World Order.) That battle to balance the weight of those who did the informing with the right to information of the "underdeveloped" peoples and to see to the equitable distribution of communication resources proved to be, as we all know, yet another failure of the many struggles waged to defend the right of the oppressed to speak, to opinion, or simply, as the constitution guarantees, to the free expression of ideas.

I believe that one of the reasons for the failure can now be seen clearly. I'll discard, for the moment, a structural analysis of our countries, which would show how they lack the political and economic conditions to make "the right to information" a reality due to the absence of real democracy, the constant abuse of power, the concentration of wealth, and the increasing marginalization of vast sectors of the population. I want to stress, beyond these conditions that define the projects for "the modernization of backwardness," as someone has called them appropriately, other aspects of the new paradoxical logics of the audiovisual cultures. The electronic concentration has produced, against all expectations, the most complete experience of information ever recorded. Societies were never so "informed" as they currently are. It is then necessary to ask how this information is given, what are the new forms of censorship, institutional and rhetorical, that act to reduce the visible real through political manipulation, or what is more complicated, through a specific *take*, that is, through the typical technical conditionings the camera allows. What is certain is that we live in overinformed societies in which it is difficult even to disqualify, as we used to do routinely, the control of news by private corporations. Such control exists, but in the present conditions of electronic expansion and of the rules of communicative exchange that this expansion and its networks prefigure, I wonder how a politics of the "redistribution" of the audiovisual space could be imagined? What would it mean, in these regimes that place "everything" before our eyes and that even change wars of destruction into an aesthetic sign, to conceive of the "democratization of culture" or of dialogue between social groups. I believe that the situation is very complex.

Canclini: I'd like to note a slight discrepancy with what Raymundo was saying. Although the general line of his analysis is very good, especially on the question of the differentiation of transparency and visibility, which I find to be very pertinent, there persist in Latin America, and notoriously in Mexico, forms of cultural development that we can call traditional for which the distinction between truth and truthfulness continues to be very important. The concern that political parties should represent us continues to be significant, and I think that the case of the PRD [the leftist electoral coalition built around Cuauhtemoc Cárdenas] in Mexico is an example of that. One could, from a postmodern perspective, view with amazement the fact that the dispute over electoral fraud still continues to be located at the center of the political struggle, but in fact this is what happens and probably will continue to happen for a long time in Mexico. For the peasants, and even for urban sectors, in Michoacán or Guerrero, who have been taking over the municipal offices and mounting very energetic political actions in defense of an electoral result that they want to coincide with the truth, with reality, to belong to the category of truth, it seems to me that certain parameters of the epistemology of traditional politics continue to be in effect.

I want to insist on this in order to avoid the risk of substituting the modern with the postmodern or the traditional with the modern. We live in a complex situation in which different temporalities coexist and in which, for vast sectors of the Mexican population, these problems of truth, truthfulness, transparency, and so on, continue to be of the utmost importance. This does not mean that even these "traditional" processes cannot be studied in terms of a theory of verisimilitude, with a degree of problematization that does not correspond with the precise political articulation the local actors make of them. But in any case, given the persistence and the central place of the political struggle in Mexico, they are modern, and even postmodern, processes, so I believe we need to be careful with these problems of political theory, like representativity and credibility.

This situates us not only before the coexistence of various historical temporalities, but before problems of scale that we still don't know how to confront very well. What is visible as a political fact for the peasants of Michoacán, so that they take over the mayor's office and demand that in their town of two thousand inhabitants the electoral results be respected, has apparently very little to do with the war in the Persian Gulf or with the big decisions of the Mexican government concerning the Free Trade Agreement with the United States and Canada. Nevertheless, one could think that, on very different levels, these facts are interconnected. And this is not simply a matter of articulating different levels of politics but rather of seeing at each level how the conditions of social action are governed by different dynamics and logics.

Mier: Néstor's observation is very interesting. The democracies Néstor is speaking about are reminiscences of other systems. I don't know whether to call them reminiscences or hybrid cultures. It's difficult, however, to call these complex systems of reciprocity and collective actions democracies. The sit-ins and demonstrations in Michoacán to protest the election results conflict with the canonical representations of what has become the almost cinematographic parliamentarianism of the Western democracies, such as the United States, Germany, and France. Compared to these, local processes of collective action, such as the sit-ins, seem like violence bordering on barbarism. Maybe what we're seeing is the exercise of political practices arising out of the tensions of hybridization in our decidedly heterogeneous cultures. One could speak of the displacement of the notion of democracy toward direct action, toward the assumption of a collective responsibility for innovation or normative reproduction, and an abrogation of specularity as a means of political control.

Zires: Considering everything that's been said, I think that it's a question of the coexistence of different political logics, logics of representativity along with the logic of the spectacle. I believe that this is happening not only in Mexico and Latin America but also in the so-called modern democracies such as those in Europe. I'm thinking about Spain, for example. Today, I read in the paper that a new Spanish newspaper has been established, whose main purpose is to counteract the dominant media slant on the Gulf War and to contribute to peace. Side by side with this phenomenon, we see protests all over the world against the war and against the present information system. For me, these protests demonstrate a series of contradictions between the respective logics of visibility and truth, of spectacle and informational representativity. Despite the great visibility of the war, despite the enormous quantity of information about what is taking place in the Gulf, the people are rebelling, or rather, *because* of this they're rebelling. On the one hand, there are pacifist interests of certain sectors of the population that do not see themselves being listened to or represented by the media chains. On the other hand, the logic of spectacle and hyperrealism is functioning so perfectly or has arrived at such an extreme that it goes beyond the notion of the visible generally accepted by the public, by the spectator, so that he or she rejects it and then applies the logic of truth and representativity.

I believe that this also deserves to be examined with more care. It is clear that the way in which information is interpreted in the case of the war, as well as in other situations, is not homogeneous. The way in which the logics of verisimilitude and truth interact varies in different social groups and in different social contexts.

Piccini: I'd like to synthesize a little of what we've been saying. I continue with my obsessions. Something that seems central to me is the increase in the volume of information and disinformation people experience every day. A little while ago, some friends were telling me that, confused by the news reports of the Gulf War they were watching on television or reading in the national newspapers, they decided to buy some European newspapers in order to get a better picture of what was going on. The surprising thing was that this new supply of reports and facts didn't help them understand the conflict or its underlying causes any better, beyond the generalities about it we all share to one degree or another. It seems that we are undergoing a serious crisis of the comprehension of reality—or that reality itself has become particularly complex—and also a crisis of belief. I understand that this is a general phenomenon in Western countries that doubtlessly becomes more acute in our own. But it is clear that we are now before a cultural paradox of massive proportions: ever-greater levels and volume of information, and ever-diminished levels of credibility. Collective beliefs have been fatally wounded. We need to determine what is the new kind of contact with reality (in quotation marks) that is gestating with the new cultures of complete visibility.

Postmodernism and Neoliberalism in Latin America

Martín Hopenhayn

The debate about postmodernism has, at its extremes, two opposite positions: On the one hand, that of "postmodern enthusiasts," who proclaim the collapse of modernity, of its cultural bases, and of its paradigms in the social sciences, politics, art, and philosophy; on the other hand, the position of the "critical modernists," who recognize the crisis of modernity as a point of inflection that does not suppose the obsolescence of modernity, but rather forms part of its inherent dynamic. From this perspective, postmodernism is no more than modernity reflecting on itself and explaining its unresolved conflicts.[1]

The critical modernists see in the postmodern enthusiasts an intellectual fad of the decade of the eighties, which, like all fads, is marked by frivolity and inconsistency. The postmodern enthusiasts, on the other hand,

---

1. In the origin of the debate, Lyotard is the postmodern enthusiast—*The Postmodern Condition* (Minneapolis: University of Minnesota Press, 1985)—and Habermas the critical modernist—"Modernity, an Incomplete Project," in *The Anti-Aesthetic*, ed. Hal Foster (Port Townsend, Wash.: Bay Press, 1983), 3–15.

see in the idea of the crisis of modernity the reflection of a wide range of political, intellectual, and cultural phenomena that transcend the academic field and permeate the sensibility of the people, daily life, and the models of communication.[2] In the following pages, we will situate ourselves in an intermediate position, one of "criticism without renunciation" of modernity, but conceding to the postmodernism debate a series of political and cultural implications that prevent us from simply dismissing it pejoratively as an intellectual fad. What I intend is to incorporate the postmodern perspective in order to enrich or re-create postponed challenges within modernity itself. I will summarize the positions of postmodernism in a schematic manner, emphasizing its ideological ambivalence and its differences with the paradigms and options of modernity. Then, I will attempt to survey the challenges that postmodernism poses in Latin America in particular by shifting the emphasis from the so-called crisis of modernity to the equally important question of the crisis of *styles* of modernization, which will lead me to consider the connections between postmodernism and the current influence of neoliberalism in Latin America.

In Lyotard's well-known definition, postmodernism is the crisis of metanarratives. Metanarratives are understood as the transcendental categories that modernity has invented in order to interpret and normalize reality. These categories—such as the advancement of reason, the emancipation of man, progressive self-knowledge, and the freedom of the will—spring from the project of the Enlightenment and function to integrate, in an articulated direction, the process of the accumulation of knowledge and the development of the productive forces and of sociopolitical consensus and control. They all refer, in turn, to an idealization of the idea of progress, that is, the conviction that history marches in a determined direction in which the future is, by definition, an improvement on the present. The metanarratives constitute the cognitive parameters that determine intelligible, rational, and predictable reality. Perceptive thought consists of using the faculties of reason to get to the bottom of phenomena—be they of nature, of history, or of society—in order to be able to predict their behavior "rationally." In this way, the metanarratives authorize us to describe and normalize; they show us how things are, where they should lead to, and how to resolve the gap between what is and what should be. In this sense, both classical liberalism and Marxism are inspired by a shared, Enlightenment origin, invoking uni-

2. Baudrillard has been perhaps the most charismatic representative of this position.

versal principles that have, for a long time, exhibited enormous mobilizing capacity.

The postmodernists question the force of the metanarratives of modernity. They point out that such axiomatic categories have lost explanatory capacity and legitimizing force. They associate this obsolescence with diverse causes, among which the following stand out: (1) the revolution of paradigms in the exact and natural sciences and its subsequent impact on the social sciences; (2) the acceleration of technological change and the consequent diversification of processes and products, which prevents the perception of society in homogeneous and extended unities and imposes increasingly higher degrees of complexity, movement, and flexibility on it; (3) the microcomputer revolution, and the resulting diffusion of data processing, which brings a proliferation of signs and languages that pulverizes the single model of rationality (our situation becomes interpretable from many possible perspectives, according to the software we use to deal with different problems we confront); (4) the loss of the centrality of the subject in a historical period in which the complexity of cultural structures and fragmentation makes the idea of a generic human identity, necessary for projects of human emancipation, collective self-consciousness, or any global utopia, inconceivable; (5) the depersonalization of knowledge through its conversion into the strategic input of new productive processes, and the multiplication of information to totally unmeasurable levels, which impedes preserving the idea of the subject as the "bearer" of knowledge and makes any ideology that pretends to integrate available knowledge into a comprehensive interpretation of the world impossible; finally (6) the "communicative ecstasy" (Baudrillard) caused by the combined effects of data processing, capital flows, and telecommunications, by virtue of which national frontiers and regional identities are dissolving under the dizzying pace of communication.

The discourse of the postmodern situates itself in a position of consummated facts. It does not present itself as an attempt to demystify modernity but rather as an ex post facto verification of the fact that modernity has already lost its mystique. The postmodernists, at least explicitly, do not pretend to precipitate the entropy of the concepts and visions that govern modernity, such as the rationality of history, progress, and integration via the homogenization of values. Rather, they claim to recognize this entropy in the condition of the present. Nevertheless, for those who have followed the debate, it is not clear whether this crisis and decline of the metanarratives of modernity is merely being described or whether it is being provoked "from outside" by the postmodern enthusiasts themselves.[3] This ambiguity comes out of the contingent ideological functions that postmodern discourse tends to assume, which we will examine later on.

The principal targets of postmodern discourse are, in summary:

1. The idea of progress. For the postmodernists, history does not march in an ascending path; it is discontinuous, asynchronic, pregnant with multiple directions and with growing margins of uncertainty about the future. There is no internal and specific rationality that regulates the movement of history but, rather, multiple, incongruous forces that give results that are unexpected, provisional, partial, and dispersed.[4]

2. The idea of a vanguard. Since there is no single rationality or directionality to history, even less recognizable and legitimate is the aspiration of a group that appropriates for itself the rational interpretation of history and that deduces a normative directionality on a global scale based on this interpretation. Whether in politics, science, art, or culture, and whether the vanguard is the party, the state, the educational elite, or an aesthetic movement, no one can claim to constitute the group chosen or destined to establish totalizing orientations. Once the category of the directionality and rationality of history is questioned, all vanguards seem to be invested with authoritarian and discretionary power.[5]

3. The idea of modernizing integration or of integrating modernization.[6] According to the criteria of modernization, being in step with the times involves increasing productivity, developing ever-higher levels of formal education in the population, and incorporating an enlightened sensibility into the masses. This is rejected by the postmoderns. The Enlightenment and the industrial utopias that are the basis of modernity and that permit the understanding of development as a progressive process of homogenization

---

3. "Postmodern culture does not guide or lead the process of secularization; it is its product. Specifically, it is the expression of a hypersecularization. Perhaps we should understand it as an ex post facto rationalization of a disenchantment." Norbert Lechner, "La democratización en el contexto de una cultura postmoderna," in *Cultura política y democratización*, ed. Norbert Lechner (Santiago: FLACSO/CLACSO/ICI, 1987), 253–62.

4. This, of course, was the lesson of Foucault. See Carlos Pareja, *Más allá del mito del progreso* (Montevideo: CLAEH, 1987); and Benjamin Arditi, "Una gramática postmoderna para pensar lo social," in Lechner, *Cultura política y democratización*, 169–88.

5. See, on this point, Octavio Paz, "The Twilight of the Avant-Garde," in *Children of the Mire* (Cambridge, Mass.: Harvard University Press, 1974), 148–64.

6. See Pedro Morandé, *Cultura y modernización en América Latina* (Santiago: Cuadernos del Instituto de Sociología, Pontificia Universidad Católica de Chile, 1984).

are put into doubt by ascribing to them an excess of normativity, an ethnocentric bias and a pretension to cultural cohesion that proves anachronistic
in light of the "proliferation of variety" of the "new times."

4. Ideologies. To the preceding is added, for good measure, the
disqualification of all ideology, understood as an integrated vision of the
world that allows one to explain a great diversity of phenomena from a few
basic principles, or from which a desired image of order, considered univer-
sally valid, can be projected. The disqualification of ideologies automatically
brings with it the disqualification of utopias, understood as images of an
ideal social order that possess an orienting force for decision-making in the
present and that provide a unified directionality toward the future. If utopian
thought has been considered, from Renaissance humanism to modernism,
as an exercise of the freedom of spirit, in postmodernity it seems more like
an authoritarian ruse.[7]

If the "postmodern narrative" declares the obsolescence of the idea
of progress, historical reason, vanguards, integrating modernization, and
ideologies and utopias, what is it that it proclaims in exchange? Basically,
the exaltation of diversity, aesthetic and cultural individualism, multiplicity of
languages, forms of expression and life-projects, and axiological relativism.
The vagueness of this proposal does not disturb its supporters, since it fits
in perfectly with the idea of the indeterminacy of the future, which, according
to them, sets the tone of the times.

In these general orientations, the postmodern narrative borrows from
multiple disciplinary sources. From anthropology and ethnology it takes cultural relativism and the critique of ethnocentrism. From philosophy it takes
the critique of humanism and of the centrality of the (universal/particu-
lar, free/conscious) subject, and from semiotics the primacy of structures
and signs over subjects. From antipsychiatry and the "radical" variants of
psychoanalysis it takes the exaltation of polymorphous desire and the critique of "philogenetic reductionism." From political theory it takes the idea
that society is composed of an inextricable interweaving of micropowers
and "local," rather than universal, power-games. From aesthetics it takes

7. This negative evaluation of utopian thought was already present in the work of Karl
Popper (e.g., *The Open Society and Its Enemies*, 5th ed. [London: Routledge and Kegan
Paul, 1966]). In a different perspective, Franz Hinkelammert also undertakes a critique
of specific forms of utopian thought in his *Crítica de la razón utópica* (San José, Costa
Rica: DEI, 1984). See also my own "Construcción utópica y práctica política," *Revista
Comunidad* 60 (1987): 3–11; and "Mayo 68–Mayo 88: Realismo y revuelta viente años
después," *El Gallo Ilustrado* 1353, Weekly of *El Día* (Mexico), 29 May 1988.

the taste for combining heterogeneous and asynchronic styles (the classical and the romantic, the baroque and the functionalist, the rococo and the futurist). And from sociology it takes the recognition of the heterogeneity and complexity of social dynamics.

All of this might lead one to think that postmodern discourse is a sane antidote to the excessively ethnocentric, rationalist, and mechanist tendencies of modern society. If that is the case, postmodernism could be thought of as an internal movement of modernity itself, a critique modernity puts into effect in order to exorcise its entropy. But, in fact, postmodernism frequently acquires very different pretensions and functions: In effect, it transforms itself into an ideology, disguising its normative judgments as descriptions, and ends up seeing what it wants to see.

The ideologization of postmodern discourse may be glimpsed when one focuses on the service that it lends to the political-cultural offensive of the market economy. Postmodernist rhetoric has been profitably capitalized on by neoliberalism in order to update its longed-for project of cultural hegemony. This project, the dream of liberalism in its formative stages, was frustrated by the universalist ethic of modern humanism, by political mobilization, and/or by social pressures. What many neoliberals saw, especially in the industrialized countries, is the possibility that reculturization, via a seductive postmodern narrative, could serve to legitimize the market offensive of the eighties, in other words, could make the desires of the public coincide with the promotion of pro-market policies and with the consolidation of a transnational capitalist system. It is no accident that elements of what we are calling the postmodern narrative have been disseminated, at least in good measure, by neoliberals and disenchanted leftists seduced by anarcho-capitalism.[8] What are the connections between postmodern critiques and the project of neoliberal cultural hegemony? Schematically, the following:

1. The exaltation of diversity leads to the exaltation of the market, considered as the only social institution that orders without coercion, guar-

---

8. "But the dream of the abolition of state power no longer functions exclusively as part of the socialist vision of the future. On the other hand, on the right side of the political spectrum, there appeared a radical conceptualization of capitalism which supports similar concepts. This union of anarchism and capitalism . . . can be made plausible by the privatization of up to now state functions" (Hans Albert, quoted in Franz Hinkelammert, "Utopía y proyecto político: La cultura de la postmodernidad," *Revista Nueva Sociedad* 91 [1987]: 114–28).

anteeing a diversity of tastes, projects, languages, and strategies. Only by expanding the reach of the market can the interventionist and globalizing excesses of the state be avoided. The state itself should be restricted to subsidiary functions in places where the market shows itself to be insufficient. Economic deregulation and privatization appear as almost ad hoc policies for the full realization of the "ludic individualism" heralded by postmodern discourse. Deregulation is the correlative in the practical sphere of the theoretical celebration of diversity. In the face of this wager, in which everything is potentially permissible, problems of social disparity, structural heterogeneity, insufficient development, and the like lose relevance.[9]

2. The critique of the vanguards translates into: (a) a critique of the transformational function of politics, unless the transformation is in the direction of privatization and deregulation (anarcho-capitalism);[10] and (b) a critique of state planning and intervention in the organization, regulation, and direction of the economy (by reducing the state to the status of one social actor among others, in order to then object to its interventionism as involving the will to domination of one actor over the rest).

3. Without an emancipatory dynamic that runs beneath events or that guides the actions of humanity, nothing permits the questioning of consumer society, waste, the alienation of work, the growing split between the industrialized and developing countries, social marginality, technocracy, or the way in which productive forces are misused.

4. The critique of ideologies culminates, in particular, in a criticism of Marxism and its humanist-socialist variants; the critique of utopias tends to

9. In this sense, a postmodern vision of Latin America is provided by Hernando de Soto's best-seller, *El otro sendero* (Bogota: Editorial Oveja Negra, 1987), translated into English as *The Other Path* (New York: Harper and Row, 1989). In this book, the Peruvian economist analyzed the extensive informal economy of Peru and arrived at the conclusion that the variety of forms it displays, which are unfolding despite state regulation, gives evidence of the benefits of the market. In this way, de Soto transformed a problem, the informal sector, into a virtue, ignoring the vulnerability of resources and the poverty that accompanies the vast majority of the informal sector's population. The book was heavily promoted in Latin America by neoliberal organizations and media, and Ronald Reagan mentioned it with enthusiasm in a speech.

10. We find an example of this in Joaquín Lavin's book, *La revolución silenciosa* (Santiago: Ed. Zig-Zag, 1987), another recent best-seller promoted by the neoliberal media. As in de Soto's book, Lavin elaborates a political-cultural strategy of market-hegemony, appropriating terms that, in the past, were linked ideologically with the criticism of capitalism ("marginality," "informality," "revolution"), in order to redirect them as functional strategies for the expansion of the market.

focus in particular on egalitarian utopias or on any ideal that proposes, as a task of the present, the redistribution of social wealth and power.

5. The critique of modernizing integration transforms structural heterogeneity into a healthy example of diversity and relativizes conventional indicators of development, such as expanded and improved services in the fields of health and education.

The synchrony between the market offensive and a cofunctional postmodernist cultural sensitizing is noteworthy. It is here that our analysis requires precision. The defense of a status quo governed by unequal competition, social inequality, the will of the transnationals, and the discretionary self-policing of finance capital cannot be automatically deduced from the verification of the crisis of the models of modernity. The discursive astuteness of postmodern neoliberalism resides in its effective articulation of euphemisms, which the interests of the centers of political and economic power, and of sectors identified with the "free" economy, can use to cover themselves with an aesthetic aura that undoubtedly makes them more seductive. It is more attractive to talk about diversity than the market, about desire than the maximization of profits, about play than conflict, about personal creativity than the private appropriation of the economic surplus, about global communication and interaction than the strategies of transnational companies to promote their goods and services. It is more seductive to speak in favor of autonomy than against planning, or in favor of the individual than against the state (and against public expenditure and social welfare policies). In this way, the social contradictions of capitalism, accentuated on the Latin American periphery, disappear behind the exaltation of forms and languages. The economic crisis—the worst we have experienced in this century—is hidden under the euphemism of a beautiful anarchy, and structural heterogeneity is converted into the creative combination of the modern and the archaic, "our" peripheral incarnation and anticipation of the postmodern.

The above suggests some of the ways in which postmodernism can be used to produce a "strategic" package of euphemisms to dress up the neoliberal project of cultural hegemony, which is the ideological correlative of the transnational offensive, in a way that penetrates the sensibility of the public. It does this, basically, by opposing an aesthetic fascination with chaos to an ethical concern with development. The negligence of the future assumes the appealing figure of a passion for the present. The postmodern narrative, however, is susceptible to many interpretations and uses. It cannot be reduced to the market offensive and to the ideological uses that some neoliberal strategies make of it.[11] This is so for a number of reasons. In the first place, many enthusiasts of the postmodern narrative are politically situated at a considerable distance from neoliberal positions.[12] In the second place, positions such as the passion for the present, aestheticism, the exaltation of diversity, the rejection of ethnocentrism, the desire for open societies, the return to pluralist individualism, cultural polymorphism, and the prioritization of creativity can be adapted to political projects of another kind. In the third place, the questioning of cultural paradigms and matrices, in light of emerging scenarios, does not necessarily lead to the defense of anarcho-capitalism. Finally, the critique of paradigms that have directed the styles of modernization and development has also generated alternative proposals and/or visions that, far from uniting with the deregulating offensive of the market, seek to mobilize social creativity in totally different directions.

The following considerations, oriented to Latin American reality, may be indicative of such directions:

1. The industrial model, centered in the substitution of imports, was discovered to have less integrating capacity than was supposed at its beginning, as much in terms of its internal insufficiencies as of exogenous variables (the heritage of Catholicism, etc.). The model also produced destructive, collateral effects, especially by imposing an imitative pattern in which, in the name of modernization, questions of cultural identity and ecological preservation were relinquished to sectors that incorporated the values and

---

11. "The everything goes [of postmodernism] is neither conservative, nor revolutionary, nor progressive. . . . In reality, what has triumphed is the cultural relativism which began its rebellion against the fossilization of class-cultures and against the ethnocentric dominance of an exclusive, correct, and authentic culture" (Agnes Heller, "Los movimientos culturales como vehículo de cambio," *Revista Nueva Sociedad* 96 [1988], 44). In the article previously cited, Lechner observes, "postmodern culture assumes hypersecularization in its tendency to separate social structures from value and motivational structures. That is, it accepts the liberal vision of politics as a market: an exchange of goods. And what happens to nonexchangeable goods? I am referring to human rights, psycho-social necessities such as social roots and collective belonging, the necessity of transcendental referents, but also to fear and the desire for certainty. I do not see any consideration of this in postmodern culture" (258). But Lechner also shares Heller's vision of the value of the relativizing function that postmodern discourse can exercise in the face of ideological and political reductionism.

12. Among them are included some figures already mentioned here (Arditi, Lechner, Pareja, Baudrillard, and Lyotard) and others from the Anglo-Saxon world, such as Hal Foster, Craig Owens, and Fredric Jameson.

expectations of industrial culture, at the same time leaving other sectors in a position of frustrated expectations, condemned to social marginality and economic informality by the same model of development that saw the desired benefits of growth pass them by. The insufficiencies or trade-offs of this model do not, however, have to impel us to a neoliberal alternative. The dynamic insufficiencies of accumulation, noted by the Economic Commission on Latin America (CEPAL) for a long time, and the process of economic growth without social equity, which has characterized our countries even in times of relative consensus regarding the modernization paradigm, do not find a remedy in the neoliberal prescriptions. On the contrary, such prescriptions sharpen the regressive tendencies in matters of social integration and balanced growth instead of blunting them. Finally, neoliberalism massively promotes imitative patterns of consumption that have very little to do with the exaltation of diversity and the criticism of ethnocentrism. To promote, in the particular, a diversity in the consumption of goods and services may well be a form of promoting, in the general, a specific, and implacable, economic logic.

2. The styles of modernization in Latin America have shown an excessive privilege of instrumental rationality over substantive rationality. Consequently, they have delegated instrumental knowledge and power to elites who have not acquired representative legitimacy and who have often tended toward technocracy. The predominance of technical reason has frequently resulted in the sacrifice of social participation in decisions and measures, and in a democracy restricted by the power of "expertise." Curiously, the uncritical exaltation that postmodern neoliberals make of the new technologies does not reverse this tendency but rather celebrates it, under the pretext that the new technologies are "spontaneously" decentralized. Faced with a similar "technologist" triumphalism, the warnings of the Frankfurt school to the effect that the crisis of modernity does not have its cause in a supposed entropy of substantive rationality or of collective utopias, but rather in the growing predominance of instrumental reason over the values and utopias characteristic of humanism acquire full force in Latin America.[13] The nature of the corporate interests involved in the deregulation of the acceleration of technological change and the productivist euphoria that accompanies it does not annul but rather confirms these "modern" suspicions.

---

13. On this point, see the classic essays: Max Horkheimer and Theodor W. Adorno, "The Dialectic of Enlightenment" and Max Horkheimer, "A Critique of Instrumental Reason," in their *Dialectic of Enlightenment* (New York: Herder and Herder, 1972).

3. It is essential to examine the role of the state in Latin American societies in more than one aspect. In the economic aspect, the centrality of the state in stimulating development has entered into a crisis of effectiveness. It is not necessary to be neoliberal to object to state hypertrophy, the gigantism of the public sector, or the rigidity of the bureaucracies. In the political aspect, the examination of the state's role is related to the new vitality of the theme of democracy, its principles and its most appropriate forms. The emphasis on social agreement, citizen participation, decentralization, civil society, and autonomy on a local or regional scale aim to minimize the coercive effects of the state and to increase its social legitimacy as an articulator of different social actors.

All of the above does not suppose the alternative of laissez-faire, however. The market has not proven to be the most efficient mechanism of decentralization, democratic participation, and autonomy. Undoubtedly, the market has made important contributions to economic dynamism under certain circumstances and in some countries. But frequently, it has required the help of authoritarian and repressive governments to avoid the conflicts generated by its discriminatory effects in matters of access to goods and services.

4. It is important to reconsider the role of planning in the economic and social ordering and directionality imposed by development. This supposes the critique of normative planning, the incorporation of new perceptual inputs in the exercise of the planner, the revision of the dominant rationalities sedimented in the practice of planning, and a greater coherence in the articulation between the technical and political dimensions in the decision processes.[14] This, however, does not force the renunciation of planning nor the reduction of it to its minimal expression. Nor does it suppose that all planning is the negation of diversity, the predominance of a technocratic caste, or the inhibition of autonomy. Planning is opposed to the negligence of the future,[15] but it does not have to sacrifice passion for the present. This future directionality can, provided it finds its appropriate forms

14. On this point, see the papers from the ILPES (Instituto Latinoamericano y del Caribe de Planificación Económica y Social), *Revista de la CEPAL*, 31 (1987); and Carlos Matus, *Planificación de situaciones* (Caracas: CENDES, 1977).

15. No one can doubt that the same transnational corporations, in large measure linked to the crisis of state planning (and the most enthusiastic about this crisis), plan all the time and invest considerable sums for this. The strategy of the acceleration of technological change and of growing diversification of products responds to an attentive job of planning by the transnationals.

of application, give meaning to the present. It is not a question of doing away with planning but of designing it in new ways to meet the challenges of postmodernity.

5. In tandem with the previous point, the critique of the directionality of our present history does not have to be confused with the rejection of all directionality. What is in question are the styles of linear development that use the present state of the advanced industrial "center" countries as the guiding model for the future. This is so for two reasons: in the first place, because of growing difficulties caused by the disproportional demands for investment capital for industrial reconversion and for competitive research and development, and the impossibility of servicing the foreign debt and stimulating internal growth at the same time; in the second place, because the social and cultural costs of an imitative development are too high and unethical under the pressure of the crisis. This crisis of directionality, however, is not resolved through deregulation. On the contrary, deregulation is simply the new version of development with a still-imitative model and, for the same reason, a specific directionality.

6. New political, economic, and technological conditions make evermore difficult the desired confluence of individual projects in a joint project for the transformation of society. The progressive demystification of socialist experiences, the social disarticulation caused by the installation of repressive political regimes and by work-force recomposition, the substitution of insurrectional options by arranged or negotiated settlements in the resolution of political conflicts—these have taken the mobilizing force away from the idea of revolution. The proliferation of corporate interests, the disintegration of the traditional working-class image, the fragmentation of identities, which makes the unitary image of a "people" seem almost metaphysical, the accelerating informalization and the proliferation of the most varied strategies of survival—all of these factors weaken the formulation of global projects of structural change capable of motivating vast social sectors. Once again, however, crisis does not suppose the collapse but rather a challenge to planning. The collapse will occur when the crisis of projects leads to a kind of laziness disguised as pragmatism, in which politics is converted into the mere administration of crisis. An unethical and unaesthetic alternative.

Among the alternative proposals and/or perceptions that attempt to find a solution to the crisis of modernization in Latin America without identifying with the neoliberal program, it would be fitting to mention the following:

1. The reappraisal of democracy for its intrinsic value and as an indispensable frame for dynamically joining a plurality of social interests and

demands. Political theory certainly offers diverse conceptions of democracy. But faced with the growing complexity of the social fabric and the consequent crisis of authority, the kind of democracy posited as desirable is one based on extensive social agreement.[16] Such an agreement is conceived as a platform for resolving conflicts between sectors with a minimum of coercion and for articulating in the most harmonious way the relations between the state and civil society, the technical and political dimensions of development, planning and the market, the micro and the macro, and the local and the national. A democracy with articulatory capacity would permit the optimization of levels of social participation, the decentralization of decision-making processes, the apportionment of resources among the various agents of development, and the equitable distribution of the benefits of growth. Finally, a democracy founded on social agreement is the most appropriate means for encouraging a culture of civic coexistence that could conceive projects with social legitimacy.

2. The reorientation of planning in tune with the new scenarios of social crisis and complexity. This supposes the relativization of mechanistic paradigms and requires working with growing levels of uncertainty about the future, open outcomes and ongoing, continuing adjustments, the activation and coordination of dispersed social energies, fields of multiple interaction, and mechanisms of cohesion that can articulate social projects without homogenizing.

3. The change of perception and attitude of social scientists in the face of reality. In the decade of the sixties, the analytical exercise of sociology was, in good measure, determined by the idea of a "militant science" that was identified with a model of the state and social organization that projected an extreme normativism in questions of the styles of development. At present, a considerable number of social scientists in the region have opted for greater disciplinary humility, from which they seek to comprehend the complexity of dynamics that are created between the multiple social actors. In a sense, the risk of global projects has been substituted by the "prudent" observation of intrasocietal articulations.[17]

16. There is much literature that points in this direction. The following examples are noteworthy: Norbert Lechner, *La conflictiva y nunca acabada construcción del orden deseado* (Santiago: Ediciones Ainavillo, FLACSO, 1984); Angel Flisfisch, "Consenso democrático en el Chile autoritario," in Lechner, *Cultura política y democratización*, 99–128; Norbert Lechner (comp.), *Estado y política en América Latina* (Mexico: Siglo XXI, 1981), and Gino Germani et al., *Los límites de la democracia* (Buenos Aires: CLACSO, 1985).
17. The influence of Alain Touraine is well known in this tendency in Latin America. Tou-

4. The reappraisal of social movements above political parties as protagonists in the rearticulation between civil society and the state.[18] Such an option follows from, in good measure, the relative incapacity of the traditional system of political parties to fulfill the function of mediation between social demands and the state apparatus. The crisis of the party system has given place to a search for new forms of doing politics, or at least the diversification of political practices. In that context, social movements appear to be the bearers of new or different logics of collective interests, in contrast to the hierarchical uniformity that characterizes party organization. The reappraisal of social movements also aims to recover the richness of the social fabric as opposed to a state that has seldom taken it into account.

5. The emergence of new social movements, or grass-root organizations, or "popular economic organizations," and the enthusiasm that this proliferation of initiatives awakens in some academicians and politicians disenchanted with conventional approaches to development.[19] These new social movements, as sociologists have taken to calling them, occupy sectors of informality that develop at the community, or local, level, and they are organized around collective strategies of survival or new forms of channeling demands. In practice, they combine diverse functions, such as the administration of scarcity, the mobilization of dispersed social energies, the de-hierarchization of production relations, the construction of collec-

---

raine posits that the reorientation of sociology toward the comprehension of social actors coincides with the political reappraisal of democracy. See his *Le Retour de l'acteur* (Paris: Fayard, 1984).

18. See, for example, Elizabeth Jelin (comp.), *Movimientos sociales y democracia emergente* (Buenos Aires: Centro Editor de América Latina, 1987); Alain Touraine, *Nuevas pautas de acción colectiva en América Latina* (Santiago: PREALC, 1984); Fernando Calderón (comp.), *Los movimientos sociales ante la crisis* (Buenos Aires: CLACSO, 1986); Fernando Calderón and Mario R. dos Santos, "Movimientos sociales y gestación de cultura política: Pautas de interogación," in Lechner, *Cultura política y democratización*, 189–98; and Enzo Faletto, "Propuestas para el cambio: Movimientos sociales en la democracia," in *Revista Nueva Sociedad* 91 (1987): 141–47.

19. For example, see Tilman Evers, "Identidade: A face oculta dos novos movimentos sociais," in *Novos Estudos CEBRAP* (1984), 11–15; José Luis Castagnola, *Participación y movimientos sociales* (Montevideo: *Cuadernos de CLAEH* 39, 1986); Luis Razeto, *Economía de solidaridad y mercado democrático*, two vols. (Santiago: Programa de Economía del Trabajo, 1984–1985); Luis Razeto et al., *Las organizaciones económicas populares* (Santiago: Programa de Economía del Trabajo, 1983); *Development Dialogue*, Special issue (Dec. 1986); and Martín Hopenhayn, "Nuevos enfoques sobre el sector informal," *Pensamiento Iberoamericano* 12 (July–Dec. 1987): 423–28.

tive identity, the socialized provision of basic necessities, the promotion of community participation, and the search for democracy in small spaces (or democracy in daily life). It is not easy to weigh the capacity of these movements to permeate the social fabric and to influence the technical and political leadership. Their emergence, however, posits a challenge, namely, to recuperate popular creativity and impel new "cultures" of development.

The postmodern debate can be fruitful in the sense that it permits, in general, the articulation of the cultural dimension of development. Its view of modernity allows us to interpret the crisis of styles of modernization as a cultural crisis. With this, new light is shed on the obscurity that presently envelops economic strategies and the policies of financial adjustment or control, and the discussion of policies and strategies is provided with a more comprehensive context from which it is possible to articulate immediate options in the operation of national projects or concrete utopias. The return to the cultural dimension of development permits the re-creation of horizons that infuse politics and policies with a mobilizing force that convenes and commits social actors. The celebration of the new social movements shows a concern for the constitution of collective identities, be they regional or sectorial. The preference for social movements, as opposed to political parties, privileges new logics of social dynamism, the search for new forms of doing politics, and an ad hoc grounding of the exaltation of diversity. The reappraisal of democracy and pluralism points to the consolidation of a democratic culture and not only a majority-elected government. The reorientation of planning puts in place a change in the paradigms of the interpretation and prediction of reality, and requires a revolution in perceptual structures, as well as in plans and programs. The reorientation of the social sciences also implies a change in the form of comprehending social reality, starting from the verification of the progressive complexity, increasing disarticulation, and polymorphism of the social fabric. In all of these forms of "groping in the dark," the tension between instrumental and substantive reason, or between means and ends, is once again at issue. Is this not, perhaps, one of the greatest cultural dilemmas of modernity? As we noted at the beginning, the postmodern debate may well be an attempt to remove the cultural base on which the road to modernization in Latin America has been constructed, be it successful or frustrated, open or truncated. But this does not necessarily imply that the invention of utopias and the design of projects has to be renounced, nor politics limited to laziness and the cynical administration of crisis. Nor does it mean that neoliberalism has to be embraced. On the contrary, it is through the thematic insistence on the cultural foundation of modernization that we can break with the neoliberal vicious circle and with shortsighted compulsion, often disguised as pragmatism.

Postmodernism requires that we open our perception to new contexts. Our battery of interpretive tools cannot remain unchanged faced with phenomena such as the acceleration of technological change, occupational recomposition, the deregulation of the financial system, the transnationalization of culture that accompanies the globalization of markets, social disarticulation, and the constriction of resources and margins of operation. Specifically, the challenge consists of enriching many of the concepts that, for a long time, permitted us to critically relate ourselves to modernity, with the aim of restoring their lost efficacy. The refunctioning of such concepts in the light of new times can lend great assistance for understanding our context and orienting our task. I am referring to concepts, or values, such as alienation, the satisfaction of social needs, structural change, social participation, personal development, social subjectivity, and emancipation from poverty and political oppression. None of these proves to be irrelevant or arbitrary today.

In the same way, it would not be sensible to renounce the interpretive and predictive richness of a structural focus on peripheral capitalism. This focus has permitted, in the past, the exercise of a notable critical and constructive capacity with respect to the styles of modernization implanted in Latin America and continues to encourage orientations and alternatives in the present.[20] Many of its suspicions and warnings regarding the models of development in force continue to be confirmed: the regressive tendency of the terms of exchange, the dynamic insufficiency of accumulation in peripheral capitalism, the difficulties of reconciling growth and equity, and structural heterogeneity, et cetera.[21] Moreover, we do not possess another interpretive focus capable of giving a specific sense of totality and coherence to the heterogeneity characteristic of the processes of modernization in Latin America. Nevertheless, this focus cannot be taken as prescriptive. Its opening to the already mentioned problematic of social complexity or progressive uncertainty necessitates a critical revision of the mechanistic paradigm with which it usually operates.

20. For example, see the recent works of Osvaldo Sunkel, such as "Las relaciones centro-periferia y la transnacionalización," *Pensamiento Iberoamericano* 11 (Jan.–June 1987).
21. In the extensive bibliography of Raul Prebisch, the following texts deserve to be cited here: "Estructura económica y crisis del sistema," *Revista de la CEPAL* (1978): 167–264, and the book *Capitalismo periférico: Crisis y transformación* (Mexico: Fondo de Cultura Económica, 1981).

In summary, the question we are considering here can be posed in the following terms: How can the postmodern debate be incorporated in order to reactivate the cultural base of development, without it leading to the postmodernism functionally inherent in the project of political-cultural hegemony of neoliberalism? How do we creatively confront our crisis of paradigms and projects, without this confrontation submerging us in a twilight "pathos" where the only option is the administration of entropy, the uncritical acceptance of a status quo that is critical of itself? How do we reinterpret the challenges of planning, the role of the state, and the program, or programs, of modernization in light of this inevitable cultural earthquake announced by the postmodern trumpets? How can we integrate the critique of ethnocentrism (and along with it, the critique of imitative models of development) without leading to fantasies, fundamentalisms, regionalisms, particularisms, or other forms of wishful thinking?

The challenges and problems that are presented are very complex and can stimulate impotence as well as creativity. The multifaceted and structural character of the crisis situates us before a moment of maximum entropy that is, in turn, a moment of intensity. That is our weakness, but also our strength. In the throes of this dilemma, we go from enthusiasm to desperation, postmoderns by osmosis in the midst of a still-pending modernization.

Postmodernism and Imperialism: Theory and Politics in Latin America

Neil Larsen

My remarks here[1] concern the following topics of critical discussion and debate: (1) the ideological character of postmodernism both as a philosophical standpoint and as a set of political objectives and strategies; (2) the development within a broadly postmodernist theoretical framework of a trend advocating a critique of certain postmodern tenets from the standpoint of anti-imperialism; and (3) the influence of this trend on both the theory and the practice of oppositional culture in Latin America. To eliminate the need for second-guessing my own standpoint in what follows, let me state clearly at the outset that I will adhere to what I understand to be both a Marxist and a Leninist position as concerns both epistemology and the social and historical primacy of class contradiction. Philosophically, then, I will be advancing and defending historical and dialectical materialist arguments. Regarding questions of culture and aesthetics, as well as those of revolutionary strategy under existing conditions—areas in which

---

1. An earlier version of this paper was presented as a lecture entitled "Postmodernism and Hegemony: Theory and Politics in Latin America," at the Humanities Institute at SUNY–Stony Brook on Mar. 2, 1989. A Spanish translation appeared in *Nuevo Texto Crítico* 3, 6 (1990): 77–94.

Marxist and Leninist theory has either remained relatively speculative or has found it necessary to rethink older positions—my own thinking may or may not merit the attribution of "orthodoxy," depending on how that term is understood.

The Philosophy and Politics of Postmodernism

One typically appeals to the term "postmodern" to characterize a broad and ever-widening range of aesthetic and cultural practices and artifacts. But the concept itself, however diffuse and contested, has also come to designate a very definite current of philosophy as well as a theoretical approach to politics. Postmodern philosophy—or simply postmodern "theory," if we are to accept Jameson's somewhat ingenuous observation that it "marks the end of philosophy"[2]—arguably includes the now standard work of poststructuralist thinkers such as Derrida and Foucault as well as the more recent work by ex-post-Althusserian theorists such as Ernesto Laclau and Chantal Mouffe, academic philosophical converts such as Richard Rorty, and the perennial vanguardist Stanley Aronowitz. The latter elaborate and rearticulate an increasingly withered poststructuralism, redeploying the grandly dogmatic and quasi-mystical "critique of the metaphysics of presence" as a critical refusal of the "foundationalism" and "essentialism" of the philosophy of the Enlightenment. These two assignations—which now come to replace the baleful Derridean charge of "metaphysics"—refer respectively to the Enlightenment practice of seeking to ground all claims regarding either truth or value in terms of a self-evidencing standard of Reason, and to the ontological fixation upon being as essence, rather than as relationality or "difference."

Postmodern philosophy for the most part adopts its "antiessentialism" directly from Derrida and company, adding little if anything to accepted (or attenuated) poststructuralist doctrine. Where postmodernism contributes more significantly to the honing down and retooling of poststructuralism is, I propose, in its indictment of foundationalism—in place of the vaguer abstractions of "presence" or "identity"—as the adversarial doctrine. It is not all "Western" modes of thought and being that must now be discarded, but more precisely their Enlightenment or *modern* modalities, *founded* on

2. Fredric Jameson, "Postmodernism and Consumer Society," in *The Anti-Aesthetic: Essays on Postmodern Culture,* ed. Hal Foster (Port Townsend, Wash.: Bay Press, 1983), 112.

the concept of *reason*. Indeed, even the charge of foundationalism perhaps functions as a minor subterfuge here. What postmodern philosophy
intends is, to cite Aronowitz's forthright observation, a "rejection of reason
as a foundation for human affairs."[3] Postmodernism is thus a form, albeit
an unconventional one, of *irrationalism*.

To be sure, important caveats can be raised here. Postmodernist
theoreticians often carefully stipulate that a rejection of reason as foundation does not imply or require a rejection of all narrowly "reasonable" procedures. Perhaps it is possible to *act* "reasonably" without the need to *prove*
that that is what one is doing. Postmodernity, at any rate, is not to be equated
with antimodernity. Aronowitz, for example, has written that "postmodern
movements" (e.g., ecology and Solidarity-type labor groups) "borrow freely
the terms and programs of modernity but place them in new discursive contexts" (*UA*, 61). Chantal Mouffe insists that "radical democracy"—according
to her, the political and social project of postmodernity—aims to "defend the
political project [of Enlightenment] while abandoning the notion that it must
be based on a specific form of rationality."[4] Ernesto Laclau makes an even
nicer distinction by suggesting that "it is precisely the *ontological status* of
the central categories of the discourses of modernity and not their *content,*
that is at stake. . . . Postmodernity does not imply a *change* in the values of
Enlightenment modernity but rather a particular *weakening* of their abso-
lutist character."[5] And a similarly conservative gesture within the grander
irrationalist impulse can, of course, be followed in Lyotard's characterization
of "paralogy" as those practices legitimating themselves exclusively within
their own "small narrative" contexts, rather than within the macroframes of
modernist metanarratives of Reason, Progress, History, and the like.[6]

Two counterobjections are necessary here, however. The first is that
any thoughtful consideration of claims to locate the attributes of reason
within supposedly local or nontotalizable contexts immediately begs the
question of what, then, acts to set the limits to any particular instance of
"paralogy," among other things. How does the mere adding of the predicate
"local" or "specific" or "weakened" serve to dispense with the logic of an ex-

3. Stanley Aronowitz, "Postmodernism and Politics," in *Universal Abandon? The Politics
of Postmodernism,* ed. Andrew Ross (Minneapolis: University of Minnesota Press, 1988),
50. *Universal Abandon?* cited hereafter in text and notes as *UA*.
4. Chantal Mouffe, "Radical Democracy," in *UA*, 32.
5. Ernesto Laclau, "Politics and the Limits of Modernity," in *UA*, 66–67.
6. Jean-François Lyotard, *The Postmodern Condition,* trans. Geoff Bennington and Brian
Massumi (Minneapolis: University of Minnesota Press, 1984).

ternal ground or foundation? Cannot, for example, the ecology movement be shown to be *grounded* in a social and political context outside and larger than it is, whatever the movement may think of itself? If reason is present (or absent) in the fragment, does not this presence or absence necessarily connect with the whole on some level? If, as one might say, postmodernism wants to proclaim a rationality of means entirely removed from a rationality of ends, does it not thereby sacrifice the very means/ends logic it wants to invoke, the very logical framework in which one speaks of "contexts"? I suggest it would be more precise to describe the measured, nonfoundationalist "rationalism" of postmodernism as simply an evasive maneuver designed to immunize from critique the real object here: that is, to preserve Enlightenment as merely an outward and superficial guise for irrationalist content, to reduce Enlightenment, as an actual set of principles designed consciously to govern thought and action, to merely the specific mythology needed to inform the project of a "new radical imaginary" (Laclau, *UA*, 77).

Clearly, a complete failure—or refusal—of *dialectical* reasoning is incurred by postmodernism's attempted retention of an Enlightenment "micro"-rationality. And this brings up the second rejoinder: postmodern philosophy's practiced avoidance on this same score of the *Marxist*, dialectical materialist critique of Enlightenment. Postmodern theory, seemingly without exception, consigns something it calls "Marxism" to the foul Enlightenment brew of foundationalism. Marxism is, in effect, collapsed back into Hegelianism, the materialist dialectic into the idealist dialectic—or, as Aronowitz somewhat puzzlingly puts it, the "form of Marxism is retained while its categories are not." (*UA*, 52). But in no instance that I know of has a postmodern theorist systematically confronted the contention first developed by Marx and Engels that "this realm of reason was nothing more than the idealized realm of the bourgeoisie."[7] I think perhaps it needs to be remembered that the Marxist project was not and is not the simple replacement of one "universal reason" with another but the practical and material transformation of reason to be attained in classless society, and that this attainment would *not* mean the culmination of reason on earth à la Hegel but a raising of reason to a higher level through its very de-idealization. Reason, then, comes to be grasped as a time-bound, relative principle, which nevertheless attains a historical universality through the social universality

7. Frederick Engels, *Socialism: Utopian and Scientific* (Bejing: Foreign Languages Press, 1975), 46.

of the proletariat (gendered and multiethnic) as they/we who—to quote a famous lyric—"shall be the human race."

But again, postmodern irrationalism systematically evades confrontation with *this* critique of Enlightenment too. It typically manages this through a variety of fundamentally dogmatic maneuvers, epitomized in the work of Laclau and Mouffe, who, as Ellen Meiksins Wood has shown,[8] consistently and falsely reduce Marxism to a "closed system" of pure economic determinism.

Why this evasion? Surely there is more than a casual connection here with the fact that the typical postmodern theorist probably never got any closer to Marxism or Leninism than Althusser's left-wing structuralism and Lacanianism. One can readily understand how the onetime advocate of a self-enclosed "theoretical practice" might elicit postmodern suspicions of closure and "scientism." Indeed, Althusser's Marxism can fairly be accused of having preprogrammed, in its flight from the class struggles of its time and into narrowly epistemological speculation, the subsequent turnabout in which even the residually rationalist categories still formally upheld by Althusser are themselves rejected for their inconsistency.[9]

But this is secondary. What I would propose is that postmodernism's hostility toward a foundationalist parody of Marxism, combined with the elision of Marxism's genuinely dialectical and materialist content, flows not from a simple misunderstanding but, objectively, from the consistent need of an ideologically embattled capitalism to seek displacement and preemption of Marxism through the formulation of radical-sounding "third paths" ("neither capitalism nor socialism"). That postmodern philosophy normally refrains from open anticommunism, preferring to pay lip service to "socialism" even while making the necessary obeisances to the demonologies of Stalin may make it appear as some sort of a "left" option. But is there really anything "left"? The most crucial problem for Marxism today—how to extend and put into practice a critique *from the Left* of retreating socialism at the moment of the old communist movement's complete transformation into its opposite—remains safely beyond postmodernist conceptual horizons.

Postmodernist philosophy's oblique but hostile relation to Marxism

8. See Ellen Meiksins Wood, *The Retreat from Class: A New "True" Socialism* (London: Verso, 1986).
9. See, for example, Laclau and Mouffe, *Hegemony and Socialist Strategy: Towards a Radical Democratic Politics* (London: Verso, 1985), 97–105.

largely duplicates that of Nietzsche. And the classical analysis here belongs to Lukács's critique of Nietzschean irrationalism in *The Destruction of Reason,* a work largely ignored by contemporary theory since being anathematized by Althusserianism two decades ago. Lukács identifies in Nietzsche's radically antisystemic and countercultural thinking a consistent drive to attack and discredit the socialist ideals of his time. But against these Nietzsche proposes nothing with any better claim to social rationality. Any remaining link between reason and the emancipatory is refused. According to Lukács, it is this very antagonism toward socialism—a movement of whose most advanced theoretical expression Nietzsche remained fundamentally ignorant—that supplies to Nietzschean philosophy its point of departure and its principal unifying "ground" as such. "It is material from 'enemy territory,' problems and questions imposed by the class enemy which ultimately determine the content of his philosophy." [10] Unlike his more typical fellow reactionaries, however, Nietzsche perceived the fact of bourgeois decadence and the consequent need to formulate an intellectual creed that could give the appearance of overcoming it. In this he anticipates the later, more explicit "antibourgeois" anticommunisms of the coming imperialist epoch—most obviously fascism. This defense of a decadent bourgeois order, based on the partial acknowledgement of its defects and its urgent need for cultural renewal and pointing to a third path "beyond" the domain of reason,[11] Lukács terms an "indirect apologetic."

Postmodern philosophy receives Nietzsche through the filters of Deleuze, Foucault, and Derrida, blending him with similarly mediated versions of Heidegger and William James into a new irrationalist hybrid. But the terms of Lukács's Nietzsche critique on the whole remain no less appropriate. Whereas, on the one hand, postmodernist philosophy's aversion to orthodox fascism is so far not to be seriously questioned, its basic content continues, I would argue, to be "dictated by the adversary." And this adversary—revolutionary communism as both a theory and a practice—assumes an even sharper identity today than in Nietzsche's epoch. Let it be said that Lukács, writing forty years ago, posits an adversarial Marxism-

10. Georg Lukács, *The Destruction of Reason,* trans. Peter Palmer (Atlantic Highlands, N.J.: Humanities Press, 1981), 395.
11. "The two moments—that of reason and that of its other—stand not in opposition pointing to a dialectical *Aufhebung,* but in a relationship of tension characterized by mutual repugnance and exclusion." Habermas, "The Entry into Postmodernity: Nietzsche as Turning Point," in *The Philosophical Discourse of Modernity,* trans. Frederick Lawrence (Cambridge: MIT Press, 1987), 103.

Leninism more free of critical tensions and errors than we know it to have been then or to be now. If, from our own present standpoint, *The Destruction of Reason* has a serious flaw, then it is surely this failure to anticipate or express openly the struggles and uncertainties within communist orthodoxy itself. (Lukács's own subsequent allegiance to Krushchevite positions—by then perhaps inevitable—marks his decisive move to the right on these issues.) But the fact that postmodern philosophy arises in a conjuncture marked by capitalist restoration throughout the "socialist" bloc and the consequent extreme crisis and disarray within the theoretical discourse of Marxism, while it may explain the relative freedom from genuinely contestatory Marxist critique enjoyed by postmodern theorists, in no way alters the essence of this ideological development as a reprise of pseudo-dialectical, Nietzschean "indirect apologetics."

This becomes fully apparent when one turns to postmodernism's more explicit formulations as a politics. I am thinking here mainly of Laclau and Mouffe's *Hegemony and Socialist Strategy,* a work that, though it remains strongly controversial, has attained in recent years a virtually manifesto-like standing among many intellectuals predisposed to poststructuralist theory.[12] *Hegemony and Socialist Strategy* proposes to free the Gramscian politics linked to the concept of hegemony (the so-called "war of position" as opposed to "war of maneuver") from its residual, Marxian foundationalism in recognition of what is held to be the primary efficacy of discourse itself and its "articulating" agents in forming hegemonic subjects. And it turns out, of course, that "socialist strategy" means dumping socialism altogether for a "radical democracy" that more adequately conforms to the "indeterminacy" of a "society" whose concept is modeled directly on the poststructuralist critique of the sign.

The key arguments of *Hegemony and Socialist Strategy*—as well as the serious objections they have elicited—have become sufficiently well known to avoid lengthy repetitions here. What Mouffe and Laclau promise to deliver is, in the end, a revolutionary or at least emancipatory political strategy shorn of foundationalist ballast. In effect, however, they merely succeed in shifting the locus of political and social agency from "essentialist" categories of class and party to a discursive agency of "articulation."[13] And

12. In the area of Latin American studies these include, *inter alia,* George Yúdice, John Beverley, Marc Zimmerman, Howard Winant, and Doris Sommer.
13. See the introductory chapter to my *Modernism and Hegemony: A Materialist Critique of Aesthetic Agencies* (Minneapolis: University of Minnesota Press, 1989).

when it comes time to specify concretely the actual articulating subjects themselves, *Hegemony and Socialist Strategy* resorts to a battery of argumentative circularities and subterfuges that simply relegate the articulatory agency to "other discourses."[14]

Ellen Meiksins Wood has shown the inevitable collapse of *Hegemony and Socialist Strategy* into its own illogic as an argument with any pretense to denote political or social realities[15]—a collapse that, because of its very considerable synthetic ambitions and its conceptual clarity, perhaps marks the conclusive failure of poststructuralism to produce a viable political theory. But the failure of argument has interfered little with the capacity of this theoretical tract to supply potentially anticapitalist intellectuals with a powerful dose of "indirect apologetics." The fact that the third path calls itself radical democracy, draping itself in the ethics if not the epistemology of Enlightenment, the fact that it outwardly resists the "fixity" of any one privileged subject, makes it, in a sense, the more perfect "radical" argument for a capitalist politics of pure irrationalist spontaneity. And we know who wins on the battlefield of the spontaneous.[16] While the oppressed are fed on the myths of their own hegemony—and why not, since "on the threshold of postmodernity" humanity is "for the first time the creator and constructor of its own history" (Laclau, *UA,* 79–80)—those already in a position to articulate the myths for us only strengthen their hold on power.

14. "[T]he exterior is constituted by other discourses." *Hegemony and Socialist Strategy,* 146.

15. Wood, *The Retreat from Class,* especially chap. 4, "The Autonomization of Ideology and Politics."

16. See Lenin, *What is to Be Done? Burning Questions of Our Movement* (Moscow: Progress Publishers, 1973): "*All* worship of the spontaneity of the working class movement, all belittling of the role of the 'conscious element,' of the role of Social-Democracy, *means, quite independently of whether he who belittles that role desires it or not, a strengthening of the influence of bourgeois ideology upon the workers*" (39); "Since there can be no talk of an independent ideology formulated by the working masses themselves in the process of their movement, the *only* choice is—either bourgeois or socialist ideology. There is no middle course (for mankind has not created a 'third' ideology, and, moreover, in a society torn by class antagonisms, there can never be a non-class or an above-class ideology). Hence to belittle the socialist ideology *in any way, to turn aside from it in the slightest degree* means to strengthen bourgeois ideology. There is much talk of spontaneity. But the *spontaneous* development of the working class movement leads to its subordination to bourgeois ideology" (40–41).

"Left" Postmodernism

In my remarks so far I have emphasized how contemporary post-modern philosophy's blanket hostility toward the universalisms of Enlight-enment thought may in fact serve to preempt Marxism's carefully directed critique of that *particular universal* which is present-day capitalist ideology and power. Does not the merely theoretical refusal of the (ideal) *ground* serve in fact to strengthen the *real* foundations of *real* oppression by ren-dering all putative knowledge of the latter illicit? When Peter Dews rebukes Foucault for his attempt to equate the "plural" with the emancipatory, the re-mark applies to more recent postmodern theory with equal force: "The deep naivety of this conception lies in the assumption that once the aspiration to universality . . . is abandoned what will be left is a harmonious plurality of unmediated perspectives." [17] In light of this perverse blindness to *particular* universals, postmodernism's seemingly general skepticism toward Marx-ism as *one* possible instance of foundationalism would be better grasped as a specific and determining antagonism. Is there an extant, living—that is, *practiced*—philosophy *other* than Marxism that any longer purports to ground rational praxis in universal (but in this case also practical-material) categories? I am saying, then, that postmodern philosophy and political theory become objectively, albeit perhaps obliquely, a variation of anticom-munism.

It might, however, be objected at this point that postmodernism en-compasses not only this demonstrably right-wing tendency but also a cer-tain Left that, like Marxism, aims at an actual transcendence of oppressive totalities, but diverges from Marxism in its precise identification of the op-pressor and of the social agent charged with its opposition and overthrow. Under this more "practical" aegis, the axis of postmodern antagonism shifts from the universal versus the particular to the more politically charged ten-sion between the center and the margin. Such a shift has, for example, been adumbrated by Cornel West as representing a particularly *American* inflection of the postmodern. "For Americans," says West,

> are politically always already in a condition of postmodern fragmen-tation and heterogeneity in a way that Europeans have not been; and the revolt against the center by those constituted as marginals

17. Peter Dews, *Logics of Disintegration* (London: Verso, 1987), 217.

is an *oppositional* difference in a way that poststructuralist notions of difference are not. These American attacks on universality in the name of difference, these "postmodern" issues of otherness (Afro-Americans, Native Americans, women, gays) are in fact an implicit critique of certain French postmodern discourses about otherness that really serve to hide and conceal the power of the voices and movements of Others.[18]

Among instances of a "left" postmodernism we might then include certain of the contemporary feminisms and the theoretical opposition to homophobia as well as the cultural nationalisms of ethnic minority groups. The category of the "marginal" scarcely exhausts itself here, however. Arrayed against the center, even as also "concealed" by its discourses and "disciplines" are, in this conception, also the millions who inhabit the neocolonial societies of the "Third World." Hence there might be a definite logic in describing the contemporary anticolonial and anti-imperialist movements of the periphery as in their own way also postmodern.

It is this marginal and anti-imperialist claim to postmodernity which I now wish to assess in some depth. In particular, I propose to challenge the idea that such a left movement within postmodernism really succeeds in freeing itself from the right-wing apologetic strain within the postmodern philosophy of the center.

The basic outlines of this left position are as follows: both poststructuralism and postmodernism, as discourses emergent in the center, have failed to give adequate theoretical consideration to the international division of labor and to what is in fact the uneven and oppressive relation of metropolitan knowledge and its institutions to the life-world of the periphery. Both metropolitan knowledge and metropolitan systems of ethics constitute themselves upon a prior exclusion of peripheral reality. They therefore become themselves falsely "universal" and, as such, ideological rather than genuinely critical. The remedy to such false consciousness is not to be sought in the mere abstract insistence on "difference" (or "unfixity," the "heterogeneous," etc.), but in the *direct* practical intervention of those who *are* different, those flesh-and-blood "Others" whom, as West observes, the very conceptual appeal to alterity has ironically excluded. As a corollary, it is then implied that a definite epistemological primacy, together with a kind

18. "Interview with Cornel West," in *UA*, 273.

of ethical exemplariness, adheres to those subjects and practices marginalized by imperialist institutions of knowledge and culture.

Among "First World" theorists who have put forward this kind of criticism, perhaps the best known is Fredric Jameson. In his essay "Third World Literature in the Era of Multinational Capitalism," Jameson argues that "third world texts . . . necessarily project a political dimension in the form of national allegory: the story of the private individual destiny is always an allegory of the embattled situation of the public third world culture and society." [19] Third World texts, then—and by extension those who produce them and their primary public—retain what the culture of postmodernism in the "First World" is unable to provide, according to another of Jameson's well-known arguments: a "cognitive map" [20] equipped to project the private onto the public sphere. As such, these peripheral practices of signification consciously represent a bedrock political reality that, for the contemporary postmodern metropole, remains on the level of the political unconscious. (It should be pointed out, of course, that Jameson's schema is largely indifferent in this respect to the modernism/postmodernism divide.) What enables this is the fact that the Third World subject, like Hegel's slave, exhibits a "situational consciousness" (Jameson's preferred substitute term for materialism). As "master," however, the metropolitan consciousness becomes enthralled to the fetishes that symbolize its dominance.

An analogous but weaker theory of the marginal as epistemologically privileged is to be found in the writings of Edward Said. In *The World, the Text and the Critic,* for example, Said chastises contemporary critical theory, especially poststructuralism, for its lack of "worldliness"—by which he evidently means much the same thing designated by Jameson's "situational consciousness." What is needed, according to Said, is "a sort of spatial sense, a sort of measuring faculty for locating or situating theory," [21] which Said denotes simply as "critical consciousness." *The World, the Text and the Critic* ultimately disappoints in its *own* failure to historically or "spatially" situate such "critical consciousness," but given Said's public commitment

19. Fredric Jameson, "Third-World Literature in the Era of Multinational Capitalism," *Social Text* 15 (Fall 1986): 69.
20. See Fredric Jameson, "Postmodernism: The Cultural Logic of Late Capitalism," *New Left Review* 146 (July–Aug. 1984): 53–92.
21. Edward Said, *The World, the Text and the Critic* (Cambridge: Harvard University Press, 1983), 241.

to Palestinian nationalism, it wouldn't seem unreasonable to identify in his call for "worldliness" a prescription for "Third-Worldliness."

Both Jameson and Said—the former far more openly and forthrightly than the latter—violate central tenets of postmodernism, of course, insofar as they posit the existence of a marginal *consciousness* imbued with "presence" and "self-identity." That is, they appear to justify an orthodox postmodernist counteraccusation of essentialism. But should this be thought to constitute a final incompatibility of postmodernism for an anti-imperialist, postcolonial standpoint, however, it suffices to mention here the work of Gayatri Chakravorty Spivak. Foreseeing this difficulty, Spivak has (in her critical reading of the work of a radical collective of Indian historians known as the Subaltern Studies Group) sought to justify such essentialism as a strategic necessity, despite its supposed epistemological falsity. The radical Third World historian, writes Spivak, "must remain committed to the subaltern as the subject of his history. As they choose this strategy, they reveal the limits of the critique of humanism as produced in the west." [22] Spivak, that is to say, poses the necessity for an exceptionalism: a conceptual reliance on the "subject of history," which as a poststructuralist she would condemn as reactionary and "humanist," is allowed on "strategical" grounds within the terrain of the "subaltern." It begins to sound ironically like the old procolonialist condescension to the "native's" need for myths that the educated metropolitan city-dweller has now dispensed with—but more on this below.

Even if the "marginal" cannot be proved to enjoy an epistemological advantage, however, its very *reality* as a "situation" requiring direct action against oppression can be appealed to as politically and ethically exemplary. Thus, in her very poignant essay entitled "Feminism: the Political Conscience of Postmodernism?" [23] the critic and video artist Laura Kipnis proposes that feminism, seemingly trapped between the "textualist" (i.e., modernist) aestheticism of French poststructuralist critics on the order of Cixous and Irigaray on one hand and North American liberal reformism (another case of "essentialism") on the other, adopt "a theory of women not as class or caste but as colony" (*UA*, 161). The efforts of a Rorty or a Laclau to salvage "Enlightenment" by ridding it of foundationalism and leaving only its "pragmatic" procedures would, in this view, be too little too

22. Gayatri Chakravorty Spivak, *In Other Worlds: Essays in Cultural Politics* (New York and London: Methuen, 1987), 209.
23. *UA*, 149–66.

late. For Kipnis, as for Craig Owens,[24] postmodernism denotes what is really the definitive decline of the West and its colonial systems of power. If those marginalized within the center itself—for instance, women—are to rescue themselves from this sinking ship, they must model their opposition on the practice of non-Western anticolonial rebels. Referring to the 1986 bombing of Libya, Kipnis writes: "When retaliation is taken, as has been announced, for 'American arrogance,' *this* is the postmodern critique of Enlightenment; it is, in fact, a decentering, it is the margin, the absence, the periphery rewriting the rules from its own interest" (*UA*, 163).

An analogous proposal for Third World revolt within the conceptual terrain of postmodernism has been issued by George Yúdice. Against the postmodern "ethics" formulated by Foucault as an "aesthetics of existence"—manifesting itself, for example, in the liberal comforts of pluralism—Yúdice suggests finding an ethical standard "among the dominated and oppressed peoples of the 'peripheral' or underdeveloped countries."[25] As a mere "aesthetic" the postmodern "explores the marginal, yet is incapable of any solidarity with it" (*UA*, 224). Yúdice terms this marginal ethic an "ethic of survival" and points to the example set by Rigoberta Menchú in her role as an organizer for the Christian base-community movement against genocidal repression.[26] "Menchú, in fact, has turned her very identity into a 'poetics of defense.' Her oppression and that of her people have opened them to an unfixity delimited by the unboundedness of struggle" (*UA*, 229). In Menchú's ethical example we thus have, so to speak, the subversive promise of "unfixity" à la Mouffe-Laclau made flesh.

Yúdice is not the first to attempt this particular inflection with specific reference to Latin America. The liberation theology that guides Menchú's practice as a militant might itself lay some claim to represent an indigenously Latin American postmodernism—"avant la lettre" insofar as Foucault and his followers are concerned. The philosophical implications of liberation theology have been worked out by the so-called Philosophy of Liberation, an intellectual current that developed in Argentina in the early 1970s. As recounted by Horacio Cerutti-Guldberg,[27] Philosophy of Liberation set out ex-

24. See "The Discourse of Others: Feminism and Postmodernism," in Foster, 57–82.
25. George Yúdice, "Marginality and the Ethics of Survival," in *UA*, 220.
26. See Rigoberta Menchú, *Me llamo Rigoberta Menchú y así me nació la conciencia* (Mexico: Siglo Veintiuno, 1983).
27. See "Actual Situation and Perspectives of Latin American Philosophy for Liberation," *The Philosophical Forum* 20, 1–2 (Fall–Winter 1988–89): 43–61. Cited hereafter in text as *LAP*.

plicitly to formulate a uniquely Latin American doctrine of liberation would be "neither a liberal individualism nor a Marxist collectivism" (*LAP*, 47). Rather, it would set itself the goal of "philosophizing out of the social demands of the most needy, the marginalized and despised sectors of the population" (*LAP*, 44). This in turn requires, according to exponent Enrique Dussel, a new philosophical method—known as analectics—based on the logical priority or "anteriority" of the exterior (i.e., the marginal, the Other) over totality.[28] Analectics are to supplant the "Eurocentric" method of dialectics. As Cerutti-Guldberg observes:

> Dialectics (it doesn't matter whether Hegelian or Marxist, since ana-lectical philosophy identifies them) could never exceed "intrasys-tematicity." It would be incapable of capturing the requirements of "alterity" expressed in the "face" of the "poor" that demands justice. In this sense, it would appear necessary to postulate a method that would go beyond (ana-) and not merely through (dia-) the totality. This is the "analectical" method which works with the central notion of analogy. In this way, analectical philosophy would develop the "essential" thinking longed for by Heidegger. Such thinking would be made possible when it emerges out of the cultural, anthropo-logical "alterative" Latin American space. This space is postulated as "preliminary in the order of Being" and "posterior in the order of knowledge" with respect to the "ontological totality." It is constituted by the poor of the "third world." (*LAP*, 50)

In Dussel's *Philosophy of Liberation,* the logic of going "beyond" the totality ultimately leads to explicit theology and mysticism. "What reason can never embrace—the mystery of the other as other—only faith can penetrate" (Dussel, 93). But the analectical method has received other, non-theological formulations in Latin America, most notably in the case of the Cuban critic Roberto Fernández Retamar, whose theoretical writings of the early 1970s[29] were aimed at refuting the possibility that a universal theory of literature could truthfully reflect the radical alterity of "Nuestra América." This is argued to be so not only as a result of the unequal, exploitative relation of imperial metropolis to periphery—a relation that is historically

28. See Enrique Dussel, *Philosophy of Liberation,* trans. Aquilina Martínez and Christine Morkovsky (Maryknoll, N.Y.: Orbis Books, 1985), 158–60.
29. Roberto Fernández Retamar, *Para una teoría de la literatura hispano-americana* (Havana: Casa de las Américas, 1975); *Calibán and Other Essays,* ed. and trans. Edward Baker (Minneapolis: University of Minnesota Press, 1989).

evolved and determined and thus subject to transformation—but because all notions of universality (e.g., Goethe's, and Marx and Engels's idea of a *Weltliteratur*) are fictions masking the reality of radical diversity and alterity.

One should point out here that Retamar's philosophical authority is José Martí, and certainly not Derrida, Deleuze, or Foucault, whom, had he been aware of them at the time, Retamar would almost surely have regarded with skeptical hostility. Dussel and the various Latin American philosophers associated with the philosophy of liberation have obvious debts to European phenomenology and existentialism, especially to Heidegger and Levinas. But here, too, a philosophical trend in which we can now recognize the idea of postmodernity as a radical break with Enlightenment develops out of what is perceived at least as a direct *social and political* demand for theory to adequately reflect the life-world of those who are, as it were, at once both marginal and the subject of history. One can sympathize with the general impatience of Latin American critics and theorists who see in the category of "postmodern" what appears to be yet another neocolonial attempt to impose alien cultural models. (Such would probably be Retamar's conscious sentiments.) But the example of the "analectical" critiques of Dussel and Retamar show, in fact, that the intellectual and cultural gulf is overdrawn and that all roads to postmodernism do not lead through French poststructuralism.

Latin American Postmodernist Culture

Do we then find a *Latin American culture* of postmodernism linked to these particular conceptual trends? I would argue—and have argued elsewhere[30]—that the recent proliferation in Latin America of so-called testimonial narratives like that of Rigoberta Menchú, as well as the fictional and quasi-fictional texts that adopt the perspective of the marginalized (see, among others, the works of Elena Poniatowska, Eduardo Galeano, and Manlio Argueta), give some evidence of postmodernity insofar as they look for ways of giving voice to alterity. Significant here is their implicit opposition to the more traditional (and modernist) approach of magical realism, in which the marginal becomes a kind of aesthetic mode of access to the ground of national or regional unity and identity. One could include here

---

30. Neil Larsen, "Latin America and Postmodernity: A Brief Theoretical Sketch," unpublished paper; and *Modernism and Hegemony*.

as well the general wave of interest in Latin American popular and barrio culture as an embodiment of resistance.

But our direct concern here is with the ideological character of the conceptual trend as such. Does the move to, as it were, *found* postmodernism's antifoundationalism in the rebellious consciousness of those marginalized by modernity alter orthodox postmodernism's reactionary character?

I propose that it does not. Basing themselves on what is, to be sure, the decisive historical and political reality of unequal development and the undeniably imperialist and neocolonialist bias of much metropolitan based theory, the "leftist" postmodernists we have surveyed here all, to one degree or another, proceed to distort this reality into a new irrationalist and spontaneist myth. Marginality is postulated as a condition which, purely by virtue of its objective *situation,* gives rise to the *subversive particularity* upon which postmodern politics pins its hopes. But, one must ask, where has this been shown actually to occur? Where have imperialism and its attendant "scientific" and cultural institutions actually given way and not simply adapted to the new social movements founded on ideals of alterity?

Jameson, whose argument for a Third World cognitive privilege gestures openly toward an anti-imperialist nationalism as the road to both political and cultural redemption from postmodern psychic and social pathologies, speaks to us of Ousmane Sembene and Lu Hsun but leaves out the larger question of where strategies of all-class national liberation have ultimately led Africa and China—of whether, in fact, nationalism, even the radical nationalism of cultural alterity, can be said to have succeeded as a strategy of anti-imperialism. As Aijaz Ahmad remarked in his well-taken critique of Jameson's essay, Jameson's retention of a "three worlds" theoretical framework imposes a view of neocolonial society as free of class contradictions.[31]

Spivak's move to characterize the subaltern as what might be termed "deconstruction with a human face" only leads us further into a spontaneist thicket—although the logic here is more consistent than in Jameson and Said, since the transition from colonial to independent status itself is reduced to a "displacement of function between sign systems."[32]

Kipnis, whose attempt to implicate *both* textualist and reformist femi-

31. Aijaz Ahmad, "Jameson's Rhetoric of Otherness and the 'National Allegory,'" *Social Text* 17 (Fall 1987): 3–27.
32. Spivak, *In Other Worlds,* 198.

nisms in a politics of elitism and quietism has real merits, can in the end offer up as models for an "anticolonial" feminism little more than the vague threat of anti-Western counterterror from radical Third World nationalists such as Muammar Khadafy. One recalls here Lenin's dialectical insight in *What Is to Be Done?* regarding the internal link between spontaneism and terrorism. Yúdice's counterposing of a Third World "ethic of survival" to a postmodern ethic of "self-formation" possesses real force as itself an ethical judgment, and one can only concur in arguing the superior moral example of a Rigoberta Menchú. But where does this lead us *politically?* Those super-exploited and oppressed at the periphery thus become pegged with a sort of subpolitical consciousness, as if they couldn't or needn't see beyond the sheer fact of survival.

Are these lapses into the most threadbare sorts of political myths and fetishes simply the result of ignorance or bad faith on the part of sympathetic First World theorists? I do not think so. Regarding current political reality in Latin America, at least, such retreats into spontaneism and the overall subestimation of the conscious element in the waging of political struggle merely reflect in a general way the continuing and indeed *increasing* reliance of much of the autochthonous anti-imperialist left on a similar mix of romantic faith in exemplary violence and in the eventual spontaneous uprising of the "people," whether with bullets or with ballots. Although both *foquismo* and the strategy of a "peaceful road to socialism" based on populist alliances are recognized on one level to have failed, the conclusions drawn from this by the mainstream Left have on the whole led only to an even more thoroughgoing abandonment of Marxist and Leninist political strategies in favor of a "democratic" politics of consensus.

Here I would refer the reader to the survey of recent intellectual-political trends in Latin America undertaken by James Petras and Michael Morley.[33] These authors note how, after the fascist counterrevolutions of the 1970s and the ensuing normalization of counterrevolutionary policy under the guise of the "return to democracy" in the 1980s, a new type of intellectual is replacing the Latin American "organic" intellectual—the Martís, Mariáteguis, Guevaras, and the like—that typified previous periods of revolutionary and radical ferment. This new intellectual they term the "institutional intellectual," alluding to the latter's frequent dependence on

---

33. See *US Hegemony Under Siege: Class, Politics and Development in Latin America* (London: Verso, 1990), esp. chaps. 1 and 5; and *Latin America in the Time of Cholera* (New York: Routledge, 1992), esp. chaps. 1 and 7.

research-funding from liberal and social-democratic foundations based in the metropolis. Writing in *US Hegemony under Siege,* Petras and Morley note the involvement of the new institutional intellectuals in various successive waves of research agendas emanating from the funding agencies themselves. These focused, in turn, on a critique of the economic model and human rights violations of the military dictatorships and on an assessment of the "new social movements" emerging in the wake of the dictatorships. Petras and Morley note how

> studies . . . of the social movements claimed that [these] were counterposed to class politics, that the class structure from which they emerged was "heterogeneous," and that the struggles of the social movements were far removed from older ideological politics. The political line in regard to social movements was in the first instance that they should separate themselves from the ideological (radical) political parties; later, with the rise of liberal electoral parties, the political line shifted and the movements were advised to channel their attention toward the "struggle for democracy." The "autonomy of social movements" was promoted when the researchers sought to separate them from the revolutionary left; "participation" in "broad democratic fronts" became the formula the researchers promoted when liberal electoral politics came to the fore.[34]

Unfortunately, Petras and Morley provide few specific names of "institutional intellectuals" or their host foundations—something that considerably weakens their otherwise highly valuable efforts. But it will not be difficult for the reader of recent "postmodern" social and political theory in Latin America to recognize in the above description of "social movement" research the work of theorists such as Arditi, Argumedo, Borón, Brunner, Escobar, García Canclini, Lechner, Nun, and others.[35]

34. Petras and Morley, *US Hegemony,* 149.
35. See, for example, Benjamín Arditi, "Una gramática postmoderna para pensar lo social," in *Cultura, política y democratización,* ed. Norbert Lechner (Santiago de Chile: FLACSO/CLASCO/ICI, 1987): 169–87; Alcira Argumedo, *Los laberintos de la crisis, América Latina: Poder transnacional y comunicaciones* (Buenos Aires: ILET/Punto Sur, 1984); Atilio A. Borón, *Estado, Capitalismo, y Democracia en América Latina* (Buenos Aires: Ediciones Imago Mundi, 1992); José Joaquín Brunner, "Notas sobre la modernidad y lo posmoderno en la cultura latinoamericana," *David y Goliath* 17, 52 (1987): 30–39; Arturo Escobar, "Imagining a Post-Development Era? Critical Thought, Development and Social Movements," *Social Text* 31–32 (1992): 20–56; Arturo Escobar and Sonia E. Alva-

This entire political trend within Latin America can, I think, be correctly grasped only as a consequence of the failure of Marxists, in particular the established Communist parties and allied organizations, to carry out a self-criticism from the left, and of the resulting shift rightward into political positions that merely compound the errors of the past. As Petras and Morley put it in *Latin America in the Time of Cholera,* the "internal crisis of the political parties of the popular classes has severely weakened the political, organizational, and ideological capacities of the oppressed majorities to respond to the prolonged decay of social life: double negativity has not yet generated a positive outcome."[36] The response of traditional Latin American Marxism to the evident failure of populism (with or without a *foco* component) as a variation on the orthodox "two-stage" model (democratic capitalism first, then socialism) has typically been to jettison the second stage entirely. One could argue with a certain justice that this collapse was inevitable, given the political mistakes already embedded in the older line. As Adolfo Sánchez Vázquez has pointed out,[37] Latin Americans inherited the Marxism of the Second International, the Marxism that regarded revolution in the Western centers of capitalism as the necessary precondition for even national liberation, much less socialism or communism on the periphery. The Marx who, after studying British colonialism in Ireland, concluded that the liberation of Irish workers from imperialism was key to the political advance of an increasingly reformist and conservative British working class, the Marx who speculated that peasant communes in Russia might make feasible a *direct* transition to socialism—this Marx was largely unknown in Latin America. Thus when the communism of the Third International adopted the two-stage model for neocolonial countries, Latin American revolutionaries had scarcely any theoretical basis upon which to dissent. (This, according to Sánchez Vázquez, held true even for so original a Marxist thinker as Mariátegui, who, perhaps because he had to go outside

---

rez, eds., *The Making of Social Movements in Latin America: Identity, Strategy, and Democracy* (Boulder: Westview Press, 1992); Néstor García Canclini, *Culturas híbridas: Estrategias para entrar y salir de la modernidad* (Mexico: Grijalbo, 1990); Norbert Lechner, *La conflictiva y nunca acabada construcción del orden deseado* (Madrid: Siglo Veintiuno and Centro de Investigaciones Sociológicas, 1986); José Nun, *La rebelión del coro: Estudios sobre la racionalidad política y el sentido común* (Buenos Aires: Editores Nueva Visión, 1989). See also David Slater, ed., *New Social Movements and the State in Latin America* (Amsterdam: CEDLA, 1985).
36. Petras and Morley, *Latin America,* 20.
37. Adolfo Sánchez Vázquez, "Marxism in Latin America," *Philosophical Forum* 20, 1–2 (Fall–Winter 1988–89): 114–28.

Marxism for theories sensitive to factors of unequal development, was ultimately led in the direction of the irrationalism of Bergson and Sorel.) Latin America is in no way unique in this, needless to say. Everywhere the dominant trend is to compound past errors with even greater ones, thus reaching the point of renouncing the very core of Marxism as such in preference for liberal anachronisms and worse.

I dwell on this because I think a truly critical assessment of an "anti-imperialist" postmodernism, as of orthodox postmodernism, requires a prior recognition of the essentially parasitical dependence of such thinking on Marxism and particularly on *the crisis within Marxism*—a dependence that, as we have repeatedly observed, postmodernism systematically tends to erase. The very insistence on a politics of spontaneism and myth, on the tacit abandonment of conscious and scientific revolutionary strategy and organization, is, I am suggesting, the derivative *effect* of developments within Marxism itself, of what amounts to the *conscious political* decision to give up the principle of revolution as a scientifically grounded activity, a praxis with a rational foundation. The contemporary emphasis on "cultural politics" one finds throughout intellectual and radical discourse in Latin America as well as in the metropolis, while useful and positive to the degree that it opens up new areas for genuinely political analysis and critique, is symptomatic, in my view, of this theoretical surrender, and more often than not simply ratifies the nonstrategy of spontaneism. One might almost speak these days of a "culturalism" occupying the ideological space once held by the "economism" of the Second International revisionists. To adopt the "postmodern" sensibility means, in this sense, to regard the "culturalization" of the political as somehow simply in accordance with the current nature of things—to so minimize the role of political determination as to eliminate it altogether. And yet, this sensibility itself is *politically* determined.

Spontaneism, however it may drape itself in populist slogans and admiration for the people's day-to-day struggle for survival and so forth, rests on an intellectual distrust of the masses, a view of the mass as beyond the reach of reason and hence to be guided by myth. The Latin American masses have a long history of being stigmatized in this way by both imperial and creole elites. This elitism begins to lose its hold on the intelligentsia in the writings of genuine "radical democrats" such as Martí and is still further overcome in the discourses of revolutionary "organic" intellectuals such as Mariátegui and Guevara, although even here vestiges of the old viewpoint remain. (Mariátegui, who saw the Quechua-speaking indigenous peasants of Peru as beings with full historical and political subjecthood, maintained

ridiculously archaic and racist views regarding Peru's blacks and Asian immigrants.) And, of course, sexism has been and remains a deadly obstacle.

But in the era of postmodernity we are being urged, in exchange for
a cult of alterity, to relinquish this conception of the masses as the rational
agents of social and historical change, as the bearers of progress. Given the
increasing prevalence of such aristocratism, however it may devise radical
credentials for itself, it becomes possible to fall short of this truly democratic
vision, to be seduced by the false Nietzschean regard for the masses as
capable only of an unconscious, instinctual political agency.

In this respect, it is important to consider what the role of the Nicaraguan revolution during the 1980s was, and especially the theory and
practice of *sandinismo,* in supplying to radical or anti-imperialist postmodernism a species of historical warrant. As Greg Dawes has recently observed in *Aesthetics and Revolution* (see especially chapter one, "Sandinismo and Postmodernism"), "terms such as *pluralism, unfixity, différance,*
and *totality*" were "frequently evoked when historians, political scientists,
and literary theorists . . . turned their gaze toward Nicaragua." Dawes as-
serts the existence of a definite "correlation between a certain type of postmodern theoretical language . . . and the 'post-Marxist' revisions incarnated
in the politico-aesthetic alterations that have taken place in Nicaragua since
1979." [38] Inspired in part by *sandinista* theoreticians themselves,[39] but above
all by the great explosion of cultural energy unleashed by the revolution,
not a few intellectuals claimed to see in the evident freedom of *sandinismo*
from orthodox, Marxist notions of class, and the former's seemingly successful attempts to utilize culture itself as a primary means of constructing
a popular-revolutionary subject, a corroboration in practice of certain basic
tenets of postmodern political theory.

The clearest example of this is, I think, to be found in John Beverley
and Marc Zimmerman's *Literature and Politics in Central American Revolutions,* as well as in Beverley's subsequent essay, "The Politics of Latin
American Postmodernism." [40] In the former work, the authors in effect argue
two fundamental theses. The first is that, due to the effects of dependent,

38. Greg Dawes, *Aesthetics and Revolution: Nicaraguan Poetry, 1979–1990* (Minneapolis: University of Minnesota Press, 1993), 25.
39. See, for example, Orlando Núñez and Roger Burbach, *Democracia y revolución en
las Américas* (Managua: Editorial Vanguardia, 1986).
40. John Beverley and Marc Zimmerman, *Literature and Politics in the Central American
Revolutions* (Austin: University of Texas Press, 1990), hereafter cited in text as *L & P*);
and John Beverley, "The Politics of Latin American Postmodernism," in Beverley, *Against
Literature* (Minneapolis: University of Minnesota Press, 1993), 103–23.

export-oriented capitalism in the region and the resulting absence of a well-developed scientific and technical culture, it is literature and above all poetry that takes on the role, in Central America, of producing the "subject position of a radicalized intelligentsia" (*L & P,* 9). Here, it seems to me, Beverley and Zimmerman make a highly compelling case. Their second thesis complicates matters, however. Invoking both the Althusserian theory of ideology as an unconscious process of subject formation and the Laclau-Mouffe theory of society as "not some essence that is prior to representation but rather the product of struggles over meaning and representation" (*L & P,* ix)—that is, society as itself the supreme ideological construct—*Literature and Politics* implicitly attributes to Central American revolutionary poetry as "ideological signifier" the power to, as it were, constitute the revolutionary society itself. True, this is revolutionary society in its subjective dimensions only; but following the Laclau-Mouffe logic, one is forced to conclude that society *has* no other dimension. Beverley and Zimmerman cite the example here of Carlos Fonseca, founder of the FSLN, whose basically literary invention of Sandino as revolutionary theorist in the so-called *Ideario* supplied a needed "ideology of armed national liberation struggle specific to Nicaragua's cultural and political experience" (*L & P,* 32). That is, if literature in Central America is a "model for politics" (*L & P,* xiii), *sandinismo* itself, as formulated by the basically literary intelligence of Fonseca (over which the poetry of Darío exercised a decisive influence) represents such a "model" in truly practical form. *Sandinismo,* and not Marxism-Leninism becomes the "necessary and sufficient ideological signifier for all social forces in the country capable of being mobilized against dictatorship and U.S. domination" (*L & P,* 32). Explicit efforts to rouse class *consciousness* become unnecessary, perhaps even counterproductive. By coming at the subject on the level of culture—that is, *unconsciously* and, as it were, from behind—*sandinismo* becomes a formula for a spontaneous revolutionary will.

What then to make of the FSLN's fall from power after their electoral loss in February 1990? In *Literature and Politics*—caught virtually in press by this unexpected turn of events—Beverley and Zimmerman concede that the "identification achieved in the period of insurrection and reconstruction between a radicalized intelligentsia . . . and the popular sectors" had "at least in part, broken down" (*L & P,* 111). They hold out the possibility, however, that a "continued radicalization and democratization at the cultural level *might* have produced a stronger bond between the revolution and the popular sectors, and that this, in turn, might have offset some of the ideological damage caused by the economic crisis and the war" (*L & P,* 112). In

Beverley's "The Politics of Latin American Postmodernism," this same hope is expressed in stronger language: "Even in defeat (and precisely because of their commitment to implement and respect democratic processes in the face of massive foreign aggression and interference) it seems to me the Sandinistas are exemplary of the emergence of a postmodern but still explicitly socialist political agency in Latin America: I believe their political project is by no means exhausted."[41]

If we take off our postmodern spectacles, however, and look at what—on the level of *sandinismo* as *economic and social policy* rather than "ideological signifier"—preceded the electoral debacle of 1990, a rather different picture emerges: that of a *conscious* decision to seek accommodation with the revolution's enemies, both in Washington and within Nicaragua itself, leaving the masses of Nicaraguan workers and peasants to suffer the consequences. As Petras and Morley report in *Latin America in the Time of Cholera* (see chapter 6, "The Electoral Defeat of the Sandinistas: Critical Reflections"), the FSLN response to the combined pressure of the *contra* war and the economic embargo was, among other things, to implement massive, IMF-style austerity measures, resulting in catastrophic economic hardships for the poor; to send in the police to break the resulting strikes and protests; to agree to elections *while* the *contra* war was still being actively pursued by Washington; to permit massive foreign funding of the pro-U.S. opposition parties coalesced in UNO; and to conduct a glitzy, U.S.-style electoral campaign, in the hopes that this sort of "ideological signifier" and "struggle over meaning" might persuade those it had betrayed that the FSLN was still their best hope for the future. As FSLN *comandante* Tomás Borge himself declared, "We sacrificed the working class in favor of the economy as part of a strategic plan."[42] Unfortunately for Borge, Ortega, and the FSLN leadership, however, this strategy failed, leaving the revolution to, as Petras and Morley put it, "fall between two chairs," unable to sell itself to the imperialists in Washington and the capitalist elites in Nicaragua itself after having first sold out the Nicaraguan masses who had supplied the "political agency" (in the form of armed insurrections) that brought the FSLN to power in the first place. And as for the "exhaustion" of their "political project," about which Beverley expresses a cautionary optimism: Petras and Morley report that *after* the election of UNO candidate Violeta Chamorro in 1990, Ortega and the FSLN directorate have, while

41. Beverley, "Politics of Latin American Postmodernism," 120.
42. Quoted in Petras and Morley, *Latin America,* 134.

threatening "government from below," actively facilitated Chamorro's "free market," neoliberal "reforms"—even, in the person of former FSLN vice president Sergio Ramírez, traveling to Washington to help Chamorro's representatives offer up the latest round of sacrifices to the World Bank and other prospective lenders.[43]

The lesson here, *qua* the question of "postmodern . . . political agency," would seem to be that there is no magical, cultural route—no matter how poetically inspired—around the stubborn political problem of class consciousness as such. Re-"articulate" and re-"signify" the social text as it would, when *sandinismo* made the calculation that a good dose of revolutionary culture would enable it to renegotiate its identity with the popular sector while its leading representatives renegotiated the economic pact with imperialism, this problem came back to haunt it with a vengeance. While the FSLN trusted to the spontaneous power of its ideological signifiers to generate a mass revolutionary will, the masses responded by spontaneously turning it out of power. Of course, in doing so, the latter demonstrated their own grievous lack of consciousness. But even to suggest, as Beverley and Zimmerman do, that this was somehow a result of insufficient "radicalization and democratization at the cultural level" is to trade in reality itself for a pair of postmodern spectacles.

Ultimately, it may be only revolutionary practice, the *activity* of strategy and organization, that can successfully trouble the political reveries of postmodernism. But the sheer history of such practice, particularly in Latin America, makes risible any theory that considers politics (in the Leninist sense) to be either too abstract to matter, or—in what finally amounts to the same thing—to be "self-produced," as Aronowitz has phrased it.

Perhaps the most eloquent refutation of spontaneist faith in "new social movements" is recorded in Roque Dalton's testimonial classic *Miguel Mármol,* in which the legendary Salvadoran revolutionary named in the title recounts a life as a communist militant in Central America. It is impossible, by citing excerpts, to do justice to the combined practical wisdom and theoretical profundity of this narrative (by which I mean Mármol's own; I leave it to subtler intellects than my own to decide whether Dalton's editorial participation in this narrative may somehow serve to render it a postmodern "historiographic metafiction," as Beverley has suggested). But one in particular speaks poignantly to the question at hand: in the third chapter of the text, Mármol discusses his return in 1930, shortly before he participates in

43. Petras and Morley, *Latin America,* 139.

founding the Salvadoran Communist Party, to his home town of Ilopango. His task is to organize a union of rural workers. At first, as he tells it, the workers reject him, suspicious of his being anti-Catholic. He is led to recall the failure of previous union organizing efforts carried out by a local teacher and a railroad engineer. "However, we suspected they had always worked outside reality, that they hadn't based their organizing work on the actual problems of people and, on the contrary, had created an impenetrable barrier between their 'enlightenment' and the 'backwardness' they ascribed to the people."[44]

Mármol, however, persists in "finding out what the people thought" (*MM*, 119)—that is, he refuses to take their initially backward reaction (defense of church authority) to mean that they lack "enlightenment." Meetings are called, and as the people begin to talk about working conditions, Mármol recalls, "it wasn't hard to hear, over and over again, concepts that sounded to me just like the 'class struggle,' the 'dictatorship of the proletariat,' etc." (*MM*, pp. 136–37). Mármol's task, then, is not that of "enlightening" the "backward" masses, nor is it simply to acknowledge "what the people thought" as sovereign. Rather, it is to collect these isolated concepts, to *articulate* them, and to lead the masses in drawing the logically necessary conclusions.

Of course, the eventual armed insurrection of 1932 toward which the practice of Mármol and the Salvadoran Communists was ultimately directed proved a miscalculation and was drowned in blood. But the fact that it could be planned at all must be considered, as it is by Mármol, a significant step forward. If, as the present situation in Central America suggests, the positive culmination of such practice still remains distant, this, it seems to me, is a reflection not of Mármol's "sectarianism" (as Dalton had, and, no doubt, the postmoderns would have it) but of his precociousness. Here, in so many words, Mármol demonstrates his profound dialectical grasp of the contradictory relation of theory to practice, of concept to reality, of culture to class, of the conscious to the spontaneous, of the "from without" to the "from within." Postmodernism, meanwhile, even at its most "left," political, and self-critical, remains cut off from the dialectical truths discovered in the practice of Mármol and of the millions of others in Latin America and across the planet who prepared it and will follow it through.

44. Roque Dalton, *Miguel Mármol,* trans. Kathleen Ross and Richard Schaaf (Willimantic, Conn.: Curbstone Press, 1982), 119. Cited hereafter in text as *MM*.

Founding Statement

Latin American Subaltern Studies Group

Introduction

The work of the Subaltern Studies Group, an interdisciplinary organization of South Asian scholars led by Ranajit Guha, has inspired us to found a similar project dedicated to studying the subaltern in Latin America.[1] The present dismantling of authoritarian regimes in Latin America, the end of communism and the consequent displacement of revolutionary projects, the processes of redemocratization, and the new dynamics created by the effects of the mass media and transnational economic arrangements: these are all developments that call for new ways of thinking and acting politically. The redefinition of Latin American political and cultural space in recent years has, in turn, impelled scholars of the region to revise established and previously functional epistemologies in the social sciences and humanities.

1. The group explains that it uses the word *subaltern* "as a name for the general attribute of subordination in South Asian society whether this is expressed in terms of class, caste, age, gender, and office or in any other way." See Ranajit Guha, "Preface," in *Selected Subaltern Studies*, Ranajit Guha and Gayatri Spivak, eds. (New York: Oxford University Press, 1988), 35.

The general trend toward democratization prioritizes in particular the re-examination of the concepts of pluralistic societies and the conditions of subalternity within these societies.

The realization that colonial and postindependence elites agreed in their views of the subaltern led the Subaltern Studies Group to question the master paradigms used in representing colonial and postcolonial societies, both in the cultural practices of hegemony developed by elite groups and in the disciplinary discourses of the humanities and social sciences that seek to represent the workings of these societies. Guha's inaugural article in the first volume of the *Subaltern Studies* series, published by the group beginning in 1982, lays out the ambition of the project to displace the casual and descriptive assumptions about South Asian colonial history embedded in the dominant models of colonial, nationalist, and traditional Marxist historiography.[2] His 1983 book, *Elementary Aspects of Peasant Insurgency*, criticizes the prejudice in previous historical scholarship favoring insurgents who present *written* agendas and carefully thought-out programs. This dependency on the written record, Guha notes, betrays a prejudice for both literacy and foreign and indigenous elites in the very construction of South Asian historiography.

Reading this historiography "in reverse" (or "against the grain," in the idiom of deconstruction sometimes used by the group) to recover the cultural and political specificity of peasant insurrections has, for Guha, two components: identifying the logic of the distortions in the representation of the subaltern in official or elite culture; and uncovering the social semiotics of the strategies and cultural practices of peasant insurgencies themselves.[3] The insight of Guha was that the subaltern, by definition not registered or registrable as a historical subject capable of hegemonic action (seen, that is, through the prism of colonial administrators or "educated" native leaders), is nevertheless present in unexpected structural dichotomies, fissures in the forms of hierarchy and hegemony, and, in turn, in the constitution of the heroes of the national drama, writing, literature, education, institutions, and the administration of law and authority.

The subaltern, in other words, is not only *acted on*, despite the tendency in traditional paradigms to see it as a passive or "absent" subject that can be mobilized only from above; it also *acts* to produce social effects that

2. Ranajit Guha, "On Some Aspects of the Historiography of Colonial India," in *Selected Subaltern Studies*, 37–43.
3. The classic statement of this double endeavor is Guha's "The Prose of Counter-Insurgency," in *Selected Subaltern Studies*, 45–84.

are visible, if not always predictable or understandable, by these paradigms or the state policies and research projects they authorize. It is the recognition of this role of the subaltern, how it curves, alters, modifies our life strategies of learning, understanding, and research, that underlies the doubts besetting these traditional disciplinary and historiographic paradigms, paradigms that are themselves related to the social projects of national, regional, and international elites seeking to manage or control subject populations and that bring in their wake the danger of filtering cultural hegemonies all the way across the political spectrum, from the elites themselves to the epistemologies and discourses of revolutionary movements looking to subvert their power in the name of the "people."

The Subaltern in Latin American Studies

The limits of elite historiography in relation to the subaltern do not come as an unexpected theoretical surprise in Latin American Studies, which has long worked with the assumption that *nation* and *national* are not popular, all-inclusive terms. The concept and representation of subalternity developed by the South Asian Subaltern Studies Group does not gain currency until the 1980s; but Latin American Studies has been involved with related issues since its inauguration as a field in the 1960s. The constitution of the field itself (and of the Latin American Studies Association as its organizational form) as a necessarily interdisciplinary formation corresponds to the way in which the South Asian group conceptualized the subaltern as a subject that emerges across, or at the intersections of, a spectrum of academic disciplines ranging from the philosophical critique of metaphysics, to contemporary literary and cultural theory, to history and the social sciences. Indeed, the force behind the problem of the subaltern in Latin America could be said to arise directly out of the need to reconceptualize the relation of nation, state, and "people" in the three social movements that have centrally shaped the contours and concerns of Latin American Studies (as of modern Latin America itself): the Mexican, Cuban, and Nicaraguan Revolutions.

We may plot the relationship of the emergence of Latin American Studies with the problem of the conceptualization of subalternity in terms of three major phases from 1960 to the present.

Phase One: 1960–1968

As is well known, although most of Latin America gained formal independence in the nineteenth century, the resulting postcolonial nation-states were ruled predominantly by white criollos who developed internal colonial regimes with respect to the Indians, the slaves of African descent, the mestizo or mulatto peasantry, and the nascent proletariats. The Mexican Revolution marked a point of departure from this white- (and male-) dominated, oligarchic, and Eurocentric model of development, depending as it did on the agency of Indians and poor mestizos not only as soldiers but also as leaders and strategists of the revolutionary upheaval. In postrevolutionary Mexico, however, in a process that has been amply studied, this protagonism was blunted at the economic, political, and cultural levels in favor of the rise of a new mestizo upper and middle class by the suppression of Indian leaders and communities, and by the resubalternization of the Indian as a "cultural" artifact of the new state apparatus (e.g., in Mexican muralism) rather than as an actual historical-political agent.

The Cuban Revolution represents a partial revival of the impulse toward a surfacing of the subaltern, in particular raising against the primacy of Eurocentric historiographic and cultural paradigms on both a practical and a theoretical level the question of the non- (or post-) European character of the social subject of Latin American history in the context of decolonization. Roberto Fernández Retamar's rereading of Fanon and the discourse of national liberation in his essay *Calibán* was an example of the new ways of conceptualizing Latin American history and identity.

This impulse influenced not only the Boom writers in literature, such as Mario Vargas Llosa, Carlos Fuentes, and Gabriel García Márquez, but also intellectuals in the social sciences, such as André Gunder Frank and the dependency-school theorists. Both groups came to see the establishment of viable economies and societies in Latin America as contingent on a radical structural "break" with the dominant system, a break that, at least in theory, would both allow and be produced by the protagonism of subaltern subjects.

The Cuban Revolution opened up cultural and political practices that were no longer satisfied with the representation of the social subject of Latin American history as the middle or upper class. The new prestige the revolution gave to Marxism among Latin American intellectuals and cultural workers provided an optimism and epistemological certainty regarding the nature of historical agency. The concept of the people as the "working masses" became the new center of representation. Among the most significant results of this shift in the field of culture were the documentary film school of Santa Fe created in Argentina by Fernando Birri, the films of the Brazilian Cinema Nouvo and Cuba's ICAIC, the Bolivian concept of "film with-the-people" developed by Jorge Sanjinés and Grupo Ukamu, the Colombian "teatro de creación colectiva," the Teatro Escambray in Cuba, and related movements in the United States like the Teatro Campesino.

But, even where this work engaged problems of gender, race, language, and the like, its insistence on a unitary, class-based subject and its concomitant assumption of the identity of theoretical-literary texts produced by elite intellectuals with this subject veiled the disparity of blacks, Indians, Chicanos, and women; alternative models of sexuality and of the body; alternative epistemologies and ontologies; the existence of those who had not entered into a social pact with the (revolutionary) state; the "lumpen." (A good dramatization of the issues involved, but one that also is "part of the problem" in its manner of posing them, was Sara Gómez's exploration of class, race, and gender conflicts in postrevolutionary Cuba in her film *De cierta manera* [One Way or Another].) The subject of history was never in question, and so neither was the adequacy of its representation (both in the mimetic and the political sense) by revolutionary sects, by the new forms of art and culture, or by new theoretical paradigms like dependency theory or Althusserian Marxism.

Phase Two: 1968–1979

The crisis of the model of protagonism represented by the Cuban Revolution comes with the collapse of Che Guevara's guerrilla group in Bolivia and of the *foco*-based guerrilla fronts generally in the late 1960s, a collapse predicated in part on the separation between these groups and the masses they sought to dynamize into revolutionary action (an eerily apt image of this was Guevara's recognition, noted in his *Bolivian Diary*, of the lack of response in the eyes of the Aymara-speaking peasants of the altiplano he was trying to organize).

The U.S. New Left and antiwar movement, the French "May," and the student demonstrations and subsequent massacre at Tlatelolco in Mexico in 1968 signal the entrance of students as political actors onto the world stage, displacing traditional social-democratic or Communist parties and formations. The cultural practices informing this insurgency are exemplified in Latin America by Violeta Parra and the *nueva trova* movement in Latin American music, or by the emergence of reggae and some forms of rock as oppositional musics. The moment is characterized politically, on the one hand, by a "generational" struggle between elite and middle sectors and a new, class-amorphous social sector, which the student-based New Left seeks to represent; on the other, by the broad alliance politics or popular frontism of movements such as the Chilean UP (Popular Unity) under Allende.

In cultural production, the emergence of testimonial and documentary forms shifts dramatically the parameters of representation away from the writer and the avant-gardes. In contrast to the ambition of the Boom novelists to "speak for" Latin America, the subaltern subject represented in the testimonial text becomes part of the construction of the text itself. The dissatisfaction with the Boom's male-centered strategy of "metafictionality" leads to a new emphasis on the concrete, the personal, the "small history," writing (or video work) by women, political prisoners, lumpen, and gays, raising, in the process, questions of who represents whom. Simultaneously, there is the initiative in academic literary criticism to construct a "social history" of Latin American literature, represented by projects such as the Ideologies and Literature group at the University of Minnesota and the Instituto de Estudios Latinoamericanos "Rómulo Gallegos" in Caracas, both nourished by the diaspora of Southern Cone leftist intellectuals in the years following 1973.

This phase also marks the introduction into Latin America of French poststructuralist theory, Gramscian Marxism, and the heritage of the Frankfurt school, which serves to destabilize some of the assumptions of the various forms of orthodox Marxism dominant in the 1960s and the model of "modernization" generated in U.S. social sciences. In response to the formalism of structuralist semiotics, a "social" semiotics stressing heteroglossia, dialogism, and the multiplicity of discourses and signifying practices gains currency, impelled by the Latin American reception of the work of Bakhtin, Voloshinov, Lotman and the School of Tartu, and the emerging field of popular culture studies in the United States and Great Britain.

Phase Three: The 1980s

The Nicaraguan Revolution, and the contingent spread and importance of liberation theology theory and practice, become primary points of reference in this phase. *Culture, democratization, global, post-*(Marxism, modernism, structuralism) become key words. High culture forms such as literature are bracketed by the critiques developed by deconstruction, feminism, black and Chicano studies in the United States, and in their place, an anthropological sense of culture as "lived experience" comes to the fore. In tandem with the emergence of projects such as the Subaltern Studies Group, or the Birmingham Center for Cultural Studies directed by Jamaican Stuart Hall, Latin Americanists begin to question deeply the persistence in Latin American modernity of colonial or neocolonial systems of representation.[4] There is a new sense that both cultural and political dynamics have begun to function in a global context that problematizes the center-periphery model of dependency theory as well as the strategies of economic nationalism that follow from it (the end of the growth cycle of the sixties and the debt crisis will be the dominant economic facts of the decade in Latin America).

The rapid development and spread of information technology is the defining technological feature of this phase, permitting, among other things, the circulation of texts and cultural practices from areas of the formerly colonial world in new, global circuits of information retrieval and exchange (the publication, subsequent reception, and current centrality in the U.S. multiculturalism debate of Rigoberta Menchú's testimonio, is one small, but significant, example of the new ways in which cultural objects are created and circulate). With the proliferation of television, the dominant new cultural form in Latin America becomes the *telenovela*, and communications the fastest growing academic field.

It is the moment, precisely, of the emergence of Cultural Studies within the Anglo-American academy, an emergence fueled by the conjunction of feminist theory and activism, the critique of colonial discourse, new forms of Marxism and social theory (Jameson, Mouffe and Laclau's "post-Marxism," Lyotard's postmodern condition), the psychoanalytic account of the construction of the subject provided by Lacanian theory, the new attention to the mass media and popular culture, and the new experiences of globality and simultaneity. With a delay of about five years, this emergence is replicated in Latin America itself and in Latin American Studies. It would be appropriate, then, to conclude this narrative of the relation of the problem of subalternity to Latin American Studies with two observations: (1) the project of developing a Latin American Subaltern Studies Group such as the one we are proposing represents one aspect, albeit a crucial one, of the larger emergent field of Latin American Cultural Studies; (2) in the new situation of globality, the signifier *Latin American* itself now refers also to significant social forces *within* the United States, which has now become the fourth- or fifth-largest Spanish-speaking nation in the world (out of twenty).

4. See, for example, Angel Rama's posthumous *La ciudad letrada* (Hanover, N.H.: Ediciones del Norte, 1984).

Founding Concepts and Strategies

It is above all the emerging consensus on the need for a democratic world order that sets the stage for our work. The ethical and epistemological nature of this consensus and the fate of the processes of redemocratization in Latin America itself are, we believe, linked in ways that impose new urgencies and challenges on our work as scholars and teachers. These involve, on the one hand, a heightened sensitivity to the complexities of social difference and, on the other, the composition of a plural, but bounded, space or platform of research and discussion in which everyone has a place. Traditional configurations of democracy and the nation-state have barred subaltern social classes and groups from actively participating both in the political process and in the constitution of academically authorized knowledge, and have not recognized their potential contributions as a pool of human capital, except by default.

What is clear from the work of the South Asian Subaltern Studies Group is the axiom that the elites represented by the national bourgeoisie and/or the colonial administration are responsible for inventing the ideology and reality of nationalism. Their way of looking at things is located within the parameters of the nation-state as constituted at points of intersection, and interest, between a formerly hegemonic colonial power and a future post-colonial system of new states, in which they will play key leadership roles. At the same time, it is what Guha calls the "historic failure of the nation to come into its own,"[5] a failure due to the inadequacy of elite leadership, that is the central problematic of postcoloniality. The new global political economy brings in its wake a conceptual movement to de-emphasize paradigms of *nation* and *independence*, a shift that accounts for the changes in terminology in the social sciences. *Consensus, pluralism, democracy, subalternity, power shift, new global order*, and *Grand Area* are examples of this mutation. They have substituted terms such as *modernization, dictatorship, party, revolution, metropolis/periphery, development, nationalism*, and *national liberation*. One of our first tasks is to track the ways in which terms mutate, and what it means to use a given terminology.

In addition to conceptualizing *nation* as at least a dual space (colonial or metropolitan/Creole elites; Creole elites/subaltern groups), the study of the subaltern in Latin America involves other structural dichotomies. As

5. Guha, "On Some Aspects," 43.

a space of counterposition and collision, the nation includes multiple frac-tures of language, race, ethnicity, gender, class, and the resulting tensions between assimilation (ethnic dilution and homogenization) and confronta-tion (passive resistance, insurgency, strikes, terrorism). The subaltern func-tions as a "migrating" subject, both in its own cultural self-representations and in the changing nature of its social pact with the state(s). According to both the mode of production narrative of classical Marxism and the mod-ernization narrative of sociological functionalism, a migrating subject must be plotted against its position in the stages of development of a national economy. In such narratives, the consent of the subaltern classes and their identity as economic categories underwrite the increased productivity that is the sign of progress and economic stability. The question of the nature of the subaltern social pact is integral to the effective functioning of govern-ments in the present, as much as to plotting their future.

De-nationalization is simultaneously a limit and a threshold of our project. The "de-territorialization" of the nation-state under the impact of the new permeability of frontiers to capital-labor flows merely replicates, in effect, the genetic process of implantation of a colonial economy in Latin America in the sixteenth and seventeenth centuries. It is not only that we can *no longer* operate solely within the prototype of nationhood; the con-cept of the nation, itself tied to the protagonism of Creole elites concerned to dominate and/or manage other social groups or classes in their own soci-eties, has obscured, *from the start*, the presence and reality of subaltern social subjects in Latin American history. We need, in this sense, to go backward to consider both pre-Columbian and colonial forms of prenational territorialization, as well as forward to think about newly emerging territo-rial subdivisions, permeable frontiers, regional logics, and concepts such as *Commonwealth* or *Pan-Americanism*.

Calling the concept of nation into question affects, in turn, "national" notions of elite and subaltern. In Latin America (and now in the United States), patterns of migration, or the recent phenomenon of resettlement, impinge on existing social and economic formations, their legal status guar-anteed by the state, and consequently on the representation and protago-nism of the subaltern. What are the boundaries of Latin America if, for instance, we consider New York the largest Puerto Rican metropolis and Los Angeles the second-largest Mexican metropolis? Or, if we are dealing with the English-speaking Afro-Caribbeans of the Atlantic Coast of Nica-ragua who call themselves Creoles and whose cultural tastes include U.S. country music and Jamaican reggae?

This insistence on thinking the subaltern from the standpoint of post-modernity does not mean that we do not intend to pursue the traces of previous cultural hegemonies in the formation of the subaltern or of the corresponding area-elites. We can find the subaltern only in the seams of the previously articulated sociocultural and administrative practices and epistemologies, in the cloning of cultural mentalities, and in the contingent social pacts that occur at every transitional juncture. According to elite writings, nationalism is an idealist venture conducted by the same elite, guided in part by a "literary" ideal of nationhood. The native elite, with its antagonism toward the colonizer, allegedly advocates the good of the people, the subaltern classes, claiming altruism and self-abnegation instead of a search for class empowerment. The history of the national bourgeoisie becomes the spiritual (auto)biography of the elite, a fact not lost on the subaltern classes and directly contributing to their political and cultural formations (the well-known resistance to Spanish-language literacy in some Indian areas and to "high culture" generally on the part of subaltern groups, for example). Not to acknowledge the contribution of the people to their own history manifests the poverty of historiography and points to crucial reasons for the failures of national programs of "popular" entitlement. Subaltern (trans)nationalism is recorded negatively only as a problem of law and order, and positively only as a response to the charisma of elite leaders, in other words, as vertical mobilization through the populist or media manipulation of groups and factions.

To represent subalternity in Latin America, in whatever form it takes wherever it appears—nation, hacienda, work place, home, informal sector, black market—to find the blank space where it speaks as a sociopolitical subject, requires us to explore the margins of the state. Our premise, again, is that the nation, as a conceptual space, is not identical to the nation as state. Our initial concepts are therefore more geographical than institutional. Our research strategies oblige us to do archaeological work in the interstices of the forms of either domination—law and order/military and police powers—or integration—learning and schooling. From the perspective of subalternity, the alternate use of police and teachers may well be coordinated strategies of transnational projects for economic extraction and territorial administration. We must be careful, in the process of conceptualizing subalternity, not to ensnare ourselves in the problem, dominant in previous articulations of "national" liberation (for example, in some forms of Puerto Rican nationalism or in Latin American literary *Arielism*), of the national elite itself as subaltern, that is, as transcriber, translator, interpreter,

editor: to avoid, in other words, the construction of postcolonial intelligen-
tsias as "sharecroppers" in metropolitan cultural hegemony. This is not to
dismiss the problem but simply to indicate that retaining a focus on the intelligentsia and on its characteristic intellectual practices—centered on the
cultivation of writing, science, and the like—leaves us in the space of historiographic prejudice and "not-seeing" that Guha identified in his studies
of peasant insurgency.[6]

To the extent that *nation* and *national* are reconceptualized as
colored, and move from criollo to mestizo, from mestizo to mulatto, black,
and Indian, from male to female, we approximate more closely the idea
of territoriality—areas, spaces, and geography—we seek to encompass.
In other words, it is the inter/national, internecine deinstitutionalized social
subject that confirms the structure of globalization, of population control
(political as much as biological), be it in terms of "prestige," "culture," or
maquiladoras. Paying attention to and acknowledging the presence of this
subject is an index of the importance of the subaltern groups, of how they
force themselves into the administrative structures and practices of domination as flesh-and-blood living beings. Since colonial and "national" epistemologies have given them the status of objects, their activity seems "erup-
tive," breaking with models of vertical mobilization and calling into question
hegemonic party/state forms of social control and representation, forcing
the state and its agents (including university professors and research foundation staff) to negotiate a more horizontal social and research dynamic or
to face the bomb in the path of their own project of making history.

We do not, however, want to simply exclude the question of the
"national" and forms of nationalism and "national-popular" mobilization,
for example, the sort involved in the Sandinista Revolution in Nicaragua
(we are influenced here by the work of Carlos Vilas on the question of

---

6. This may indicate one point of difference between the Subaltern Studies proposal and
those of, for example, Roberto Fernández Retamar or Edward Said, with which it shares
many concerns. In his foreword to *Selected Subaltern Studies*, Said puts Guha and
the members of the group in the company of Fanon, Salman Rushdie, Gabriel García
Márquez, Ngugi wa Thiongo, C. L. R. James, et cetera (ix–x). This is appropriate to the
extent that their work is, in Said's words, "a hybrid," partaking jointly of Western and
non-Western concerns and theory. But where Said and Retamar envision a *new type
of intellectual* as the protagonist of decolonization, the, admittedly paradoxical, intent of
Subaltern Studies is precisely to displace the centrality of intellectuals and intellectual
"culture" in social history.

the identity of the social subject of the revolution).[7] Neither do we want to establish a fissure between the theoretical and the political. The subaltern is not one thing. It is, to repeat, a mutating, migrating subject. Even if we agree with the general concept of the subaltern as the masses of the laboring population and the intermediate strata, we cannot abjure the inclusion of nonworking subjects unless we want to run the risk of repeating the mistake of classical Marxism on the question of how social agency is constructed. We need to access the vast (and mobile) array of the masses—peasants, proletarians, the informal and formal sectors, the sub- and underemployed, vendors, those outside or at the margin of the money economy, lumpens and ex-lumpens of all sorts, children, the growing numbers of the homeless . . .

We need to conclude this statement, however, with a recognition of the limits of the idea of "studying" the subaltern and a caution to ourselves in setting out to do this. Our project, in which a team of researchers and their collaborators in elite metropolitan universities want to extricate from documents and practices the oral world of the subaltern, the structural presence of the unavoidable, indestructible, and effective subject who has proven us wrong—she/he who has demonstrated that we did not know them—must itself confront the dilemma of subaltern resistance to and insurgency against elite conceptualizations. Clearly, it is a question not only of new ways of *looking at* the subaltern, new and more powerful forms of information retrieval, but also of building new relations between ourselves and those human contemporaries whom we posit as objects of study. Rigoberta Menchú's injunction at the end of her famous testimonio is perhaps relevant in this regard: "I'm still keeping secret what I think no-one should know. Not even anthropologists or intellectuals, no matter how many books they have, can find out all our secrets."[8]

7. Carlos Vilas, *The Sandinista Revolution: National Liberation and Social Transformation in Central America* (New York: Monthly Review Press, 1986).
8. Rigoberta Menchú, *I, Rigoberta Menchú: An Indian Woman in Guatemala*, trans. Ann Wright (London: Verso, 1984).

A Disenchantment Called Postmodernism

Norbert Lechner

What does it mean to discuss so-called postmodernity in Latin America? A long experience of frustration has made us skeptical of debates that might be valid in Europe or North America but are foreign to Latin American reality. Postmodernism has been a controversial notion, and it is still too early to evaluate its reach. But there undoubtedly exists a new state of mind that deserves our attention.[1] Moreover, we live in a period of transnationalization that involves not only economic but ideological changes as well; the "cultural climate" is also becoming internationalized, and the themes of the European and North American debate—even if only as an intellectual "fashion"—are part of our reality, too.

What do we mean by *postmodernism*, anyway? The interpretations are multiple and frequently contradictory. For some, modernity has ex-

---

1. It is significant for the history of the social sciences in the region that CLACSO celebrated its twentieth anniversary with a conference entitled "Latin American Identity, Premodernity, Modernity and Postmodernity." See *David & Goliath* (Buenos Aires) 52 (1987). No less revealing is the interest the theme awakens in journals of neoliberal inspiration; see, for example, the special issue of *Estudios Públicos* (Santiago) 27 (1987).

hausted itself, giving rise to a new age. For others, what is involved instead is a critique that is interior to an incomplete project of modernity.[2] In any case, it is with reference to modernity that we consider our situation. It must be said that the question of postmodernism is fundamentally a consideration of our *time*. Moreover—and above all else—the debate over postmodernity, initiated in the fields of philosophy, aesthetics, and architecture, has now transformed itself into a *political question*. Has the reforming impulse of modernity exhausted itself? This is, although premature, the basic question. And it is from this point of view that I intend to examine a possible change in our political culture.

The phenomenon which, without a doubt, characterizes the political situation of Latin American countries today is disenchantment.[3] This disenchantment can seriously affect the process of democratization by weakening its political roots. As such, it is usually judged negatively, and there is no lack of historical experience to justify this fear. The danger of a disenchantment with democracy is real; but for this very reason, it is important to analyze that possibility more thoroughly. There have always been periods of certainty and periods of disenchantment; in a sense, there can only be disenchantment where there are illusions. One speaks, for example, of an excess of expectations that democracy cannot fulfill. But more than an excess, what seems to be involved is a change of the subjectivity invested in politics. In my opinion, so-called postmodernity is above all disenchantment with modernity, a modernity that, in turn, Max Weber defined as a "disenchantment of the world." That is to say, it entails a kind of "disenchantment with disenchantment"—a paradoxical formula that reminds us that disenchantment is, more than a loss of illusions, a reinterpretation of desires. As such, this disenchantment called postmodernity could be a point of departure for rethinking politics in Latin America.

On Modernity

Latin America is born under the sign of modernity in a double sense. On one side, the European discovery of America (along with the Renaissance, the Reformation, and the philosophy of the Enlightenment) contrib-

2. See the well-known essay by Jürgen Habermas, "Modernity, an Incomplete Project," in Hal Foster, ed., *The Anti-Aesthetic: Essays on Postmodern Culture* (Port Townsend, Wash.: Bay Press, 1983).
3. For Argentina, see Fabián Echegaray and Raimundo Ezequiel, *Desencanto político, transición, y democracia* (Buenos Aires: Centro Editor, 1987).

utes to the shaping of modern, Western thought. The encounter with the New World alters the consciousness of historical time; since curiosity about the new brings so many material benefits to Europe, "the new" is constituted as a value in itself. The conquest of America marks a decisive milestone for undertaking the conquest of the future. Not only the temporal coordinates but the spacial coordinates are de-centered as well. The encounter with the Indian—the other—posits a new scale of differentiation that immediately challenges identity itself. The world map is modified and, contingently, the narrow mental space in which the traditional social order of Europe conceived of itself is also altered.[4]

If Latin America is discovered in the origin of modernity, its identity is constituted, in turn, under the impact of modernity. The wars of independence at the beginning of the nineteenth century confronted our countries with the challenge of modernity represented by the French Revolution: How to institute society only on the basis of the social itself without resorting to a transcendental legitimization? The question is as urgent today as it was then.

Since Weber, we have understood modernity as the process of disenchantment with the religious organization of the world. Religious society was characterized by the absolute anteriority and alterity of a divine principle as an inviolable guarantee of order. This radically separate foundation, as well as the world-order itself, was totally removed from human disposition. Modernity consists of a break with this transcendental foundation and the recovery of social reality as a system determined by human disposition. By affirming their autonomy, human beings are irredeemably charged with organizing their own cohabitation.

Modernity is, above all, a process of secularization: the slow transition from a *received order* to a *produced order*.[5] The emphasis is double. On one side, the social *production* of order: The world ceases to be a predetermined system that we must submit to and becomes the object of human will. How do we make ourselves responsible for the world with our meager resources of character and control? On the other side, *order* itself: There no longer is an absolute law nor a sacred tradition that prosecutes

4. See Tzvetan Todorov, *La Conquete de l'Amérique: La Quéstion de l'autre* (Paris: Seuil, 1982).
5. The idea is from Marcel Gauchet, *Le Désenchantment du monde* (Paris: Gallimard, 1985).

human will, and it is humankind that has to limit itself. On what general principles can social order be based when everything is submitted to criticism?

Questions like these, which, with more or less drama, accompany the development of modernity, suggest the magnitude of the challenges that a "produced order" posits. In the midst of that revolution, whose radicalism we can hardly imagine today, perhaps the main problem of modern society has been to assure itself of its own identity, that is, to assure itself of "itself" as a society.[6] Starting from itself, it has to create its own normativity. And precisely because it is self-determined, this produced order can no longer claim any guarantee whatsoever. If the radical alterity of divine foundation previously excluded conflicts concerning the form of social cohabitation, both the existing order as well as the order that should exist now find themselves subject to dispute. Not only the rights of this or that estate but rather the meaning and legitimacy of order itself find themselves permanently questioned. With no transcendental or ontological escape hatch, modern society is inexorably self-referential. This explains its incessant attempts to give itself identity, as well as the extreme sensitivity with which it reacts to any unexpected threat to its self-image.

Modern politics arises alongside this radical autoreferentiality. Secularization transfers to politics the integrating function that religion previously fulfilled. If religion constituted the last instance on which all the manifestations of the given order were based, politics is now accorded a privileged position in the production of social order. The substitution of divine foundation by the principle of popular sovereignty institutes the centrality of politics in a double sense: (1) as a conscious action of society concerning itself and, (2) as the representation of society as a collective order. In general, the first aspect is emphasized, but the second aspect is no less productive. More to the point, that society recognizes and affirms itself as a collectivity is the premise that enables it to act on itself. Therefore, a decisive question of modernity is the following: Can modern society politically elaborate a reasonable identity?

There are two problems here. I have already alluded to one: How to articulate a plurality of wills, in principle unlimited, in a collective will that by definition establishes limits? The articulation of plurality and collectivity is precisely the pretense of democracy. Nevertheless, from its beginning,

6. This is, of course, the theme of Jürgen Habermas's *Der philosophische Diskurs der Moderne* (Frankfurt: Suhrkamp Verlag, 1985).

there is a great distance between this theoretical claim and its practical institutionalization. The diversity of actually existing "peoples," or the heterogeneity of society, contradicts the homogeneity that the concept of the rule of the people presupposes.[7] The idea of popular rule evokes an already existing "people" when, in reality, this new identity has yet to be created. To be more exact: Democracy (as a principle of legitimacy) presupposes an identity that democracy (as a principle of organization) can never produce as something permanent and definitive.

The second problem may be formulated as follows: Inasmuch as politics is only a partial aspect of life, can it "represent" society in its entirety? A premise of all modern democratic theory is the possibility of elaborating a representation of unity through specifically political means. Such a "community" is constituted, explicitly or implicitly, through reference to a general will. The fictitious and abstract character of "the general," however, is always immediately open to criticism. This criticism may be restricted to the mechanisms of representation (obligatory voting, et cetera), but already for Marx it was not a question of insufficiency inside the political sphere but rather of the incompetence of politics as such to legitimize the social order. The representativity of politics is the problem.

These difficulties explain the diverse attempts to situate the issue of identity in a structure different from politics, specifically, from democracy. It is sufficient to recall in this regard Marx's thesis that "the anatomy of civil society has to be sought in the political economy," which used class as the identifying referent, or de Tocqueville's idea of a sociocultural integration resulting from the similarity of customs, feelings, and beliefs as the basis of North American democracy. The most important attempt of this sort, however, is nationalism. Independent of how the nation is defined (in essentialist, ethnic, or linguistic terms, as a "manifest destiny"), the nationalist impulse clearly illustrates some of the contradictions posed by modernity.

The first contradiction lies between the assigned centrality of politics as the *locus* of popular rule and the social determination of identity. As in Marx and de Tocqueville, in the idea of national identity, the unity of the social process is conceived as a given external to politics. Historically, it should be the state that effectively realizes unification, but the state's action is legitimized only insofar as it "represents" a socially defined entity. This

7. François-Xavier Guerra offers a good introduction to the Latin American independence period in these terms in "Le Peuple souverain: Fondemonts et logiques d'une fiction," mimeograph, EHSS-CLACSO Seminar, Paris, 1987.

fact reduces the productivity assigned to politics: The politically elaborated collective will always remain subordinated to an ultimate instance outside of politics (national unity, the economic structure, cultural tradition).

The second contradiction involves the search for a historical identity in a predominantly "futurist" age. If modernity is characterized by a break with tradition, the issue of identity, on the other hand, is projected onto the past. By means of a retrospective construction, the unity of social life is located before politics as an a priori. For this reason, the rich diversity of elements and alternatives of the real is usually reduced to a unique and linear "history" from which all intersections and discontinuities have been erased. The result is a fictitious identity, because it is based on an artificially homogenized past created with the aim of legitimizing the present—a self-enclosed identity, with little capacity to modify itself in accordance with the innovations of the social process.

There is a third contradiction between the universalist criteria of democracy and the particular characteristics of the nation-state. Modern society is founded upon the unlimited rule and general will of its citizens, and, at the same time, on the institutionalization of determined values. While in principle democracy rests on a cosmopolitan citizenry that does not accept any limit other than constitutional order, the nation-state is formed by a population preselected according to quasi-natural categories: The (national) community is defined exclusively by opposition to other nations. A nationalist identity basically focuses on difference as an (international) division of friends and enemies. What is different is foreign, and vice versa.

Since the question of democratization has been our main preoccupation in Latin America in the last ten years, it makes sense to look at the contribution of postmodernism to a new theory of democracy.

The Disenchantment with Modernization

A primary dimension of postmodern disenchantment is the loss of faith in the possibility of a theory that possesses the key to understanding the social process in its entirety. Our age is characterized by the suspicion of any kind of all-encompassing metadiscourse. This distrust comes out of an antitotalitarian suspicion that behind knowledge or any pretension to truth is hidden a relationship of power. In this way, postmodern criticism pursues the relativization of all norms, seeing the "will to power" as the real force structuring that magma of differences that is the social, institutionalizing a system. Opposing the social to society seeks to recover the infinite complexity of "life" as against "form." The historical "moderns" were very familiar with this tension, as the extensive discussion at the beginning of the century testifies. The "social system" is certainly not a neutral structure. All criticism feeds on doubt, and it is necessary to be suspicious of the objective power in the existing structures. An indeterminate negation of all power, however, cannot manage to discern between legitimate and illegitimate institutions. The postmodernist critique of power approximates an anarchist posture, with—unless the question of legitimacy itself is obsolete—the danger of ending up as a purely testimonial and ineffectual form of rebelliousness. Postmodernist deconstruction has the unquestionable merit of emphasizing complexity as a central phenomenon of our society, but I wonder whether it also offers us the means to shape that complexity.

The rejection of a unitary social metadiscourse is based on the supposition of the coexistence of diverse rationalities—a trivial point if it alludes to the process of differentiation engendered by secularization, where, as we know, with the loss of the unity provided by religion and metaphysics, the social fields differentiate themselves quickly, each developing according to its own specific logic. The philosophers of the Enlightenment already recognized cognitive-instrumental, moral-practical, and aesthetic-expressive rationalities as differentiated spheres in this sense. But the recognition of such differentiation was always accompanied by the search for some principle of universal validity. Modernity was conceived as a tension between differentiation and unification within a historical process that tended toward a final harmony. Nowadays, the Enlightenment optimism about the convergence of science, morality, and art to achieve the control of natural forces, social progress, and human happiness has disappeared. The reconciliation of the good, the true, and the beautiful appears as an illusion of modernity. The disenchantment with this illusion is, in effect, postmodernity: The *differentiation* of distinct rationalities is now considered as a *schism*.

The break with modernity, then, consists in rejecting the reference to totality. Nevertheless, the scope of this new disenchantment remains ambiguous: Is the reference to an articulated totality of the different fields rejected because it is not possible or because it is no longer necessary? Can we really do without a notion of totality, thought of in other terms, perhaps? In my opinion, the postmodern debate leaves a basic question unanswered: Does the tension between differentiation and unification continue to be a practical problem, or is it an obsolete issue?

Disenchantment always has two faces: the loss of an illusion and, for that very reason, a resignification of reality. The constructive dimension of the current disenchantment resides in the *praise of heterogeneity*. We are in the presence of a new dynamic, at the same time threatening and stimulating. Threatening because it destroys landscapes that were familiar to us and that allowed us to move with foresight. It does not matter that the certainty was illusory; the important thing was the existence of some shared references. Now everything is accelerating and nothing is in its place. The new dynamic can provoke creative vitality as well as an often paralyzing feeling of precariousness. Why take for granted that homogeneity favors peaceful understanding while heterogeneity is a source of conflict?[8] For too many years, we have denounced the "structural heterogeneity" of Latin America as an obstacle to development, without considering that it could foment a much more dense and rich interaction than the desired homogenization.

Nevertheless, our criticisms of heterogeneity were not completely unfounded. They were born of the concern about an increasingly eroded community. It is from the point of view of a threatened identity that we see heterogeneity as a fragmentation to be rejected. This is a reasonable criticism when, in fact, heterogeneity does not produce a greater social dynamism without being complemented by some notion of community. If that is the case, maybe we should reformulate the problem. Instead of continuing to stress the heterogeneity of our societies, we should reexamine our idea of community. Maybe the problem is the notion of society we are using. More than a "crisis of consensus," what is involved in postmodern disenchantment may be a crisis of our concept of consensus.

The fragmentation of society into segmented camps increases apace, but so does the will to restore an organic integration. The will to synthesis can do little else but express itself through an act of violence when the objective conditions for integration are not present. Our dictatorships are fundamentally that: the imposition of an organic unity on a heterogeneous and complex reality. We can go beyond authoritarianism only to the extent that we can arrive at a different understanding and appraisal of our societies than that of a dispersed and eccentric modernity. We lack, however, a theory of modernity that recognizes the existence of diversity, the value it has and the necessity to give it a formal, if not substantive, coherence.[9]

8. Magaroh Maruyama offers a suggestive comparison with Oriental thinking in "Diferentes paisajes mentales," *Letra Internacional* (Madrid) 5 (1987).

9. Xavier Rupert de Ventos, "Kant responde a Habermas," *Fahrenheit 450* (Buenos Aires) 2 (1987).

It seems to me that this change of focus is one of the positive contributions that the postmodern turn makes to our concern about democracy. Historically, the fear of heterogeneity as a threat to social integration has been extended to the political field. Latin American democracy has always been permeated by a distrust of plurality, seen as an improper questioning of national unity. In recent years, the experience of authoritarianism and postmodernist culture, mutually reinforcing one another, have disputed the apparently univocal meaning of that unity. Ethnic and cultural pluralism, the diversity of economic structures, and political-ideological tolerance have begun to be valued. Social difference is positively reappraised. It is not solely identified with social divisions and inequalities. There arises a new sense of "fair" and proper differences. This is the postmodernist contribution, with the proviso that, in Latin America, it is not limited to the celebration of heterogeneity as an aspect of civil society. Here, the reappraisal of heterogeneity continues to refer to the issue of political order. How does one distinguish legitimate diversity from illegitimate inequities?

In criticizing "master narratives," postmodernism poses at its center the question of the ordering of social life. But what alternative does it offer? As a consequence of its rejection of notions of totality, it does not concern itself with the institutionalization of the collective. Even more, postmodern disenchantment usually expresses itself precisely as a loss of faith in the state. The state is perceived, more than anything else, as an apparatus of domination, always suspected of seeking totalitarian control. This distrust of the "philanthropic ogre," to use Octavio Paz's phrase, is certainly justified; where the state assumes the tasks of collective responsibility it tends to eliminate individual responsibility. But in its rejection of the totalitarian inclination of the state, postmodernism usually discards the state as such. Its anti-institutionalism disavows the symbolic dimension of the modern state. With its divine foundation eroded, society is obligated to create a new instance that will enable it to structure its divisions; in modernity, the state is the medium through which the body politic recognizes and affirms itself as a collective order. This representation of the "whole" by means of the state finds itself doubly questioned today, both in theoretical terms and as the result of the process of secularization itself.

For Niklas Luhman, for example, the functional differentiation of modern society leads to a linking of subsystems, the state being one of many, without any privileged status to represent the social system in its totality:

> No system of functions, not even the political, can take the place of hierarchy and its summit. We live in a society which cannot represent

its unity in itself, as this would contradict the logic of functional differentiation. We live in a society without a summit and without a center.
The unity of society no longer comes out of this society. . . . Systems
of functions can only legitimate themselves. That is, no system can
legitimate another.[10]

Robert Bellah arrives at a similar conclusion from a different point of view.
In modernity, politics, formerly a public and sacred sphere, experiences the
progressive advance of privatization and secularization. "Such a privatized
and secularized politics," he writes, "though celebrated by many political
scientists, seems unable to stimulate not only patriotism but even respect.
Being of uncertain legitimacy itself, it cannot supply social legitimation and
instead becomes the source of widespread cynicism and disaffection." [11]

In our countries, the metaphysical halo that the state irradiated has
also disappeared; the patriotism with which nineteenth-century theater,
painting, and poetry exalted the state as the incarnation of national unity
seems anachronistic to us today. The present-day state ends up reduced to
one of its three branches, the executive, which, in turn, increasingly carries
the stamp of its bureaucratic machinery. The image of the state changes
from a collectivity to a bureaucracy. Even this finds itself threatened by privatization. To the extent that the state becomes a "political market" of particular interests, it becomes difficult for citizens to recognize the *res publica*
in it. The symbolic dimension of the state disappears, and, as a bureaucracy
or market, it now seems to run exclusively in terms of formal-instrumental
rationality.

We arrive here at a decisive point for understanding postmodern disenchantment. That all-encompassing discourse some interpeters of postmodernity attribute to a planning, controlling, objectifying, and systematiz-
ing intellect—in short, to totalizing reason—is nothing more than formal
rationality. In my opinion, the problem is not so much reason in its Enlightenment tradition as the identification of reason with formal rationality. The
postmodernist critique underlines the differentiation of the diverse aspects
of social life without paying sufficient attention to that formal rationality that
crosses the specific logic of each field, generating a kind of "systematic
integration" that is imposed behind the backs of the citizenry. Frequently,

10. Niklas Luhman, "The Representation of Society within Society," *Current Sociology* 2,
no. 35 (1987): 105.
11. Robert Bellah, "Legitimation Processes in Politics and Religion," *Current Sociology*
2, no. 35 (1987): 95.

social demands are administratively absorbed before they can even enter the political arena. Political-parliamentary debate appears as an irrelevant "theater" in the face of the absolute predominance of formal rationality. This rationality is undoubtedly indispensable, but it does not assure the articulation of the social process by itself. Therefore, a politics that is exclusively guided by a calculation of means and ends fails. The inability to represent society in its entirety, which Luhman imputes to politics, in reality corresponds to formal rationality.

It is necessary to relate postmodern disenchantment to this predominant mode of formal-rational politics. It is not a disenchantment with politics as such but rather with a specific way of doing politics and, in particular, with a politics incapable of creating a collective identity. Reversing the point of view: I do not see, in the postmodern praise of heterogeneity, a rejection of all ideas of collectivity; on the contrary, I see an attack on the false homogenization imposed by formal rationality.

Seen this way, postmodernism does not oppose the project of modernity as such but rather a specific modality of it (although certainly not a minor one). It involves a disenchantment with that process of "rationalization" that Max Weber considered characteristic of modernity. Weber saw the rationalization of the world as a system of complementarity.[12] Once the unity that religion provided is lost, the relativization of values necessitates their privatization. Social life can only be organized as a peaceful coexistence if faith, moral norms, and aesthetics are relegated to the jurisdiction of the private sphere as concerns of individual consciousness. The privatization of subjectivity is complemented by the formalization of the public sphere; politics, law, and the economy are subordinated to a value-neutral, formal rationality. This dualism between the public and private spheres, between procedures and values, is undoubtedly an emancipatory act. There is nothing worse than a moralizing power that demands not only obedience but also love and faith. With the separation of politics and faith, of power and love, individual autonomy takes form. But that promise of autonomy with which modernity is initiated is soon contradicted by the irresistible advance of the market and the bureaucracy. The rationalization of the world once again leads back to a closed system.

What Max Weber contemplated with anxiety is today accepted with-

---

12. I base this on Karl Otto Apel, "The Situation of Humanity as an Ethical Problem," *Praxis International* (October 1984): 257. Also see Richard Bernstein's introduction to *Habermas and Modernity*, Richard Bernstein, ed. (Oxford: Oxford University Press, 1986).

out the least hesitation. Little by little, a monist vision of capitalism crystallizes. In the concept of modernization, modernity has been reduced to the deployment of formal rationality. The social process is thought of exclusively in terms of the equilibrium of the system. Political modernization is defined in an ahistorical way by the development of the diverse capacities of the system (symbolic, regulatory, extractive, and distributive), whose functional requirements replace the old categories of sovereignty, representation, will, et cetera, politically neutralizing the question of order. Democracy is "cleansed" of any roughness and resistance to formal rationality to the point that all *pathos* is also eliminated from politics. The moral commitment and emotional ties on which democratic order rests are weakened, and finally, for the citizenry, one political regime is the same as another.

In sum, postmodern disenchantment refers to modernization and, in particular, to the managerial-technocratic style of doing politics. This interpretation seems to me to be supported by some tendencies that are within our immediate view. I am thinking, for example, about the concern for human rights. More than a vindication from the state, this concern involves the questioning of a state that can only deal with a plurality of views by excluding them from the political field. It is not the split between politics and morality that is in question here but rather the resulting reduction of politics to a value-neutral rationality. Another example is the interest in everyday life. To speak here simply of privatization would be to accept the previously mentioned distinction between the public and the private spheres, when, in reality, it is precisely a question of breaking with some of the implications of this dualism. Again, the distinction between different spheres is not being disputed here; what is rejected are the quasi-ontological limits in which political activity remains cloistered by the distinction. Finally, I mention the demand for radical pluralism. I mention it because it is not simply a matter of vindicating a plurality of political actors or a plurality of rationalities differentiated according to fields. The demand is radical in that it points to a plurality of rationalities within the *same* political field, thus rejecting a single "political logic." This is expressed in the "informal politics" that the new social movements introduce with their renunciation of institutionalization and formalization. This reaction certainly can become premodern, and even irrational, but this is not an inevitable consequence if we know how to read the underlying desires.

These examples seem to me expressive of postmodern disenchantment. Our societies want to be "modern," of course, but we should not confuse modernity with modernization. Postmodernity involves, I repeat, a disenchantment with modernization and not with modernity. What is revealed as an illusion is the pretension of making formal rationality the principle of totality. In this sense, the term *postmodernity* itself is ambiguous. On the one hand, it implies a break, but only with a specific modality of modernity. That this modality is hegemonic does not imply, however, that we cannot conceive and develop the project of modernity in another form. This is precisely the challenge posed by the present debate. On the other hand, we cannot speak of a break, since postmodern disenchantment does not abandon the tension between differentiation and articulation that, as we have seen, characterizes modernity. Postmodern disenchantment has not made the basic problem disappear. On the contrary, the examples mentioned above indicate a rejection of the segmentation of the diverse aspects of social life, even though they do not formulate an alternative notion of the collective. The problem of community is present precisely in its absence. I believe that we cannot shape the complexity of modern society without a collective referent.

Postmodern disenchantment contemplates, in my opinion, a double challenge: It invites us (1) to rethink the project of modernity, and (2) to do this by emphasizing the articulation of social differences. In short, it proposes that we reverse our focus: Instead of asking ourselves, starting from a supposedly given unity, how much plurality we can tolerate, postmodernity entails assuming social heterogeneity as a value and of then asking how it can be articulated in a collective order.

The Disenchantment with Redemption

Another current dimension of disenchantment is the *loss of faith in progress*. This has to do with the way modernity modifies our consciousness of time. The modern age ceases to pay homage to some exemplary past and defines itself with an eye toward the future. Time accelerates, quickly devaluing any acquisition, while the new is consecrated as a value in itself. The artistic or political avant-garde, the symbol of innovation, replaces tradition.

The belief in the value of the new makes progress a central category of modernity. The idea of progress permits the structuring of an open future, neutralizing the possible flight from meaning by means of a teleological construction: By believing in the meaning of history, we are assured, above all else, of the meaning of the present. Here, we see the effects of secularization, which, at the same time that it abolishes the sacred vision of the world, must also find a new way to channel expectations of a better life. The heavenly promises of harmony and happiness are now projected to the human realm and, specifically, to politics. Hence the *pathos* of progress. Let us not underestimate this fact: From it democracy is nourished. It is the belief in a more open and just society that allows us to justify sacrifices and to overlook the repeated insufficiencies of the one we live in. In reality, if the idea of progress creates illusions, it also relativizes disillusions. (If disillusions were permanent, who would believe in democracy nowadays?) A radical disenchantment proves to be intolerable, because it corresponds, in effect, to the utopia of a completely autonomous society, identical with itself. Therefore, the current debate about postmodernity does not escape the question of the future: Once our illusions of progress are critiqued, what expectations can we have? Thinking about the relevance of the democratic "creed" for the affective rooting of political institutions, I propose revising the theme of disenchantment as postmodernity from this point of view.

Postmodernity presumes an exhaustion of secularization; the innovative capacity of society has expanded and accelerated to such a point that it standardizes progress and finally empties it of content. The differentiation of all fields continues apace, but in that infinite unfolding of novelties, it becomes increasingly more difficult to appreciate something really new. Accustomed to an endless sequence of innovations, the gaze is exhausted by déjà vu. The changes are marginal and predictable, forming a chain of repetitions. The future ends up diluting itself in the present and ceases to have value. The promises of a new society appear as a fata morgana that dissolves as soon as we try to approach it. A case in point is the resignification of socialism in recent years. For many decades, socialism was, in spite of the recurring criticisms, a symbol of social progress and, as such, an alternative to capitalism. Suddenly, in a short period of time, socialism stops being perceived as an alternative. What happened? Perhaps more than a strictly political phenomenon what is involved may be a cultural revolution: The idea of a progressive emancipation seems to have lost meaning. In its place, the image of an eternal return becomes attractive again. Postmodernism expresses this new state of mind, denouncing progress as an illusion.

But here, too, postmodern disenchantment has a double face: the dismantling of illusory progress is translated into a *praise of the present*. This reappraisal seems positive to me, of course. For too long, we have lived the present as a mere waiting room for the future, sacrificing even hard-won liberties on the altars of the "promised land." Disenchantment recuperates the present, giving it an inherent dignity.[13]

This means, above all, renouncing any escape forward. Abandoning a futurist perspective that focuses on problems exclusively through some model of a future society, we open ourselves to the existing tensions and contradictions. They lose their pejorative connotation. I have already noted the reappraisal of heterogeneity by postmodernism, which allows us to confront social complexity without reflexively seeking to reduce it immediately. Today, it is not so much a question of tolerating a discourse that embodies a common or majority view as it is of fomenting a multiplicity of meanings, without presupposing an ultimate instance. From this point of view, uncertainty is a distinctive feature of postmodernity. But this has a limit. Beyond a certain point, disenchantment ceases to be a beneficial loss of illusions and is transformed into a dangerous loss of meaning.

It seems reasonable to suppose that there are hard nuclei of meaning, given by the material conditions of life, among them the structuring of time in the past, present, and future. We cannot dispense with such a construction of continuities and discontinuities without being devoured by an infinite present. What is madness but this absence of limits? We would once again be living in the sixties if the juvenile slogans of some European circles were, in fact, true. The graffiti "no future" or "everything goes" speak to us of an unhinged world. Both assertions refer to one another reciprocally: If "everything goes," then there is no way for us to imagine a future; and if we do not have a notion of the future, then we are lacking any perspective for choosing between the multiple possibilities of the moment and, effectively, everything is possible. Postmodern de-structuring reflects, in a conscious or unconscious manner, a crisis of project. On the one hand, the future is seen more as a result of the undesired or unanticipated effects of human action than as deliberate construction. (In other words, the future would not only be open but also essentially opaque; politics would intervene occasionally, resolving minor conflicts but not directing the course of history. If our will is blind, why should we be interested in politics?) On the other hand, there is a crisis of project inasmuch as our images of the desired order have faded. Neither capitalism nor socialism, neither the Left nor the Right, offers a "model" that summarizes the majority's aspirations. Desires seem

13. Among others, see Josep Ramoneda, "Una teoría del presente," *Letra Internacional* (Madrid) 6 (1987).

to vanish without crystallizing in a collective imaginary. In short, it seems that we do not know what we can do or even what we want. Postmodernity expresses, then, not only a crumbling of the idea of the future, but also of history itself. We are already in "posthistory."

There are those who rationalize disenchantment as a new value. Apparently radical, this attitude is profoundly conservative: It prefers to adapt itself to the supposedly natural course of the world. The fear of the misfortunes that our dreams lead to now censors our desires. Disenchantment engenders weariness, and fatigue persecutes us. It is enough to look at ourselves and to remember the poet:

> I am telling you that life is in the mirror, and that you are the original, death. . . . You are dead, never having lived before. Anybody would say that, not being alive now, you were in other times. But, in truth, you are the cadavers of a life that never was. A sad fate.[14]

César Vallejo said this, too: There is no life without dreams. Life always dreams of a better life. We long for another future, but what future? What is desirable?

This feeling of precariousness and bewilderment is what appears as a theme under the name of postmodernity. As in the disenchantment with modernization, the disenchantment with progress does not eliminate the problem of the future. The question continues to be present among us, and an adequate interpretation of disenchantment must take it into account. As I see it, disenchantment with the future is fundamentally a loss of faith in a specific conception of progress: the future as redemption.[15]

The belief that we can save our souls through politics is a substitute for the religious vacuum left by secularization. This gives rise to a process of "de-transcendentalization," which transfers eschatological expectations to human history, projecting them to the future as the end of social development. The future is then reduced to utopias conceived as achievable goals. From this confusion of the imaginary and the empirical, of the ideal and the real, arises the illusions of a happy ending and eternal harmony. In the name of its feasibility (and possibly its proximity), all sacrifices are justified. That is to say, the idea of redemption basically operates as a mechanism of legitimation: We affirm ourselves to ourselves, against all odds, projecting

14. César Vallejo, Trilce, poem LXXV.
15. See Joel Whitebook, "The Politics of Redemption," Telos 63 (1985); and Ferenc Feher, "El paradigma de la redención," Leviatan (Madrid) 28 (1987).

ourselves to a safeguarded future. But does not all politics rest on such illusions? Machiavelli already shrewdly perceived that society requires illusion, not as a "Machiavellian" deception but rather as a project for the future that enables it to assure itself of its fleeting present. Paradoxically, illusion is an element of certainty: We assert our identity through promises of perpetuity. If so, if politics is always based on motivational beliefs, what distinguishes the paradigm of redemption? The search for redemption points to a plenitude beyond history, separated from any empirical condition of existence. It does not recognize mediation between the present and a radically different future. The expectation of the new is intensified to such a degree that the future has value only as an absolute discontinuity. Redemptive politics usually produces an aesthetization and moralization of politics, when it does not lead to terrorism. What distinguishes the belief in redemption from other political cultures is the faith in a total break and the advent, ex nihilo, of an integrally different system. The objective is not to *change* the existing conditions but to *break* with them.

The enchantment with redemptive politics coincides with a monist vision of social reality. I am thinking of those approaches that see capitalism as an inexorable logic of alienation, a one-dimensional system from which it is impossible to escape without jumping outside of it. Revolution would be this leap to a new order, just as monolithic as the one it replaced. If the monist vision has a revolutionary strategy, it is just the opposite when postmodern culture abandons the idea of a specific hegemonic rationality and at the same time renounces a strategy of rupture. For if we consider that the social process is intersected by different rationalities, its transformation can no longer consist in "breaking with the system" but rather in reforming it. This opens a new perspective for redefining reformism as more than a simple difference of strategies with regard to revolution. On the contrary, it would be necessary to understand reformism as a disenchanted conception of the social process. To reform is to discern between conflicting rationalities and to reinforce the tendencies that we consider the best. The result would not be a pure and definitive system; on the contrary, our societies would continue to be as contradictory and precarious as life itself, and as such, creative processes.

In this way, disenchantment, which arises, in a sense, out of the crisis of the political, can, in the end, be politically fruitful. The postmodern sensibility foments an experimental and innovative dimension in politics: an art of the possible. But this possibility rests in turn on the premise of *a renewed consciousness of the future*. We trust in political creativity only to the extent that we have a perspective of the future. Seen this way, the problem is not the future but rather the concepts we have of it. A better future is not just around the corner, within reach of faith or science. But neither is the future an "unripe grape," which it is better to forgo. Maybe, as Rupert de Ventos puts it, we lack the courage to recognize that "the grapes are ripe and beyond our reach; that they are desirable and unreachable; that there are problems that we cannot solve, but neither can we stop posing them."[16] In this sense, postmodern disenchantment can renew the reforming impulse of modernity.

16. Rupert de Ventos, "Kant responde a Habermas," 65.

Postwork Society and Postmodern Subjectivities

María Milagros López

Puerto Rico is in the process of becoming a postwork society. This phenomenon, which has been noticeable since at least the mid-1960s and has not yet concluded, encourages the emergence of ways of life that do not presuppose the centrality of work or its supporting reproductive apparatus in individuals, families, and communities. In the current global division of labor, Puerto Rico occupies a contradictory location, making it a kind of laboratory for experiments on the consequences of incomplete strategies of economic, political, and cultural modernization.

When observers of global transformations deal with the restructuring of class, labor, industry, and welfare in the 1970s and 1980s, they seldom notice locations where the process has already culminated in a massive expulsion of the workforce. For countries such as Puerto Rico, it is not a matter of the re-skilling or de-skilling of the workforce, nor of the growth of the industrial reserve army as such. What becomes evident instead is the consolidation of a "two-speed" society and the proletarianization or, better yet, the subproletarianization of the whole of society, a process that cuts across (although differentially) all classes. The middle sectors experience subproletarianization as the closing off of the opportunities for mobility that seemed to be available from after the Second World War until the end of the 1960s; but it is also viewed, perhaps more importantly, as involving a "cheapening" of the quality of life, a loss of values and of the traditional modes of Puerto Ricanness often associated with preindustrial times, and the spread of criminality.

Some authors have adopted the notion of peripheral postindustrialization to explain the Puerto Rican condition. This idea attempts to capture the coexistence of export-led forms of industrialization that have allowed, in conjunction with federal subsidies, comparatively high standards of consumption, high fixed ratios of capital, and a place in the high-finance international circuit, alongside high levels of unemployment, bankruptcy, and violence, a crisis of governability, and all the social problems associated with underdevelopment and premodern, preindustrial scarcity.

I want to argue that Puerto Rico's inability to make the transition during this century from the formal to the real subsumption of labor has created the conditions for the appearance of ways of life that can be properly designated "postmodern" subjectivities. That is, the incompleteness of the modernization project has allowed for accommodations and resistances that, at this historical conjuncture, conflate pre- and postmodern forms of life and work that lay claim to rights, needs, entitlements, enjoyment, personal dignity, and self-valorization outside the structure of wages or salaried work. Although these forms, many of which are "cultural" in character, have rarely received the attention they deserve (or are seen as aberrant) from the perspective of the dominance of a modernization model of development that assumes full employment as a goal, they preserve the impulse of alternative ideas and demands around work proposed by groups such as Autonomia Proletaria in Italy during the 1970s, Ratkommunismus in Germany, the movement for workers' councils or workers' self-management (*autogestión*), and Zero Work. While the articulations of new forms of democracy and freedom in the workplace these groups put forward are thought of primarily as pertaining to a certain "fordist" level of development, organization, and militancy of the working class, I believe they are also found in a context such as ours, which can be better described as the realm of the lumpenproletariat, the supernumeraries, or the underclasses. It is worth recalling here, with regret, the lack of importance attached to these sectors in orthodox Marxist thinking, where they are seen as a superfluous population unable to assume forms of historical agency and protagonism (see Marx himself on the Paris lumpenproletariat in *The Eighteenth Brumaire,* for example).

Similarly, the notion of an industrial reserve army presupposes the existence of the industrial army and an advanced capitalist division of labor across the whole of society. Short of reducing entire countries in the era of global capital to the category of lumpen nations and thereby losing the specificity of each, such a notion is insufficient for our purposes—not to mention more mainstream sociological analyses ranging from notions like the culture of poverty, the impossibility of delaying gratification, excessive present-orientedness, teenage pregnancy, unemployment, overcrowding, cultural deprivation, external locus of control, field dependence, and narcissistic-borderline personalities to more recent discussions of the urban underclasses that share as common denominators the psychologization of the impossibility of salaried work or nonadherence to the industrial regime of work—in short, a concern with the obstacles to becoming a, or the, subject of modernity in unmodern conditions. By contrast, can the ensemble of notions of postmodernity—irony, pastiche, the carnivalesque, the decentered, postnational, postcolonial, and postclass subject—be sufficient to render an adequate account of the paradoxical equations addressed here? Are we elliptically approaching Nietzsche's politics of *ressentiment?*

Economic Restructuring in Puerto Rico

In what is probably the most comprehensive study of Puerto Rico's current political economy, Emilio Pantojas rehearses an explanation of what he calls its "capitalist-colonialist-pre-modern-modern-postmodern para-dox."[1] Puerto Rico's first stage of capital importation and export processing strategies (after the Second World War) did not assume the development of local- or state-owned industries. Instead, it was based on attracting U.S. capital in export-oriented light manufacturing industries. Today these strategies are known variously as the Puerto Rican model, the industrialization by innovation model, the Korean model, or the *maquiladora* model. The result was an increased dependency on the importation of capital and an external control of the economy that did not have as its priority the local economic infrastructure or its needs. As early as the 1940s and 1950s, Puerto Rican peasants and workers expelled from the countryside due to rapid agribusiness transformations ended up in U.S. urban centers as cheap labor. At that time they already stood for a significant portion of an internationalized labor market. Those displaced workers alleviated the island's unemployment and

1. Emilio Pantojas, *Development Strategies as Ideology: Puerto Rico's Export Led Industrialization Experience* (Boulder: Lynne Reiner, 1990), 158.

allowed the development strategy to continue with a measure of success. The viability of the "development strategy," in other words, was based on the exclusion of a large sector of the working population from the productive process. In a complementary way, for Puerto Rican women, sterilization, family planning, and a variety of experimental forms of birth control were strongly enforced.

By the beginning of the 1970s, however, the strategy collided with global restructuring, without an internal agenda to fall back upon. In the "New World Order" of the 1980s, Puerto Rico lost its importance as a haven for cheap labor—after all, U.S. minimum wages now apply there—leaving a quaint national culture and tourism and a new form of tax shelter for transnational capital, the so-called "936" corporations. This precipitated a shift from the development strategy to what Pantojas calls a "high finance strategy" that facilitates transactions that are "foreign but local," as the slogan of one of our banks has it.

My purpose here is not, however, to reconstruct Puerto Rico's modern economic history but rather to examine the processes that since the 1970s have generated the conditions of impossibility for wage or salaried work there. What is clear is that as long as the active population of the country keeps growing, the domestic industrial structure, in its high-tech, export-oriented mode, and the global restructuring of capital will reduce the absorption capacity of the economy dramatically. To summarize some highlights: the overall rate of labor participation in Puerto Rico has been declining since 1950. In the same period, agricultural workers in particular declined by 69 percent. From 1950 to 1964 approximately forty thousand Puerto Ricans migrated every year to the United States. Despite the impetus of the development strategy, the contribution of manufacturing to employment from 1950 to 1987 has remained steady at 18 percent. Unemployment rates, the official ones, are three times those of the United States; in 1991 the official rate was 15.2. The median age of the unemployed is twenty-five.

In 1983, reports of the national planning board stated that 42.1 percent of all Puerto Rican families had all their members outside of the work force, and 11.2 percent had all of their members unemployed. By 1985, 53.5 percent of all Puerto Rican families had their members outside of the work force. In 1983, 62.4 percent of all Puerto Rican families were under the official poverty level. By 1987, 45 percent of the population received some form of direct welfare assistance, and it was thought at the time that 17 percent more qualified for help. Half of the families who receive PAN (the direct cash assistance program that supplanted food stamps) are female heads of households. The informal economy, according to government figures, accounted for 30 percent of the gross national product in 1990. Not accounted for is the illegal but extensive commerce in drugs, sex, and weapons. The global figures of supply and demand of the educated labor force indicate that educational programs and academic, technical, or professional post-secondary institutions have produced a total of graduates that exceeds job opportunities at the rate of three to one. The development of neoartisanal production of handicrafts and similar ventures has been gradually taking place with the government's blessing and regulation. To believe the government, it would seem that having your own small business in the carport (*un negocito en su marquesina*) is an act of liberation, entrepreneurship, and self-reliance. Doing for yourself (*autogestión*) has become paradoxically an official state discourse.

The unemployment figures alone, however, misrepresent the true situation.[2] Vázquez Calzada, a respected demographer at the University of Puerto Rico, has argued the case for a new index, which he calls the idleness index (*la tasa de ociosidad*). According to him, the economically inactive population (the part of the population that neither works nor searches for waged or salaried formal work) is as important as the officially unemployed in rendering an account of the place of work in the life of the country.[3] In 1950, almost 60 percent of the population sixteen years of age and older was economically active—that is, working or searching for work. Since then the numbers have steadily declined, reaching their lowest level in 1982 (41 percent). In 1986 the employment rate in the United States was 61 percent, while for Puerto Rico it was 35 percent, one of the lowest in the world. The proportion of economically inactive males in Puerto Rico in 1987 was the highest in the world; for women it was the sixth highest. The group of economically inactive is comprised of students, houseworkers, the mentally or physically handicapped, the retired, and the voluntarily unemployed. This last group describes those who have stopped searching for work due to lack of interest or skills, bad living conditions, or perceived lack of knowledge or experience.

2. For example, in situations of crisis not only does unemployment grow but many people give up on the search for work. This actually causes the official unemployment rates to go down.
3. J. Vázquez Calzada, "La ociosidad: El gran problema de la sociedad puertorriquena" (manuscript, Graduate School of Public Health, Division of Medical Sciences, University of Puerto Rico).

Unemployment seems to be most acute among males from twenty-five to thirty-four years of age—so much so that statisticians assume that these subjects *have* to be working in the informal economy—and among young adults in general. Among males, 72 percent of those between the ages of sixteen and nineteen and 45 percent of those between the ages of twenty and twenty-four are searching for work or have completely withdrawn from the search for work. For all other age groups the figures are 20 percent or higher. These conditions generate the structural framework for the rise of criminality in Puerto Rico. The gridlock of the educational process and the very limited and limiting job market make illegal activities an almost overdetermined outcome.

Since the 1960s the United States has essentially subsidized the failure of the development strategy in Puerto Rico. By defining Puerto Rico as a strategic spot in the Caribbean and holding it hostage as an induced consumer society, U.S. policy produced a situation where, from the early 1970s onwards, the country could no longer survive without a steadily increasing flow of federal transfer payments. These funds go to individuals in the form of veteran's benefits, Medicare benefits, Social Security pensions, scholarships, student loans, U.S. civil service pensions, housing assistance, nutritional assistance, assistance to families in disaster areas, private nonprofit institutions, and others. The Puerto Rican state receives $70.3 million; other funding goes to the private sector, municipal governments, nonresidents, federal government agencies, and industries subsidized by the U.S. government. The total of U.S. transfers in 1991 was $4.958 billion; the gross national product for the same year (in 1954 constant dollars) was $5.674 billion. We arrive thus at almost a one-to-one ratio between production and subsidies. The figure lends credence to the unconfirmed notion that only 10 percent of the population does not receive some direct subsidy from federal transfers.

The massive influx of federal transfer funds has allowed the maintenance of the population's standard of living by in effect subsidizing personal consumption. The persons made redundant as wage or salaried workers have turned to their own entrepreneurial skills—in many cases of a very elementary nature but creative nonetheless—to service the demand for goods and services that this subsidized consumption generated. This helped launch the growth of the tertiary sector as well as that of the informal economy. It also contributed to the consolidation of economic dualism and to the general instability of the economy. On the other hand, the permanent nature of economic stagnation and the pressure exerted to sustain the level of consumption growth before 1970 has made the government itself the largest and most important employer in the country (about 30 percent of the economically active population has state or state-related jobs). This, in turn, has contributed to the lowering of wages for public workers and decreased their productivity. Inefficient primary sectors have been subsidized to the extent of their political clout, absorbing available resources for investment and reducing the general productivity and competitiveness of the economy.

The government's strategy has ceased to be oriented toward economic growth, turning instead to a redistributive role to sustain basic consumption and the standard of living of the population. The conversion to a politics of distribution, with Social Security as a paradigm of economic politics, has produced a high degree of state dependency among the population.[4] The efforts to modify the characteristics of the workforce, its birth, death, and migration rates, have, in fact, worked. Today, the population of Puerto Rico has a demographic profile similar to that of the developed countries. The government is betting on a future that includes decreased birth rates, a steady flow of emigrants to the United States, and a more restrictive immigration policy to control the flow of incoming Caribbean workers from the West Indies, the Dominican Republic, and Haiti, among others. The government also speaks of budgeting social time and controlling employment participation rates, claiming that Puerto Rico needs to develop competitive niches to find its place in the global economy, encourage professionalism in all sectors, and diversify the economy to make it less dependent on 936 industries. This implies, of course, diminishing the role of government itself as an employer.[5]

Except for the preeminent role the government plays as an employer, however, Puerto Rico has followed the path of the developed countries in recent years—the turn to a service economy, with more severe damage to

---

4. For Vázquez Calzada these massive transfers have generated an acceptance and even a reinforcement of idleness as a way of life. He argues that people have been pushed further into poverty by making them dependent on sources of financial aid. From 1970 to 1980 family income derived from salaries was reduced from 75 to 65 percent and that derived from personal means went from 15 to 7 percent, according to the Department of Labor and Human Resources.

5. For example, a document called "2004: The Strategy" (1987) calls for turning away from a politics of redistribution of federal funds toward a policy of ensuring the "same" economic opportunities for everyone. The new criterion for salary and wage scales should be productivity. In education, for example, teachers' salaries should be proportionate to their pedagogical success.

local agriculture and not enough emphasis on communication and transportation. The Government Development Bank reluctantly acknowledges that the rise in inflation for 1990 was sharper than that of the United States. Comparative time, wages, and per capita income, on the other hand, are much lower—the average salary is $4.95 per hour, and per capita income is estimated by the World Development Bank at $5,530, suggesting a picture of a high cost of living for a population with low wages.

The new development strategies being proposed can therefore be expected to further burden the working classes, deepen the decrease in public services, freeze salaries, increase privatization, reduce jobs in the public sector, and foster a more punitive work discipline. The dependence on productivity considerations will probably result in the further polarization of a dual society. The sub–working classes will be subjected to stricter containment practices, surveillance, normalization, and incarceration, in view of the fact that the process of expulsion from the job market is irreversible. The legitimization of a more authoritarian state is possible for several reasons, not the least of which is the elastic imaginary of fear and insecurity that calls for police intervention to protect the citizenry from the dangers that lurk. Fear of violence and criminality has sustained the hegemony of Puerto Rico's fragile democracy in times of considerable social effervescence. Official and unofficial discourses chastise the unemployed and welfare recipients in an increasing wave of middle-class intolerance that is, remarkably, endorsed by radicals as well as conservatives. The right moves to implement neoliberal economic policies. The more vocal left denounces the dependence on federal transfers as the source of social evils promoted by the imperial will of the United States and calls for self-initiated, autonomous projects that will emancipate the country from its situation of political and economic dependency. Unfortunately, this call, while clearly well intended, ignores the contemporary restructurings in the global division of labor and capital and makes the neo- and subproletarian sectors shoulder the burden of the failure of modernization. What might be an alternative policy?

Postwork Selves

Social workers in New York City often refer to their clients as having an "entitlement attitude." These clients are especially difficult and demanding and show little appreciation for the social worker's efforts or the grants received. At times they may be loud, but generally they seem distant, impermeable to behavioral modification recommendations, beyond reach. I believe this "attitude" is part of the emerging postwork subjectivities that accompany economic postmodernity. In the context of contemporary Puerto Rico, these modalities invoke a political and cultural imaginary that no longer relies on the centrality of salaried work, wages, and rights as traditionally envisioned by the left. To continue on the path of insisting on that centrality is therefore, as I suggest above, to join ranks with a conservative discourse that refuses to recognize the consequences of the transformations in the social division of labor. It also implies a de facto deepening of the punitive discourses against poor women and children insofar as they constitute the direct beneficiaries of federal transfers and welfare services. It is not only in Puerto Rico that one finds a surprising and sinister convergence of left-right discourses on the evils of welfare and the loss of the work ethic. For example, for feminists who have based their strategy on the equal incorporation of women in the workplace, the struggles for the extension of the social wage and the insistence of some welfare mothers on staying at home and raising their children seem tantamount to an act of treason.

One variant of the punitive discourse on welfare is represented by Linda Chavez's controversial book *Out of the Barrio: Towards a New Politics of Hispanic Assimilation,*[6] and particularly its chapter on the Puerto Rican exception. *Out of the Barrio* portrayed a picture of slow but steady improvement for Hispanics and their contributions to American society. The one exception: Puerto Ricans! Traditionally, this was seen as a consequence of Puerto Ricans' difficulty in assimilating to U.S. society. One of every two Puerto Ricans in the United States in 1990 was foreign born (that is, born on the island), and one third of Puerto Ricans in the United States live under the official poverty line. Chavez claims, however, that the problem is more the disproportionate number of Puerto Rican single female–headed households and their dependence on welfare. She evokes the inevitable specter of women heads of households receiving larger welfare stipends as they have more children and therefore being rewarded for self-destructive behavior. Bilingual education is also for Chavez a contributing force to making the wrong choices. For Puerto Ricans, she claims, it has resulted in increased segregation within U.S. society during the last twenty-five years.

In a comprehensive study of the life histories of poor and working-

6. New York: Basic Books, 1991.

class Puerto Rican women, Benmayor, Juarbe, and Torguellas respond that

> by this logic, it is more beneficial to be denied legal rights, as an incentive to work hard and to prosper! What this view fails to appreciate is that the struggles in Latino and other immigrant, minority communities illustrate a very different concept of citizenship than that which governs the above arguments. Our research and that of our colleagues in the IUP Cultural Studies group contends that it is through the cultural community more than the legal canon that Puerto Ricans and other Latinos define active citizenship and base their claims for equity and full participation in society.[7]

The women in the Benmayor, et al. study did have an entitlement attitude. They believed that, in spite of not having husbands, they still had a right to have children and to care for them appropriately. In a paradoxical way, they claimed their rights and space in the dominant patriarchal discourse by asserting their rights as mothers. They articulated a vernacular conception of rights, including mothering, jobs, health care and education for their children, and cultural specificity.

Just as work-ethic discourse can be shown to be gendered, the discourses around welfare fundamentally refer to women and not to lazy (male) drones, what we call on the island *los gordos y coloraos*. In the United States, out of thirteen million persons on welfare, nine million are children. Nancy Fraser has argued in this respect that "what some writers are calling the coming welfare wars will be largely wars about, even against women. Because women constitute the overwhelming majority of social-welfare program recipients and employees, women and women's needs will be the principal stakes in the battles over social spending likely to dominate national politics in the coming period."[8]

Women are asked to inscribe themselves in the discourse of patriarchy that valorizes them (particularly because of the structural educational, professional, and historically and socially acquired handicaps) fundamen-

---

7. Rena Benmayor, Rosa Torguellas, and A. L. Juarbe, *Responses to Poverty among Puerto Rican Women: Identity, Community, and Cultural Citizenship* (New York: Center for Puerto Rican Studies, 1992), 78.
8. Nancy Fraser, *Unruly Practices* (Minneapolis: University of Minnesota Press, 1989), 144.

tally as wives and mothers while it also looks down on them as being reproductively irresponsible, a causal factor in all of society's evils. For welfare women, it becomes a process of moving in and out of patriarchal discourses and modes of subjection. The husband is aware of a competing structure that will keep the mother and the children alive, and the mother can negotiate spaces of self-assertion, while the state resents her reproductive capability but cannot entirely repress it. (Although in Puerto Rico it came close, with 35 percent of women in reproductive years having been sterilized as an outcome of a population control project.)

"We are poor, but we have dignity," notes one of the participants in the Benmayor study. For the authors of the study, this entails a claim to cultural citizenship that affirms the right to equal participation in the society. Through the right to difference, "cultural identity comes to bear on claims for social rights in oppressed communities. . . . Affirming the right to equal participation in a society through culture brings into view the resources, rather than the deficits of a community. It also posits human agency. . . . Drawing on what is sometimes referred to as cultural capital they make concrete claims on the social structures that oppress them, even if these claims do not always produce positive results."[9] For poor and working-class women, defining as work only that which is paid labor is artificial, since the jobs performed for wages are usually an extension of the work performed at home. Regardless of the context, the women see themselves as fulfilling their productive obligations in society, performing the type of work that they as women were entrusted to carry out. Consequently, even when becoming welfare recipients may have represented a last choice, the women in the study did not see this as a strategy for cheating the state but rather one that enabled them to continue to exercise their reproductive and social responsibility. They redefined the discourse of opportunity as presented to them. They affirmed their prerogative to have children, to insure their survival, and to fulfill the obligations that were assigned to them. These values, as the authors of the study rightly point out, are not different from those of white, middle-class women. But they also conclude that many of the Puerto Rican women's struggles were articulated in terms of a different concept of rights and entitlement than that which informed the country's prevailing legal and political canons.[10]

The notion of *dignidad* may be a clue to the cultural factors that have

9. Benmayor et al., *Responses to Poverty*, 4.
10. Benmayor et al., *Responses to Poverty*, 70.

helped engender a culture of rights or social needs, as we may tentatively call it. In any case, it is a notion of the right to demand from the state a certain amount of material satisfaction, however minimal, for those for whom the very uneven and contradictory process of modernization has not paid off. It also has to do, I believe, with a deeply ingrained sense of the right to enjoy life in spite of everything.

The sociosemantics of everyday life in Puerto Rico speak of forms of cultural resistance to suffering that are both fatalistic and celebratory of life itself. The music, the humor, the festive spirit attest to a sense of community, however ephemeral, that serves as a backdrop against which inevitable everyday fatalities are also understood. *A mí me matan, pero yo gozo* (they may kill me but I still enjoy life) signifies the slippage that allows for survival, resistance, and enjoyment under minimalist conditions. The literary work of contemporary Puerto Rican writers such as Ana L. Vega, Luis Rafael Sánchez, and Edgardo Rodríguez Juliá has aptly described this slippage. The rise of a form of welfare state since the late 1960s, the consolidation of mass consumption, the back-and-forth migratory movement to and from the United States, where forms of welfare were first known and made available to the Puerto Rican population, have in paradoxical ways come to reinforce an entitlement attitude vis-à-vis the state.

The claim could be made that entitlement is the response of the "dangerous" classes to a history of dispossession, if the phenomenon did not also entail the strengthening (with the tongue-in-cheek acquiescense of its subjects) of an increasingly interventionist and authoritarian state. Enjoyment, then, as a political category, in the phrase of Žižek, operates as much to conduct a negativity with respect to the state, capital, and work discipline as in the subsumption of the population to their logic. In psychoanalytic terms, as Žižek notes, enjoyment is the surplus that comes from our knowledge that our pleasure involves the thrill of entering a forbidden domain—that is, that our pleasure involves a certain displeasure.

> Lacan's fundamental thesis that superego in its most fundamental dimension is an *injunction to enjoyment:* The various forms of superego commands are nothing but variations on the same motif; Enjoy! Therein consists the opposition between law and superego: Law is the agency of prohibition which regulates the distribution of enjoyment on the basis of a common, shared, renunciation (the symbolic castration), whereas superego marks a point at which permitted enjoyment, freedom-to-enjoy, is reversed into an obligation to enjoy—

which, one must add, is the most effective way to block access to empowerment.

The uncanny excess that perturbs the simple opposition between external social law and unwritten inner law is therefore the "short-circuit" between desire and law—that is to say, a point at which desire itself becomes law, a point at which insistence upon one's desire equates to fulfilling one's duty, a point at which duty itself is marked by a stain of (surplus) enjoyment.[11]

The subject's duty is then to claim his or her dignity and conditions for enjoyment. While dignity and enjoyment seem to belong to different nomenclatures, both address that which rightfully belongs to each human being.

A duality with respect to power has been judged a central aspect of postmodern subjectivity. It corresponds to emergent modes of life that are described as nomadic in terms of the instability of work as well as in the lability of affectivity, sexuality, responsibility, and other traits that by contrast are associated more closely with the authorial "modern individual," centered, owner of his/her discourse, and responsible for his/her actions.

Whether the "entitlement attitude" signals the emergence of postmodern subjectivities or a recognition of premodern sensibilities that were never fully subsumed under modernity and thus remained undomesticated seems an unresolvable question. It would presuppose, to begin with, the acceptance of the premodern-modern-postmodern trichotomy, which is itself a historical and political enigma and tends to reify chronology. This has led some Latin American writers to speak of the "always/already" postmodern character of our societies, referring to the pastiche produced by coexisting modes of production and coexisting ethnic cultures that seem to bridge centuries and contain mythical overlappings of time, as in the novels of Boom.

In the context of Puerto Rico, the existence of a premodern semantic basin that contains enjoyment as a guiding imaginary does not guarantee the concept's radicality. Rather, its radicality, if any, relies on its refusal to follow the imperative: act so that your activity in no way impedes the free circulation and reproduction of capital.[12] For Žižek, psychoanalysis is more than ever charged with the task of delimiting the space of possible resis-

11. Slavoj Žižek, *For They Do Not Know What They Do: Enjoyment as a Political Factor* (London: Verso, 1991), 239.
12. Žižek, *Enjoyment*, 270.

tance created by new forms of hysterical refusal. It needs to assume and to understand these forms as they challenge the logic of capital. To find proper names for this, he claims, is now the task ahead for the left.[13]

Objective needs, subjective needs, and needs interpretation

The changing notions of need and entitlement have to do with the historical specificity of capitalist mass society, generalized consumption, rights of consumption, and the extension of welfare. Contrary to the notion that consumer society operates univocally to corrupt citizens, it can be seen as a contradictory process where access to consumption is democratized and leads to expanded conceptions of citizenship and social rights. This brings into play the question of "relative deprivation."

Relative deprivation argues that poverty is always relative, measured against contemporary expectations and living standards. Michael Katz explains the epistemological and political force of the concept:

> As liberals renewed their concerns with poverty in the 1960's, relative definitions seemed the defense of conservatives. After all, no one in America was poor by the standards of the third world or even by the standards that prevailed throughout much of American history. By combining a relative definition with international examples, conservatives appeared to diminish the plight of America's poor and erode the will to action. By contrast, a fixed, objective standard denoted the persistence of poverty and offered a target for social policy. (Some social scientists tried to combine the virtues of both approaches by setting the poverty line at a fixed proportion of median income. Had that prevailed poverty would seem a much worse problem in contemporary America because the relation of the poverty line to median income had shifted downward.) Nonetheless, during the 1970s objective definitions of poverty became more appealing to conservatives. Set low, combined with in-kind-benefits, objective definitions allowed conservatives to minimize the extent of poverty and relax efforts to reduce it. At the same time, relative definitions began to shore up liberal policies because they maximized the extent and consequences of poverty. By emphasizing the importance of contex-

13. Žižek, *Enjoyment,* 271.

tual standards, they could shake complacent assumptions of social progress and counter comparisons in the Third World.[14]

Other authors, however, have vigorously attacked the notion of relative needs and the cultural construction of needs hypothesis as responsible for the weakening of the welfare state, and claim that this approach has added strength to the New Right. In their eyes, the poststructuralist, postmodern discourse on the situational nature of needs serves to undermine the objective character of scarcity and suffering. They claim that there are basic needs that can be satisfied by adequate forms of distribution and that the responsibility for this should fall squarely on the state's shoulders. If basic needs are the evidence of serious harm, we should be able to define them. Other basic needs relate to personal autonomy—having the ability to make informed choices about what should be done and how to go about it.[15]

While I agree with much of this argument, a source of tension remains in relation to the question of agency. The argument depends on a notion of human agency that corresponds to the paradigm of the centered subject, capable of deferring gratification and therefore much needed for organizational and action purposes. This notion, however, compromises efforts to deconstruct the discourses of modernity. Perhaps the limits of the capacity of theory to serve as a mobilizing tool are being approached here, and what appears is a contradiction between theory and practice.

Nancy Fraser puts forth as an alternative the notions of "interpretative" needs and interpretative needs politics to problematize discourses around needs in contemporary welfare discussions. She wants "to sketch a picture according to which the social welfare apparatus is one force among others in a large and highly contested political arena. . . . The social is a site of discourse about problematic needs, needs that have come to exceed the apparently (but not really) self-regulating domestic and official economic institutions of male-dominated capitalistic societies."[16]

The struggle to define the interpretation of needs is crucial in the struggle to meet basic needs, in other words. How are needs codified in order to include or exclude people? Fraser prefers a needs discourse over a rights discourse. The politics of needs interpretation designed to bring

14. Michael Katz, *The Undeserving Poor: From the War on Poverty to the War on Welfare* (New York: Pantheon, 1989), 168.
15. See, e.g., Len Doyal and Doyal Gough, *A Theory of Human Need* (New York: Guilford Press, 1991).
16. Fraser, *Unruly Practices,* 156.

into relief the contested character of needs talk in welfare-state societies, however, does not necessarily imply an antagonistic relation with respect to the discourse of rights, and more particularly with taking up social rights as a politico-organizational banner. They may be complementary. Needs interpretation addresses the recognition of a variety of needs discourses in society and their competition in establishing social policy. The emergence of needs-talk "presuppose[s] shifts in the boundaries between political, economic and domestic spheres of life." [17] It attempts to problematize people's needs as objective on the one hand and socially constructed on the other. It focuses on the contextual character of needs and their shifting political value in terms of both hegemonic and counterhegemonic practices. "To treat justified needs claims as the basis for new social rights is to begin to overcome obstacles to the effective exercise of some existing rights." [18]

To push the limits of the state in struggling for the recognition of needs and rights is, I think, the politically appropriate and urgent response elicited by the conditions of postwork society.

New Subjectivities: Pre or Post?

Tu amor es un periódico de ayer,
que yo jamás procuro ya leer,
sensacional cuando salió en la madrugada,
a medio día ya noticia confirmada,
y en la tarde, materia olvidada . . .
—Héctor Lavoé

What I am calling emergent postwork modes of life and subjectivity seem to be permeated by a sense of a *lack of respect*. This notion finds its way into everyday remarks about our social situation. *La gente ya no respeta* (people no longer show respect): a complete imaginary of a way of life that is coming to an end is invoked by this expression. It connotes a loss of cordiality in everyday personal encounters, a sense of distrust of the other, a fear of crime, a fear of dying, a recognition of an increase in illegal activities, in divorce, in beserk actions by drug users, in runaway sexualities, in the loss of motherhood as a sacred value and the loss of purity and chastity as women's attributes, in children's disaffection with school, in people's lack of interest in low-wage jobs, in the loss of status and credibility

17. Fraser, *Unruly Practices,* 200.
18. Fraser, *Unruly Practices,* 201.

of politicians and professionals, in white-collar corruption (bankers most importantly), in the loss of local agriculture and of preindustrial relationships to nature, and so on. It conjures up our own fears of social decadence and a nostalgia for the centrality of personal dignity.

For those of us who also see the institutions of modernity as domination discourses, this sense of fatalism and lack of respect also contains much resistance to generalized oppressive material conditions of existence. Ways of life that can no longer presuppose formal waged or salaried jobs, job permanence, and the discipline of labor find alternative discursive practices in what Maffesoli calls the "conquest of the present."[19] The conquest of the present tries to abandon self-sacrifice as the mediation necessary to achieve pleasure. It is profoundly distrustful of any public discourse that call for the deferral of gratification for the sake of the future—whether these come from the government, the left, religions, or personal relations and commitments.

Maffesoli points to the recent increase in religious sentiment in France to illustrate the duality of this process. While formal religions are prescriptive and future oriented, the ones that seem to capture popular support today are those that emphasize affective and corporal expression. The fundamentalist groups that constitute themselves as affective-expressive communities are thriving. In them, the present is reenacted in everyday rituals, support groups, and the encouragement of the expression of feelings. Charismatic Catholicism and Pentecostal and evangelical sects have been on the rise in Puerto Rico in the last decades. They have been nurtured by the tradition of *santería* and spiritism as widespread practices, particularly among the popular sectors.

Nomadism in the sphere of work—temporary jobs, job instability, job migration—corresponds to affective nomadism in that both seem to preclude the possibility of stable, long-term commitments. Women's discourses—not restricted to poor women—about men's reluctance to commit themselves in affective and sexual relations, as condensed in everyday conversations, the media, and the explanations for the high divorce rate, lend partial support to this hypothesis. Proximity is the overarching concern. You've got to love the one you're with. *La luz de alante es la que alumbra! Y que me quiten lo bailao.* These are popular ways of emphasizing the situa-

19. Michel Maffesoli, *La Conquête du présent* (Paris: Presses Universitaires de France, 1979).

tional character of personal relations. Intensity is highly valued, but only for as long as it lasts.

This attitude does not entail a disregard for the other. On the contrary, what is negatively valued in it are the instrumental reasons for relating to one another. It is a tragic recognition of the ephemeral nature of sociality, which does not rule out solidarity. Perhaps it can be thought of as an exacerbation of the romantic imaginary accompanied by a hyperrealism about the contingency of desire. *El relajo, el gufeo, el velloneo* as modes of "getting along," are ways of coming to terms with duality and the equivocality of relationships in Puerto Rican cultures. They invoke premodern forms that are translated and extended in the contemporary situation into postmodern sensibilities. If these modalities of being present-oriented were identified by the culture of poverty thesis of the 1960s and 1970s—before the last international crises of capitalism and its globalization solution—they are now generalized in the whole of Puerto Rican society. I do not mean to accept the notion of the culture of poverty, which I consider yet another modernizing discourse that went awry. By recalling it, I only wish to emphasize an ironical turn in the postmodern—that we are all, tendentially, part of the culture of poverty: *¡Cuando llegará el día de mi suerte, la esperanza de mi muerte, te juro que mi suerte cambiará!*

The prevailing notions of men as providers and women as homemakers and mothers—always a tenuous one—is giving way to a notion of a general disappropriation of work and family as normative. For runaways from state and capital—not by choice—other ways of establishing communities and socialities have to emerge. I had been at first puzzled by but then became an admirer of the commodity clubs in Puerto Rico, for example. For some time now, people who own a special brand of car have had clubs that organize mutual help activities—exchanging parts and services—as well as social activities and leisure get-togethers on weekends. The commodity—in this case the car, an object of private consumption that should, by its nature, isolate consumers—becomes the centerpiece for a form of sociality that would be incomprehensible by traditional conventions of socializing. What do Toyota Corolla owners have in common? The question has been rendered irrelevant. The commodity offers an occasion for proximity. Perhaps "hot rod culture" in the United States is a good analogue that also involves forms of nonwage labor, intensity, and solidarity.

The taking over of public spaces by the poor and working poor and the young—displacing fearful middle and upper strata who wall themselves into private housing projects—speaks of a reordering of social space. The spatialization of fear takes very definite forms in the metropolitan and suburban areas of Puerto Rico. One is reminded of Mike Davis's descriptions in *City of Quartz* of contemporary architecture in Los Angeles.

The rapid expansion of the informal economy is also a visible feature of everyday life in Puerto Rico. Vendors of chewing gum, fruits, cakes, and flowers, as well as windshield cleaners, are fixtures on many streets and corners. Consumption organizes daily life alongside the fear of criminality for the middle and upper strata. The shopping mall has replaced the park and the plaza for people of all ages, pretty much as it has in the United States. This is to say that a politics of the right to consumption would find a preexisting consciousness already in place among the population.

In Puerto Rico, the middle classes and the intellectuals had come to think in terms of a fairly homogenous "Puerto Rican" cultural heritage, disrupted, if at all, only by class particularities. However, the Nuyoricans, the subproletarians, and the recent immigrants from the Dominican Republic have tested the limits of cultural, linguistic, and racial tolerance. The use of "national" cultural products and symbols of national identity, amply encouraged and subsidized by the state, has had to compete with an extension of the notions of the popular and the growing importance of (often imported) mass culture forms like the telenovela. One could venture, in fact, that the manipulation of the "national" from above by state cultural apparatuses is losing its capacity for mobilization.

The Politics of Unwork

Why have sectors of the left in Puerto Rico and elsewhere become complicit in the punitive discourses directed against the unemployed, those on welfare, the "underclass," and other such groups? The explanations range from their own ambivalent stance vis-à-vis the state and state regulation to their predominantly middle- and upper-middle-class composition. But it is also the case that a "labor metaphysics" still dominates labor and leftist ideology. As Stanley Aronowitz argues, "Trade unions and socialists are prepared on the ground of solidarity to propose shorter hours to spread work and thus support the less fortunate among the working class, but to suggest a campaign to reduce work on social and ideological grounds remains highly suspect."[20]

20. Stanley Aronowitz, "Why Work?" *Social Text* 12 (1985), 19.

André Gorz has been perhaps the most vocal advocate of a "politics of unwork" from a socialist perspective. Gorz has argued that due to conditions of technological innovation we have in fact reached the possibility of the end of work society. He proposes a fixed quota of work assigned to each child at the moment of birth in order to distribute whatever work it is necessary to perform among the population. Leisure and free time and the search for personal creative satisfaction would allow new forms of social exchange and use values to appear. Reduced compulsory working time would facilitate the emergence of a new morality and new ways of being for others.[21]

Does this new morality move people closer to contestatory practices? Cingolani argues that the decommodified sectors constitute, in contemporary capitalist societies, the clientele of the welfare state and the constituency of the new social movements—hence their political ambivalence towards the state. Their ambition is the revalorization of personal singularity, creative leisure, solidarity, nonconformity, and gratification outside of consumerism, family life, and compulsory forms of sexuality. Spontaneous sexuality, personal dignity outside of hierarchy, and the autonomous control of time—to be able to get up and lie down according to the body's clock—are their guiding principles. They express an interest in moving away from the traditional social markers of race, class, and gender. Discourses that insist on circumscribing the ideological terrain are abandoned. There is an apparent contradiction here with the current emphasis on identity politics as the basis of new social movements in the United States. All habits associated with belonging to a particular discourse go against the desire to remain socially anonymous, flexible, capable of entertaining a multiplicity of close personal relations that do not, however, stifle one's expression of one's own personal singularity. The emphasis is placed more on nonconformity than on happiness itself.[22] Rémy, in his analysis of the postmodern mass, states that "individuals avoid ideologically marked spaces. This is particularly the case in countries such as Switzerland and Belgium where there is a preference for the ideologically neutral where personal preferences of other sorts can be expressed. This can lead, in its limits, to the valorization of situations where one cannot be identified."[23]

21. André Gorz, *Les Chemins du Paradis* (Paris: Galilee, 1983).
22. Patrick Cingolani, *L'Exil du Précaire: Récit de vies en marge du travail* (Paris: Meridiens-Kliensjeck, 1986).
23. J. Rémy, "Société de masse," in *Masses et Post-modernité,* ed. J. Zylberberg (Paris: Librairie Meridiens, 1986), 55.

We are witnessing, in other words, forms of transindividual citizenship that are not based on social identity, in sharp contrast with the ascendance of identity politics. Ideological accusations of false consciousness and alienation have been quick to be made. The Colletivo Strategie, based in Milan, insists that this is precisely the strategy of capital and its ideologues. They argue that the mass cannot, due to its own nature, constitute a representation of itself. By remaining atomized within the mass, or at least thinking of ourselves as such, we are left isolated in the face of the massifying discourses of capital and the capital-state.[24]

The "lite" subjects described by Cingolani want to break away from the circuit of production—to achieve consumption from a passive, contemplative position. From a material being they want to become a "being of forms." They are clients of alternative medicine and "poor tourism" who walk through the large cities. It is not that they despise family or tradition; it is more as if they do not feel interpellated by them. They are people of the surface (without a pejorative connotation), "lite," with a personality that is not strongly marked. They tend not to attach much importance to formal education, though many have finished high school and had some college. Their knowledge is more of a "counterfeit" type, marginal to institutional knowledges. For them, there is not a public sphere defined by the exercise of reason. Their relationship with the law is one of indifference. At times, it can be illegal, but what they represent is more a rupture with formal respect for the law that does not become a rupture with morality. Time is the essential mediation in their lives, their project, and becomes their most radical questioning of the social structure and its rigid demarcation of times to grow, times to study, reproductive time, retirement time, work time, and leisure time.[25]

However, Cingolani questions the contestatory character of these practices:

Their precarious subversion does not belong to the register of having but of being. They do not search for the valorization of an identity. . . . it is not a matter of having more and prolonging a way of life, it tries to avoid the hurt. If, as we have said, precarious behavior is not a reaction, it does not presuppose either or at least not yet, a

24. "The mass, dispersed, as a result of the loss of mediations, does not achieve a representation in itself." Colletivo Strategie, "The Technotronic Society," in *Compulsive Technology,* ed. T. Solomanides and L. Levidow (London: Free Association Books, 1985), 36.
25. Cingolani, *L'Exil,* 130.

struggle. In this the precarious delineates a map of another conflictual scene where the demand for "indirect salary" might be raised. This would entail a solidification of identities, and marked antagonisms from which a war of positions would ensue. . . . It is not only, as some would have it, in the subversion of order that the mechanisms of concrete conditions of domination operate; paradoxically they also take place in alterity and insubordination. The roads to liberation and emancipation could very well be the spaces in which a new form of dispossession is consolidated, even as they allow the presence of conflict and criticism.[26]

In other words, the discourse of unwork, taken out of the context of a struggle for the extension of a social wage and for new social rights and an expanded notion of citizenship, may readily find a correspondence with those who want to further expel from the workplace sectors of the population that position themselves in some way or other against the regime of labor discipline.

This concern should encourage us to present alternative analyses of the transformations that have taken place in the sphere of work and in the realm of the welfare-state policies directed towards the unemployed and poor. A counternarrative has to be developed that can render an alternative vision of the recomposition of the working and subworking classes. Such a narrative would contribute to offsetting the rearticulation of the punitive discourses on the loss of the work ethic and lumpenization.

While it is beyond the scope of this study to offer or consider alternative economic proposals that might accompany such a narrative, Fred Block has posed concisely what is at stake in them. He writes:

For some years now, many advocates of an expanded welfare state have suspected that the kinds of social reforms they believe in would diminish the efficiency of a market economy. In a time of affluence, they were willing to argue that the society could afford some reduced efficiency as a means to greater justice. As the economy became increasingly troubled, this argument was no longer viable. But no new argument emerged to fill the gap; many on the political left continued to advocate social justice, but they did so with the usually silent concern that the reforms they advocated would probably deepen the society's economic difficulties. The consequence was a certain

26. Cingolani, *L'Exil,* 172.

lack of self-confidence and a loss of persuasiveness. When the left could not make a convincing case for the economic viability of certain reforms, it lost the support of earlier liberal allies. The result was the loss of initiative to the political right, which had no hesitation in claiming that its reforms would solve all economic problems.

What has been argued here is that the pursuit of social justice and the pursuit of economic efficiency are compatible. Once one clears away the mystifications of self-described realists, it is apparent that we are again in a situation, like the 1930's in which major institutional reforms can promote equality, democracy and a stronger economy. The essential point is the recognition that the political preferences of the business community and the pursuit of economic efficiency are not the same thing. The vitality of the American political economy can be restored, but it will have to be done, once again, against the resistance of those whom Franklin Roosevelt called "the malefactors of great wealth"—the big business people who confuse their narrow self-interest with the needs of society.[27]

For Block, the realist position—which posits the need to increase internal competitiveness by carrying out austerity programs that favor private investment, tax breaks at the top, increased productivity, and decreased welfare—has become an equivocal common sense that has no empirical support from economic data analysis. What is needed are more, not fewer, disincentives to work to allow an incoming younger labor force entry to a labor market already oversaturated due to the effects of technological redundancy. One of Block's proposed solutions is the reduction of the work week to allow for what were traditionally unpaid but socially necessary or beneficial activities; as he puts it, "greater employment and income security, more democracy at the workplace, greater options for adult education and training, more extensive family and community services and more flexible working time are all aspects of a post-industrial transformation of work that would make the economy more efficient."[28]

Fox Piven and Cloward have argued that the whole debate on welfare is fundamentally over ways to discipline the labor force, to consolidate an assault on the conditions of work for all workers. In these debates, they

27. Fred Block, *Post-Industrial Possibilities* (Berkeley: University of California Press, 1990), 56.
28. Block, *Post-Industrial Possibilities*, 154.

claim, salaried or wage work and the nuclear family are treated as inviolable assumptions, thus limiting analytical and political options. The real issue is what makes workers slightly more self-reliant and gives them leverage on the labor market: "The income supports that reduce insecurity and make people more independent also blunt the force of market incentives and disincentives. After all, desperate people without any protections at all, will work at any job no matter how harsh the terms. This is the heart of what the conflict over the welfare state is about, and it is what conflicts over relief have always been about."[29] According to Fox and Cloward, the "progressive" intellectuals and welfare researchers who have joined with neoliberal economic policy realists in confirming the need to reduce public spending, especially welfare benefits, because these foment dependency, "have underplayed political conflict in favor of a consensual and evolutionary interpretation of the development of welfare programs. . . . A class conflict perspective has fallen out of fashion and out of favor, and this at the very historical moment when the welfare state is embattled by class forces."[30]

The protests of the 1960s and 1970s that pushed the state to provide welfare have been deleted or underemphasized in these discourses. In so doing, the existence of welfare programs seems to result from the increasing rationalization of the state and its bureaucracy. I have noted that in Puerto Rico we are witnessing a sinister convergence of left and right discourses around the need to end dependency and restore the work ethic. The collaboration of once radical intellectuals in administering the funds to end dependency is done in a self-righteous spirit of preserving "Puerto Ricanness" and the true moral fiber of the population against the corrupting influence of American dollars. Somehow, the middle- and upper-class origins of these intellectuals and the absence of deprivation in their own experience are present in these assertions. There must be a better way of putting forward anti-imperialist revindications that does not place the burden on the shoulders of the poor.

There was a time not long ago when there were regrets that subproletarian sectors were untheorized historical subjects or that the lumpenproletariat had become almost a residual category. But who's sorry now? And therefore, why work? The question may seem blasphemous, but unwork is inscribed within work. The struggle over time goes on in the fac-

29. Francis Fox Piven and Richard Cloward, "Welfare Doesn't Shore Up Traditional Family Roles: A Reply to Linda Gordon," *Social Research* 55, 4 (1988): 60, 80.
30. Fox Piven and Cloward, "Welfare," 90–91.

tory and office. From the point of view of capital, frequent breaks, whether sanctioned or not, machine breakdowns, informal sabotage, slowdowns in production, lateness, absenteeism, and longer vacations are forms of unproductive labor. These disruptions of the workday are manifestations of the tendency toward progressive diminution of work in late capitalist societies. This is not only a cultural question but a serious field of struggle over the production and appropriation of economic surplus. In times of severe competition on a world scale, capital has bent every effort to tie workers more closely to the machine, monitoring their output and trying to impose productivity norms on sectors historically immune from such measures. On the other hand, our work domestication seems to undo itself every morning when we question it one more time. The conditions for less toil and more leisure, less drudgery and more pleasure, less domination and more democracy, are already present. It is a matter of the redistribution of work and leisure and a transformation of the notion of work itself. But what comes after work?

In Conclusion

I have often wondered what other places in the world there might be with similar experiences to ours in Puerto Rico—with the possibility of "life on other planets," it cannot be that we are alone. Are we an anticipatory model of global postmodernity, or a curious, not quite yet postcolonial aberration? Is Hawaii a mirror we should be looking into? Already one of the United States, it is seeking to redefine its national and ethnic identities within that context. As Friedman suggests, for Hawaiians postmodernity refers to the way in which the fragmentation of Western identities is expressed in simultaneous local processes, including the nostalgic turn in the gentrification of tourism, the increasing clout of Hawaiianness, and the potential new identifications that emerge for villagers who are classified as "traditional" while at the same time they are up to their ears in modern activities.[31]

Like us, Hawaiians are also represented as a mongrel, lazy, criminal race that has nothing in common with the idyllic past and seems resistant to being incorporated into the normative disciplines of modernity. They too search, from a postnational location, for an insertion in global culture and

31. Jonathan Friedman, "Narcissism, Roots, and Postmodernity: The Constitution of Self in the Global Crisis," in *Modernity and Identity,* ed. Friedman et al. (Cambridge: Basil Blackwell, 1992), 347.

within their own specificities. The search from this contradictory location for a redefined notion of citizenship is not necessarily at odds with identity politics. Rather than subscribing to the notion of citizenship proposed by Chantal Mouffe,[32] which requires a universal citizen who can represent a plurality and serve as an articulating principle that implicates the different subject positions of the social agents with multiple alliances, I tend to agree more with Iris Young's proposal that modern citizenship has been constructed on a separation between the public and the private that has presented the public as the realm of homogeneity and universality while relegating difference to the private. This tends to erase the historical marks of oppression and to oblige alliances among equals to start from scratch. For Young, the crucial problem is that the public sphere of citizenship has been presented as expressing a general will held in common. She favors a repoliticization of public life that would not require the creation of a public sphere in which citizens leave behind their particular group affiliations and needs in order to discuss a presumed general interest or common good. In its place, she proposes the creation of a "heterogenous public" that provides mechanisms for the effective representation of all voices.[33] While, for Mouffe, this risks essentialism, I find it more of a recognition of the historical, nonerasable nature of affiliations that are not subject to changes in formal theorizing and that recognize the importance of affectivity and desire. This redefined notion of citizenship should allow, in our case, for a struggle for the extension of the social wage, the revival of policies of broad-based guaranteed income, and the redefinition of work and labor in postwork conditions. The democratization of leisure instead of the policing of idleness is what is at stake.

I would like to conclude by reiterating the guiding concern of this text. When I look around and experience my context, I sense an air of insecurity and fear in those who have made very strong commitments to the values of modernity. A mood of apocalyptic doom seems to pervade the middle and upper classes and those in charge of administering everyday life in ungovernable times. For the rest, an uncanny will to live, to enjoy, to *¡matar el tiempo, antes de que el tiempo nos mate!* (kill time before time kills us!), the easy smile, and the perennial *buena gentismo* of *tó' el*

32. Chantal Mouffe, "Feminism, Citizenship, and Radical Democratic Politics," in *Feminists Theorize the Political,* ed. Judith Butler and Joan Scott (New York: Routledge, 1992), 369–84.
33. Iris Young, "Polity and Group Difference: A Critique of the Ideal of Universal Citizenship," *Ethics* 99 (1989): 250–74.

mundo es güeno (everybody's OK) are sufficient to imagine the generalized resilience and goodwill of the population—this, and the need to collaborate in the weaving of a counternarrative of those Marx somewhere calls "the whole indefinite disintegrated mass thrown hither and thither," of the margins turned centers, and, more importantly, of their transformation into the crucial object of a new political imaginary are the pivots of my concern here. Whether these new postwork subjectivities represent forms of transgression or accommodation, the carnivalesque and its populist utopia or Nietzsche's politics of *ressentiment,* is uncertain. Whether they are "good" forms of resistance, leading categorically to a more democratic and just society, or "bad" forms of disorganized, short-term victories through negativity—the morality of the slave, who prevails by ceasing to be acted upon—they represent in the present the triumph of impermeability, silence, indifference, and sabotage, challenging our notions of contestatory practices and questioning the common sense erected around rational, "straightforward" conceptions of struggle and development. They ask us to rewrite the narrative of modernity in our own work and lives.

Feminism: Modern or Postmodern?

Raquel Olea

The meaning of the concepts of postmodernism and postmodernity remains notoriously imprecise. What is certain is that the discussion they have given rise to is dominated by the same masculine discourse that, as always, has hegemonized the explanation of reality. Latin American feminist women, however, also feel interpellated by these concepts to the extent that they challenge us to reexamine the role of women—and of feminist thought—in the production of culture and society.

In this respect, we have more questions than answers. Is contemporary feminism modern or postmodern? Can we speak of postmodernity from our colonized and hybrid Latin American reality? Was there a Latin American modernity? Are we still in it? Is Latin America premodern, or postmodern *avant la lettre?* How have women participated in modernity? Is it possible for us, as feminists, to continue thinking our utopia (is feminism a utopia?) when one of the signs of postmodernity is the end of utopias?

There is a general consensus among social scientists, philosophers, and cultural critics that modernity originated in the eighteenth century with the French Revolution, its ideas of liberty, equality, and fraternity, and its project to incorporate all human subjects in the construction of a dynamic, future-oriented society based on the pursuit of increasingly progressive goals. The cult of reason, the project of human liberation, the domination of nature by "man," and technological and industrial development appear to be (among others) the necessary conditions for the construction of modern society. At the cultural level, modernity is signaled by aesthetic iconoclasm and the autonomy of the artwork, conditions exacerbated in the modernist vanguards of this century. At the psychic level, the desire for fame, power, and property are the characteristic features of modern man (or woman).

The crisis of modernity, and with it the appearance of the postmodern, mark the failure of an epoch that could not achieve its goals, giving way instead to disillusion and despair. The postmodern celebrates the present alone, as in the slogan *No Future*. The renunciation of belief in the possibility of total transformations of society, the crisis of reason and of the notion of the subject (the masculine subject of representation in particular), and the negation of history and the future, as symptoms of a new epoch, also locate women in a position of distance from a modernity that we never protagonized in the first place. To refer to modernity from feminism is in fact to mark the absence of women in a social project that included us only ambiguously.

Feminism as a discourse has constructed itself, on the one hand, on the periphery of the hegemonic authority of masculine discourses, which have constituted themselves as the only valid ones for creating knowledge (philosophical, political, sociological, etc.), and, on the other hand, in the fissures that have appeared in the way these discourses experience the crisis of their norms and projects of self-affirmation and reproduction. Perhaps feminism's most notable contribution to the critique of modernity has been to make evident in it the continuity of one of the central contradictions of a social system structured by polarities: the contradiction of gender. As an instrument of historical analysis for examining, from different perspectives, the relations between men and women, the concept of gender illuminates the inner nature of a social project founded on the superiority of a One [*Unos*] that has its reverse in the subalternization of a gendered Other [*Otras*]. The patriarchal system is built on contradictions of ethnicity, race, class, age, culture, and identity, which together delineate the margins of an exclusive and repeated map, a map on which it is no longer easy to find paths to any sort of utopia. In this sense, the crisis of modernity expresses, more than the deficiencies of political systems and social organization, the crisis of the ways in which our culture has articulated how we think, or can think, about the dimensions, possibilities, and needs of human beings.

The origins of the present-day women's movement coincide with those of modernity itself. We have to accept the fact that feminism arises as a product of the Enlightenment and its hope of incorporating all subjects in the construction of modern society. As Celia Amorós puts it: "The premises of feminist demands are in the Enlightenment concept of the subject as a new space of universality, which opens itself up in principle as a space of inter-subjectivity, without the limitations that in antiquity were given by the institution of slavery." However, she continues, "woman was not conceived as a subject of the social contract, nor as the interpreter of her own will." [1] It follows that if in fact modernity has reached its end, it exits leaving for all time an unpaid debt to women.

If women were not part of the social contract, as Amorós suggests, it was because modernity restructured the assignment of the social spaces corresponding to the masculine and the feminine according to the needs of the liberal bourgeoisie and its economistic concept of functionality and profitability. Masculine was the open space of the public sphere, of the *agora,* of individualization, of discursive elaboration, of symbolic and cultural production (of "production" itself in the narrow sense), of the agents of history, of modernization and social and economic progress. Masculine was the space of adventure and discovery—yesterday geographic, today spatial. Masculine was, in sum, the space of the power that constructs projects of civilization and society. Feminine, by contrast, was the closed space of the private, of unpaid domestic labor performed without a contract, the space of the reproduction of labor power and of the species.

In both spaces, Enlightenment reason constructed systems of norms and prohibitions. We know that the new bourgeois order and the discourse of the family organized the space of private life, of the intimate, of desire and female virtue at the margin of the public. We also know, however, that it was toward this space, the place of useless energies, that the maximum social repression was directed by means of discourses—religious, scientific, and juridical—that established the standards of morality, mental health, and normality for the woman, seen as the pillar of the family, which was in turn seen as the basic unit of bourgeois society.

But in its initial contestation of women's inequality and its demands for women's rights, feminism itself was also a product of Enlightenment ideology and was regulated by the parameters of the liberal project, which in principle or in fact opened up a new legal status and new spaces of partici-

1. Celia Amorós, *Mujer: Participación, cultura política y estado* (Buenos Aires: Editorial de la Flor, 1990).

pation for women. Within liberalism, women obtain access to public space by offering there, under conditions that continue to be set by patriarchal hegemony and representation, their bodies, their labor power, and their subjectivity, underwriting with this act their gradual and uneven incorporation into the ideology of progress.

In the context of the social and political project of capitalist ideology in particular, women participate in modernity and in modernization as one more object of representation in a masculinist vision of the world, one more object of the desire of Western "man" for domination and total control. The evolved product of this incorporation of woman in modernization is the "modern woman": the successful, emancipated professional, the object of consumption and use-value for the dominant ideologies and the patriarchal system. A construction, it goes without saying, of masculine desire, according to its principles of function and utility—the same principles that also determined its degradation of the environment and the domination it exercises over subaltern groups and minority cultures. The advances in medical technology and the media serve to underwrite a production of images of woman that range from the happy housewife—the queen of private space, surrounded by her electronic servants—to the intelligent and seductive corporate executive, the transvestite invader who can triumph in the public sphere. The place of woman as an optimal object of consumption is likewise reproduced along a spectrum that goes from simple sexual offer to more elaborate images of perversion and sexual sophistication in pornography.

During the first half of this century, and continuing more or less into the 1970s, feminism projected itself as a movement for the emancipation and liberation of women that was interior to (or in alliance with) ideologies that sought a transformation of the mode of production—in particular, those of socialism. If the capitalist system were to change, so the argument went, so also—automatically—would the situation of woman. By becoming detached from her function as mother, sole and central support of the structure of the bourgeois family, woman would be incorporated fully into "productive" labor, into production. This would be the motor of her true liberation, independence, and social equality. Today we know, however, that this proposal can entail a reinforcement rather than a transformation of the traditional woman's role, to which is simply added the role of also being a, or the, economic provider for the household. In the context of socialism, women were to carry out their political practice within the socialist parties, which prioritized class contradictions. Women's sections were created to fight for specific demands, but always within the symbolic place that the patriarchy had assigned. Socialist ideologies did not envision in their foundational principles a deep questioning of relations of power.

In modernity, women have of course also formed their own movements or parties, but these have been built around specific goals that, once achieved, lead to an impasse in these organizations, so that they sometimes end up disbanding. An example of this is the long historical silence of the Chilean feminist movement after the achievement of full rights of citizenship for women in 1949. It has been only recently that some sectors of feminism have begun to create autonomous spaces for feminist theory and critique and for the transformation of patriarchal relations. This new feminism constitutes itself in an important production of theoretical knowledge, on the one hand, and as a space of cultural critique, on the other. Rather than opposing neoliberal capitalist ideology or the socialist ideologies represented in particular by Marxism, this feminism proposes instead the "deconstruction" of the system of patriarchy as such. To that end, it has introduced into the language of social analysis the concepts of patriarchy, sexual gender, and public/private space; a critique and revision of sexual identities; and proposals for the construction of a new subject form for women. These theoretical constructs, in turn, have been important factors in the political struggles of women. For example, the slogan "the personal is the political" has allowed women in many countries to win specific legal rights pertaining to divorce, abortion, child care, and the like.

In addition, as a response to the deification of reason as representing the one and the universal, the practices of feminism in recent decades involve a revalorization of the experiential, of the body, and of practice itself, as modes of construction of rationalities that arise from logics rooted in the coporeality of women's experience, a dimension that is notably absent in the discourse of Enlightenment. Feminist scholarship today is undertaking, in different disciplines, a rehistoricization of the place that women have occupied in Western society, as a way both of making ourselves visible and of installing a difference that cancels the pseudo-objectivity of masculine discourses.

That modernity, as a cultural project, is elaborated from the perspective of a masculine subject, or, better, that it postulates the subject of representation as centered, unitary, and in principle masculine, and that this subject is now in crisis: these are among the main themes of the modern/postmodern debate. The recognition that woman as historical subject was absent from the project of modernity as such can serve to induce feminism to agree with the thesis of Habermas that modernity is "an incomplete project."[2] On the other hand, the feminist project of constructing a new subject form of woman, a subject other than—an "other" subject—the dominant masculine one, with the consequent need for a cultural transformation that this implies, could be seen as an aspect of what Albrecht Wellmer has called the "not yet formulated project of postmodernity."[3]

From the perspective of feminism, these alternatives, rather than being exclusive, are variables generated by the same crisis: the impasse the different discourses of phallocentrism find themselves in, in the face of their own self-imposed imperative to complete projects, close out historical epochs, and open up new times—in other words, to make more efficient the power of speculative reason to constitute the beginning and end of things. What is in evidence is the crisis of a cultural system that has not only left out the greater part of humanity but also built its system of values and powers on the suppression of all those human faculties that imply difference with a masculine, adult, and European One.

This is why the modern/postmodern debate as such has not concerned Latin American feminist discourse in a central way. Our own ambiguous integration as women in cultural processes deriving from Eurocentrism always/already prevents us from positioning ourselves in relation to our own complex reality. Whether we in Latin America live in premodernity, or in a "peripheral modernity," or a confused postmodernity; whether all these phases and processes coexist in mixed and subordinate fashion in the passage to a truncated and perpetually incomplete modernity: these are questions we can answer only by reference to metropolitan discourses.

Women have been subjects neither of the project of modernity nor of the crisis of this project; historically absent from the pacts of discursive, social, and political power, our recent incursion into the public sphere still situates us in the margin, outside of the spaces valorized by the dominant culture. It has been in this liminal space that feminism in the last several decades has installed itself as both a theoretical discourse and a social movement with the capacity to intervene in and modify forms of social functioning. Feminism comes from "no-where" to spaces where its discursivity does not yet have a history, where it does not yet have the capacity even to negotiate or enter into alliances.

2. The phrase is Jürgen Habermas's, in his essay "Modernity—An Incomplete Project," reproduced in translation in Nicolás Casullo, El debate modernidad/postmodernidad (Buenos Aires: Punto Sur, 1989).
3. Albrecht Wellmer, quoted in Casullo, Debate.

The egalitarian and rights-oriented feminism produced by modernity has given way in the last twenty years to a more all-embracing theoretical-political questioning of the structures of power. Some have called this new kind of feminism, which insists on operationalizing the concept of difference as the expression of a minority social subject always deferred by mascu- line power, postfeminism. I prefer the notion of a feminism of difference, which is marked by its engagement with poststructuralist thought. It prob- lematizes critically the uses of the concept of difference, sexual difference, the difference of women's experience, and how difference as a signified fixes subject position. As such, it also takes on the debate between pro- and antiessentialist positions as ways of understanding male-female gender difference.[4]

The feminism of difference I am talking about is concerned not only with the greater participation of women as a result of the more evolved forms of technological-patriarchal society; it also seeks through its own practices and production of symbolic and cultural capital to construct subjectivity from the position of a female subject of representation, other and legitimate in its otherness. As I have noted, its dissemination of the concept of gender as a category of social and historical analysis questions in particular the cognitive force of the ethical and aesthetic categories of modernity that have falsely universalized a pseudo-objective analysis of cultural produc- tion. Today, it is no longer possible to ignore the fact that sexual gender difference is the mark of a production that originates in other physical ex- periences, an other—even if still inarticulate—subjectivity, other subject positions. In turn, it is no longer possible to ignore the mark of gender in the instincts, drives, or fantasies that spring conditionally from a female body or a male body. To operationalize the opposition male/female implies, consequently, a critical historicization of cultural and symbolic orders, of power relations, and of all the forms of social functioning of patriarchy. To think in terms of gender implies that feminism itself must assume a critical stance in relation to questions such as: What is the feminine? Is there a natural or essential difference between men and women? How have sexual identities been constructed? Are there only two sexual differences in the range of human experience? How is sexual difference itself conditioned by historically given variables of class, culture, and religion?

Feminism has often been accused in the past of lacking theory;

4. On these points, see Virginia Vargas, "El movimiento feminista latinoamericano: Entre la esperanza y el desencanto (apuntes para el debate)," mimeographed document (San- tiago de Chile: Centro de Analisis y Difusión de la Condición de la Mujer, 1991).

this is no longer the case today. But it is also necessary to add that feminism does not see theoretical reflection as the sole mode of production of thought. In the practices that women develop in their autonomous groups; in their physical labor; and in workshops on sexuality, on the relations between women or between mothers and daughters, and on alternatives to compulsory heterosexuality, forms of thought and proposals for civilization are also being produced. Women's practices in writing and other forms of artistic expression, for example, embody forms of thought that arise from erotic drives, from hysteria, or from the primary relations of the child with the mother, that transcend false concepts of morality and normality to reveal a repressed and suppressed dis-identity that is seeking to constitute itself.

In these endeavors, feminism is no longer a horizon of expectations only for women. Its concerns are no longer located exclusively in demands for women's rights or full and equal participation in society as it is. Instead, to these demands has been added a wager in favor of the possibility of a general social and cultural transformation that will involve other sectors and other forms of critical discourse. Contemporary feminist discourse proposes a project of cultural change that can no longer be contained in an autonomous "women's" space. Nor can women continue to insist that we speak only from a position of oppression and victimization, which we attribute to an inequality that seems to be without remedy. It is our own discourses and practices that, in dialogue with other critical proposals and with the system of dominant representations, legitimize us in our identity or identities. In this sense, feminism does not seek a "room of its own" in which to institutionalize its utopia; rather, it installs itself in the place historically denied to women, the space of the public sphere, of discursive competence and the pacts of power: the space in which the discourses and projects of civilization and society legitimize themselves in a process of dialogue between equals, at the same time open and cyclical and permanently in flux, which produces the new forms of thought and social life. Moreover, it has also become clear that today it is no longer possible to refer to feminism itself as a univocal space; the multiple differences between women evidence the diverse positionalities that are interior to it.

Feminism conceived in this way, as a space of symbolic production based on the experiences, practices, and reflections of women, elaborated from the position of woman as a subject of representation, transcends the "modern" form of a feminism that struggles for the full incorporation of women in a civilization and culture designed essentially by and from a masculine subject. To determine whether this is "postmodern," however, is not something that is a matter of urgency for us, for the reasons I have noted. We know that we don't want to be a "model kit," even less a closed system of thought that grants itself certainty in its interpretation of the real. Feminism attempts instead to open a door to dimensions and zones negated by patriarchal culture; it attempts to examine human potentials and residues that allow us to think, still, the possibility of constructing a more human and more open civilization and culture.

Modernity, Identity, and Utopia in Latin America

Aníbal Quijano

Perhaps for many, to take up the modern/postmodern debate in relation to Latin America is not something whose importance is immediately evident. For others, the topic is more of a fashion than a serious way of thinking about the problems of our modernity. Nevertheless, it seems to me that this question is not so simple or banal. It is not only a European–North American discussion or a snobbish, vulgar imposition of a topic foreign to Latin America. On the contrary, the question of modernity involves power on its most extensive, global scale. Therefore, even if modernity were an exclusively European–North American phenomenon, it would not be inconsequential for us.

In the European concern with the "end of modernity" or in North American "antimodernity," it is impossible not to detect the peculiar odor of certain areas of the European zeitgeist that preceded (or directed?) the Second World War, areas that incubated the ideological germs that sought to destroy the seeds of liberty, equality, solidarity, and democracy produced as part of the original, liberating promises of rationality and modernity. Perhaps the horizon facing Johannes Huizinga was no less dark when, at the beginning of the 1930s, he decided to publish his worried reflections with the cautionary title *In the Shadow of Tomorrow*. Our present horizon does not necessarily have to darken with new fascisms, nazisms, Stalinisms, wars, ovens, famines, and trials. All of this is not necessary, but it is implicated in the debate.

None of this is foreign to Latin America. Not only because the entire world is involved, but also because, for us, the debate about modernity implies seeing ourselves from a new point of view whose perspective can reconstitute our ambiguous relationship to our own history in a new way. A way of ceasing to be what we have never been.

Latin America and the Production of Modernity

We still have not liberated ourselves from a failed or deficient "modernization," in operation especially since the Second World War. That experience blocked, in many people, any other concept of modernization; it made us see ourselves as little more than belated and passive recipients of modernization and could not prevent a skepticism about its promises, because of which many of us now find ourselves ahead of the present debate. Nevertheless, although Latin America may have been, in fact, a latecomer to, and almost passive victim of, "modernization," it was, on the other hand, an active participant in the production of modernity.

The history of modernity itself began with the violent encounter between Europe and America at the end of the fifteenth century. From then on, there followed, in both worlds, a radical reconstitution of the image of the universe. It is not necessary to insist here on the implications of the Conquest for the Ptolemaic image of the universe. What was important at the time was the recognition of the imperative to study, explain, doubt, discuss, and investigate all that exists and happens in the universe, and to modify ideas, images, and experiences correspondingly—that is, to reconstitute on a new, experimental basis the relations between human beings and the universe, and their relations with themselves.

The secularization of authority in the production and communication of experience and knowledge was legitimized and consolidated with the encounter between Europe and America. Henceforth, all knowledge would owe its production and legitimacy to the employment of the characteristic human aptitudes for making experiences common property, announcing discoveries, translating, and developing cognitive frameworks. This new cultural imperative, and the resources and procedures destined for its satisfaction in the Europe of that time, was reason, or rationality. And the new social intersubjectivity it brought in its wake was what we are accustomed to calling modernity.

The primordial moment of this vast mutation of intersubjectivity, without which it would have no meaning, occurs in the social image of time: The past is replaced by the future as the privileged seat of the hopes of humanity. Until then, all previous images of the universe lay in the past, because they came from it. All explanations, indeed all legitimacy, were associated with this past. Hope was an insistence on a return to a golden age. More accurately, it was nostalgia.

What characterizes the European labyrinth of the fourteenth and fifteenth centuries was not only the erosion of the central institutions of society and culture and the exacerbated violence of their conflicts but also, or perhaps even more decisively, the loss of control or confusion about historical alternatives. Absent a historical sense of the future, no perspective was able to give meaning to events nor to the constitution of a social project that envisioned a time yet to come, as opposed to the mere prolongation of the past.

The production of the European utopias at the beginning of the sixteenth century gives testimony that this labyrinth begins to be left behind and that history begins to be projected toward, or charged with, the future, with meaning. Those first forms of a new historical consciousness, in which the beginnings of European reason and modernity were situated, were not only a new elaboration of their own past. Their most powerful images, those that gave the utopias their immense motivating force and their longevity, were dependent above all on the seminal contribution of Andean rationality to the new European imaginary that was being constituted. Andean social institutions and forms of thought, established around reciprocity, solidarity, the control of chance, and the joyous intersubjectivity of collective work and communion with the world (or, in European terms, by the unity of the tree of life) provided models for the utopias. None of this came from the European past, and all hope of it had to be located in the future.

This copresence of Latin America in the production of modernity not only continued but became more conscious throughout the period of the crystallization of modernity, especially during the eighteenth and the beginning of the nineteenth centuries. If one considers the characteristic traits of the Enlightenment—the interest in the scientific investigation of the universe and the resulting discoveries; the acceptance of the often radical intellectual risks implied in this behavior; the critique of existing social reality and the complete acceptance of the idea of change; the disposition to work for reforms, against social prejudices, arbitrary power, despotism, and obscurantism—if these are the initial features of the movement of modernity, they are as documentable in colonial America as in Europe during the eighteenth century.

On both sides of the Atlantic, groups such as the Societies of Friends of the Nation, were organized to pursue these goals. These intellectual and political circles formulated the same questions, worked on similar projects, and published and discussed common matters. That is precisely what Humboldt would find, without being able to conceal his surprise, in the course of his journey through America. The fruits of Enlightenment were tasted at the same time in Europe and America.

Nor was the movement of ideas simply from Europe to America. A Peruvian, Pablo de Olavide, forced to emigrate from Peru by the colonial authorities, befriended Voltaire, joined the group of French encyclopedists, and played an active part in the political experiences of the Spanish reformers of that period. Persecuted by the Inquisition, Olavide was defended by all of the European circles of the Enlightenment, and it was Diderot himself, also Olavide's personal friend, who published the first bibliography of his works.

The intellectual and political movement of the Enlightenment, in other words, was produced and practiced simultaneously in Europe and America. In both worlds, a battle had been mounted against the religious obscurantism that blocked the development of knowledge and personal freedom of choice; against the arbitrariness and inequality of the relations of social power in a context in which the crisis of feudal society was still not overcome; against the despotism incorporated by the monarchic state; against anything that might be an obstacle to the reorganization of society on the basis of reason.

All of this was even more profoundly felt in America than in Europe during the eighteenth century, because its colonial situation reinforced despotism, arbitrariness, inequality, and obscurantism. It is not surprising, then, that the Societies of Friends not only spread throughout all of Latin America but also frequently enjoyed a more intense activity there than in Europe. Contrary to the usual model of cultural transmission in the narrative of modernity, it is useful to remember, for example, that intellectual and political nationalism, one of the clearest consequences of the reformism of the Enlightenment, developed earlier and in more politically concrete forms in America than in Europe, where it did not enter the arena of political debate and conflict until almost a century later, toward the end of the nineteenth century.

The "Metamorphosis" of Modernity in Latin America

If modernity, as a movement of social intersubjectivity, could occur at the same time in Europe and Latin America, this was due not only to the communication existing between both worlds, but also to the fact that they were going through the same sociohistorical process: the apogee of the mercantilism of the seventeenth and eighteenth centuries. The problem with Latin America, however, was that just when its modernity seemed to enter the phase of the demarcation of its specificity and maturity with respect to Europe, when it began to define itself as a new social and cultural possibility, it fell victim to its colonial relationship to Europe and was subjected to a literally Kafkaesque "metamorphosis." While in Europe, mercantilism started to transform itself into industrial capitalism, in Latin America, especially from the last third of the eighteenth century on, the parallel transformation was halted, and the economy began to stagnate due to the double effect of the continued restrictions imposed by the political economy of the Iberian metropolis and the displacement of economic power in favor of England. So, while in Europe modernity was part of a radical mutation of society, feeding off the changes prepared by the emergence of capitalism, in Latin America, from the end of the eighteenth century on, modernity was linked to an adverse social context, in which the decline of the economy and the breakdown of the mercantilist system permitted the social sectors most antagonistic to it to occupy the leading positions in the elaboration of Latin America's independence from Europe.

In this way, the same modernity that remade in Europe not only the sphere of intersubjective relations but also, increasingly, the material, social relations themselves, becoming, as a result, the mode of everyday life in society, in Latin America remained confined to the intersubjective sphere, blocked from its possibilities of entering the materiality of society, and even there it was repressed, persecuted, forced to seek refuge in the practice of enlightened minorities.

This was, without a doubt, an authentic "metamorphosis." For a long time, modernity would exist for us as pure intelligence, self-enclosed, incommunicado, and almost incommunicable. The intellectuals could think with the tools of modernity while their society became less and less modern, less rational. This helps to explain why the liberal intelligentsia, once colonial subjugation was ended, could not manage to liberate itself from the chimera of a modernization of society without a revolution, and why many intellectuals, often the most brilliant, ended up simply submitting themselves to the servitude of the new models of power and society that were being exported from Europe and later the United States. Modernity ceased to be produced and coproduced from Latin American cultural soil.

The Internal Conflict of Modernity in Europe

This "metamorphosis" of modernity in Latin America is not a phenomenon disconnected from the European history of that movement. It resulted, to a decisive degree, from Latin America's colonial relationship to Europe, and its consolidation and prolonged duration (which has still not completely ended) were, in turn, associated with the fact that in Europe, domination could impose, in its own service, the almost complete instrumentalization of reason against liberation.

From its very beginnings, the European Enlightenment contained an unbridgeable split between tendencies that saw reason as the historical promise of the liberation of humanity from its own ghosts, from social injustice and the prisons of power, and, on the other hand, tendencies that saw rationality in instrumental terms, as a mechanism of power, of domination. The first tendencies were particularly disseminated in Mediterranean and Latin Europe; the second in Nordic Europe and especially in what today is Great Britain. The split between the two became clearer and sharper in the course of the eighteenth century; it was involved in the conflict between England and Spain and, later, between England and France over the course of the French Revolution and control of the Americas, and became definitive with the imposition of English hegemony over Europe and, subsequently, over most of the rest of the world in the nineteenth century.

The imposition of English hegemony, linked as it was to the spectacular expansion of British industrial capitalism, consolidated the hegemony of the tendencies in the movement of the Enlightenment that conceived of reason primarily in instrumental terms. The association between reason and liberation was occluded. Henceforth, modernity would be seen almost exclusively through the crooked mirror of domination. The age of "modernization," instead of modernity, had begun: that is, the transformation of the world, of society, according to the requirements of domination and control, specifically, of the domination of capital, stripped of any purpose other than accumulation. The ax that had cut off the Moor's head could be turned in a different direction and allowed to prolong its pale efficiency.

For Latin America, this inflection of the history of modernity was more than decisive—it was catastrophic. The victory of the instrumentalization of reason in the service of domination was also a profound defeat for Latin America, which, because of its colonial situation, had associated modern rationality more than anything else with liberation. Latin America would not again encounter modernity except under the guise of "modernization."

The subsequent predominance of the United States in capitalist imperialism and the imposition of "Pax Americana" after World War II not only consolidated and globalized the hegemony of instrumental reason (the association of reason and domination) over "historical reason" (the association between reason and liberation); it also exacerbated its consequences immeasurably. For it has been under this empire that all instances of society and each of its elements have ended up subjugated to the demands of capital. And it has been precisely during the period of its rise that Latin America, in particular, came to be one of the victims of "modernization."

The victory of instrumental reason was even more profound and tragic because it also involved ideas and social movements that emerged as the bearers of the original liberatory promises of modernity, only to succumb themselves to the force of instrumental reason. What is worse, these ideas and movements attempted, not without success for a long time, to present instrumental reason as nothing less than liberating rationality itself. In this way, they contributed to the further occlusion of the association between reason and liberation. Everyone knows what I am referring to: Socialism did not manage to be anything other than "actually existing socialism"—that is, Stalinism in any of its local variants.

Why, then, all things considered, should we be surprised that the term modernity now appears to designate only "actually existing modernity"—that is, the reign of instrumental reason?

Whose Modernity Is in Crisis?

It is a historical irony, then, that the present attack on modernity should come precisely from the bastions of instrumental reason. I say this because the postmodernism of a sector of the French intelligentsia (some of whose members came from, or had to define themselves against, a Stalinist Left, others who did not discover in time that the mask and the face of "actually existing modernity" were the same thing) and the antimodernism of a sector of the North American intelligentsia (not a few of whom are also former leftists) are precisely dedicated to destroying what little remains of the original association between reason and social liberation.

The postmodernists contend that after nazism and Stalinism, no one can still believe in the "master narratives" of modernity or its promise of liberation. The North American antimodernists, for their part, sustain that these promises were never more than chimeras, and that order and authority are the only expressions of modernity. Both of them propose that the technology of power is the only aspect of modernity that is worth defending anymore.

If all efforts for the liberation of men and women from domination, servitude, social inequality, arbitrary authority, despotism, obscurantism, and the like, are in vain, if all hopes of achieving the complete realization of individual faculties and collective joy are chimerical, if they are only something that history reduced to "master narratives" of impossible aspirations, then it should be admitted that the promises of modernity are not only not rational, they are decidedly irrational. The only thing that really remains, then, is power. The rational thing would be to surrender oneself to it. In this way, the seduction of power offers itself to us as an alternative to modernity.

The effect of historical reason, that is, of rationality as a project for the liberation of society, is subjugated to a new and more insidious siege. Social and political forces equivalent to those that, like nazism and Stalinism, produced the weakening—in truth, almost the eclipse of historical reason—emerge again in search of the definitive destruction of all projects to liberate society from the present holders of power.

This, in essence, is the nature of the present crisis of modernity. Nevertheless, it would be pointless and, worse, dangerous not to see that it is not only a matter of the struggle between instrumental reason and historical reason. If the liberating promises of modern rationality were able to be marginalized and subordinated to the necessities of power, first under the hegemony of British and then later North American imperialism, and if the alternative movements, the heirs and bearers of the promises of modernity, ended up converting these promises into "actually existing socialism," it is improbable that all of this should happen only because historical reason is defended only by the weakest sectors of society. It is more likely that in the constitution of modern rationality itself in Europe, elements that not only weakened the liberating force of rationality but also made it possible to disguise and to substitute this force, have been present from the beginning.

It turns out that liberating rationality was not itself constitutionally immune to the seduction of power. This is because, as I noted, modern rationality is connected from its Enlightenment origin on to the relations of power between Europe and the rest of the world. But if European reason could wither so quickly into instrumental reason, perhaps this is also because it had to nourish itself, from the start, from a tree of knowledge broken off from the tree of life precisely as the price of the association between reason and domination.

In this sense, in the present crisis of modernity, it is European identity itself, the European constitution of modern rationality, that is in question. This is not only a matter, consequently, of a confrontation between instrumental and historical reason in the abstract. It involves, more profoundly, the European model of the constitution of liberating rationality. It is European, and now European–North American, hegemony over the history of modernity and rationality that is now in crisis.

"Metamorphosis" and the Tension of Subjectivity in Latin America

During the sixties, we discussed more than anything else in Latin America the problems of our society and how to change it. Now we are more anxious to establish our identity. This is not surprising. What is behind our search for identity every time Latin America is in crisis is that the formative elements of our reality have not lost their tension among themselves, thus slowing down and impeding the process of historical sedimentation that could make the ground of our social existence more dense and firm, and our need to always be in search of our identity less urgent or recurrent.

The connection of these questions with the trajectory of modernity in Latin America opens a very extensive problematic that it would not be pertinent to discuss here at great length. Let me take up a few elements that seem central and exemplary to me. I suggested before that the "metamorphosis" of modernity in Latin America, as one of the consequences of colonial domination, served to excessively prolong a system of power whose beneficiaries were social groups that embodied the most perverse results of colonial domination, that were the least touched by modern rationality, and that today, with "modernization," have managed to maintain their hegemonic positions.

The problem of Latin American culture, however, is not only due to the traumatic "metamorphosis" its modernity was subjected to at the end of the eighteenth century but also to the uninterrupted reproduction of its dependence with respect to European–North American domination. One of the most insistent expressions of the tensile character of Latin American subjectivity is a permanent note of dualism in our intellectual manner, our sensibility, our imaginary. This dualism cannot be simplistically explained by the opposition between the modern and the nonmodern, as the apologists of "modernization" continue to attempt to do. Rather, it derives from the rich, varied, and dense condition of the elements that nourish this subjectivity, whose open contradictions also continue to fuse together in new meanings and consistencies that articulate themselves in a new and different structure of intersubjective relations. The slowness and perhaps precariousness of this process of production of a new and autonomous cultural universe is not disconnected from the very same factors that reproduced colonial domination and then the hegemony of instrumental reason, and that have been reinforced under the pressures of "modernization."

Perhaps the best example of the presence of this note of dualism in the Latin American intelligentsia is Mariateguí. A Marxist, considered today perhaps the greatest Latin American Marxist, Mariateguí was at the same time *not* a Marxist. He openly believed in God. He proclaimed that it was not possible to live without a metaphysical conception of existence; and he never ceased to feel close to Nietzsche. His discoveries concerning the specific character of Latin American social reality could not be understood outside of this tension in his thought and personal attitude, perhaps because outside of it he probably would not have made them. (In any case, those who were looking at the same reality at more or less the same time with a methodology tied to European rationalism managed to do little more than find the reproduction of Europe in Latin America.)

A similar tension runs through everything and almost everybody in Latin America. It is not just that we read European books and live in a completely different world. If it were only this, we would be little more than "exiled Europeans in these savage plains," as some have defined us, or we would have as our main aspiration to be accepted as Europeans, or even better, as Yankees, which is undoubtedly the dream of many others. We could not, therefore, stop being what we never were and never will be.

One of the many meanings that is beginning to form Latin American identity is that here, because of the "metamorphosis" of our modernity, the relation between history and time is completely different than in Europe or the United States. In Latin America, what is a sequence in other countries is a simultaneity. It is also a sequence. But in the first place, it is a simultaneity. What in Europe were stages of the history of capital, for example, here constitute both historical stages of and the present structural grounds for capital: Forms of the "primitive accumulation," competitive capitalism, monopoly capitalism before the Second World War, still tied to national imperialisms, and transnational capitalism today are all active, manifested in a pyramid structure of levels of domination rather than stages in a sequence. But neither could one completely deny their disposition as stages. Time in this history is simultaneity and sequence at the same time.

It is a question of a different history of time, and of a time different from history. This is what a lineal perspective and, worse, a unilineal perspective of time, or a unidirectional perspective of history (such as the "master narrative" of the dominant version of European–North American rationalism), cannot manage to incorporate into its own ways of producing or giving "reason" meaning within its cognitive matrix. Although we are always made anxious by the signs of its presence, we have not been able to completely define or assume our own historical identity as a cognitive matrix because we have not successfully liberated ourselves from the control of this rationalism.

For many of us, this was the most genuine meaning of our searches and confusion during the period of the agitated debates over dependency theory. It is also true, however, that we were able to get at the question of our identity only intermittently. It was no accident that it was not a sociologist but a novelist, Gabriel García Márquez, who, by good fortune or coincidence, found the road to this revelation, for which he won the Nobel Prize. For by what mode, if not the aesthetic-mythic, can an account be given of this simultaneity of all historical times in the same time? And what but mythic time can be this time of all times? Paradoxically, this strange way of revealing the untransferable identity of a history proves to be a kind of rationality, which makes the specificity of *that* universe intelligible. That is, in my opinion, what García Márquez basically does in *One Hundred Years of Solitude*. And that, without a doubt, is worth a Nobel Prize.

In Latin America, the past runs through the present in a different way than is pictured in the premodern European imaginary: not, that is, as the nostalgia for a golden age that is, or was, the continent of innocence. Among ourselves, the past is, or can be, a personal experience of the present, not its nostalgic recovery. Our past is not lost innocence but integrated wisdom, the unity of the tree of knowledge with the tree of life, that which the past defends in us as the basis for an alternative rationality against the instrumental rationalism that dominates our present. Here, rationality is not a disenchantment with the world, but rather the intelligibility of its totality. The real is rational only inasmuch as rationality does not exclude its magic. Juan Rulfo and José María Arguedas, in the privileged seats of the heritage of the original rationality of Latin America, narrated this fact. But the formula that names this alternative rationality for international consumption, "magical realism," a contradiction in terms for European rationalism, comes, not by chance, from Alejo Carpentier, the most intellectual, or if you prefer the most European, of the Latin American narrators who had the audacity and the fortune to make (recalling one of his titles) "the trip to the seed," in the course of which his European intellectual formation was taken to the limit of all of its tensions and reconstituted from the recognition of what he called a "marvelous real."

This tensile relation between past and present, simultaneity and sequence of historical time, and the note of duality in our sensibility, could not be explained apart from the history of domination of Latin America by Europe, the copresence of Latin America in the initial production of modernity, the split between liberatory and instrumental rationality, and the eventual hegemony of instrumental rationality.

Because of the uninterrupted reproduction of our dependence in this history, every time there is a crisis in European rationality and, consequently, in the intersubjective relations between the European and the Latin American, the process of the sedimentation of our own identity also enters into crisis, and we once again leave in search of our absent identity. Today, this problem is more pressing than at other times: While the Creole-oligarchical culture that appeared after the "metamorphosis" of modernity has irrevocably lost the social bases of its reproduction and is in advanced decay, it is not clearly evident yet who will have the subsequent hegemony.

Rationality and Utopia in Latin America

The "unfinished" character of our culture is a product of the way in which the elements that originate from this relationship of domination and conflict are reorganized and redirected when the bases and institutions of power have been corroded and partially dismantled by the eruption of the dominated in the foreground of the historical stage—in other words, when the basic elements of our universe of subjectivity become original again. The anxious demand for identity is stronger in the countries and among the groups where the pressures of the transnationals to form a new version of Creole-oligarchical culture (which was, it should be remembered, a neocolonial culture) have not managed to displace cultural identities produced by Indian and African cultures. With this resistance, a new utopia is beginning to be formed, a new historical meaning, a proposal of an alternative rationality.

It should not be surprising that this process is most notable in areas that have inherited sources of original culture that still survive and flow anew, as in Mexico-Mesoamerica and the Andean world. Is not the writing of José María Arguedas an expression, an instance, of this utopia? He had to choose between Spanish, the dominant language, and Quechua, the dominated language, to express the needs of the dominated population to communicate. He chose to write in the dominant language, contriving in the process, however, to achieve the transmission of some of the expressive possibilities of the dominated language. His was a program of linguistic subversion, really something like the creation of a new literary language.

This method led Arguedas to another discovery. What sort of narrative structure would be the most effective for representing, as he wanted to, the magmatic constitution of a new society, a new culture on the sandy, coastal deserts where the masses of immigrants from the sierra gathered in a world agitated by the tense dialogue between the dominant and dominated cultures? El zorro de arriba y el zorro de abajo, his posthumous novel, contains his answer. Once again he had to opt for a narrative structure derived from the dominators, the novel, but with the condition that the world of the subaltern caught up in this somber conflict would be the real content of the product. This is a program of narrative subversion, a subversion of paradigms of historical becoming and agency: the end point of a project of cultural subversion initiated by a linguistic subversion.

In this moment of our history, we must admit to ourselves irrevocably that we have never been, and will never be, just like European–North Americans, in the mode of the self-image sought after by the old Creole-oligarchical culture or the new version of it that some would like to simulate. The dominant culture was not imposed, nor will it be imposed, by the extinction of the dominated cultures. Nor, on the other hand, will the liberation of the dominated cultures be the equivalent of some kind of resurrection. In this sense, Arguedas's proposal, implicit in all of his work, should be recognized, as Angel Rama already suggested, as the model of a historical project that it is necessary to realize consciously—that is, as nothing more nor less than the cultural utopia of Latin America.

Arguedas's utopia could not have been articulated as such were it not for the prefiguration of other and greater subversions. Any utopia is, after all, a project for the reconstitution of the historical meaning of society. The fact that such a project was first lodged in the aesthetic or symbolic-expressive sphere does nothing other than indicate, as always, that it is within that sphere that the possible transformations of the historic totality are prefigured. Is this not what was at issue in the debates of our European counterparts Lukács, Adorno, Benjamin, and Brecht before the Second World War? Was not aesthetic liberation seen as, in effect, the antechamber of a possible social liberation?

The Latin American utopia as the proposal of an alternative rationality acquires all of its specificity when it is confronted by what has been perhaps the crucial question in the present debate about modernity, and not only in Latin America: the question of the private versus the state (or, as the current slogan has it, of society versus the state). This question is, in my opinion, the result of a double process: on the one hand, the clustering of postmodernists and antimodernists around a kind of neoconservatism that sings paeans to the seductions of power; on the other hand, the discovery that the mask and the face, the dream and the reality, were the same in "actually existing socialism." The result is an offensive based on the enchantments of the power of private capital and an unexpected confusion in the other camp that gradually gives in to these enchantments.

The private versus state question has emerged as the axis around which not only the problems of the economic crisis are debated but also those which concern every other instance of social reality. The private is seen, from a political and cultural point of view, as supportive of liberty and democracy because nationalization accompanied the despotic organization of bureaucracy under Stalinism; from the point of view of economic rationality, the private is celebrated because the bureaucratic sclerosis caused by nationalization ended up retarding the growth of the economy.

Despotism really exists under Stalinism, but it finds its match in the operations of the transnational corporations, which are also despotic. It is true that private capital is the source of the dynamic power and success of these corporations. Capitalism, as a system capable of producing a free and prosperous existence for the vast majority of the world's peoples, and certainly for most of us in Latin America, however, continues to be a chimera. For the exploited and dominated of the world, this confrontation between unrestricted capitalist property and absolute state property cannot be recognized as the only alternative. In truth, it is a trap that ends in an impasse. Both are faces of the same instrumental reason and lead to the same frustrations of "modernization" and "populism" in our countries.

Neither proposes anything other than a power always hanging over the vast multitude of the dominated.

In Latin America, the state sphere has ended up being efficient for the controllers of the state, the private sphere for the controllers of capital. Nevertheless, in our experience, there is not only one kind of private sphere. There is a private sphere that effectively functioned, and functions today, for the direct producers involved in it, not because it is capitalist but precisely because it is not. I am thinking, of course, of what Mariateguí pointed to: The experience of the Andean communities before their adaptation to mercantilism shows the possibility of a communal form of the private, of "civil society," or institutions outside the state. This was what enabled Arguedas to learn to love in them the joy of collective work, the freedom of enterprises decided by all, and the effectiveness of reciprocity.

No one should think that I am proposing the return to Andean communalism or to the systems of reciprocity of the ancient agrarian societies of our continent. Neither will they return, nor would they be able to satisfy the complex needs of contemporary society if they did. Nor do I mean to suggest the immediate dissolution of all forms of social power except the uncoerced association of free citizens that appears in some of the formidable utopias of the anarchist movement. Instead, what I propose is what Arguedas shows: that in the very center of Latin American cities, the masses of the dominated are building new social practices founded on reciprocity, on an assumption of equality, on collective solidarity, and at the same time on the freedom of individual choice and on a democracy of collectively made decisions, against all external impositions.

What is involved in this is a way of rearticulating two cultural heritages: from the original Andean rationality, a sense of reciprocity and solidarity; from the original modern rationality, when rationality was still associated with social liberation, a sense of individual liberty and of democracy as a collective decision-making process founded on the free choice of its constituent individuals. We do not have to remain prisoners of the alternative between the private or state forms of capitalism, nor of any of the faces of instrumental reason. Latin America, because of its peculiar history, because of its place in the trajectory of modernity, is the most apt historical territory to produce the articulation of elements that up to now have been separated: the happiness of collective solidarity; the adventure of complete individual self-fulfillment. We do not have to renounce either of these elements because both are part of our heritage.

If one looks at the United States, one finds that the ideology of social egalitarianism was more profoundly established there than in any other known society. In general, all the others were hierarchical societies, not just in socioeconomic terms (the United States has no particular advantage over them in that area) but also in intersubjective relations. It does not seem an accident, however, that this ideology of social egalitarianism was the other face of the most exacerbated individualism, because the latter is not possible without the former. The North American utopia that is expressed in contemporary science fiction reveals that the only idea systematically absent in it is precisely the idea of social solidarity. I believe that this is also an expression of the exacerbated power of instrumental reason in that culture.

Latin America, by contrast, is beginning to constitute itself through new social practices of reciprocity, solidarity, equity, and democracy, in institutions that are formed outside or against the state and private capital and their respective bureaucracies. Latin American identity, which cannot be defined in ontological terms, is a complex history of production of new historical meanings that depart from legitimate and multiple heritages of rationality. It is the utopia of a new association between reason and liberation.

Cultural Peripheries: Latin America and Postmodernist De-centering

Nelly Richard

The narratives of encounter and disencounter between Latin America and postmodernity are particularly difficult to analyze:

First, because of the aloofness of the features that name this disperse configuration called "postmodernity," an exact definition is not guaranteed. A mixture of modes (*modos*) (doubt in philosophy, parody and simulacrum in aesthetics, deconstruction in critical theory, skepticism in politics and relativism in ethics, syncretism in culture, etc.) and fashions (*modas*) (pastiche and citation in architecture, post-Marxist disenchantment, narcissist play and cool detachment, neutral eclecticism in cultural taste and bland pluralism in social values, etc.) makes it so that the confusion between postmodernity and postmodernism(s) is the enveloping frame for a diffuse feeling that accompanies the epochal changes marked by the *dissemination* and *contamination* of meaning: a crisis of totality and pluralization of the fragment, a crisis of singularity and a multiplication of differences, a crisis of centrality and the proliferating overflow of the margins.

Second, because of the unevenness of Latin America's own internal matrices, which integrate unequal historical-cultural processes in each country: Peru, Chile, and Argentina do not share the same antecedents

of modernity, modernization, or modernism. The unfolding of cultural tendencies has not been uniform and the mixture of myth and history, ritual
and progress, tradition and market, has taken root unequally among them.
Therefore, the dispositions of each of these countries to postmodernity,
considered as the critical balance of the achievements and frustrations of
a modernity encrusted according to regionally specific dynamics of forces
and resistances, are not comparable.

In spite of these problems, we can probably agree on a general definition of the category *postmodernity*, synthesizing its main features: the
fracture of the ideals (subject-history-progress as the absolutes of reason)
that monologically regulated the civilizing process of the dominant Western modernity; the subsequent heterogenization of signs and the multiple
voices of meaning; the passage from the macrosocial phase of integrating
powers to the microsocial phase of disintegrating forces; the abandonment
of certainties and the resignation to the partial and the relative as the fragmented horizons of a new theoretical-cultural landscape situated under the
vacillating sign of doubt; and the disembodiment of the social-real converted into mass-mediated artifice through images whose spatiality and
temporality have lost historical texture and density.

The physiognomy of "we" (as the Latin American site of the questions of whether and how postmodernity affects us), however, is so dis-
similar that it fragments the subject of enunciation into incompatible parts.
Even if only as a polemical notation of a "difference" activated against the
dominant international postmodern, "Latin America" designates a zone of
experience (call it marginalization, dependency, subalternity, de-centering)
common to all the countries situated at the periphery of the dominant,
Western model of centered modernity. How does the discourse of the postmodern, which theorizes the failure of this centered modernity, intervene in
(disorganize, reformulate) the way that Latin America has had of imagining
itself under modernist dependency?

The fractured syntax of postmodernity allowed the Center to be the
first to meditate about its crisis of centrality and about recovering the transversal proliferation of its margins. The periphery, one of the margins now re-
integrated into the rhetorical complex of the disintegrated, sees itself today
forced to re-diagram its axis of polemical confrontation due to this perverse
inflection of the Center, which aims at appropriating the periphery's alterity
and its anti-hegemonic protagonism. Part of the challenge revolves around
the conversion of the postmodern theme to a Latin American key, a project
that raises the question of the value, insurgent or resigned, of the new re-

lations of authority and cultural power between: Latin American marginality and the postmodern defense of the margins, the crisis of authority and the metanarrative of the crisis, the theory of de-centering and the center-function of this theory as a symbol of cultural prestige, and the rhetoric of difference and the politics of difference. I want to pose this question in the context of the relations of the terms (*model*/*copy* or *original*/*translation*) that structured the behavior of the Latin American periphery faced with the universalizing paradigm of the Center: dependency and imitation as colonialized inflections, but also parody and recycling as decolonizing strategies. Do the disarrangements introduced by the postmodern, registered in the chains of meaning that surround the idea of the Center, alter or not the distributions of cultural power that separate decision makers and followers, "strong" subjects and "weak" subjects on the stage of discourses, practices, and institutions?

Model and Copy: The First World Ceremony

To be the peripheral extension of models centrally promoted by the metropolitan networks means to belong to a culture distinguished as *secondary* with respect to the anteriority and superiority of the model, to a culture of "reproduction," in which each image is an image of an image reproduced until the very idea of an original is lost in the distance. Accustomed to images by means of copies deformed by illegitimate substitutions, I am, as a Latin American, obligated, in the absence of the originals, to take advantage of my deficit of originality, exaggerating the *copy* as a self-parodying vocation, pasting over cosmetically my lack of identity-property with the device of the disguise, the allure of the borrowed or stolen, the ornamentality of the artificial.

The rhetorical exacerbation of this fascination with the copy as the plagiarizing rite and illusionist comedy of a "Latin Americanness" that owes more to the derivative fiction of appropriation than to an original truth of its own, would appear to assign to the colonial imaginary the task of protagonizing initially that distribution of parodic figurations we celebrate today as postmodern. This Latin American neo-baroque, retro-reading of the copy as a signifying exercise of cultural transvestism (cosmetic prowess, allegory of dubbing, transfigurative mimicry) is stimulated by postmodern artifice. The postmodernist decline of postmodernism permits, thanks to the reappraisal of the copy, the following inversion of scene: From dependent and imitative, always behind the latest international slogan of the new, Latin America now becomes the precursor of the postmodernist simulacrum in the simulations and dissimulations already contained in the colonial signature that feigned obedience to the European code, while diverting its icons toward alternative messages. This reversal of roles (from backward to advanced, from secondary to principal, from extra to protagonist) reverses the colonialist sanction that punished repetition with the denigration of the "déjà vu," inasmuch as the "déjà vu" of the copy is now the adulterated hypothesis that the periphery theatricalizes in order to ridicule the dominant European belief in the integrity of the model. In a postmodern manner, it is true, but using cultural pastiche as a form of satire that reverses the First World hierarchy of the model of imitation, although the model itself may have become, in the post-auratic phase of this hierarchy, the desecration of the model. In *refunctioning* the copy as its colonial heritage, the periphery disorders the foundational protocol of the before and after, reinaugurating itself caricaturistically as the *pre* of the *post*.

Thus, we arrive at one of the tricks of meaning elaborated by the Latin American periphery. It uses (abuses) the postmodernist model in international competition (the parodic quote) in order to auto-consecrate itself postmodernistically as both pretender and impostor in the ceremony of the precedences and successions of the First World, in order to auto-consecrate itself as the usurper of the role of master of ceremonies.

Up to what point does this strategy of reversal effectively disadapt the mechanism of authority fixed between the *original* (the postmodern text of the center) and the *translation* (the postmodern reading of the periphery)?

De-centerings versus Re-centerings: The Rhetorical Subterfuge of "Difference"

Original and *translation* are the marked terms of a hierarchy (in the first sense, the canonical reference) that validates the superiority of the Center—prescription and control—in relation to the periphery—dependence and obedience. The postmodern mutation upsets several of the instances of domination that sustained that hierarchy: The contaminating and disseminating multiplicity of meaning affects the assumption of unanimity of voice according to which the originals were the depositories of a foundational truth; the center-functions have experienced various disintegrating processes that have led to the explosion of its images of totality as a homogeneous fiction. It is necessary to find out whether these upheavals of meaning in the center-functions were also successful in destabilizing the network of control of cultural power symbolized by the institutional complex (universities, endowed chairs, libraries, etc.) that protects the privilege of a certain "subject position" in complicity with its advantages, epistemological and operational, over subaltern positions.

The postmodern discourse of the other is distinguished by its recuperation of the divergent and the alternative, of the minority. This new heterological disposition would appear to benefit the resurgence of all those cultural peripheries until now censured by European-Western dominance and its universalist foundation in a self-centered representation. Postmodernism decrees its own role in decreeing the end of Eurocentrism, claiming that its critique of modernity has damaged the superiority of the European model by weakening its fantasies of domination through the relativization of absolutes and the delegitimization of universals. This fall of the model invites the subcultures of the margin or periphery to be prominent parts of the new antiauthoritarian modulation of a postmodernity finally respectful of diversity.

Following the lesson of the same postmodernity that raised suspicions about scientific method, however, we also need to *doubt* this new "centrality" of the margins that suddenly recompenses categories up until now out of circulation, such as the feminine or the Latin American. Feminism (the sexual key to the critical dismantling of the apparatus of representation of hegemonic masculinity) and Latin Americanism (the dissident practice of the transcultural fragment) are categories relegitimized by the new movement toward the borders of the center culture. But women and the Third World are categories more *spoken for* by postmodernity, without obliging the cultural institution to loosen its discursive monopoly over the right to speak, without ceding to them the much greater right to become autonomous subjects of enunciation, to assume a critical *positionality* itself capable of intervening (disorganizing) in the rules of discourse that determine property and pertinence (*pertenencias y pertinencias*).

Celebrating difference as exotic festival—a complement of otherness destined to nuance, more than subvert, the universal law—is not the same as giving the subject of this difference the right to negotiate its own conditions of discursive control, to practice its difference in the interventionist sense of rebellion and disturbance as opposed to coinciding with the predetermined meanings of the official repertory of difference. If the Latin American no longer fits with the search for "identity" (essentialist nostalgia for the self as origin and being), neither does it fit submissively with the silhouette of difference, the merely functional marking of the postmodern rhetorization of otherness. The Latin American empowers itself more as a demand to know why the identity/difference conflict continues to be arbitrated by the discursivity of the First World. Even when their current hypothesis is that of de-centering, those who formulate it continue to be surrounded by the reputation, academic or institutional, that allows them to situate themselves in "the center" of the debate at its densest point of articulation. If it is a question of heterogeneity, of fragmentation and plurality, it will be necessary to de-symbolize difference, opening it to a *differential multiplicity* of practices not included in the arena of theoretical-cultural prestige of the authorized signature. To escape from the control of the centrist signature and to destabilize its power of auto-referentiality are strategies to be undertaken by the deviant/devious (*desviante*) resources of the peripheral citation, of the fragment mobilized by a *situational* politics of critical resignification of the very operation of cultural transference.

The Peripheral Center of Postmodernism:
On Borges, García Márquez, and Alterity

Carlos Rincón

Recently, Peter Buerger tried, like Lukács before him, to interpret literary modernism by resorting to the Hegelian premise that a double alienation between the subject and the object and between 'man' as an individual and 'man' as a member of a species are basic characteristics of modern (bourgeois) society.[1] Proceeding from this premise, he catalogs the variety of narrative modes in which the subject seeks (unattainably) to become one with surrounding objects. The historico-philosophical foundation of Buerger's investigation assumes the continuity of literary modernity and its Eurocentric determination. Is it possible to ascertain a threshold between the modern and the postmodern at a point where Buerger wants to see nothing but continuity? Or, better, what is the "other" that allows the identity of the postmodern itself—as the recognition of the end of Eurocentrism and Western hegemony—to appear?

Against the horizon of new forms of culture and social reproduction, the art of narrative plays a different role today than it did in the early 1960s, when the term *postmodernism* was introduced for the first time in

---

1. Peter Buerger, *Prosa der Modern* (Frankfurt am Main: Suhrkamp, 1988).

North American literary discussion to characterize novels that sought the de-hierarchization of the modernist separation of elite and mass cultures. A selection of Borges's *Ficciones* (written mainly between 1935 and 1944) was published in English in 1962, coincident with the declaration of "the end of the modern." Foucault invoked Borges a few years later in the preface to *Les Mots et les choses*. And, in short order, the novels of García Márquez, Cortázar, and Fuentes, among others, were rapidly assimilated to the canon of literary postmodernism.

The enthusiastic reception of these Latin American texts by a relatively saturated literary and socioeconomic European–North American modernity also repressed the complex overdeterminations of class, culture, peoples, gender, and history in Latin America's own "uneven" modernity at the end of its most intensive period of growth (1950–1970) and in the midst of its most dramatic crisis in this century. These overdeterminations traverse the relationships to history and power that these texts try to work out and condition their reception and cultural function in Latin America itself. The question I want to raise in this context, however, is not whether the assimilation of Latin American writers such as Borges or García Márquez to the canon of metropolitan postmodernism is a hegemonic reduction of the different to the same; rather, I am interested in how the force of (their) alterity is constitutive of the "postmodern condition" itself, which is precisely the center's loss of its status as such.

In the early 1940s, Borges represented in the "Library of Babel" the modern's ambition in the allegorical figure of an old man on a toilet ("the sedentary librarian") who is playing with the idea of combining the aleatory with the mystical and who hopes to show the hidden order of the universe with his game. I want to tell here the story of the genesis and structure of another Borges story, "Pierre Menard, Author of *Quixote*," which emblematically stands for modern literature (in a sense, for literature as such).

We know from Adolfo Bioy Casares that early in 1939, he intended to write a story with Borges and Silvia Ocampo, which they began but never completed. The basic idea was coined by Borges: A young French provincial writer's attention is drawn to a long-dead writer, whose manuscripts he starts looking for and begins to study. Although the master is famous, at least in some circles, the young writer finds his work insignificant. Finally, he gains access to the unpublished manuscripts and discovers brilliant outlines that were never developed. One that particularly attracts his attention is a catalog of literary rules and prohibitions. Bioy Casares was of the opinion that there was hidden in the catalog the irony of the master's own fate: "The

writer without works, an illustration of the impossibility of writing with absolute clarity." One of the prohibitions, namely to express neither praise nor
reproof in a review, was attributed to a certain Menard, who, Bioy Casares
explains, is the "hero of 'Pierre Menard, author of Quixote;' both the published and the not written stories were invented in the same year, possibly
on the same days, for, if I am not mistaken, Borges wrote his 'Pierre Menard'
on the afternoon we made up the list of prohibitions." [2]

The image of Borges as the "modern among the moderns," or the
"modern master," as he was called by Paul de Man, is corroborated by
many of his activities in the thirties, including his work as editor of the foreign language section of the women's magazine El Hogar from 1936–1939.
It was here that Borges introduced Joyce and reviewed the latest arrivals
by Broch, Mann, Faulkner, Hemingway, Huxley, Babel, Woolf, Larbaud, and
Valéry. It is likely that Borges found the literary and hermeneutic model
for the "secret work" of Pierre Menard in one of the fragments of Valéry's
Tel Quel:

> The pleasure or the boredom that a book written in 1612 may afford
> to a reader in 1912 is almost merely accidental. What I want to ex-
> press by that is that so many and such new circumstances play a
> role here, which never would have been imagined by even the most
> sensitive and clear-sighted author of 1612. The books of the past are
> bathed in today's glory with the same intelligence that is typical of a
> fire or a worm in a library when destroying this or that one. [3]

Just before this passage, Valéry introduces a new figure, the "profi-
teur who listens and takes advantage. I give him ideas and he develops and
does something with them." What also coincides with the binary opposition between visible work and underground (nonrealizable) work in "Pierre
Menard" is Valéry's assessment of the limits of positivistic literary history:
Such a project is guided by the "visible work" and cannot take into consideration what happens "inside" the author. The tone of self-irony that inflects
the picture of the provincial writer in the unwritten story clearly alludes to
such provincials as Borges, Bioy Casares, and Ocampo as they seek to
understand, from Argentina, Valéry's work. Paul de Man has pointed out that
Borges considers the author's vanishing from the picture he has created
as an expression of "poetic greatness." This form of projection also de-

2. Adolfo Bioy Casares, La otra aventura (Buenos Aires: Emecé Editores, 1983), 181.
3. Paul Valéry, Oeuvres II (Paris: Gallimard, 1960), 632.

termines the relation between Valéry and Monsieur Teste. What, however, complicates Menard's attempt to rewrite the *Quixote* is that it exists within a framework of relations of "ironies, parodies, reflexes, and prospects."[4]

Modern criticism has deployed two strategies of reterritorialization in relation to "Pierre Menard": an analytical re-Oedipalization of the content of the story, and a reading of the story in terms of the aesthetics of reception. What occurs in the first case is the idea of desire as an interpretation machine with its own inherent code and demands. Thus, we have Oedipus, castration, and familiarization ("killing one's father," "death wish"); death of the father (2 Feb. 1938) when Borges was thirty-eight; growing dependence on the mother due to his loss of eyesight ("incest taboo" and "desire for love"); self-punishment through a severe accident and blood poisoning late in 1938 ("fear of castration" and "fear of punishment"); identification, although on another level, with the writing profession, which his father had not been successful in ("sublimation"—the text of "Pierre Menard, Author of *Quixote*" was published in the journal *Sur* in May 1939). "By attempting to symbolically kill himself, Borges killed the 'ego' that was a reflection of his father. He assumed a new identity [the identity of the author of fantastic texts] after the mythical experience of death and resurrection."[5]

In Nouvelle Critique's infancy, Gerard Genette interpreted Borges's story in order to elaborate on the relationship between the work and the reader and on the idea of reading as a form of written work.[6] More than twenty years after the change of perspective in literary theory that he introduced had resulted in a new draft for a historical theory of aesthetic experience, Hans Robert Jauss read "Pierre Menard" as an enactment of the literary process that leads from the aging of the modern into the postmodern. "Pierre Menard" elucidates, in particular, the starting point of reception aesthetics: Things that are repeated have no identity as time goes by.[7]

I do not intend to pursue these modern or modernist readings any further; rather, I wish to elaborate on how "Pierre Menard" is *different*, and on how it thus outlines a different way to read Latin American texts, because the structural features of their narrative apparatus, as well as their discontinuous and heterogeneous formal processes and their hybrid genre

4. Paul de Man, "A Modern Master," *New York Review of Books* (March 1964), 9.
5. Emir Rodríguez Monegal, *Borges: Una biografía literaria* (México: Fondo de Cultura Económica, 1987), 296.
6. Gerard Genette, *Palimpsestes* (Paris: Seuil, 1982), 325.
7. Hans Robert Jauss, "Die Theorie der Rezeption—Rückshau auf ihre unerkannte Vorgeschichte," unpublished typescript, 18–20.

specification, tend to go in other directions, directions that point to a histori-cally specific, changed matrix for experience.

After the Great Depression, in the thirties, Argentine society entered a rapid process of industrialization. With the arrival on the scene of new social factors, changing values, and new demands, traditional sociocultural facts and ways of life were robbed of their strength. The systems previously underlying the exchange of goods and information gradually lost control. Culturally, this resulted in changes brought about by the rapid urbaniza-tion of consciousness and the restructuring of social communication via the mass media. Relationships to power that were frozen or blocked gave way to a mobile field of power relations where populism could find fertile soil. To the "downfall" of Europe, as experienced by the crisis-stricken periphery, was added the problem of looking at the future directly into the sun. The individual's conscious understanding of society became badly shaken, so that each individual world was experienced as unreliable and transitory in the sudden pluralization of the social environment.

The specific form of the crisis of Argentine culture, art, and literature in this context was not that of "modernity": that is, the experience of the anomie of modern life or the need for a compensatory aesthetic counter-world by the now unsure of itself bourgeois subject. Parallel to changes in the sociocultural system of reproduction introduced by the mass media and mass-produced and spread images was the development of ambivalent art works, such as Borges's story, which do not involve a descriptive reproduc-tion of reality, which unfold within imaginary settings and times and relate to an intermediate level of reference: a reality of images and collective sym-bols as the basic screens for perception. Borges was a great consumer of detective stories and Hollywood movies, but neither of these could fulfill for him the "modern" function of a reconciliation between the discursive and the associative, between soul and world. In "Pierre Menard," the reader is expected not only to take part in producing and developing meaning but also to play within and with the limits of the artificial, but possible, world and with the real world as a reference.

Moreover, the textual dynamics of "Pierre Menard" refer to a life of the unconscious that does not correspond with the role of the classical Oedipal triangle in modern society, but rather to the empirical features of an economy based on desire. Oedipus—"a colonization that has been carried out by different means" (Deleuze and Guattari)—is the internal colony. Dreams of colonized peoples show that desire is more important than any-thing the society can convey through parents or anything that happens in the family triangle: The unconscious runs rampant throughout society.[8] Once desire is set in motion, it connects and binds itself to other desires, constantly presupposing and producing processes of delimitation and re-coding. What dominates in Borges's "The Garden of Forking Paths" (1941), and signals the end of the fantastic as a possibility of narration, is not the alienation between subject and object nor the modern strategy for the sta-bilization of the ego through repression, nor even Oedipus, but rather a now happy schizophrenia that plays with systems, including writing, and re-organizes logocentric narrative structures by means of a narrator-authority that constantly shifts from authorial discourse to narrative action. Calvino found that in "Pierre Menard," Borges succeeded in inventing himself as a narrator:

> He found the egg of Columbus which made it possible for him to es-cape from his block that kept him (he was forty) from switching over from trivial prose to narrative prose because he acted as if the book he intended to write had already been written by another unknown author, an author from another language circle or another culture, and as if he wanted to plagiarize, summarize, and review just this hypothetical book.[9]

In a review of Valéry's "Introduction á la Poétique," Borges unravels the paradox in the two approaches to literature he finds in Valéry: that the history of literature is the history of the intellect as the producer and the consumer of literature, and that the works of the intellect only exist in the reader's here and now. Borges considers that, with the simultaneous discovery of literary narrative's process of arching over everything (Joyce) and the challenge to its autonomy by the mass media, it is now possible to establish paradox as a law of the universe. The idea of modernism might be sufficient to characterize the unwritten story planned by Borges-Bioy Casares-Ocampo, with its ironization of literary practice and literary life, but it would not be enough to master the multiple coding of "Pierre Menard" and the radical heterogeneity of its inherent problems. Pierre Menard is able to write the *Quixote* although it already existed, which is to say that the existence of the imaginary does not presuppose, for Borges, the cate-gory of the subject. There is no pre-existent identical subject. He considers

8. See Gilles Deleuze and Félix Guattari, *Capitalisme et Schizofrenie: L'Anti-Oedipe* (Paris: Editions de Minuit, 1972), 209–16.
9. Italo Calvino, *Sei proposte per il prossimo millenio* (Turin: Einaudi, 1988), 49.

the subject an essential consequence of discourse: a (collective) chain of assertions. Jauss has underlined that Derrida's deconstruction of logocentrism does not go beyond "Pierre Menard" in this sense. Geoffrey Hartman similarly states in his characterization of Derrida's "philosophical antimask," that for him, Derrida is "in line with Mallarmé and, *nolens volens*, a cousin of Borges's." [10] What Borges is asking is how the fictitious reality of the "individual" is thinkable and what (indispensable) values are linked with the real fiction of the "individual" under conditions where the autonomous (modern) subject comes into crisis.

Borges is an intruder in Euro-American modernism in the sense of a cultural *extopia* of a peripheral marginality, of a modernity that is not yet and never will be completed. The hermeneutics of the Yale Critics, or Genette, or John Barth, represent a "completed" modernity that represses the experience of the other in order to domesticate it. This is what, in a different context, the modern liberal imagination of Conrad, Forster, and Camus did with what frequently was an ontologically given other, but not a historically concrete one. What is different in Borges's fiction is a historical (and political) dimension that goes beyond the strategies of the modern: the fact that the primacy of the original (*Don Quixote*) and the hierarchy of metropolis and periphery, model and copy, have been overcome. From this "misplaced" perspective, it is possible for him to turn the concept of culture upside down in a labyrinth game and to measure the existing system of the established culture against the logic of the non-place and the paradox. The refusal of Telos in the face of philosophy of history coincides with a self-reflexivity that is no longer bound to the anthropocentric tradition of Enlightenment.

This brings me to another narrative in which the problem of the subject's constitution is also placed in the foreground. It deals with the erection of a building, a "crypt," and it is begun over and over again in García Márquez's writing. Each new circle of the narrative starts its task anew to find out what is hidden in the event and to determine its importance. This involves the staging of a (the original) scene that includes, each time, other subjects, name-bearers, and places. The story is textualized in a local artifact, in an enclave—a crypt—that is isolated from public space so that "things"—a body—can be embedded in it. What the endurance of this artifact and its contents evidences is the violence of the conflict created by the tension of libidinous desire there. One could say that Thanatopoetic lust

---

10. Geoffrey Hartman, *The Fate of Reading* (Chicago: University of Chicago Press, 1975), x.

starts up the machinery of the narrative, mobilizing mimetic power and illusion in order to conceal and protect what is in the crypt. Let me use three examples of the story in García Márquez's novels *Leaf Storm, One Hundred Years of Solitude*, and *Love in the Time of Cholera* to demonstrate its cryptic structure as a kind of given, but eternally lost, text that is continually being made over in something like a transferential process of remembering and reworking.

In *Leaf Storm*, a child, his mother, and the colonel who is the child's grandfather stand in front of a dead man in a room that is usually kept locked. The dead man is the colonel's friend, who hung himself the night before. The colonel prepares everything for the funeral, as he promised his friend he would, in spite of the indignation of the inhabitants of Macondo. The dead man's identity—he was a French physician who turned up there one day presenting the colonel with a letter of recommendation—had always remained mysterious and the subject of conjecture. As in *Antigone*, which is the novel's referent, a curse hangs over Macondo, which may bring about its apocalyptic destruction. The incapacity of the inhabitants of Macondo to understand themselves and their situation goes hand in hand with the fact that it is impossible for them to recognize the stranger as the other and as one of their own kind (this incapacity could be read as their inability to know or "decipher"). The closed interior of the locked room represents the first textualization of the crypt that preserves a dead man (who is revived by the narrative).

The theme of the other, the double, and the crypt also runs through *One Hundred Years of Solitude* from the first page on. García Márquez's text connects the novel with the epic under the sign of myth. It carnivalizes narration. The imagination is the power of recollection and the plan of the future; fiction becomes the acquisition of history. The persistence of sexual endogamy and of the failure to establish a relationship with the other brings the constant possibility of the return of a crypt and the body preserved in it. Melquíades, the gypsy, the stranger, the first one to die and be buried in Macondo, enjoys a special relationship with the founding patriarch. He is, consistent with the theme of the double, the cofounder of Macondo. The room in which he lives and writes his chronicle splits the system of place that the house of the Buendía, which has been erected both to keep a dead man alive and to bury him, represents. In the enclave of the room, which is isolated from the course of time, time itself becomes a spatial interior. Here is where Melquíades takes down the cryptic manuscripts containing Macondo's many generations of hallucinatory history before they can be decoded in the middle of the apocalyptic catastrophe at the end and thus become the book we are reading. The crypt develops into a forum in which Macondo's fate and its inhabitants' incapacity to know themselves are discussed; it is the place that preserves a "living" dead man.

In *Love in the Time of Cholera,* the crypt is on the opening page itself. In order to make it possible to tell the story, the cryptic mechanism and its economy of desire must be set in motion, and the hermetically sealed room of the photographer Jeremiah de Saint-Amour must be established as the crypt. This stranger, who originally came from the French Antilles, arrived one day in Cartagena and became a protégé of the physician Juvenal Urbino. On the day before the story opens, he commits suicide with potassium cyanide. His name in Spanish is "Santo Amore," holy love. Jeremiah de Saint-Amour, in his own way, personifies the *vita nuova,* the way of life of the other and the secret that allows each day the resurrection in this world of postmodern tupidity and modern ravages of life for those who condemn the masters of power to nonexistence.

From a psychoanalytic point of view, the text is a "poorly closed" crypt, which hides and reveals at the same time. The crypt itself is the "monument of a catastrophe," which presupposes an initial (hypothetical) trauma and, retrospectively, a reconstruction of its scenography and scene. Nicolas Abraham and Maria Torok have worked out the general premises and communication patterns for this in their interpretation of Freud's case of the Wolf-Man. They take off from the recognition that the scene of the Wolf-Man's trauma "with all its libidinous force and 'contradictions' is enclosed in the crypt."[11] As a result of denied or impossible grief, the never completed cryptic enclosure takes place at the boundary line that separates internalization and incorporation from one another and contrasts one with the other. The crypt is between the "dynamic unconscious" and the "ego of the internalization," which is in the middle of the ego's general area of space. For in the inner ego, the enclave (of all internalizations) is surrounded by the crypt, which is a general space of incorporation. Incorporation into the ego embodies an economic answer to traumatic object loss. It is this "incorporated object," then, that the ego uses to identify itself.[12]

11. Nicolas Abraham and Maria Torok, *Kryptonimie: Des Verbarium des Wolfsmanns* (Frankfurt am Main: Suhrkamp, 1979), 10.
12. Derrida comments, in his foreword to the Abraham-Torok book: "Such a maneuver is alien to the internalization process and, strictly speaking, is against it. I act as if I absorb the dead person, alive, intact, 'not damaged' (eviscerated), in order to be able to deny myself in a necessarily ambiguous way my being able to love him, as in the internalization

García Márquez has often referred to the fact that he was raised from birth by his grandparents in a house with many women and numerous servants, among whom were two male Indian and one female Indian, Memé. He first met his mother when he was five and went to live with his parents when he was eight. When he was five, a man known as Don Emilio committed suicide in Aracataca by swallowing potassium cyanide. Don Emilio was a disabled war veteran, a Belgian goldsmith, and a friend of his grandfather's, Colonel Nicolás Ricardo Márquez Mejída. Don Emilio and the colonel spent hours on end playing checkers. Don Emilio killed himself after seeing the film *All Quiet on the Western Front* with the colonel and the young García Márquez at the local cinema. This is the same film Jeremiah and Urbino see in *Love in the Time of Cholera*. There is another parallel: Urbino misses Sunday Mass, as Colonel Márquez had to, when he buried Don Emilio's remains in the cemetery for suicides. Three years later, after García Márquez had started living with his parents, his grandfather died under similar circumstances as Juvenal Urbino does in the novel. The boy experienced this loss without showing any clear signs of grief; although only eight years old, he experienced that grief is impossible.

This is as far as my "paleontological" reconstruction of the narrative crypt, taking its hypothetical character for granted, goes. García Márquez's constructions form the links in a mnemonic chain, whose energy and intensity make it possible for secrecy and mystery, irony, ceremony, and imagination (the source of the poetic changes that come to work in them) to become manifest. It is obvious that none of these narrative crypts is able to reproduce the original crypt, so that the chain is an infinite one with a dynamism driving toward the next link, the next novel, or the retelling of the story in the form of an (auto)biography. But this would also mean that García Márquez unveils his "secret" in order to hide it even better. Nothing can close the crypt; its contents are inexhaustible (utopian) and libidinous.

One can read in this project a historically conditioned and situation-specific psychogenesis of the (de-centered) subject and its structural illusions that deviates from the metropolitan logic of the modern. From its very

---

process of so-called 'normal' grief when the dead person is a living part in me in an un-damaged—eviscerated—way. . . . [T]his helpless (progressive, slow, difficult, mediated, ineffective) internalization process loses ground to incorporation, which is phantasmic, unexpected, sudden, magic, and sometimes hallucinatory. . . . No doubt, the ego, in order to resist the internalization process, identifies itself in an obscure and imaginary way with the lost object and its 'life beyond the grave.' No doubt, this endocryptic identification . . . remains phantasmic, cryptomatic" (13–17).

beginning, the interrelations in *One Hundred Years of Solitude* oscillate between the present, past, and future; life and death; and the real and the imaginary. As such, they differ from Oedipal desire and the bourgeois ego's subject effect, which occurs either as a nomadic center of action that eliminates subjectivity in favor of individuality or produces an alienated subject marked by anomie, fear of existence, and private revolt, whose modern literary form is the *Bildungsroman*. What the composition of Macondo as a chronicle (*crónica*) presupposes, instead, is a global view of overlapping cultures and time periods. This makes it possible for García Márquez to articulate Latin America's history in a form that goes beyond the *grand récits* of Enlightenment, the phenomenology of self, and the philosophy of history.

What characterizes García Márquez's fiction is that it links "chronicle" with a massive unfolding of the unconscious's primary processes. Once experience has been made visible, objectivized, in narrative, any imaginary and affective contents encountered along the way can be used to describe things and ideas, opposites can be juxtaposed, and subjectivity's official boundaries can be tested and crossed. This narrative treatment of primary psychic processes involves, like "Pierre Menard," a reaction to the new logics of mass culture, tuned to the structural needs and desires of a (secondary) narcissism that requires an egotistical (fickle and individualistic) satisfaction.[13] There is a difference between the subject effect in García Márquez's fictions and the dismantled, distraught (de-Oedipalized) subject found in novels such as Barth's *Sabbatical* and Robert Coover's *Gerald's Party*, or in the inhabitants of Pynchon's San Narciso. García Márquez's "meta-fictions" typologically resemble the North American postmodern texts. But the interpretative challenge that they represent is more complex.

Let me illustrate this in the following way: Brian McHale uses the confrontation between worlds in postmodern fiction to prove his theory that pastiche has an ontological character, unlike modernist collage. He draws on *One Hundred Years of Solitude* to recall the fact that the inhabitants of Macondo accept supernatural things and events as real but react to everything that is banal and everyday with surprise. Their reaction occurs under a complete reversal of signs:

> In Macondo, not only is the fantastic banal but because of a kind of chiasmus, the banal also becomes fantastic. The dialogue between

13. Stuart Ewen, "Mass Culture, Narcissism and the Moral Economy of War," *Telos* 44 (1980), 77.

the normal and the paranormal continues, in *One Hundred Years of Solitude*, although their relative positions have been reversed. *One Hundred Years of Solitude* is still a fantastic text, despite—or indeed because of—its banalization of the fantastic.[14]

What bothers me here is not only the terminological and conceptual vagueness, nor the validity of categories such as the banal, paranormal, and fantastic, nor the question of how the imaginary and the real are organized and what desire and reality are in *One Hundred Years of Solitude*. Rather, it is the occlusion of the importance of combined and uneven development in the production and sociocultural relevance of the text's effects. From an epistemological point of view, there has been a clear degradation of the unusual, which puts Macondo's sense of provable reality into question so that, although Macondo is far from the modern disenchantment of magic, products of modern civilization have still been introduced to it through the enclave economy. The reaction of Macondo's inhabitants, however, is unlike that of inhabitants of societies that are dominated by technical, economic, and administrative rationality. The miracles that happen in Macondo—the ascension of Remedios the Beautiful or the levitation of Father Nicanor— are dealt with within the context of social knowledge, whereas the wonders of technology—the gramophone, movies, and the telephone—put reality's boundaries to the test and, as such, are a danger to the mental integrity of the inhabitants and the community. Therefore, the narrative articulation of epistemological crisis as it exists in Macondo, even though it connects with similar changes in production, in communication, and, consequently, in perception, cannot be compared with an epistemology such as Pynchon's, which is founded upon a denial of causality and of the modern's chronological teleology. Because of its situation-bound difference, *One Hundred Years of Solitude* articulates an epic, carnival-like critique of reason, which must be assessed parallel to, but independent of, the philosophical critique of instrumental reason, the psychoanalytic and semiotic critique of the subject, and radical skepticism about the validity of great narratives in the metropolis.

It is perhaps appropriate to mention at this juncture Habermas's claim that the (Western) model of modernity is the only valid, "reasonable" social structure. The claim is founded on the assumption that Western rationalism, and thus the possibility of communicative rationality, has been realized

14. Brian McHale, *Postmodernist Fiction* (New York and London: Routledge, 1987), 76–77.

and generalized by modernization and by the dissolution of magic in the world.[15] The functions of the premises used by Habermas became clear in the twenty-year discussion on development and underdevelopment, and on the limits of European and American modernization theories and their counterarguments, the theories of structural dependency. Richard Morse has shown that instrumental reason—that is, the "objective" intellectualization of the world—has not been fully internalized yet in Latin America and that society is still understood by the individual as a structural exterior.[16] Today, the simultaneous occurrence of things that are not simultaneous has come to mean in Latin America a peripheral modernity, in which the dissolution of magic in the world is not going to be decisive. In the history of Latin America, which has its own version of the West's history, the function of the concept of the modern has been changed. Just as "wild" capitalism lacks institutional mechanisms for normative integration and social engineering, the processes of differentiation and individualization in Latin America and the trend toward secularization have been shifted onto historically concrete situations of dependence. Latin America is not only "partially modern," it seems also to belong to three historical worlds at once, and it is legitimate to ask whether its identity can be plotted on any abstract time line.

Habermas's critique of postmodernist architecture leads to an apology for the modern's linking of form and function. Just as his concept of communicative rationality ignores the colonization of the public sphere and the unconscious by the electronic mass media, his insistence on function(alism) ignores its history in the periphery. Urbanistics is the field par excellence in which the fate of the modern's project in Latin America can be observed. The utopian urge of the modern inspired Le Corbusier's plans for the reconstruction of Buenos Aires and Bogotá. The impossibility of modernizing misery he encountered theoretically is as instructive for the paradoxes of the modern and of its loss of authority in the periphery as the failure of the city of Brasília. Even more symptomatic of the crisis brought on by modernist urbanistics is the immediate future of the megalopolis of São Paulo, which will have 26 million inhabitants by the millennium and will virtually have grown into Rio de Janeiro over a 400 kilometer chain of satellite towns. (Parallel to this are the disastrous interventions in the ecosystem of

15. Jürgen Habermas, *Der philosophische Diskurs der Moderne* (Frankfurt am Main: Suhrkamp, 1985), 9.
16. Richard Morse, *El espejo de Prospero* (Mexico: Siglo XXI, 1982), 178.

the Amazon rain forest or the development of Latin American narcotics into one of the most flourishing industries of the subcontinent and of the world.)

The concept of difference in relation to Latin American cultural production becomes relevant if one takes into consideration that the obstacles that have to be overcome to thematize it are as great as those involved in "wild anthropology." This is evident in the ongoing debate in literary studies at American universities about "emerging literatures" and related questions of field and canon formation. It was in order to intervene in this debate that Jameson published his now famous essay on Third World literature. Particularly interesting is the way he uses there the categories of identity and difference in order to consider the relationship between First and Third World literatures. In a Hegelian tour de force, Jameson reduces the heterogeneity of Third World literature to a single exclusive dimension, the "experience of colonialism and imperialism," which still has not been recognized in the metropolis. It follows that "all texts from the Third World necessarily . . . are national allegories," where the process of allegory formation is understood as a relation between the private and the public, the individual and the collective, and history of the individual and history of the "tribe." [17]

In Latin America, where the nation-state was used as a lever by capitalist modernization and where the dream of a modernized democratic state has been thwarted, the role of nationalism as a legitimizing ideology is openly challenged today by literary theory and criticism and by those social and political movements that have developed on the periphery of hegemonic "national" projects. Instead, the appreciation of traditions and the mingling of cultural levels in Latin American literature find their parallel in the hybridization of different genres. Neither the concepts of the national and the allegorical nor the exclusiveness of colonial and imperialist experience exhaust the possibilities of the heterogeneity of Latin American fiction. The specific features of these texts resist being represented by interpretations such as Jameson's, which repress, and thus deny, their difference.

In tandem with the idea of "national allegory," Jameson has introduced the concept of "magic realism" into the debate about the postmodern.[18] To my mind, this concept, which was originally intended to counter the epistemology of social realist narrative, has not served, from the very beginning, to determine a clearly defined aesthetic problem. The controversial

17. Fredric Jameson, "Third World Literature in the Era of Multi-National Capitalism," *Social Text* 15 (1986): 69.

18. Fredric Jameson, "On Magic Realism in Film," *Critical Inquiry* 12 (1986): 301–32.

versions of its history by Roberto González Echevarría and Emir Rodríguez Monegal that Jameson refers to were broken off in the early 1970s, and the concept itself was nearly completely abandoned by literary studies as impractical. It did, however, become increasingly popular with the authors themselves and with their readers. In particular, the massive reception of García Márquez and Borges made it an international literary phenomenon. Magic realist novels blossom in literature from peripheral Soviet republics, in Commonwealth literature, in French-speaking African and Caribbean literature, in the United States, and in Western Europe.

In spite of what he admits are the concept's "terminological confusions," Jameson lets himself be led astray by its "power of temptation" as "a possible alternative to the narrative logic of the contemporary postmodern" (302). From the "first world's point of view . . . as opposed to the Latin American conception," and with a "private and personal" treatment, Jameson analyzes three features he considers "fundamental for a certain magic realism" in three films: *Cóndores no entierran todos los días* (1984, Columbia), *La Casa de Agua* (1984, Venezuela), and *Fever* (1981, Poland). These features are: (1) their particularity as historical films; (2) the fact that color is used in them as a source of fascination for its own sake, as a supplement to the narrative; (3) their concentration, reduction, and simplification of the narrative itself through violence (or eroticism) "for the sake of watching or viewing in the cinematic present."

Jameson differentiates magic realist and postmodernist handling of film color and relations between visual and narrative dynamics. His first "very provisional hypothesis" is that magic realism depends on "a kind of historic raw material" that "shows the overlapping or parallel existence of pre-capitalist and just developing capitalist or technological features" (311). In Latin American criticism of the sixties, the thesis that entire strata of the past are arranged in the present in layers, one upon the other, and that Latin American society, like any other historical society, consists of an overlapping of such layers and of the coexistence of various modes of production without one dominant mode was common. The problem here is that everything and nothing was explained by this idea. According to Jameson, research into internal and structural psychic distances by means of the movie camera and the development of "new forms of relationships to being" in magic realist films are only possible because they contain "a new type of historicism," in which the historical experience of de-centering has stopped being accidental. He concludes that there is a necessary and fundamental relation between the "intensities of colors and bodies in these films and their process of de-narrativization" that proves to be a process of "ideological analysis and deconstruction" (323). It is exactly in this aesthetic tension between expressivity and narration that Jameson identifies magic realism in film.

I have two questions here: If Jameson is trying to show magic realist film as a possible alternative to the narrative logic of metropolitan postmodernism, would it then be possible, mutatis mutandis, to develop a similar hypothesis on the level of prose fiction? And, if so, isn't there an ideological short circuit in supposing that North American postmodernist fiction—and I am thinking not only of historical novels such as Doctorow's or political novels such as *The Public Burning* but also of Pynchon's texts—is as distant from a new kind of historicism as Jameson thinks? Today, there is both an epistemological candor that is questioning history as a narrative fiction with formal coherence (Hayden White), and a new ability to make fiction an essential means of cognition in a reality considered as discourse and construct. There is a de-centered, and de-centering, relationship toward history in the works of Borges and García Márquez that I have been discussing, or in testimonio. These texts are part of a counter-narration that qualifies the Western modern's stories of Enlightenment and historical teleology. They correspond to a change in what is called historical consciousness and contribute to the constitution of a historical conception of history. They make it possible, therefore, to historicize the postmodern itself. Their alterity as narrative extopias contains in a way McHale does not consider a political dimension that is related to their ability to criticize the center from the periphery.

The real issue, however, is not the alternative of postmodernism or magic realism but differences that may be perceived outside of such categories as identity, analogy, and opposition. The only way to describe Latin American fiction's place within the context of such a historicized postmodernity and the now mutated concept of "World" literature is as a peripheral center in a situation where centers have multiplied by themselves and have become sites of autonomous creativity, in contrast to a model in which the periphery was thought to mark both the distance from, and subordination to, the center.

This is how to think the relation between, for example, Pynchon's *Gravity's Rainbow* (influenced by Borges) and García Márquez's *Love in the Time of Cholera*: Both are "love stories," but with a difference. Pynchon says that he shares with García Márquez a view of "fiction as a subversive medium," and that the two of them play "this high form of the game we appreciate in fiction." He praises *Love in the Time of Cholera* as only novelists writing about themselves can do:

> Let us assume that it were not only possible to swear eternal love but to keep the promise in reality—to live a long, meaningful, and authentic life on the basis of such pledge, to invest the granted share of valuable time in the matter we set our hearts on. This is the extraordinary premise of Gabriel García Márquez's new novel. It dares to suggest that lovers' oaths given on the supposition that man is immortal—for many a juvenile idiocy—may, nevertheless, be rewarded . . . at a much later date in life. This is to effectively explain the resurrection of the body, an unavoidable revolutionary idea today. . . . [We have arrived] on the shore of a Caribbean . . . plagued by a history that has killed so terribly many people without their ever having said a word, or they spoke, disappeared without being heard, or they were heard but nothing was written down. Writing in a revolutionary and good way is the duty to break the silence.[19]

The history of means-to-end rationality has displaced imagination time and again. Today, the imaginative way of thinking, which was given new value by romanticism, and then surrealism, has begun to correct rationalism's self-expansion. This new turn of mind emphasizes the qualitative mutation that the electronic mass media have created with their upgrading of the imaginary and their inclusion of fiction in the production cycle of commodities and images. Pynchon's characters call themselves Benny Profane and Oedipa Maas, Genghis Con, and Herbert Stencil, Jr. They are designed to be clichés. In their modern industrial world, there are indications of a great plot: the "Tristerosystem," which is a secret society of the downtrodden and injured that has been waging guerrilla warfare against the prevailing order since the Middle Ages. But this is still something like the strategy of a critical—or compensatory—modernity.

Characters from the Caribbean world of *Love in the Time of Cholera*, on the other hand, are called, for example, Florentino and Urbino. Their aura is taken from the living models of the perfect courtier and courtly love in the *Divine Comedy*, where the ideal is to be faithful to only one woman, the one in whom love has condensed and who leads to divine love, the *vita nouva*, models put into practice in Urbino's little princely court, or in

19. Thomas Pynchon, "The Heart's Eternal Vow," *New York Times Book Review* 93 (1988), 1, 47, 49.

Castiglioni's *Courtier*, which is a (textual) utopia of love. In Tuscany, the "Cavalieri d'Amore" and the "Fideli d'Amore"—one of them may have been the Florentine Dante—entered into an alliance, a cross between a militia and a heretical sect, under the name of "Santo Amore" and the cult of "Donna Unica."

It is probably emblematic that both *Gravity's Rainbow* and *Love in the Time of Cholera* cannot come to a conclusion. The multi-coding of the rainbow in Pynchon's novel can be compared with the boat trip upstream and downstream at the end of García Márquez's novel, which returns to the same image that it began with: two elderly people standing on board a boat. What happens to the Newtonian cosmic system in *Gravity's Rainbow* happens also to the courtly love life-style models in *Love in the Time of Cholera* at the beginning of the modern era. The love paradigm of "Santo Amore" turns into a private male fantasy, which is contrasted to the public ecological catastrophe. The double movement of remembering and working through, which Lyotard refers to as the task of the postmodern ("réécrire la modernité"), can be found in both García Márquez and Pynchon. Both compose elements of resistance to a cultural hegemony whose containment strategies have not worked for them. García Márquez's reading of modernity, however, puts it, and Pynchon's novel as well, into a differently conceived historical constellation.

In Carlos Fuentes's novel *Cristobal no nato*, three caravels land in 1992 on the western coast of Mexico, the country with the largest city in the world. This time, however, they come from the East, from Japan. It has become evident, since the 1970s, that the Pacific is becoming one of the major poles of economic power in the world. Europe—that is, the Mediterranean maritime basin—was the economic and cultural center of the early modern world system. In the seventeenth century, the center shifted to the north and to the Atlantic Ocean; today, to the Pacific Basin. Latin American novels' characteristics of discovery and recognition make it possible to use them, not only in Latin America, to decode one's own historical and political experience and the phenomenon of reality's fictionalization. Of course, the logic of the social and cultural world is an open one of "effects not desired," as Pierre Bourdieu has shown. But recognition of the alterity of Latin American fiction shows a way to experience the alien and its differentness so that the historical question of the other, and the discovery (of the history) of the other, which the modern never took upon itself, need not be evaded any longer.

Reading and Discursive Intensities: On the Situation of Postmodern Reception in Brazil

Silviano Santiago

The distinction between spectacle (or cultural event) and simulacrum (or electronically produced mass entertainment) is common among critics who anchor themselves in classic modernist values in order to understand the historical moment we are passing through, the moment, that is, of the postmodern. According to these critics, in the field of symbolic or cultural production, postmodernity is the overwhelming and abusive proliferation of electronic images, of simulacra, to the detriment of spectacle.

In Fredric Jameson's image,[1] the field of experience of postmodernity is bounded by the walls of an electronic version of Plato's cave: The postmodern subject no longer can gaze directly, with its own eyes, at the

1. A condensed version of Jameson's postmodernism essay was published in Brazil in the journal *Novos Estudos CEBRAP* (São Paolo) 12 (June 1985), and became one of the focuses for the wide-ranging debate on postmodernity that ensued. For this, see, for example, Silviano Santiago, "O narrador posmoderno," in *Las malhas da Letra* (São Paulo: Companhia das Letras, 1989); Roberto Schwarz, "Brazilian Culture: Nationalism by Elimination," *New Left Review* 167 (1988); Luiz Costa Lima, "Posmodernidade: contraponto tropical," in his *Pensando nos trópicos* (Rio de Janeiro: Rocco, 1991); Roberto Cardoso Oliveira et al., *Pos-modernidade* (Campinas: UNICAMP, 1988); and Heloisa Buarque de Hollanda ed., *Pos-modernidade e política* (Rio de Janeiro: Rocco, 1991). [*Trans.*]

real world of the referent, the thing-in-itself, but is obliged, instead, to find mental images of the world on the walls of its confinement. For Jameson, the triadic conception of the sign (signifier, signified, referent) remains intact. Instead of privileging the referent, as both traditional and modernist theories of realism did, postmodernism affirms the exclusivity and omnipresence of the electronic image—that is, in semiotic terms, of the signifying chain. For the theorists of symbolic production in the era of late capitalism, reality (if the concept may be permitted in the company of the postmodern) appears more and more in representations of representations.

The distinction between spectacle and simulacrum is correct and should be maintained. It carries with it, however, an excessively negative evaluation of postmodernity. One rapidly becomes aware that the distinction is used strategically to privilege the realm of direct experience, *in corpore*, and to disqualify experience obtained through technologically produced images, *in absentia*. Thus, spectacle (as presented in museums, theaters, concert halls, etc.) is "authentic" culture, while simulacrum (by which is meant, above all, television) is a bastard product of cultural commercialization. Spectacle leads to reflection, while simulacrum serves only to kill time. The distinction aims, finally, to blame the mass media for the contemporary debasement of public life. For its proponents, what is at stake is the preservation, at all costs, in a democratic or would-be democratic society, of the possibility of public opinion, a possibility they believe can be attained only through a devastating critique of the mass media and the proliferation of images they furnish for mass consumption.

In a culturally "underdeveloped" country such as Brazil, the problem represented by the spectacle/simulacrum distinction becomes particularly acute. It also exists in the advanced countries, but less so, because these countries developed mass public education in the nineteenth century and underwent a subsequent democratization (in relative terms) of higher education, particularly in the decade of the sixties in this century—a phenomenon connected to the cultural radicalism of that period, which, as we know, had as its epicenters Berkeley and the Sorbonne.

In Brazil, by contrast, not even mass literacy was instituted at its "proper" moment—that is, by the end of the nineteenth century. This historical lag is at the core of our national classic, *Os Sertoes* (1902). Its author, Euclides da Cunha, suggested in vain, after the "crime" of Canudos,[2] that

2. Under the leadership of a holy man called Antonio Conselheiro (Antonio the Councilor), the poor peasantry of the interior (*sertão*) of the state of Bahia staged a rebellion against the central government in the town of Canudos. The military destruction after a

the task of reconstruction of the ruined *sertão*, or backlands, be entrusted to teachers. He believed that if the young Republic wanted to take responsible steps in its desire to modernize Brazil, it should send teachers to all corners of the country instead of relying on successive military expeditions.

If the conflict between spectacle and simulacrum in the advanced countries does not always result in the victory of the first, it at least produces a stalemate. Libraries, museums, theaters, concert halls, and books compete—more importantly, coexist—with television. There exists a broad public capable of paying for extremely expensive spectacles like grand opera, and a larger, less-privileged (economically, geographically, and culturally) public for the retransmission of opera on television or videocassette. The globalization of culture, a characteristic postmodern phenomenon today in the hegemonic countries, is only possible thanks to the technological means of reproduction of images. On the other hand, certain "spectacles" no longer exist as such, because they originate in the first place as simulacra (that is, they are produced solely by electronic transmission).

In Brazil, the debate between spectacle and simulacrum, cultural modernism and mass consumer society, already has a history. It begins with, and passes through, the discussion of the question of the extremely limited consumption of books and literature by the Brazilian public. In an essay published in 1973, when the military dictatorship was in the process of restructuring literacy education,[3] our greatest modern critic, Antonio Candido, discussed the relationship between literature and underdevelopment, calling attention to the fact that in Latin America, there existed a "prior negative condition" for the enjoyment of literature, that condition being the small size of the reading public. The modern writer of the underdeveloped periphery, Candido felt, was fated to be a "producer for minorities," given that the masses were "marginalized in a folkloric era of oral communication."[4]

The dilemma Candido identified so starkly seemed to have a correspondingly simple solution: For the market in books to improve and for Bra-

---

brutal and prolonged siege of the town, which da Cunha witnessed as a military engineer, was justified on "positivist" grounds by the newly proclaimed Republic as a question of civilization versus barbarism. *Os sertoes* has been published in English under the title *Rebellion in the Backlands* (Chicago: University of Chicago Press, 1944); the incident is also the basis of Vargas Llosa's recent novel, *The War at the End of the World*. [*Trans.*]

3. The dictatorship created something called the Movimiento Brasiliero de Alfabetizacão (MOBRAL) to replace the popular literacy workshops championed by Paolo Freire.

4. Antonio Candido, "Literatura e subdesenvolvimiento," *Argumento* 1 (São Paulo) (October 1973).

zilians to emancipate themselves as citizens, it should be enough for them to become literate. Already in 1973, however, Candido found this conclusion problematic because of the acute and (for him) pernicious interference of the mass media in the relation between literary high culture and its newly alphabetized potential audience. At the time, he wrote:

> As they acquire literacy and are absorbed in the process of urbanization, [the masses] pass into the domain of radio, television, comic books, constituting thus the basis of mass culture. . . . Alphabetization therefore does not increase proportionally the number of readers of literature, as we think; rather it impels the newly literate, together with the still illiterate, directly from the stage of oral folklore into the kind of urban folklore that mass culture in effect is.

In other words, in Brazil, or more generally for Candido in the underdeveloped countries as such, the newly literate or semiliterate masses produced by modernization would bypass the book and literary high culture on the way, so to speak, to television. The costly project of phonetic alphabetization mounted by the dictatorship would be of little or no use for the social and intellectual improvement of the population. This was the message ciphered in his 1973 article.

Candido's conclusion was anguished and compelling: Any process of phonetic alphabetization will encounter, in the countries of the periphery, a voracious and determined enemy, mass culture, which creates what he called a "catechism in reverse." Jesuit catechism in Brazil during colonization depended on ecclesiastical drama and spectacle to convert Indians and Africans to Christianity and the dominant Western values; similarly, Candido felt, the mass media, in our own day, employs the production of simulacra to indoctrinate the peasantry and urban proletariat. Through techniques such as subliminal suggestion, the media "impose values which are in themselves dubious and in any case quite different from those the cultured person seeks in art and literature." Since this is a catechism "in reverse," however, it was, for Candido, even less progressive than its colonial antecedent, which had the basically positive and high-minded goal of instilling the best of Christian thought and European high culture. The catechism of the media aims instead at restoring the mass of poor Brazilians to a state of barbarism.

A progressive modernist, Candido believed in the Enlightenment principle that access to art works and their fruition as cultural forms signified a higher stage in the process of human emancipation. Consequently, he saw: (1) the mass media as the great enemy that had to be fought by educators and intellectuals who were genuinely committed to the project of modernity; and (2) the traditional values imposed by high culture as the only values worth preserving, in spite of the fact that the economic, social, and political state of both the contemporary world and contemporary Brazil suggested a different, and perhaps easier, road. There befell the defenders of high culture such as Candido the inglorious, and difficult, task of resisting the lure of the mass media in a country with an illiterate or semiliterate majority. The sense that this task was ultimately doomed to failure posed a question Candido's article neither posed nor answered directly: In a country such as Brazil, was literacy as such, in fact, less than useless in producing an "informed" citizenry?

Let me approximate an answer via three criticisms of Candido's article, abstracting its argument from the historical moment in which it appeared and which conditioned and justified its language and concerns. My dialogue here is with my contemporaries, although the current defenders of Enlightenment values in the underdeveloped world have not come up with a more devastating rationale than Candido's. The acquisition of literacy, as they understand this, was, indeed, the path of human emancipation a century ago, when the access to modern knowledge depended crucially on the degree of reading skills an individual possessed. In the nineteenth century, and at the beginning of our own, there was no access to even the bare minimum of information necessary for an understanding of the variety and complexity of human societies and their current and historical configurations without books or magazines.

This situation began to change, however, with the advent of film newsreels seen by millions of spectators in different parts of the world; it changed even more with the documentary (it is enough to mention the importance of this paradidactic genre in a country such as England in the 1930s, and the role played by the Brazilian Alberto Cavalcanti in its production); and it changed once and for all with the massive introduction of television into the households of the literate, illiterate, and semiliterate alike.

Granted this point, however, there arises a double task for those of us who propose to go beyond an Enlightenment model of cultural citizenship: on the one hand, rethinking what is meant by *literacy* in a mass society such as Brazil, which did not go through compulsory alphabetization at the appropriate stage of its national development and which, by the same token, did not participate in the expansionary boom in higher education in the sixties; on the other hand, determining what is meant, or should be meant, by *reading* today, when it is the "texts" furnished by the mass media that are the main form of cultural consumption.

A person of good faith, a citizen, even one who is illiterate, has a quantity of information at his or her disposal today that exceeds, by far, the quantity of information available to a person of good faith, a citizen, even one who was literate, fifty years ago. The problem—then and now—is knowing how to transform this excessive, anarchic, and always biased information into knowledge, how to channel it so that the person-citizen can use it to understand and to intervene in the society and world he or she lives in. What we now know is that in the underdeveloped world, this will not happen through the immensely difficult strategy of phonetic alphabetization alone.

A second criticism follows from the first and has to do with a contradiction in the contemporary field of aesthetic judgment itself. High culture (that is, the culture of the written book or text, of the "unique," or "original," artwork) increasingly valorizes and incorporates cultural products that less and less depend on the distinctions between elite and pop, original and copy, oral and written. It would be impossible, for example, for a reader to capture accurately the sense of Manuel Puig's fiction without a knowledge of radio soap operas (*Boquitas pintadas*) or Hollywood "B" films (*The Kiss of the Spider Woman*). As Jameson and other theorists of postmodernism point out, it is becoming increasingly difficult to make out the dividing line between avant-garde high culture and commercial art. The artists themselves are investing their creative imaginations in new areas: They are discovering that they have to develop new ways of "reading" cultural productions that are not embodied in writing, understanding that there exists in the mass dissemination of simulacra a universe that needs to be explored in order to develop an aesthetic sensibility and strategies that are relevant to the present. They are, in effect, telling their "readers," "You have to learn to appreciate other forms of 'reading,' as we did, in order to be our contemporaries. You should approach pop culture with fewer preconceptions." The absence of preconceptions is the condition sine qua non of any aesthetic experience whatsoever.

A third criticism of the defenders of cultural modernism concerns a symptomatic problem in their analysis of television. They confuse the medium as such with the ways it is being used by foreign and Brazilian cultural industries. There is in this a veiled form of obscurantism, properly pilloried in some of Pynchon's novels, which, in effect, amounts to a prejudice against technological progress as such, as if it were a matter of being against the airplane because it permitted the dropping of the atom bomb on Hiroshima. (What deserves our total, unlimited disapproval is the atom bomb and the fact of its being used against a civilian population. By contrast, the airplane is a vehicle that can be used to help more quickly the victims of a disaster.)

In the case of the mass media, the confusion between *product* and *medium* derives from the privileging in modernist criticism of the analysis of the *production* of cultural commodities rather than of their *reception*. First, the medium is a priori devalued, although the problem of quality, in many cases, has to do with the product. Second, and even more important and disheartening, with the critical devaluation of the product, its "reader" is also a priori devalued. The current theorists of classical modernism are prone to state categorically that only a second-class spectator or an illiterate could be interested (in anything but an ironic or distanced way) in this type of product. Medium, producer, product, and spectator are thus confined to a low-quality ghetto, in a total communication system that, in turn, is viewed with complete pessimism by these theorists. From the confusion of medium and product, it follows that the simulacrum is nothing more than a diabolical part of this system, which, by contagion, also becomes diabolical. As the popular saying goes: If you stop here, you must dance here (*vacilou, dancou*).

Let me take as an example of this confusion the case of a Catholic Mass (spectacle) that is broadcast on television (simulacrum). If we emphasize the mode of production of the simulacrum, we will see a team of technicians who, with their lights and equipment and their loud voices, are disrupting the service and distracting the fervor and contrition of the church-goers. If we emphasize its mode of reception, however, we will observe that many of the participants *in corpore* are not that interested or involved in the service, are there perhaps only for status reasons. On the other hand, there is nothing to prevent marginal and economically or geographically underprivileged sectors of the population from participating with genuine conviction and feeling, through the broadcast, in a religious ritual that would otherwise have been restricted to the congregation in the cathedral in the city. Only through the simulacrum is what Walter Benjamin called "the experience of the poor" possible today.

It is a question, then, of locating the tonic of possibility in the *act of reading*. This should be understood as an activity that transcends the experience of knowledge transmitted by phonetic writing. In a mass society of peripheral capitalism such as Brazil, we should look for the ways to improve the interpretation of both spectacles and simulacra by ordinary citizens.

This means that the production of meaning ceases to be a monopoly of restricted minorities who are, in conditions of inequality, better trained and thus more sophisticated. With that change, the singular, or authoritarian, interpretation made by a legitimizing group (traditionally, professional critics or experts) also disappears. Meaning in symbolic and/or cultural production becomes plural and unattainable in its plurality. The "total" meaning (or the totality of meanings) becomes the product of a purposiveness that is no longer necessarily articulated by the traditional institutions of knowledge and their acolytes.

This shift in perspective involves more than a theoretical question that can be resolved simply by "taking thought," above all because we still situate ourselves as intellectuals in the hermeneutics of profundity instituted by modernity. I limit myself here, then, to simply suggesting that it is time for us to rethink radically the problem of cultural enjoyment and evaluation in mass society. More immediately, however, we need to confront the educational propaganda of the current government in Brazil, which retains an Enlightenment model of literacy. (I am referring here to the literacy program that Collor's Ministry of Education tried to implement before his impeachment, which found a powerful ally in Brizola, the social democratic governor of the state of Rio de Janeiro.) It is unthinkable that the head of a household, a worker, who every night informs himself or herself (well or badly) via TV news about what is happening in Brasilia, or Berlin, or Moscow, or the Persian Gulf—it is unthinkable that such a person should be pressured in the adult stage of his or her life to become literate in order to qualify as an emancipated citizen. Such a person cannot be compared with the Citizen of the Future posited at the end of the nineteenth century. Adult literacy training, in the form that was promoted by Collor's Ministry of Education, represents a step away from, rather than a means of access to, full citizenship. Literacy courses taken at home after an exhausting workday, with the television on, are a waste of time, pure and simple. What is needed, instead, is to find ways to turn the adult worker into a more conscious reader of his or her symbolic and cultural universe, of the walls of the electronic cave. On these are "printed" the evening news as well as the novel, the broadcast of a classical music concert as well as a debate about public policy among intellectuals on educational television.

Finally, we should be aware that simply demanding a priori better quality from the cultural producers of simulacra is not going to advance things much. Better programs, given a public that is not prepared to receive them, won't work. "A failure with the public," the Ibope (Brazil's version of the Nielsen Index) will say, and everyone will echo this. Nor will the improvement of the quality of mass cultural products come from the pressure of the state (this particular one, or even one that is more progressive politically) on the groups that control their production, or from the transference to the state, by the state, of that control. It will come, instead, from the improvement in the level of taste of the spectators, of the consumers, and this must be the task of an education oriented to our times. The spectators—that is, the new "readers," more or less literate, more or less demanding, more or less expert in their experience of mass media—are who will define the standards of excellence in the future, as the critical establishment and the university did in the past. It is not a question of excluding criticism and the university but of taking away the authority that they imagined conferred on them, the sole or final power of judgment.

Every literary critic knows that a bad book can produce a good reading, and a good book a mediocre one. Hardly anyone insists anymore that only the classics should be read. The political discussions of the 1980s taught us that so-called universal values are bound up with ethnic, social, sexual, et cetera, *centralisms*. The struggle of subaltern and minority groups for their own identity and rights passes necessarily through the search for, and recovery of, cultural objects that have been judged inferior by the modern tradition on the basis of its own centered ("objective") standards of taste. The value of a cultural object itself, however, depends on the sense that it is given by a new reading, above all if this deconstructs prior readings that are based only on prejudice and inertia.

Spectacle and simulacrum are, therefore, neither good nor bad in themselves. It depends. They are there to be taken up—or *not*—by the impassioned reason of the citizen-reader.

Aesthetics and Post-Politics: From Fujimori to the Gulf War

Beatriz Sarlo

I will attempt a review of some images and texts from different sources: a photograph of Fujimori; a newspaper account of how another photograph was taken of Mario Vargas Llosa while he was running against Fujimori as a candidate for the presidency of Peru; a novel, *El oido absoluto* (The Absolute Ear), by the Argentinean Marcelo Cohen; and the coverage of the Gulf War as it appeared on North American television, which, in turn, furnished the image of the war to the rest of the world.[1] There is no absolute necessity in the examples that I have chosen, nor are they arbitrary. Their disparity is sustained by a zeitgeist they seem to share and by some ideas of my own about the impregnation of the political by the aesthetics and ideology of the mass media. In a sense, I will be framing here a question that,

1. Marcelo Cohen, *El oido absoluto* (Barcelona: Muchnik Editores, 1989). The photo of Fujimori was published in the *Washington Post*, along with the story about the photo of Vargas Llosa, in March 1990. This paper incorporates two previous publications: "Basuras culturales, simulacros políticos" (Cultural garbage, political simulacra), *Punto de Vista* 37 (July 1990); and "La Guerra del Golfo: representaciones pospolíticas y analisis cultural" (The Gulf War: Post-political representations and cultural analysis), *Punto de Vista* 40 (July 1991).

at the same time, is a hypothesis (converted into science fiction and into a warning by Cohen's novel): What happens when the public sphere is taken over by the electronic media, when the loss of scale and distance involved in media presentation turns it into a *mise-en-abyme* and politics into icon, image, or simulacrum?

The electoral campaigns in Argentina, Brazil, and Peru in recent years have exhibited a dense network of borrowings between political discourse and the mass media: Television announcers burst into the arena putting the candidates on the defensive, and the candidates, in turn, take to the political stage in scenographies derived from sports shows or rock aesthetics, composing their gestures with as much care as their rhetoric. The Peruvian elections, decided in June 1990 with Fujimori's victory, were, above all in the first stage of the campaign, the occasion for symbolic constructions that did not always correspond to traditional forms of political discourse. These constructions embody the features of a practice that could be called, at least provisionally, post-politics.

The Photos

Fujimori does not know karate. Nevertheless, one of the photos of his campaign showed him dressed in a white karate robe in the act of breaking in half a brick of considerable size with the edge of his right hand. The brick in the photo had previously been broken (perhaps with a karate-chop struck by a real black belt) and arranged between two boards, behind which Fujimori stood, imitating the gesture, although clearly concentrating more on posing for the photo than on striking the blow. The white robe reinforced the classic image of the candidate: someone who dresses in white gives the effect of showing an exterior as pure as his intentions should be. It also evoked an avenging angel and, if one looks at the picture quickly, instead of a fake black belt, one might see the image of an angry prophet. Angel, prophet, karate expert: It was all the same, because the objective was accomplished if Fujimori successfully appeared *not* to be a politician. In a baroque way, because of the complexity of the double negation involved, Fujimori did not want to appear to be what he was not—that is, a politician—so in order not to look like a politician, he disguised himself as a black belt.

At about the same time, and in the same city of Lima, his rival, Mario Vargas Llosa, who wanted to appear as an intellectual whose moral principles drove him into politics, posed for a photo in the backyard of his home. Those in charge of taking the picture had blocked off the swimming pool with a little wall of cardboard and tin, against which were arranged a group of poor people, made to look Indian and shabbily dressed, a boy with a dirty face, and some other props. The theme of the photo, which was included in a campaign video, was the visit of the candidate to a slum. But everything—the visit, the slum, the candidate himself—was reconstructed as if in a studio, in a way Golden Age Hollywood would have admired. Vargas Llosa, a realist writer, after all, knows more about representation than about symbols. Fujimori, a Japanese, trusts more in symbols than in representations. Both of them, however, love simulacra and wanted to use their power.

Fujimori not only dressed up as a *karateca*, but he was also photographed dressed as a samurai and, in general, thoroughly exploited his Japanese ancestry, which gave him the aura of a desirable semi-foreigner: Not only did he not present himself as a politician, he did not even worry about seeming to be not completely Peruvian; better yet, whatever he lacked as a Peruvian he gained as an industrious, practical, likable, innovative (and traditionalist at the same time) Japanese. A miracle. When he was still a candidate, Menem was also familiar with the power of costumes and styles: a nineteenth-century caudillo with sideburns, a fat and friendly provincial with an accent, a man of great faith with the papal gestures and simple prose he used to speak to the poor, a sportsman, and a ballroom dancer. He had perhaps the most important quality for the current political battles whose arena is television: photogeneity. He knew how to move gracefully in Cecil B. DeMille–like scenes, such as the time he entered, dressed in phosphorescent white, a completely darkened soccer stadium so that the solitary spotlight that illuminated him was like a ray of stellar material projecting him as the head of a comet.

What happens when this paraphernalia takes the place of politics? The aesthetics of television and advertising present a new model of politics to a public sphere that itself has become saturated by the mass media. The figures of the caudillo, the performer, and the parliamentarian fuse together in that of the *communicator*, modeled on the principle of the sound bite— high impact and frequency per unit of time, small doses of information or a lot of undifferentiated information. "Intellectual" discursive forms are despised by a communicative populism that copies the strategies of the media, hoping to put itself in touch with a popular culture found in the traces that the media leave in the collective imaginary. For the aesthetics of advertising, the truth is indifferent, not because it recognizes truth as a construction but rather because truth is simply superfluous in the face of the hyperrealism of broadcast news or the audiovisual simulation of discourses. The photograph of Fujimori and the scenic montage of the Vargas Llosa type are only two examples of the new style of political construction.

It is irrelevant whether Fujimori is a samurai or a black belt. Nobody asks themselves this useless question, because everybody knows that what he or she is seeing is a disguise. The question, rather, is why it seems appropriate to do this sort of thing in order to win a political campaign, and why so many people seem to approve of it. Political symbols have changed, and if they were never really "symbols of reason," the latest Latin American examples (to which could easily be added Collor de Melo wearing his T-shirts decorated with slogans that change weekly) allow us to foresee the triumph of the simulacrum above all other modalities of symbolization. The symbols of the public sphere, along with its discursive genres, are replaced with a scenography that is no longer even a stage but rather stage-craft, constructed by and, above all, for the mirror of the mass media. Double staging, Chinese boxes of politics as a spectacle that is meant not to be viewed directly but to be taped, photographed, and televised: the mass-media utopia of MacLuhan is today.

The games of *mise-en-abyme* are complemented by the production of moments of extreme closeness: the candidate touches and allows himself to be touched (a test that Vargas Llosa held up under very poorly) or sends out missionaries to the people (literally, in the case of Fujimori, who had priests and monks working for him). Here the stage disappears completely, because it requires a distance negated in the proximity of bodies and a detachment impossible in door-to-door campaigning. North American politicians will sometimes have breakfast at the home of one of their local supporters. At these breakfasts, politics is not discussed: Seated at the family table, with both the children and the adults fascinated by the closeness of someone who is made for television, politics is impossible. It resides in the middle distance.

Both the artificial distance of the photographic simulacrum and these moments of extreme closeness have a scale that corresponds poorly to politics. As in Disneyland, scenarios are presented in which things and people are bigger or smaller than in real life. This disjuncture of scale is at the heart of their fascination, their ability to produce benevolent and happy kitsch sensations. When the scale of the spectacle is changed, the scale of the spectator is modified as well. All perspectives run toward the grand scenario, which enlarges those who occupy it; later, or at the same time, it all will be, or is, reproduced in miniature on the television screen (which may itself be part of the scenario). Or just the opposite, the politician descends from the stage to assume a human scale, but those who touch and speak to him continue to see him on the gigantic or diminutive scale in which they have *truly* known him. To "come down to Earth" or to "mount the stage" are not actions but changes of state. The trick photographs of Fujimori and Vargas Llosa are also changes of state: the passkeys of post-politics.

Without the artifice of double staging, without the kitschy charm of being bigger or smaller than real life, without these representations of life designed not to be seen directly (with the immediacy and distance of theater) but to be transmitted through another medium, the speeches would sound bad. When Vargas Llosa truthfully said what his administration would be like without faking a visit to a slum in his backyard, he lost thousands of votes. It was a rare moment in which the political represented itself truthfully. More experienced politicians, such as Menem, or mysterious beginners, such as Fujimori (when he was a candidate), know that the first thing to be perceived in a political speech is its form: the religious form, for example, which inflects its cadences (and not only in Latin America). What is a politician saying when he says "God bless you" or "with the help of God"? Like a boomerang, religion takes revenge on the process of secularization that runs through the history of the public sphere. The appeal to God is not a simple matter of hypocrisy but rather the establishment of a common and egalitarian territory: God permits the reinforcement of a simulacrum of the equality of destiny. Before God, equality is not formal but real. God introduces, once again, a dizzying change of scale into political discourse.

A corresponding change of scale is a product, on the other hand, of "knowledge." The discrete Fujimori, himself an engineer, understood the new power of the technocrat, as someone who has acquired now the prestige of both the traditional *letrado*, or man of letters, and the modern intellectual. Fujimori did not use a technological discourse; rather, he presented himself as a technician. With the efficiency of a futurist samurai, he offered technology as a respite from politics. This operation, which is not new, manages to imaginarily close the gap between society and politics, producing a special kind of collective delegation among those who claim to possess this knowledge. Unlike politics, technological knowledge needs not to convince but to teach. Its argumentative strategy leaves persuasion behind in order to impose itself through demonstration. Politics is obliged to speak of the relationship between ends and means, to adopt means that are in accord with values, to decide when a conflict of interest emerges, whereas technology puts itself forward as the only appropriate discourse for ends that are otherwise not submitted for discussion. If politics needs to compare options (what is more: needs to *produce* options), technology without politics presents itself as the *only* option. If political choices are increasingly more complex and, consequently, difficult to communicate to public opinion, technology pretends to dispense with the need for public opinion because it presents its reasons as the only viable ones.

This imaginary suture of the split between society and politics when technology takes the place of politics is itself a technologically produced simulation of knowledge, a simulacrum that does not explain but rather points to itself. Marking itself as the inexplicable icon of a complexity that it sees as the cause and not the effect of its discourse, technology requires faith. The trust that politics demands is not enough for it. Among the shattered myths of modernity, technology triumphantly marches on.

When a politician presents him- or herself as a technocrat (or when he/she delegates politics to technology), he/she also sutures another gap: the one between intellectuals and society. More precisely, technocratic post-politics does not need the intellectuals who, as a category, have lost or abandoned the public sphere from which they arose historically. The intellectuals and politicians of modernity imagined that it was possible to build bridges between society, knowledge, and politics, even though they recognized at the same time that these divisions were constitutive. The technological icon requires a world where these divisions are, by definition, irreparable in their practical dimension and blocked in their symbolic dimension.

The technological icon and the simulacrum produced by the mass media compress society, projecting the image of a unified cultural scene, a *common place* where oppositions (which could be transformed into conflict) are dissolved in polyglotism: Mass-mediated culture and politics seek to produce the illusion of a shared culture that can unite actors whose symbolic and material power is very different. If this guarantees cohesion, it is not at all clear that *that* cohesion is desirable.

The Novel

These issues intersect in Marcelo Cohen's novel *El oido absoluto*, which offers, in the form of a science-fiction dystopia, a hypothesis about the present. In Lorelei, the city in which the novel takes place, the banal happiness of mass culture has become fully realized. The inhabitants of all the countries of the world have the right to visit Lorelei once during their lives; by contrast, Lorelei's inhabitants cannot leave the city without permission. For some, it is the place of a kind of permanent marginality; for the vast majority, it is the scene of the "happy days" to which they feel they have a right. In Lorelei, the abundance of images functions as a sought-after reward for its visitors, who cannot understand the symbolic routinization it imposes on the life of its own residents.

Founded and governed by a bolero singer, Lorelei displays the paternalist features of a *soft authoritarianism* that combines the suppression of politics with the degradation of the popular. Padded by a thick tapestry of media-generated images, Lorelei shows that an abundance of images also effectively produces symbolic impoverishment. Nobody who visits it and is won over by its charm can undertake the operations necessary for the construction of some meaning, because in Lorelei, there are no signs—only simulacra of signs: a gigantic collage of cultural garbage.

The government of Lorelei can be imagined as an extraordinary electronic switchboard: Laser beams write messages in the sky. One of these defines the philosophical ideal of the city: "One nation, one in work. One nation, one in song." With this fusion of the practical and the aesthetic, we have arrived at the end of history, where conflict has been resolved by the technical production of a complete symbolic unity built around the idea of happiness. Every morning, Campomanes, the bolero singer and benevolent dictator, broadcasts a message that is anxiously awaited: It is always the same and, nevertheless, its repetition is necessary, because it tranquilizes and unifies. The daily message is the locus of identification between the inhabitants and the visitors. Precisely because it does not communicate anything, because it does not open discourse but rather closes it, because it repeatedly refuses to produce disharmony, because it protects what is known from what is not (the unspoken), the voice and image of Campomanes are indispensable in Lorelei. Campomanes has the triviality of the bolero: He speaks without force, with the uninterrupted flow of an obscene serenity.

Other messages written with lasers in the sky describe the instability of the outside world: Governments fall, politicians are assassinated, violence and hunger punish all nations that are not like Lorelei. The residents of Lorelei have arrived there after passing through prisons and rehabilitation camps, after marginality, drug addiction, and political failures: Their histories belong to what we call *history*. Therefore, the government of Lorelei views the residents with distrust, watches them, and humiliates them with the label "social indefinites." They are the *memento mori*, the skull on the playing field. Nevertheless, Lorelei needs them not only as manual laborers but as the reminders of a world where conflict still exists.

Lorelei is surrounded by a belt of garbage, and the decomposing material, enclosed in containers, emits an odor that evokes nature. The authorities police this zone with particular care, to keep people from seeing the garbage. The spectacle of decaying nature would produce a fissure in the perfect surface of the media-produced simulacrum of nature that Campomanes has designed for his city. Lorelei does not destroy nature the way predatory capitalism does. It simply replaces nature, covering it over with machines that imitate it: lasers, projections, holographs, electronic sounds, robots that represent men and women along the roads bidding welcome to the city. The world is duplicated in an abyss: "A terrestrial globe which transmitted telephotographs of the five continents from the roof of a fortified house"; Girl Scouts and Boy Scouts sell pictures of Iberian fauna. Nature has been expelled from Lorelei to conserve only produced images, artifices that lack authenticity and that cannot therefore generate a sense of the sacred, nor any distance or conflict. Happiness has finished with history, mechanical reproduction with nature, Campomanes's technical and communicative providence with politics. The symbolic misery of this state seeks the superabundance of the simulacrum and the icon. Everything is scenography and, as a consequence, no scene can be constructed in which a middle distance is possible, the separation between stage and spectator from which some kind of meaning can be produced. Campomanes circulates his discourse to the point of saturation in a communicative space totally constituted by the mass media. His government administers the images and sounds in an absurd cultural collage that, incorporating all nations and languages, negates differences instead of accentuating them. It is the communicative populism of an authoritarian regime devoid of politics.

The emblems of another culture different from the banal poetics of Lorelei languish in the margins of the city where the "social indefinites" live. There, the necessity that governs everything can secretly change into chance or violence; the order that stipulates the perceptions and sensations in the center of the city is disorganized at its borders; the compact, electronic space unravels and the laser messages can literally be read at a distance. Bereft of a plan of their own, the margins preserve aspects of the outside world: music, moral indignation, emotional solidarity, art made with scraps from previous cultures and not with the prefabricated pieces of electronic culture. More than an alternative society, this marginal space in Lorelei seems like a reminiscence of another historical period. The defeated remember and, as often happens today in many of the big cities of the West, they build a submerged city out of rusty leftovers: something like a flooded city, an ambiguous object that clearly differentiates itself from the one-dimensional icons of Lorelei.

Television

The questions presented in a futurist allegorical key by Cohen's novel made themselves dramatically present in the television coverage of the Gulf War. In accordance with the aesthetics of electronic war, the actual images of the bombs exploding on the computer screens of the aircraft seemed less real than those of a video game; at the same time, they entered into the stock of images that the networks transmitted in tandem with their centralized information technology to produce what amounted to a unified planetary gaze on the military scenario. The war was electronic and controlled by remote for two reasons: the new forms of combat and the new forms of representing combat. Neither of these was decisive in itself, but together they made possible a "natural" (so to speak) fusion of military and communicative technologies.

Accustomed to other wars, we waited for the moment when the casualties would appear, the "concrete particular," the specific. But this war had only two dimensions, not because we viewed it on the two-dimensional screen of our televisions but because the referents of its representation were also two-dimensional: As in a structure of *mise-en-abyme*, what was on the screen of one monitor was transmitted through the screen of another monitor. The complex visual mannerism of the representation was established by distance and aerial perspective; the poor resolution of the human and geographical details was counterpointed by the high resolution of the definitive destructive moment, the explosion of the bomb. The reification of the war in this communicative syntax destabilized the particular and dispensed with resources that tend to construct a sense of verisimilitude. In the abyss of successive screens, one could almost believe that the war wasn't happening. The scarce close-ups of the war were shown in press conferences whose own *mise-en-scène* called for foreground and middle-ground shots that the representations of the combat itself avoided. There were also those "human-interest" stories inspired by Hollywood stereotypes: soldiers—men and women, whites, Hispanics, and blacks—leaning against their jeeps, dressed in camouflage, prepared but not tense, determined yet smiling (with that typically North American use of the smile that contradicts other gestural conventions). The close-ups and human interest stories furnished the gossip pages or "local" news of the conflict, so to speak. The picture they invoked was completely out of bad movies: war as a nonhierarchical game, respectful of legitimate differences, open to all minorities. In this way, the American army's system of recruitment, which favors the enlistment of the poor, of Hispanics, blacks, and women not for democratic reasons but because they are the ones who have, in fact, the fewest career opportunities and choices, found in the televised representation of the war an icon of freedom of choice and equality of opportunity.

The other overriding image of the war was ecological destruction. In this case, the referent (because it implied the possible death of the planet) lent itself to the extreme close-up rather than to the *mise-en-abyme* of video-game aesthetics: The picture of the albatross covered with oil was an icon spectacularly suited to a nonpolitical use of the ecological program, to the romanticizing of conservation and environmentalism in a hypostasis of the political. The public could get angry with Saddam Hussein for immediately understandable reasons (the defense of nature) and could echo the ecological laments, now void of any politics and replete with a sentimentalism that did not always extend to Iraqi children, women, and the elderly. That the destruction of the ecosystem, in fact, began, and continues, with the irrational use of energy sources in the West, a phenomenon that if imitated by all the countries of the Third World would rapidly make the planet uninhabitable, was conveniently occluded; instead, the catastrophe was seen as something inaugurated by the homicidal and barbarous actions of Saddam Hussein. The deeper causes of the conflict, which have to do as much with California's crowded highways as with Saddam Hussein's savage irrationality, were out of the picture.

Like the invasion of Panama, the Gulf War was a televised intervention. Saddam Hussein and Noriega could not be defended in and of themselves, and the regimes they led were also indefensible for too many reasons. Those who proposed nonviolent alternatives to war were obliged, therefore, to appeal to general principles and universal values. To think about the war from a nonmilitary perspective was extremely difficult and required ideological dispositions, habits of discussion, and analytical capacities that are generally acquired in the exercise of political deliberation and debate.[2] By contrast, the Gulf War was imposed with the support of slogans that derived from the media aesthetics of both the new and old schools: an intense dramatization of the characters, a system of representation that forces immediate identifications; the suspension of analysis and value clarification in favor of the constitution of a unified field of allies and enemies; and an identification of the values supposedly at stake in the war with those of "our" way of life. It will be said that all wars produce these effects of alienation and that jingoism is not the product of the audiovisual representation of this particular one. True, but in this case, what it would have been necessary to know in order to debate the war was rhetorically expelled by the narrative of the mass media. In the rhetoric of friends and enemies, political deliberation is impossible.[3]

Let me take up again the point that the electronic aesthetic renounces representation not by virtue of a sense of the crisis of representation or its critique (which would be the starting point of the historical avant-garde in this century) but rather through the substitution of the sign by the simulacrum. This is what happens in the video game (of which Latin American cities are now full), where the screen simulates nature, cultural objects, and human beings in a way that does not refer to a referent other than the one produced by the possibilities of the software itself. The increasing naturalism of the simulacrum[4] in these games is invariably accompanied by the knowledge that there is no temporally previous referent for the image, that the simulacrum is, instead, the result of the encounter between software and player. Nothing refers to a reality outside of the game nor to the problems that the existence of an outside posed in the past for both elite or popular art. The images are simulacra in the strongest sense, and this increases, rather than diminishes, their hypnotic power: Since there is no question of the truth or the real here (however one wants to define them), all questions have to do with effectiveness, skill, speed, and distance. The modern obsession with the distinction between levels of representation (which also has to do with the modern obsession with language) disappears because levels of representation no longer exist. Differentiated scenarios do not exist

2. Something similar occurred during the Malvinas War, equally removed from the point of view of representation and also difficult to think about outside of the simplifying contexts of triumphant patriotism that the military dictatorship imposed.

3. See the analysis of this problematic in Prieto Ingrao, "Contra la reducción de la política a guerra" (Against the reduction of politics to war), *Punto de Vista* 20 (May 1984).

4. I am referring to the new software programs that simulate naturalistic human figures and to what is coming to be known as "virtual reality," as in the film *Total Recall*.

in the sense that everything is the staging of a simulacrum. Transformed into a video game, the Gulf War presents the problems of a video game, affecting at the discursive level the possibilities of symbolic processing, and naturalizing as a simulacrum something that possesses concrete outside referents. There is nothing to decipher except that which appears on the screen; even the question of whether an exterior reality can manage to postulate itself as a referent will be processed according to the rules of representational Manichaeanism that govern media aesthetics.

The representation of the war also borrowed from the video clip. Like the video game, a clip *completely* constructs its reference; it does not produce its estrangement from the concrete particular by abstraction but rather through recourse to fragmentation and to what could be called *simulated narration*. This refers to a syntax of fragments that operates as if they were narration without really being it, not because they openly negate narrative diegesis but because they present an action that lacks both progression and repetition, overall structure and individual characters, spatial-temporal relationships or the negation of these, and a hypotactic system or any other kind of subordination. Narration without law, the video clip imposes itself as a space where values are not negotiated, where perceptions are not disorganized because they do not come out of an organized perceptual discourse in the first place, where narration is not abandoned but simply ignored. A pure product of the chemistry of image transformation and of montage techniques introduced over a half-century ago and now recycled, the video clip considers speed its principal virtue. The referential disorder of the video clip has a lot in common with the referential absence of the video game.

At this point, I would like to introduce some historical perspective into this phenomenology. If it cannot be said that the realist novel and the serialized story, or its lower-class double, the *feuilleton*, molded nineteenth-century perception by themselves, it is possible, on the other hand, to assert that the mode of organization provided by the poetics of realism formed part of the cultural apprenticeship that accompanied the process of alphabetization and education that constituted a new kind of public (notably in the popular sectors). The reorganization of narration by realism displaces or mixes with other narrative possibilities (those of folklore, religion, and myth). It was precisely with nineteenth-century aesthetics that a public sphere was constituted in Latin America, in a process that extends from the cultural nationalism of the romantics to the social Darwinism of the positivist liberals. The novel was the depository of discursive and practical skills that could be exercised in political agitation, journalism, and in the organization of social networks, including the first unions, mutual aid associations and co-operatives, public libraries, and popular universities.[5] Politics and pedagogy were united in progressive Latin American thought at the end of the nineteenth and the beginning of the twentieth centuries, notably in the socialist paradigm but also in anarchism and advanced democratic liberalism.

We still do not know enough about the cultural impact of the new audiovisual forms, which are no longer emergent but dominant; in any case, the media representation of the war should not seem too strange from a Latin American perspective where, as we have seen, elections in many countries are already subject to a spectacular audiovisual processing, with media experts serving as frontline agents for the candidates and media "spots" producing some of the most significant symbolic condensations of their campaigns. The aura of the politicians such as Fujimori, Menem, and Collor is more related to the star system of the media than to the *cursus honorum* of institutions.

Celebration or Critique?

In the last ten years, several Latin American countries have gone from military dictatorship, to redemocratization, to rightist governments such as those of Fujimori, Menem, and Collor that now are dispensing with the values that had reconfigured political culture in a democratic direction at the beginning of the eighties. This, on one hand. On the other hand are the changes in the electronic, audiovisual sphere, and in popular and youth cultures, changes that are heralded or lamented under the label of post-modernism, but that basically signify a distanced relationship to politics considered in traditional institutional terms, with the public sphere seen as a space of generalizable, collective practices. Or, if one wants to put it optimistically, a withdrawal of politics toward areas that are difficult to define in terms of the known separation between the private and the public.

The hegemony of the mass media over the public sphere confirms, a quarter of a century later, the predictions of MacLuhan. Should we celebrate the transformations of modernity because, like the Lucky Man of Lindsay

---

5. On this point, see Leandro Gutiérrez and Luis Alberto Romero, "Sociedades barriales, bibliotecas populares y formación de la cultura de los sectores populares" (Working-class neighborhoods, popular libraries, and the cultural formation of the popular sectors), *Desarrollo Económico* 29 (April–June 1989).

Anderson's film, or Dr. Pangloss explaining the world to Candide, we always find reason for hope? Is it possible to live our present as if it were a past: a formation that can be the object of explanatory discourse but not a point of opposition or resistance? This somewhat juvenile and somber optimism mirrors the pessimism that accompanies it like a shadow.

In the face of the latest video clip, the latest video game, and their prolongations in the aesthetics that the media decants to politics, critical thought should not renounce the tension that precisely made it significant in the constitution of the public sphere. But at the same time, the Adornian dissatisfaction with the present puts limits on a critique that would seek to compete for an ideological and political place in the public sphere. We are trapped in a double bind, children of the crisis of modernity but, at the same time, constituted in it; submerged in the obscene communicative abundance of the culture industry, we vacillate between the temptation to convert it to the religion of ideas or destroy it as an infernal deus ex machina, the latest weapon invented by capitalism in its implacable and progressive occupation of the cultural dimensions of life.

It seems to me that we cannot offer theoretical answers that improve on the populist celebration of the fait accompli when we confuse the desires of the public with the strategies of the culture industry, forgetting the processes of social conformation of taste and the habits of symbolic consumption. At risk is the possibility of the loss of the public sphere as a global space that posits itself as alternative and complementary to the atomization of the public in totally regionalized issues (by sex, ethnicity, age, etc.). This would be the truly grave consequence, celebrated or not, of postmodern dispersion. Perhaps, between the authoritarian dream of the total transparency of meanings and practices and the nightmare of a world occupied by a single discourse unified through the rhetoric of the electronic media, the possibility of optimism has been done away with. Nevertheless, in its own way, the principle of criticism can help to avoid hopelessness.

National by Imitation

Roberto Schwarz

We Brazilians and other Latin Americans constantly experience the artificial, inauthentic, and imitative nature of our cultural life. An essential element in our critical thought since independence, it has been variously interpreted from romantic, naturalist, modernist, right-wing, left-wing, cosmopolitan, and nationalist points of view, so we may suppose that the problem is enduring the deeply rooted. Before attempting another explanation, let us assume that this malaise is a fact. Its everyday manifestations range from the inoffensive to the horrifying. Examples of inappropriateness include Father Christmas sporting an Eskimo outfit in a tropical climate and, for traditionalists, the electric guitar in the land of samba. Representatives of the 1964 dictatorship often used to say that Brazil was not ready for democracy, that it would be out of place here. In the nineteenth century people spoke of the gulf between the empire's liberal façade, copied from the British parliamentary system, and the actual reality of the system of labor, which was slavery. In his "Lundu do Escritor Difícil" Mário de Andrade [1] ridiculed his fel-

---

1. *Mário de Andrade* (1893–1945), novelist, poet and critic, was the acknowledged leader of the modernist movement in Brazil and bore the brunt of the initial scandal that it caused. The language of his *Macunaíma: The Hero without Any Character* (1928) synthesizes idioms and dialects from all the regions of Brazil. [*Trans.*]

low countrymen whose knowledge spanned only foreign matters. Recently, when the São Paulo state government extended its human rights policy to the prisons, there were demonstrations of popular discontent at the idea that such guarantees should be introduced inside prisons when so many people did not enjoy them outside. In this perspective, even human rights seem spurious in Brazil. These examples, taken from unrelated spheres and presupposing incompatible points of view, show how widespread the problem is. They all involve the same sense of contradiction between the real Brazil and the ideological prestige of the countries used as models.[2]

Let us examine the problem from the point of view of literary studies. In twenty years of teaching the subject I have witnessed a transition in literary criticism from impressionism, through positivist historiography, American New Criticism, stylistics, Marxism, phenomenology, structuralism, poststructuralism, and now Reception theories. The list is impressive and demonstrates our university's efforts to overcome provincialism. But it is easy to see that the change from one school of thought to another rarely arises from the exhaustion of a particular project; usually it expresses the high regard that Brazilians feel for the newest doctrine from America or Europe. The disappointing impression created, therefore, is one of change and development with no inner necessity and therefore no value. The thirst for terminological and doctrinal novelty prevails over the labor of extending knowledge and is another illustration of the imitative nature of our cultural life. We shall see that the problem has not been correctly posed, although we may start by accepting its relative validity.

In Brazil intellectual life seems to start from scratch with each generation.[3] The hankering for the advanced countries' latest products nearly always has as its reverse side a lack of interest in the work of the previous generation of Brazilian writers, and results in a lack of intellectual continuity. As Machado de Assis noted in 1879, "A foreign impetus determines the direction of movement." What is the meaning of this passing over of the internal impulse, which is today much less inevitable than it was then? You do not have to be a traditionalist or believe in an impossible intellectual autarky to recognize the difficulties. There is a lack of conviction, both in the constantly changing theories and in their relationship to the movement of society as a whole. As a result little importance is attached to work itself

2. For a balanced and considered opinion on the subject, see Antonio Candido, "Literatura e subdesenvolvimento," *Argumento* 1 (Oct. 1973).
3. This observation was made by Vinicius Dantas.

or to the object of investigation. Outstanding analyses and research on the country's culture are periodically cut short and problems that have been identified and tackled with great difficulty are not developed as they deserve. This bias is negatively confirmed by the stature of a few outstanding writers such as Machado de Assis,[4] Mário de Andrade, and now Antonio Candido. None of them lacked information or an openness to contemporary trends, but they all knew how to make broad and critical use of their predecessors' work, which they regarded not as dead weight but as a dynamic and unfinished element underlying present-day contradictions.

It is not a question of continuity for its own sake. We have to identify a set of real, specific problems—with their own historical insertion and duration—that can draw together existing forces and allow fresh advances to be made. With all due respect to the theoreticians we study in our faculties, I believe we would do better to devote ourselves to a critical assessment of the ideas put forward by Silvio Romero,[5] Oswald and Mário de Andrade, Antonio Candido, the concretists, and the CPCs.[6] A certain degree of cultural density arises out of alliances or disagreements between scientific disciplines, artistic, social and political groups, without which the idea of breaking away in pursuit of the new becomes meaningless. We should bear in mind that to many Latin Americans Brazil's intellectual life appears to have an enviably organic character, and, however incredible it may seem, there may be some relative truth in this view.

Little remains of the conceptions and methods that we have passed under review, since the rhythm of change has not allowed them to attain a mature expression. There is a real problem here, part of that feeling of inappropriateness from which we started out. Nothing seems more reason-

4. *Joaquim Maria Machado de Assis* (1839–1908) is regarded as the greatest of all Portuguese-language novelists. He wrote nine novels and two hundred short stories, including *Epitaph of a Small Winner* (1880), *Dom Casmurro* (1890) and *Esau and Jacob* (1904), which are considered to be far ahead of their time. [*Trans.*]

5. *Sílvio Romero* (1851–1914) wrote the first modern history of Brazilian literature, a work which is still of interest today, despite the scientistic language of the period. [*Trans.*]

6. The *Centro Popular de Cultura* (CPC) was established in 1961 at the start of the social ferment that ended with the military coup in 1964. The movement was created under the auspices of the National Union of Students, which wanted to fuse together artistic irreverence, political teaching, and the people. It produced surprisingly inventive cinema, theater, and other stage performances. Several of its members became major artistic figures: Glauber Rocha, Joaquim Pedro de Andrade and Ferreira Gullar, among others. The convergence of the student and popular movements gave rise to completely new artistic possibilities. [*Note supplied by Ana McMac*].

able, for those who are aware of the damage, than to steer in the opposite direction and think it is enough to avoid copying metropolitan trends in order to achieve an intellectual life with greater substance. This conclusion is illusory, as we shall see, but has strong intuitive support. For a time it was taken up by nationalists of both the Right and the Left in a convergence that boded ill for the Left and, through its wide diffusion, contributed to a low intellectual level and an overestimation of ideological vulgarity.

The search for genuine (i.e., unadulterated) national roots leads us to ask: What would popular culture be like if it were possible to isolate it from commercial interests and particularly from the mass media? What would a national economy be like if there were no foreign admixture? Since 1964 the internationalization of capital, the commodification of social relations, and the presence of the mass media have developed so rapidly that these very questions have come to seem implausible. Yet barely twenty years ago they still excited intellectuals and figured on their agenda. A combative frame of mind still prevailed—for which progress would result from a kind of *reconquista,* or rather from the expulsion of the invaders. Once imperialism had been pushed back, its commercial and industrial forms of culture neutralized, and its allied, antinational section of the bourgeoisie isolated, the way would be clear for the flowering of national culture, which had been distorted by these elements as by an alien body. This correct emphasis on the mechanisms of U.S. domination served to mythologize the Brazilian community as object of patriotic fervor, whereas a class analysis would have made this much more problematic. Here a qualification is necessary: such ideas reached their height in the period of the Goulart government, when extraordinary events, which brought about experimentation and democratic realignments on a large scale, were taking place. The period cannot be reduced to the inconsistencies of its self-image, indicative though they are of the illusion inherent in populist nationalism that the outside world is the source of all evil.

In 1964 the right-wing nationalists branded Marxism as an alien influence, perhaps imagining that fascism was a Brazilian invention. But over and above their differences, the two nationalist tendencies were alike in hoping to reach their goal by eliminating anything that was not indigenous. The residue would be the essence of Brazil. The same illusion was popular in the last century, but at that time the new national culture owed more to diversification of the European models than to exclusion of the Portuguese. Opponents of the liberal romantic distortion of Brazilian society did not arrive at the authentic country, since once French and English imports had been rooted out, the colonial order was restored. And that was a Portuguese creation. The paradox of this kind of purism is apparent in Lima Barreto's character, Policarpo Quaresma, whose quest for authenticity led him to write in Tupi, a language foreign to him.[7] The same goes for Antonio Callado's *Quarup,* in which the real Brazil is found not in the colonial past— as suggested by Lima Barreto's hero—but in the heart of the interior, far from the Atlantic coast, with its overseas contacts. A group of characters mark the center of the country on a map and go off in search of it. After innumerable adventures they reach their destination, where they find . . . an ants' nest.

The standard U.S. models that arrived with the new communications networks were regarded by the nationalists as an unwelcome foreign presence. The next generation, however, already breathing naturally in this air, considered nationalism to be archaic and provincial. For the first time, as far as I know, the idea spread that it was a worthless enterprise to defend national characteristics against imperialist uniformity. The culture industry would cure the sickness of Brazilian culture—at least for those who were willing to delude themselves.

In the 1960s nationalism also came under fire from those who thought of themselves as politically and artistically more advanced. Their views are now being taken up in the context of international mass media, only this time without the elements of class struggle and anti-imperialism. In this "world" environment of uniform mythology, the struggle to establish an "authentic" culture appears as a relic from the past. Its illusory nature becomes evident, and it seems a provincial phenomenon associated with archaic forms of oppression. The argument is irrefutable, but it must be said that in the new context an emphasis on the international dimension of culture becomes no more than a legitimation of the existing mass media. Just as nationalists used to condemn imperialism and hush up bourgeois oppression, so the antinationalists invoke the authoritarianism and backwardness of their opponents, with good reason, while suggesting that the reign of mass communication is either emancipatory or aesthetically acceptable. A "postmodern" critical position, perhaps, but one that is fundamentally conformist. There is another imaginary reversal of roles: although the "glo-

7. Policarpo Quaresma is the hero of the novel *Triste fim de Policarpo Quaresma* (1915) by Alfonso Henriques de Lima Barreto (1881–1922). The hero is a caricature patriot, if a sympathetic character, who gradually becomes disillusioned with the state of Brazil.

balists" operate within the dominant ideology of our time, they defend their positions as if they were being hunted down, or as if they were part of the heroic vanguard, aesthetic or libertarian, of the early twentieth century; they address the authorities in the manner of one who is starting a revolution.

In the same order of paradox, we can see that the imposition of foreign ideology and the cultural expropriation of the people are realities that do not cease to exist just because there is mystification in the nationalists' theories about them. Whether they were right or wrong, the nationalists became involved in actual conflicts, imparting to them a certain degree of visibility. The mass media postmodernists, though right in their criticisms, imagine a universalist world that does not exist. It is a question of choosing between the old and the new error, both upheld in the name of progress. The sight of the Avenida Paulista is a fine illustration of what I mean: ugly mansions, once used by the rich to flaunt their wealth, now seem perversely tolerable at the foot of modern skyscrapers, both for reasons of proportion and because of the poetry that emanates from any historically superseded power.

Recent French philosophy has been another factor in the discrediting of cultural nationalism. Its antitotalizing tendency, its preference for levels of historicity alien to the national milieu, its dismantling of conventional literary scaffolding such as authorship, "the work," influence, originality, and so on—all these destroy, or at least discredit, that romantic correspondence between individual heroism, masterly execution, and collective redemption which imbues the nationalist schemas with their undeniable knowledge value and potential for mystification. To attack these coordinates can be exciting and partially convincing, besides appeasing national sensibility in an area where one would least expect this to be possible.

A commonplace idea suggests that the copy is secondary with regard to the original, depends upon it, is worth less, and so on. Such a view attaches a negative sign to the totality of cultural forces in Latin America and is at the root of the intellectual malaise that we are discussing. Now, contemporary French philosophers such as Foucault and Derrida have made it their business to show that such hierarchies have no basis. Why should the prior be worth more than the posterior, the model more than the imitation, the central more than the peripheral, the economic infrastructure more than cultural life, and so forth? According to the French philosophers, it is a question of conditioning processes (but are they all of the same order?)—prejudices that do not express the life of the spirit in its real movement but reflect the orientations inherent in the traditional human sciences. In their view, it would be more accurate and unbiased to think in terms of an infinite sequence of transformations, with no beginning or end, no first or last, no worse or better. One can easily appreciate how this would enhance the self-esteem and relieve the anxiety of the underdeveloped world, which sees itself as tributary to the central countries. We would pass from being a backward to an advanced part of the world, from a deviation to a paradigm, from inferior to superior lands (although the analysis set out to suppress just such superiority). All this because countries that live in the humiliation of having to imitate are more willing than the metropolitan countries to give up the illusion of an original source, even though the theory originated there and not here. Above all, the problem of mirror-culture would no longer be ours alone, and instead of setting our sights on the Europeanization or Americanization of Latin America we would, in a certain sense, be participating in the "Latin Americanization" of the central cultures.[8]

It remains to be seen whether this conceptual break with the primacy of origins would enable us to balance out or combat relations of actual subordination. Would the innovations of the advanced world suddenly become dispensable once they had lost the distinction of originality? In order to use them in a free and nonimitative manner, it is not enough simply to divest them of their sacred aura. Contrary to what the above analysis might lead us to believe, the breaking down of cultural dazzlement in the underdeveloped countries does not go to the heart of a problem that is essentially practical in character. Solutions are reproduced from the advanced world in response to cultural, economic and political needs, and the notion of copying, with its psychologistic connotations, throws no light whatsoever on this reality. If theory remains at this level, it will continue to suffer from the same limitations, and the radicalism of an analysis that passes over efficient causes will become in its turn largely delusive. The inevitability of cultural imitation is bound up with a specific set of historical imperatives over which abstract philosophical critiques can exercise no power. Even here nationalism is the weak part of the argument, and its supercession at the level of philosophy has no purchase on the realities to which it owes its strength. It should be noted that while nationalism has recently been almost absent from serious intellectual debate, it has a growing presence in the administration of culture, where, for better or worse, it is impossible to escape from

8. See Silviano Santiago, "O Entre-lugar do discurso latino-americano," in *Uma literatura nos trópicos,* São Paulo (1978); and Haroldo de Campos, "Da razão antropofágica: diálogo e diferença na cultura brasileira," *Boletim Bibliográfico Biblioteca Mário de Andrade,* 44 (Jan.–Dec. 1983).

the national dimension. Now that economic, though not political, space has become international—which is not the same as homogeneous—this return of nationalism by the back door reflects the insuperable paradox of the present day.

In the 1920s, Oswald de Andrade's "anthropophagous" *Pau-Brasil* program also tried to give a triumphalist interpretation of our backwardness.[9] The disharmony between bourgeois models and the realities of rural patriarchy is at the very heart of his poetry, the first of these two elements appearing in the role of absurd caprice ("Rui Barbosa: A Top Hat in Senegambia").[10] Its true novelty lies in the fact that the lack of accord is a source not of distress but of optimism, evidence of the country's innocence and the possibility of an alternative, nonbourgeois historical development. This *sui generis* cult of progress is rounded out with a technological wager: Brazil's innocence (the result of Christianization and only superficial *embourgeoisement*) plus technology equals utopia; modern material progress will make possible a direct leap from prebourgeois society to paradise. Marx himself, in his famous letter of 1881 to Vera Zasulich, came up with a similar hypothesis that the Russian peasant commune would achieve socialism without a capitalist interregnum, thanks to the means made available by progress in the West. Similarly, albeit in a register combining jokes, provocation, philosophy of history, and prophecy (as, later, in the films of Glauber Rocha), Anthropophagy set itself the aim of leaping a whole stage.

Returning once more to the idea that Western culture has been inappropriately copied in Brazil, we can see that Oswald's program introduced a change of tone. Local primitivism would give back a modern sense to tired European culture, liberating it from Christian mortification and capitalist utilitarianism. Brazil's experience would be a differentiated cornerstone, with utopian powers, on the map of contemporary history. (The poems of Mário de Andrade and Raul Bopp[11] on Amazonian slothfulness contain a similar

9. *Oswald de Andrade* introduced European avant-garde ideas into Brazil. His *Manifesto da Poesia Pau-Brasil* (1924) and *Manifesto Antropófago* (1928) are the most daring writings of the "modern movement" (*Modernismo*) that emerged in 1922, attacking academic values and respectability and championing poetry written in the Brazilian vernacular. [*Trans.*]

10. Rui Barbosa (1849–1923) was a prominent liberal politician regarded in the early twentieth century as a model of culture, linguistic purity, and erudition. He achieved an almost mythical status, becoming known as "The Eagle of the Hague" for his diplomacy at an international conference there in 1906. In Oswald's phrase, obviously, it is the incongruity of such false representatives of high culture in Brazil that is underlined.

11. The greatest achievement of Raul Bopp (b. 1898) was his "cannibalist" poem "Cobra Norato" (1921), an exploration of the Amazon jungle. [*Trans.*]

idea.) Modernism therefore brought about a profound change in values: for the first time the processes underway in Brazil were weighed in the context of the present-day world as having something to offer in that larger context. Oswald de Andrade advocated cultural irreverence in place of subaltern obfuscation, using the metaphor of "swallowing up" the alien: a copy, to be sure, but with regenerative effect. Historical distance allows us to see the ingenuousness and jingoism contained in these propositions.

The new vogue for Oswald's manifestoes in the 1960s and particularly the 1970s appeared in the very different context of a military dictatorship that, for all its belief in technological progress and its alliance with big capital both national and international, was less repressive than expected in regard to everyday habits and morality. In the other camp, the attempt to overthrow capitalism through revolutionary war also changed the accepted view of what could be termed "radical." This now had no connection with the provincial narrowness of the 1920s, when the *Antropófago* rebellion assumed a highly libertarian and enlightening role. In the new circumstances technological optimism no longer held water, while the brazen cultural irreverence of Oswald's "swallowing up" acquired a sense of exasperation close to the mentality of direct action (although often with good artistic results). Oswald's clarity of construction, penetrating vision, and sense of discovery all suffered as greater value was attached to his primal, "de-moralizing" literary practices. One example of this evolution is the guiltlessness of the act of swallowing up. What was then freedom against Catholicism, the bourgeoisie, and the prestige of Europe became in the 1980s an awkward excuse to handle uncritically those ambiguities of mass culture that stand in need of elucidation. How can one fail to notice that the *Antropófagos*—like the nationalists—take as their subject the abstract Brazilian, with no class specification, or that the analogy with the digestive process throws absolutely no light on the politics and aesthetics of contemporary cultural life?

Since the last century, educated Brazilians—the concept is not meant as a compliment but refers to a social category—have had the sense of living among ideas and institutions copied from abroad that do not reflect local reality. It is not sufficient, however, to give up borrowing in order to think and live more authentically. Besides, one cannot so much as conceive of giving them up. Nor is the problem eliminated by a philosophical deconstruction of the concept of copy. The programmatic innocence of the *Antropófagos,* which allowed them to ignore the malaise, does not prevent it from emerging anew. "Tupi or not Tupi, that is the question!" Oswald's fa-

mous saying, with its contradictory use of the English language, a classical
line, and a play on words to pursue the search for national identity, itself
says a great deal about the nature of the impasse.

The problem may appear simpler in historical perspective. Sílvio
Romero, despite many absurdities, made a number of excellent remarks
on the matter. The following extract is taken from his book on Machado de
Assis, written in 1897 to prove that this greatest Brazilian writer produced
nothing but a literature of Anglomania, incompetent, unattuned, slavish:

> Meanwhile a kind of absurdity developed . . . a tiny intellectual elite
> separated itself off from the mass of the population, and while the
> majority remained almost entirely uneducated, this elite, being par-
> ticularly gifted in the art of learning and copying, threw itself into
> political and literary imitation of everything it found in the Old World.
> So now we have an exotic literature and politics, which live and
> procreate in a hothouse that has no relationship to the outside tem-
> perature and environment. This is the bad side of our feeble, illusory
> skill of mestizo southerners, passionate, given to fantasy, capable of
> imitation but organically unsuited to create, invent or produce things
> of our own that spring from the immediate or remote depths of our
> life and history.
>
> In colonial times, a skilful policy of segregation cut us off from for-
> eigners and kept within us a certain sense of cohesion. This is what
> gave us the so-called Minas group of Arcadian poets who flourished
> in the interior, gold-mining area of the country in the latter half of
> the eighteenth century: Basilio, Durão, Gonzaga, Alvarenga Peixoto,
> Claudio and Silva Alvarenga, who all worked in a milieu of exclusively
> Portuguese and Brazilian ideas.
>
> With the first emperor and the Regency, the first breach [opened]
> in our wall of isolation by Dom João VI grew wider, and we began to
> copy the political and literary romanticism of the French.
>
> We aped the Charter of 1814 and transplanted the fantasies of
> Benjamin Constant; we mimicked the parliamentarism and constitu-
> tional politics of the author of *Adolphe,* intermingled with the poetry
> and dreams of the author of *René* and *Atala.*
>
> The people . . . remained illiterate.
>
> The Second Reign [that of Emperor Pedro II, which lasted from
> 1840 to 1889], whose policy was for fifty years vacillating, uncertain
> and incompetent, gradually opened all the gates in a chaotic manner
> lacking any criteria or sense of discrimination. Imitation, mimicking of

everything—customs, laws, codes, verse, theatre, novel—was the general rule.

Regular sailings assured direct communication with the old continent and swelled the tide of imitation and servile copying. . . .

This is why, in terms of copying, mimicry and pastiches to impress the gringos, no people has a better Constitution on paper . . . , everything is better . . . on paper. The reality is appalling.[12]

Sílvio Romero's account and analysis are uneven, sometimes incompatible. In some instances it is the story that is interesting, in others the ideology, so that the modern reader will want to examine them separately. The basic schema is as follows: a tiny elite devotes itself to copying Old World culture, separating itself off from the mass of the population, which remains uneducated. As a result, literature and politics come to occupy an exotic position, and we become incapable of *creating things of our own that spring from the depths of our life and history.* Implicit in this demand is the norm of an organic, reasonably homogeneous national culture with popular roots— a norm that cannot be reduced to a mere illusion of literary history or of romanticism, since in some measure it expresses the conditions of modern citizenship. It is in its opposition to this norm that the Brazilian configuration—Europeanized minority, uneducated majority—constitutes an *absurdity.* On the other hand, in order to make the picture more realistic, we should remember that the organic requirement arose at the same time as the expansion of imperialism and organized science—two tendencies that rendered obsolete the idea of a harmonious and auto-centered national culture.

The original sin, responsible for the severing of connections, was the copy. Its negative effects already made themselves felt in the social fissure between *culture* (unrelated to its surroundings) and *production* (not springing from the depths of our life). However, the disproportion between cause and effects is such that it raises some doubts about the cause itself, and Sílvio Romero's own remarks are an invitation to follow a different line of argument from the one he pursues. Let us also note in passing that it is in the nature of an absurdity to be avoidable, and that Romero's argument and invective actually suggest that the elite had an obligation to correct the error that had separated it from the people. His critique was seeking to make the class gulf intolerable for *educated people,* since in a country recently

12. Sílvio Romero, *Machado de Assis* (Rio de Janeiro, 1897), 121–23.

emancipated from slavery the weakness of the popular camp inhibited the emergence of other solutions.

It would seem, then, that for Romero the origins of our cultural absurdity are to be found in the imitative talent of mestizo southerners who have few creative capacities. The *petitio principii* is quite transparent: imitativeness is explained by a (racial) tendency to that very imitativeness that is supposed to be explained. (The author's argument, we should note, itself imitated the scientific naturalism then in vogue in Europe.) Today such explanations can hardly be taken seriously, although it is worth examining them as an ideological mechanism and an expression of their times. If the Brazilians' propensity for copying is racial in origin, why should the elite have been alone in indulging it? If everyone had copied, all the effects of "exoticism" (lack of relation to the environment) and "absurdity" (separation between elite and people) would have vanished as if by magic, and with them the whole problem. It is not copying in general but *the copying of one class* that constitutes the problem. The explanation must lie not in race but in class.

Sílvio Romero goes on to sketch how the vice of imitation developed in Brazil. Absolute zero was in the colonial period, when writers "worked in a milieu of exclusively Portuguese and Brazilian ideas." Could it be that the distance between elite and people was smaller in that epoch? Or the fondness for copying less strong? Surely not—and anyway that is not what the text says. The "cohesion" to which it refers is of a different order, the result of a "skillful policy of segregation"(!) that separated Brazil from everything non-Portuguese. In other words, the comparison between stages lacks an object: the demand for homogeneity points, in one case, to a social structure remarkable for its inequality, and in the other case to the banning of foreign ideas. Still, if the explanation does not convince us, the observation that it seeks to clarify is accurate enough. Before the nineteenth century, the copying of the European model and the distance between educated people and the mass did not constitute an "absurdity." In highly schematic terms, we could say that educated people, in the colonial period, felt solidarity towards the metropolis, Western tradition, and their own colleagues, but not towards the local population. To base oneself on a foreign model, in cultural estrangement from the local surroundings, did not appear to be a defect— quite the contrary! We should not forget that neoclassical aesthetics was itself universalist and greatly appreciated respect for canonical forms, while the theory of art current at that time set a positive value on imitation. As Antonio Candido acutely observed, the Arcadian poet who placed a nymph in the waters of the Carmo was not lacking in originality; he incorporated Minas Gerais into the traditions of the West and, quite laudably, cultivated those traditions in a remote corner of the earth.[13]

The act of copying, then, did not begin with independence and the opening of the ports,[14] as Sílvio Romero would have it. But it is true that only then did it become the insoluble problem which is still discussed today, and which calls forth such terms as "mimickry," "aping" or "pastiche." How did imitation acquire these pejorative connotations?

It is well known that Brazil's gaining of independence did not involve a revolution. Apart from changes in external relations and a reorganization of the top administration, the socioeconomic structure created by colonial exploitation remained intact, though now for the benefit of local dominant classes. It was thus inevitable that modern forms of civilization entailing freedom and citizenship, which arrived together with the wave of political emancipation, should have appeared foreign and artificial, "anti-national," "borrowed," "absurd," or however else critics cared to describe them. The strength of the epithets indicates the acrobatics which the self-esteem of the Brazilian elite was forced into, since it faced the depressing alternative of deprecating the bases of its social preeminence in the name of progress, or deprecating progress in the name of its social preeminence. On the one hand, there were the slave trade, the latifundia and clientelism—that is to say, a set of relations with their own rules, consolidated in colonial times and impervious to the universalism of bourgeois civilization; on the other hand, stymied by these relations, but also stymying them, there was the Law before which everyone was equal, the separation between public and private, civil liberties, parliament, romantic patriotism, and so on. The ensuring of the stable coexistence of these two conceptions, in principle so incompatible, was at the center of ideological and moral preoccupations in Brazil in the nineteenth century. For some, the colonial heritage was a relic to be superceded in the march of progress; for others, it was the real Brazil, to be preserved against absurd imitations. Some wanted to harmonize progress and slave labor, so as not to have to give up either, while still others believed that such a reconciliation already existed, with deleterious moral results. Sílvio Romero, for his part, used conservative arguments

13. Antonio Candido, *Formação da literatura brasileira* (São Paulo, 1969), vol. 1, 74.
14. In the wake of his flight to Brazil, to escape Napoleon's invasion of Portugal in 1807–8, in which he was escorted by the British fleet, King João VI opened the ports of the colony for the first time to non-Portuguese (largely British) shipping.

with a progressive intent, focusing on the "real" Brazil as the continuation of colonial authoritarianism, but doing so in order to attack its foundations. He scorned as ineffectual the "illusory" country of laws, lawyers, and imported culture: "No people has a better Constitution on paper . . . The reality is appalling."

Sílvio Romero's list of "imitations" not to be allowed through customs included fashions, patterns of behavior, laws, codes, poetry, drama, and novels. Judged separately against the social reality of Brazil, these articles were indeed superfluous imports, which would serve to obscure the real state of impoverishment and create an illusion of progress. In their combination, however, they entered into the formation and equipping of the new nation-state, as well as laying the ground for the participation of new elites in contemporary culture. This modernizing force—whatever its imitative appearance and its distance from the daily course of things—became more inseparably bound up with the reality of Brazil than the institution of slave labor, which was later replaced by other forms of forced labor equally incompatible with the aspiration to enlightenment. As time passed, the ubiquitous stamp of "inauthenticity" came to be seen as the most authentic part of the national drama, its very mark of identity. Grafted from nineteenth-century Europe onto a colonial social being, the various perfections of civilization began to follow different rules from those operating in the hegemonic countries. This led to a widespread sense of indigenous pastiche. Only a great figure like Machado de Assis had the impartiality to see a peculiar mode of ideological functioning where other critics could distinguish no more than a lack of consistency. The historian Sergio Buarque de Holanda remarked: "The speed at which the 'new ideas' spread in the old colony, and the fervor with which they were adopted in many circles on the eve of independence, show quite unequivocally that they had the potential to satisfy an impatient desire for change and that the people were ripe for such change. But it is also clear that the social order expressed in these ideas was far from having an exact equivalent in Brazil, particularly outside the cities. The articulation of society, the basic criteria of economic exploitation and the distribution of privileges were so different here that the 'new ideas' could not have the same meaning that was attached to them in parts of Europe or ex-English America."[15]

When Brazil became an independent state, a permanent collabo-

15. Sergio Buarque de Holanda, *Do imperio à república,* vol. 2 (São Paulo, 1977), 77–78.

ration was established between the forms of life characteristic of colonial oppression and the innovations of bourgeois progress. The new stage of capitalism broke up the exclusive relationship with the metropolis, converting local property-owners and administrators into a national ruling class (effectively part of the emergent world bourgeoisie), and yet retained the old forms of labor exploitation, which have not been fully modernized up to the present day. In other words, the discrepancy between the "two Brazils" was not due to an imitative tendency, as Sílvio Romero and many others thought; nor did it correspond to a brief period of transition. It was the lasting result of the creation of a nation-state on the basis of slave labor—which, if the reader will forgive the shorthand, arose in turn out of the English Industrial Revolution and the consequent crisis of the old colonial system. That is to say, *it arose out of modernity itself.*[16] Thus Brazil's backward deformation belongs to the same order of things as the progress of the advanced countries. Sílvio Romero's "absurdities"—in reality, the Cyclopean discords of world capitalism—are not a historical deviation. They are linked to the finality of a single process that, in the case of Brazil, requires the continuation of forced or semiforced labor and a corresponding cultural separation of the poor. With certain modifications, much of it has survived to this day. The panorama now seems to be changing, thanks to the desegregationist impulse of mass consumption and mass communications. These new terms of cultural oppression and expropriation have not yet been much studied.

The thesis of cultural copying thus involves an ideology in the Marxist sense of the term—that is, an illusion supported by appearances. The well-known coexistence of bourgeois principles with those of the ancien régime is here explained in accordance with a plausible and wide-ranging schema, essentially individualist in nature, in which effects and causes are systematically inverted.

For Sílvio Romero, imitation results in the lack of a common denominator between popular and elite culture, and in the elite's low level of permeation by the national. But why not reverse the argument? Why should the imitative character of our life not stem from forms of inequality so brutal that they lack the minimal reciprocity ("common denominator") without

---

16. See Emilia Viotti da Costa, *Da monarquia à república: Momentos decisivos* (São Paulo, 1977), chap. 1; Luis Felipe de Alencastro, "La traité negrière et l'unité nationale brésilienne," *Revue française de l'histoire de l'Outre-Mer* 46 (1979); and Fernando Novais, "Passagens para o Novo Mundo," *Novos Estudos CEBRAP* 9 (July 1984).

which modern society can only appear artificial and "imported"? At a time when the idea of the nation had become the norm, the dominant class's *unpatriotic* disregard for the lives it exploited gave it the feeling of being alien. The origins of this situation in colonialism and slavery are immediately apparent.

The defects normally associated with imitation can be explained in the same way. We can agree with its detractors that the copy is at the opposite pole from originality, from national creativity, from independent and well-adapted judgments, and so on. Absolute domination entails that culture express nothing of the conditions that gave it life, except for that intrinsic sense of futility which a number of writers have been able to represent artistically. Hence the "exotic" literature and politics unrelated to the "immediate or remote depths of our life and history"; hence, too, the lack of "discrimination" or "criteria," and, above all, the intense conviction that all is mere paper. In other words, the painfulness of an imitative civilization is produced not by imitation—which is present at any event—but by the social structure of the country. It is this which places culture in an untenable position, contradicting its very concept of itself, and yet culture was not as sterile, at the time, as Sílvio Romero would have us believe. Nor did the segregated section of society remain unproductive. Its modes of expression would later acquire, for educated intellectuals, the value of a nonbourgeois component of national life, an element serving to fix Brazilian identity (with all the evident ambiguities).

The exposure of cultural transplantation has become the axis of a naive yet widespread critical perspective. Let us conclude by summarizing some of its defects.

1. It suggests that imitation is avoidable, thereby locking the reader into a false problem.

2. It presents as a national characteristic what is actually a malaise of the dominant class, bound up with the difficulty of morally reconciling the advantages of progress with those of slavery or its surrogates.

3. It implies that the elites could conduct themselves in some other way, which is tantamount to claiming that the beneficiary of a given situation will put an end to it.

4. The argument obscures the essential point, since it concentrates its fire on the relationship between elite and model whereas the real crux is the exclusion of the poor from the universe of contemporary culture.

5. Its implicit solution is that the dominant class should reform itself and give up imitation. We have argued, on the contrary, that the answer lies in the workers gaining access to the terms of contemporary life, so that they can redefine them through their own initiative. This, indeed, would be in this context a concrete definition of democracy in Brazil.

6. A copy refers to a prior original existing elsewhere, of which it is an inferior reflection. Such deprecation often corresponds to the self-consciousness of Latin American elites, who attach mythical solidity—in the form of regional intellectual specialization—to the economic, technological and political inequalities of the international order. The authentic and the creative are to the imitative what the advanced countries are to the backward. But one cannot solve the problem by going to the opposite extreme. As we have seen, philosophical objections to the concept of originality tend to regard as nonexistent a real problem that it is absurd to dismiss. Cultural history has to be set in the world perspective of the economics and culture of the left, which attempt to explain our "backwardness" as part of the contemporary history of capital and its advances.[17] Seen in terms of the copy, the anachronistic juxtaposition of forms of modern civilization and realities originating in the colonial period is a mode of nonbeing or even a humiliatingly imperfect realization of a model situated elsewhere. Dialectical criticism, on the other hand, investigates the same anachronism and seeks to draw out a figure of the modern world, set on a course that is either full of promise, grotesque, or catastrophic.

7. The idea of the copy that we have been discussing counterposes national and foreign, original and imitative. These are unreal oppositions which do not allow us to see the share of the foreign in the nationally specific, of the imitative in the original and of the original in the imitative. (In a key study, Paulo Emilio Salles Gomes refers to our "creative lack of competence in copying." [18]) If I am not mistaken, the theory presupposes three elements—a Brazilian subject, the reality of the country, the civilization of the advanced nations—such that the third helps the first to forget the second. This schema is also unreal, and it obscures the organized, cumulative

17. See Celso Furtado, *A Pre-Revolução Brasileira* (Rio de Janeiro, 1962), and Fernando H. Cardoso, *Empresario industrial e desenvolvimento económico no Brasil* (São Paulo, 1964).
18. Paulo Emilio Salles Gomes, "Cinema: trajetória no subdesenvolvimento," *Argumento* 1 (Oct. 1973).

nature of the process, the potent strength even of bad tradition, and the power relations, both national and international, that are in play. Whatever its unacceptable aspects—unacceptable for whom?—Brazilian cultural life has elements of dynamism that display both originality and lack of originality. Copying is not a false problem, so long as we treat it pragmatically, from an aesthetic and political point of view freed from the mythical requirement of creation *ex nihilo.*

Postmodernism, Postleftism, and Neo–Avant-Gardism: The Case of Chile's *Revista de Crítica Cultural*

Hernán Vidal

In my opinion, the nucleus of the postmodernist problematic in Latin America is not in the game of understanding the taxonomies of postmodernism but rather in the attempt to redefine the actual links between aesthetics and politics in an age of catastrophic social changes. It is for this reason that I propose here the study of one of these attempts, that of the *Revista de Crítica Cultural*, a publication initiated in May 1990 in Santiago, Chile, and published three times a year under the editorship of Nelly Richard. The *Revista de Crítica Cultural* assembles personalities of varied trajectory in the artistic and cultural avant-garde that arose in Chile between 1973 and 1990. The journal also recruits works from Latin American and U.S. or European intellectuals identified with postmodernist or poststructuralist positions.

The paradox involved in this study is that it is being undertaken by someone who disbelieves in postmodernist arguments: even more, from the perspective of my own historical materialism, I suspect that to discuss the profile of the forms of subjectivity generated within the unequal and combined development of dependent societies under the label of "postmodern sensibility" is a theoretical diversion, an ideological trap, and a waste of time. I do not think, however, that it is a waste of time to try to understand the way in which a particular group of progressive intellectuals assumed, and responded to, under the label of postmodernism, the social trauma initiated in Chile by the coup of 1973 and the subsequent military dictatorship. I am interested, in other words, not in the concept of postmodernism as such (in its own "metanarrative," so to speak) but in understanding why and how what I will call the neo–avant-garde represented by the *Revista de Crítica Cultural* appropriates the postmodernist problematic and introduces it into Chilean cultural practice as a focal point for political and artistic agitation. What I propose is to paraphrase or transcribe here, in collage fashion, passages from articles by the core contributors of the *Revista*, attempting to produce by these means, against the grain of the journal's own inclination to indeterminacy and the fragmentary, a totalization of its positions, which its own editors have deferred or surrendered to the will of its readers.[1] I want to profile three issues in particular: (1) the journal's "postmodernist" redefinition of Latin American identity; (2) following on this, its repudiation of traditional leftist politics in favor of new forms of cultural micropolitics; and (3) its relationship to the process of redemocratization initiated in Chile toward the end of the 1980s.

The Assumption of the Ontological Monstrosity of the Latin American

I do not believe it is an insult to say that the core contributors of the *Revista* consciously and aggressively assume the notion of the "copy" as one of the articulating forms of postmodern identity. They start from the premise that Latin American history was marked, from its origins on, by a vertical sense of dependence in its relationship to Europe and the United States. Because of this, Latin Americans do not produce knowledge; they are recipients who import and translate it to their medium. This produces a radical ontological alienation, described as a "peculiar ambivalence," insofar as the accumulation of cultural tools in Latin America does not respond to needs that arise from the task of founding and living in the immediate surroundings:[2] "It is like belonging to a tradition of which you are not the

---

1. For this reason, where a number of quotations from a single article occur in the text, I have identified them in the notes only by a general reference to the article rather than to specific page numbers.
2. The quotations that follow are from an interview by Francesco Chiodi with Carlos Pérez

legitimate addressee and in relation to which, therefore, you are delivered to possibilities which are not adequately adjusted to your history, to your landscape, which displace you from your territory, which you cannot define in a precise way. What I want to say is that Europe is constituted before the gaze of a Latin American as other, but curiously as an other which you are inevitably a part of." For this reason, the Latin American space has remained replete with "copies," "reproductions," and "simulacra," all of which generate an obsessive nostalgia for the "originals." From this stems the belief that identity is "referred [to the Latin American] in spectral terms," from a mythical space called "Europe," a place in which the concrete multiplicity of European national identities is dissolved, which therefore "only exists in the Latin American imaginary," and which at a distance "requires that attitude of reverence which is characteristic of relations of dependence and domination": "Latin America, considered culturally in relation to itself, is, to the extent that I understand it, but I insist that this is the personal opinion of a Chilean, the history of this non-identity, of this inappropriate identity."

The negation of historical identity denounces the Latin American as a monstrous being that, in its creative capacity, has only the option of an infinite "game" of the "modification" and "distortion" of the originals. This reveals a malignancy that is prone to "ironic manipulation" and the "resources of ambiguity" and that "becomes explicit [in] the process of degeneration suffered by European discourse as a result of its transference to Latin America." In this degenerative distortion, the Latin American attains an "unrestrained liberty of the imagination," which, by means of "excess," "disarranges," "de-centers," and "violates" the original "models" to the point of making them "irreconcilable" with their copies. In the meantime, "Europe" seeks to discipline and to subdue the Latin American, preventing it from intruding into its own space in its complete monstrosity, dressing it up, trivializing it to the point of changing it into an "invisible" or "simply nonexistent" entity: "I believe that Europe has codified this reality that is Latin America and has blocked all newness, if there is any, which comes from such territories; it has blocked it by installing it in certain stereotypes of, let's put it this way, the exotic. Since the sixties, for example, . . . the image of the raised fist, revolution, indigenism." But, perversely, the Latin American takes revenge on the bad faith of "European" reception by causing its distortion

of the editorial board of the Revista de Crítica Cultural, published in the Revista under the title "La no-identidad Latinoamericana: Una visión peregrina," no. 3, year 2 (1991): 28–32.

of originals to become an "impure mirror," a "blurry mirror," a "shattered mirror" that changes the European into "a monstrous face," "inverted" and "fragmented."

Latin America has been shaped by a psychic system that, in the manner of the identification of the Latin America with Caliban discussed years ago by Roberto Fernández Retamar, assumes the confrontation of a threatening native id with an introjected European superego. The Latin American subject feels judged and victimized, therefore, according to the most archaic and brutal cultural experiences of its history, experiences that reactivate images of the trauma of the Conquest and colonization, condemning it thus to a neurotic existence in the sense that these images are situated in a permanent present, they are relived infinitely and are never overcome.

Nevertheless, with the assumption of this historic monstrosity, the Latin American initiates a "voyage" of "therapeutic virtue": "As a traveller I am going to an encounter with myself, and at the end of this search what is waiting for me is the recognition that my center is always somewhere else; it is the serene acceptance that I construct myself upon an error, upon a fundamental impropriety; that between the synopsis and the original film there is another film, mine." Being one's own film would imply recovering the capacity to examine the surroundings previously saturated by the terror of European magnificence in order to situate the imposed culture in more human and objective terms, thus arriving at the possibility of narrating history without concealment or pathogenic reverence. The aim of this voyage "is to realize that the brilliance of the copies can be more spectacular; that because of their pretensions, their distortions, their impurities, they are more interesting than the self-satisfied original; or, simply, that the original does not exist anymore or is no longer interesting to anyone." Finally, the voyage should lead to a liberating catharsis of energy and the establishment of a cultural identity based on that which was previously only a deficiency and nonidentity: "The alteration suffered because of this transit offers a healthy result: the disappearance of all residue of reverence and the recognition that I am as foreign in Europe as I am in my own home."

If the therapeutic voyage ends with a consciousness of the cultural deterritorialization of the Latin American and with the construction of an identity based on the irreverent manipulation of previously revered symbolic codes, it is because it is propelled by an intimate relationship between self-aggression and the capacity for (aesthetic-political) subversion. It is not surprising, then, that other articles in the Revista de Crítica Cultural expand this at once "therapeutic" and "vanguardist" theme into what is, in effect, a psychoanalysis of Latin American and Chilean culture.

The origin of monstrous identity is indirectly attributed to the irresolution of Oedipal conflict in the colonial moment of the formation of the mestizo as an inferior, secondary caste.[3] In assuming the Spanish symbolic system, in order to insure himself of a family name, a kinship, a lineage and, therefore, a place in society, the male-gendered mestizo did not feel forced to abandon his incestuous desires for the sexual possession of the Indian mother. It was a common practice among the conquistadors to give their Indian concubines to men of socially inferior rank: "For the white father the Indian mother was not an object of competition with the mestizo child because before him she found herself devalorized, degraded to the condition of a slave and concubine. This fact, which could not pass unnoticed by the bastard son, about whom it is known that he always has a special affection for the mother, was enough to encourage in him the incestuous fantasy that his mother belonged to him because of a tacit concession by the father." The consequence is that the mestizo surrenders himself to "a simulacrum of the resolution of the Oedipus complex, not based on the overcoming of his incestuous desires towards the mother and his death-wish against the father, but on their denial."

This denial implies an incapacity of synthesis of opposing terms and generates an always latent and directionless violence in the mestizo bastard: "Illegitimacy is naturally understood as the irregularity of the civil status of the mestizo. But the term hybrid, applied as a qualifier of the nature of the mestizo, requires a supplementary etymological specification. Hybrid derives from the Greek word *hybris*, which means 'unrestrained violence and insolence, lechery and lust' and also 'to break loose, to become unbridled.'" Hybris manifests itself at the same time as the "treason" (to the culture of father) and "exploitation" of the "Indian half-brothers" associated with the maternal culture; but since "because of its [subaltern] location in the place of the Law, [the hybris] has no possibilities of directly expressing itself against the one who sustains it, the destructive tendencies revert towards the interior as self-reproaches and feelings of self-contempt."

Subsequent attempts at Oedipal resolution lead, therefore, to "delirious constructions," such as the mythic amalgamation of maternal and

---

3. The quotations that follow are from César Delgado Díaz del Olmo, "Psicosis y mestizaje," *Revista de Crítica Cultural*, no. 3, year 2 (1991): 38–44. This is a fragment of the text "Psicosis y mestizaje," published in *Vertical* (Arequipa, Peru), no. 3 (1989).

paternal negativities in another monster, "the 'birthing' man and the phallic woman," precursors of machismo. However, this monstrous fusion also leads to an impasse, because it continues to symbolize the Law of the Father: In it are present the father who humiliates, as well as the mother who is silent, who "embodies the reproach of the Law violated" with the prolongation of incest. These acute fluctuations result in a "national character" affected by a "psychosis of oppression." One of its symptoms is the "repudiation of the paternal culture assimilated through colonial imposition, and which is manifested as a rejection of the westernization of the country." The other "is the fixation on the land symbolized as mother," which supports the "geographical nationalisms" characteristic of Latin Americans.

These arguments come to an abrupt end with the suggestion that the resolution of the Oedipus complex comes about with the displacement of national identity from its archaic centering in the "Name of the Father" toward the "name of the nation." This displacement would be "related to the formation of a genuine culture, which is not an 'amalgam' of paternal cultures, but rather the product of the union of cultural difference. And in the formation of individual personality, the evolution is determined by the dialectic of the articulations of the Law and transgression."

This is why it is important to determine the origin of the primordial violence that energizes the culturally renewing symbolic combinations that are imagined in postmodernity. The irresolution of the Oedipus complex results in identities characterized by shading, vagueness, ubiquity, nomadism, and the instability and imprecision of temporal and spatial contours. Out of this could arise personal identities resistant to authoritarianism and dictatorship, identities that both sustain and are produced by the games of masks and transvestism associated with postmodernism.

In the case of Chile in particular, another article argues, the impulse for aggression against the father was initiated by a process of "reverse and sideways" *mestizaje*.[4] The destructive meaning of the colonial war between the Spanish and the Mapuches was displaced onto the sexual domination of the opponent, be it actual or figural, homosexual or heterosexual: "Let us make [this meaning] explicit in a single word: dishonor, which comes out of the homosexuality implicit in said relation. . . . [T]he taking of another's woman, even if she is his daughter or sister, is a way of reducing him, of

---

4. The quotations that follow are from Rolf Foerster G., " 'Terror y temblor' frente al Indio-Roto," *Revista de Crítica Cultural*, no. 3, year 2 (1991): 39–44.

stripping him, of humiliating him. . . . To make love with another's woman is equivalent to making a woman out of him, to killing him in a symbolic way."

But the domination of female bodies as the annihilation of the (male) other occurred as an asymmetrical relationship between the two factions. While for the Spanish, the captive Indians were only concubines and their children were looked down upon, the Spanish women captured by the Mapuches were considered legitimate wives, and their children were respected and loved enough to arrive at the rank of chief. For the Spaniard, this ethnic absorption implied an even more insidious defeat than the military one: "the Spanish confront a monster capable of digesting, interrogating and consuming them. The very existence of these processes, their feasibility, turns the Mapuches into a phantom, a subject worthy of terror. The normal thing for the Spanish is the reverse attitude to the other: if he cannot be negated (reduced), then he should be annihilated, expelled or vomited. This makes it so that the Mapuche appears with greater force, as a potential of monstrosity."

This cannibalistic and/or homosexual threat against the European is universalized in forms of Latin American popular culture, such as carnival. In such manifestations, the circulating European symbolic capital is "spontaneously" recycled in "strategies of cannibalism and carnivalization,"[5] which parody the imported icons in order to transform their meaning, removing them from their consumerist instrumentality and using them for a cultural reaffirmation. In the carnival of 1987 in Rio, a samba school presented a skit entitled Tupinicópolis: "Its theme was the Tupi Indians, the happy inhabitants of an unrestrained city, who, in the middle of neon and strobe lights, ride their supersonic Japanese motorcycles and listen to rock, wearing the 'Tupi look': brightly colored pumps, phosphorescent feathers and blenders as hats." This suggests that even at the popular levels, there is a consciousness that Latin American cultural identity is tied to pastiche, kitsch, and transvestism. "[T]he culture of Latin America, like the majority of the post-colonial or third-world cultures, was in some sense postmodern before the post-industrialized centers, pre-postmodern . . . or 'retro-futurist,' so to speak."

Moreover, this nomadic cannibalism has infiltrated the very center of the empire with the massive Latin American migration to the United States

5. These, and the quotations that follow, are from Celeste Olalquiaga, "Tupinicópolis o la ciudad de los Indios retrofuturistas," *Revista de Crítica Cultural*, no. 3, year 2 (1991): 9–14.

in recent years, where, in accordance with its "anti-Oedipal" nature, it has begun to introduce elements of its language, music, food, and iconography into the dominant social and cultural codes. This absorption, in turn, has been a factor in the production of postmodernity in the United States, contributing, in particular, to the obsolescence of the ideology of the melting pot, with which the hegemonic North American culture rationalized the selective integration of the successive waves of immigration. This ideology concealed the real existence of an exclusionary distinction between the American and the ethnic, based on the articulation of the exotic as the characteristic that isolated the new communities from the mainstream. The Hispanic presence in the United States lends itself, instead, "to more dynamic reformulations of the intricate cohabitation of cultures." Now, one would have to speak of a "'mosaic,' a place in which the elements meet not in order to be dissolved and fused but rather to construct a panorama together."

In tandem with this line of argument, the tourist, industrial, and brothel cultures of Tijuana, the border city between Mexico and the United States, appear in the *Revista* with all the enthusiasm and fascination of an anthropologist who has discovered a new topic of investigation, as the monumental epitome of symbolic Latin American deterritorialization.[6] It is a space in which identity is a symbolic short circuit that can only be defined as "post-Mexican, pre-Chicano, pan-Latin, trans-national, artist-American . . . it depends on the day of the week or the project in question"; a space in which the grotesque of donkeys painted as zebras serves as a consciously theatrical and fraudulent prop, because "faced with the lack of other kinds of things, unlike in the south where there are pyramids, here there is nothing like that . . . [it is] as if something has to be invented for the *gringos*," because of "this myth that the North Americans bring, which has to do with crossing the border towards the past, the savage, and the spirit of can-do."

Postleftism and Cultural Vanguardism

"I would say that subversion . . . understood as a modification of cultural content, is a law intrinsic in any process of the transference, translation and retranslation of a discourse. It is not a question, then, of a deliberate action, except perhaps in the case of certain artistic vanguards of this cen-

6. The quotations that follow are from interviews in Néstor García Canclini, "Escenas sin territorio: Estética de las migraciones e identidades en transición," *Revista de Crítica Cultural*, no. 1, year 1 (1990): 9–12.

tury that explicitly posit the problem and make of it the source of their work of experimentation and production."[7] For the intellectuals grouped around the *Revista de Crítica Cultural*, the moment of consciousness of the necessity of assuming the position of an artistic vanguard occurred in the period following the military coup of 11 September 1973. This is also the moment in which they sought their differentiation from the Chilean partisan Left. After the coup, the parties of the Left continued the prevailing political discourse that valued their identity as "vanguards of the people." In defeat, they acted to safeguard the personal security of their members and leaders, to rebuild their cadres in secrecy, to promote the public continuity of a truncated political memory, to maintain the force of their symbols, to open safe spaces for meeting, reflection, and study, to organize mass opposition to the dictatorship, and, on the part of some sectors, to begin, toward the end of the seventies, to prepare the conditions for a national insurrection and armed struggle. In pursuit of these ends, they generated an art of direct political commitment, which sought the figurative reconstruction of a national-popular subject and the highly emotional expression of its daily struggles through testimonial literature and protest art. By contrast, the postmodernist neo–avant-garde that would come to be represented by the *Revista* distanced itself from direct political activity and, retreating to the "margins," sought to intensify the break with the past, to accept and refunction the psychosocial fragmentation and trauma instituted and administered by the repression in order to systematically reveal and deconstruct the symbolic codes that supported it.

In retrospect, this move implied that, from its field of specific activity, a group of independent intellectuals sought to make a complementary, or even more radical, subversion of the dictatorship than that of the traditional parties of the Left. The parties posited the immediate tasks of reorganization and mobilization of the base; the artistic neo–avant-garde, by agitating in Chile the problematic of postmodernity, posited the long-term dismantling of the dominant symbolic codes in Chilean political culture. The neo–avant-garde, however, characteristically refused this possibility of complementarity of projects and, instead, attacked the partisan Left in order to build up its own identity. As Nelly Richard put it:

> There was a certain arrogance in speaking about postmodernism because of the way the postmodernist discourse attacks the Latin American generation which heroically subscribed to the third-world

7. Pérez, "La no-identidad Latinoamericana," 31.

faith in revolution and the new man: postmodernism as a *theory of excess and the aesthetic of indifference*, the hyper-mediated product of the super-exposition and explosion of the self-fulfilling images of the market, violated two morals: that of poverty and that of social and political commitment, which served as vindicating images to the Latin American conscience of the sixties. This utopian-revolutionary intellectuality resents as ridicule the postmodern irony that plays at discrediting the ethical backing of its militant discursivity.[8]

The recent history of relations between artists and leftist vanguard parties in Chile has been marked in general by complementarity and contradiction. Complementarity, in the relation between the parties and the individual artist, which provided the latter with a social legitimization that related his or her work to the struggle for the emancipation of the people, and in the use the party could make of the image of the artist as yet another icon of its capacity to assemble and mobilize the material and spiritual forces of the nation. The vanguard parties are human conglomerations of varied social origin and cultural competence. Their political line is the result of a calculation for the cohesion of tendencies that incorporate the aspirations of socially subordinated classes, sometimes intensely archaic in their use of symbols and values, as well as those of intellectuals and artists of great innovative capacity. In the years after Stalinism, the Chilean leftist parties all accepted and cultivated freedom of expression in artistic and cultural matters; but in some intellectual sectors of the Left, the idea that revolutionary political vanguardism should correspond to an integral vanguardism in cultural and artistic codes became prominent. Such a position, which makes modernism in effect *the* "politically correct" cultural form of the Left, has the disadvantage of depreciating the traditionalist expressivity of non-intellectual partisan sectors whose commitment and personal performance is, on other grounds, irreproachable. If this was a contradiction in the relation between artists and parties prior to 1973, however, it is simply elided in the practice of the *Revista*, which takes place behind the back, so to speak, of the parties as such. Overestimating the effectivity of the tools of their cultural practice, at an extreme the artists claim to be more effective revolutionaries than those who act in party structures, imputing to the vanguard parties a continued hegemony of the symbolic codes of bourgeois repression. But to discredit popular expression in any of its forms is

8. Nelly Richard, "Latinoamérica y la postmodernidad," *Revista de Crítica Cultural*, no. 3, year 2 (1991), 16.

unacceptable for parties that make the subaltern classes the paradigmatic subject of social transformation. For this reason, the contradiction between political and artistic vanguards continues to be latent, even though the party bureaucracies have tended to ignore it and leave it unresolved, reaffirming, nevertheless, the freedom of artistic expression, while the avant-gardist intellectuals have abstained from direct partisan militancy.

Although this virtual polemic was never openly manifested, it intensified during the dictatorship. In secrecy, the leadership of the vanguard parties made demands of militant discipline that required the sacrifice of personal emotional and intellectual concerns for the sake of feverish activism. The existentially precarious situation of the militants was aggravated by living a strange duality: in a normal routine in order to camouflage their subversive activities, while at the same time as militants subject to the reality of brutal repression, fear, physical exhaustion, tension, and the neglect of health. In these conditions, the frustration of many militants was translated into a loss of confidence in the ability of the party leaders to arrive at a minimal general consensus that would posit an economic and political alternative to the dictatorship.[9] Faced with the considerable effectiveness of the military repression and the persistence through the years of the political animosities that had led to the crisis of 1973 (and in the 1980s with the unraveling of the Communist bloc itself), the party directives to the bases would appear to correspond to an already expired language, totally devoid of the ability of understanding the real. With all of this, in the eyes of many intellectuals, the leftist parties, in general, took on the aspect of cold and impersonal machines, disposed to the unnecessary sacrifice of a great number of militants for "reasons of state," particularly those parties that were preparing for the armed struggle.

This situation explains affirmations of the *Revista* group, such as the following: "Against the heroic finalism of this capital M Meaning (be it Revolution or Dictatorship), [our] practices constructed a *counter-epic* of disarmament and the precariousness of signs. They broke the doctrinaire verticality of self-enclosed meaning (ideology) through a horizontal poetics of the suspensive and the discordant: all which ridiculed the belief in a finite reality or in an ultimate signified, and exploded the totalism of univocal meanings."[10] As opposed to the sacrifices demanded by party leaderships,

9. See the testimonial by Maggy LeSaux, "Aspectos de la militancia de izquierda en Chile desde 1973," *SUR* (Santiago, Chile), 49 (1985).
10. Nelly Richard, "En torno a las diferencias" (unpublished manuscript), 2.

the neo–avant-garde preferred to view the great popular mobilizations of the national protests initiated in 1983 as spontaneous and independent manifestations.

This antipartyism also follows, in a sense, from two aspects of the group's psychotherapeutic version of cultural vanguardism we considered earlier: the necessity of destroying the exotic stereotypes (such as "the revolutionary") with which European discourse has subjugated the Latin American; and the rejection of the "paternal" Westernism that accompanies the aggression toward the half-brother, self-aggression, and self-denigration. These suppositions based on the existence of a Latin American collective unconsciousness are, undoubtedly, highly questionable in themselves. Nevertheless, I suspect that behind them is hidden the notion of a *necessary sacrifice* made possible as a result of the supposedly *unnecessary sacrifice* of the militancy imputed to the vanguard parties. There is, after all, a strong dose of human emotion and the consciousness of being intensely unjust to Marxist-Leninist militancy when Richard speaks (in the passage cited above) of "arrogance" and "aggression" against the "Latin American generation which heroically subscribed to the third-world faith in revolution and the new man." The reality is that in Chile, the disappeared, the assassinated, and the tortured were not, generally speaking, neo–avant-garde intellectuals, but ordinary militants. Nevertheless, in a political culture such as the Chilean, one traditionally channeled through parties or other organizations closely influenced by the parties, whose ideologism became inflexible in the periods previous to, and following, the military coup, the possibility of introducing an independent critical game implied the conscious assumption of the role of isolated pariah and traitor in the eyes of many militants, a Borgesian Judas disposed to accept ignominy and vituperation as necessary in order to personify one of the contradictory elements that energizes the dialectic of history. This posture displaces the identity of this neo–avant-garde from art toward religion, something particularly evident in the *Revista*'s valorization of the cabalistic and mystical Marxism of Walter Benjamin.

To refer to "borders," "limits," and the "margins" implies installing the imagination in that hypothetical place in which the conscious work of humanity materializes the difference between nature and the realm of culture. The margins are the territory of the taboo, of the prohibitions against incest, of the preference for cooked food, et cetera, which glorify the task of the construction of culture and prevent human regression to nature. The margins are also the territory of the sacrifices realized by human bodies in order to maintain and renew the empire of the constructed culture. For this reason, they are also the space of the sacred and of the rituals that celebrate the sacred as proof that the gods want culture to survive, the festivals celebrating the fruits of labor achieved with the exhaustion of human bodies. In the festivals of antiquity, accumulated wealth was squandered and hierarchical disciplines were momentarily suspended in order to reaffirm a feeling of community among equals, thus instantiating a possibility of communal religiosity that disappears with capitalism and the secular modern state.

The postmodernist opposition between the center and the margins has been based on arguments like these.[11] It reflects not only a will to sacrifice on the part of a national collectivity but also a nostalgia for a human community immediately prior to the modern state. It defines its own conception of the "good life" and the ethical and aesthetic ideal of the human being in conflict with an apparently external and distant bureaucracy that distorts and sacrifices actual forms of community on the altars of an abstract and impersonal "national" reason of state. In order to express this nostalgia, the neo–avant-garde finds itself forced to adopt a poetic and visionary posture that gives it license to escape not only history but also all the accumulation of explanatory discourses of historical teleology throughout the ages of humanity. From this posture, the apocalyptical end of modernity as a scientific-bureaucratic project is declared. The defeat of modernity signifies, in effect, the defeat of humanity. Therefore, humanity must now seek a new orientation guided only by desire. The bard or critic should replace the scientist as the leader of humanity:

> The time of ruins is expressed in the fragmentization of the real, and only the listener, the interpreter, can restore the meanings of these fragments, of these inert and isolated elements, deciphering the extreme and opposing ideas that take shelter there. In interpretation, the fragment is saved from its definitive nullity, the idea is trapped, and the verb is re-created. In the ruin, prehistory, catastrophe, and the secret are enclosed. The road to knowledge, then, is to contemplate from the vantage point of that which is exhausted or used up the reappearance of the signifieds that capture a time of culture.[12]

11. They have been spread in Chilean intellectual circles in particular through the work of Pedro Morandé, *Cultura y modernización en América Latina* (Santiago de Chile: Instituto de Sociología de la Pontificia Universidad Católica de Chile, 1984).
12. Nicolás Casullo, "Walter Benjamin y la modernidad," *Revista de Crítica Cultural*, no. 4, year 2 (1991): 35–40.

Let us wager that the disconnected word of art or literature in the rotation of codes continues to shake the programmatic rationality of science, politics, ideology. . . . Let us wager that the figurative density and impracticality of the aesthetic motif continues to scandalize, because of the utopian overflow of forms saturated with luxury and pleasure, the principle of the surrender in the instrumental languages translated by practical reason to a simple and resigned logic of efficacies.[13]

With this poetic license, an imaginary return can be projected to a prehistoric age in which human bodies are manifested as mere biological material, still derelict, still not signed by the symbolism of the discourses of bureaucratic power: "Archaic bodies which can only appear as nocturnal scenes of an epic and liberating dream, where the yearning for insurrection can pierce the other body, which although it lies nude is already irreversibly covered by the discourse which invested the first skin once and for all."[14] Such a voyage would permit one to observe and, therefore, demonstrate the forms in which human beings finally "fell" into the sexual and gender discriminations of the symbolic order. In the last instance, what is projected is the recuperation of the 'Natural Man', with this difference:

The ethical construction of the personality and convictions of this 'Natural Man' does not depend on a previous and now archaic communal morality but on a humanist posture of altruistic character. Recognition of the other, piety toward the other, the concession of reciprocity in dialogue, recognition of the desires, not of the rights, of the other, and friendship are the effect of individual affirmation, not of the renunciation of individual liberty in the name of an illusory 'common good'. The 'Natural Man' is not a kind of Hobbesian ideal-type prior to the signing of the social contract; nor that theoretical subject of Marxist-Christian-Anarchist ontology that will inherit the Earth after the final revolutionary judgment. It is rather a matter of dissident and communal groups that develop libertarian lifestyles *outside* the principle of the hierarchic sovereignty characteristic of the state.

13. Nelly Richard, "Estéticas de la oblicuidad," *Revista de Crítica Cultural*," no. 1, year 1 (1990): 8.
14. Diamela Eltit, "Las batallas del Coronel Robles," *Revista de Crítica Cultural*, no. 4, year 2 (1991): 19–21.

The proposal of the 'Natural Man' is then one of a *Society of Friends* where politics itself vanishes.[15]

With its repudiation of party politics, its enmity to all bureaucratic centralism, its rejection of all the epics of the conquest of state power, and its distrust of the discourses of the scientific totalization of the social process, the politics furnished by the postmodernist avant-garde is marked by the uncertainty of knowing that it must deploy itself in absolutely unknown territories and forms of activity, legitimated at most by the assumption of the good faith of the individuals involved. An inventory of the ideologemes of (post-)political action in the *Revista* shows that there are really only two: (1) gestic forms of theatricality, or postmodernist "performance"; (2) a micropolitics of the quotidian with which the defeated in Latin American history, throughout the centuries, have challenged power without openly confronting it.

The first is defined as a "posturing of the margin,"[16] which arises "from the borders of legitimized writings, from the consciousness of failure as a way of distancing oneself from that which history posits as victorious models, and from the ruins of a culture which has congested its past in the consideration of its present."[17] With this "posturing," new gestures which elasticize the [social] institution and make it more daring and creative can be attempted. Even here, however, guilt as self-aggression and self-denigration can intrude. There is a total lucidity on the part of the group that the "rhetorical alloys" and "new gestures" of postmodernism are nothing more than an imitation of the social destabilizations caused by the effects of transnational finance capital, installed under the auspices of state terror and neoliberal ideology in Chile. The resulting financial speculation has aggravated enormously the effects of dependency, producing a "crisis of development, frustration of expectations of social mobility, breaches of productivity, atomization through the demobilization of the masses, loss of collective referents, or the fading of the future."[18] Speculation creates

---

15. Cristián Ferrer, "De Prometeo a Proteo," *Revista de Crítica Cultural*, no. 4, year 2 (1991): 46–48.
16. Richard, "Estéticas de la oblicuidad," 8.
17. Casullo, "Walter Benjamin," 39.
18. This quotation and those that follow are from Martín Hopenhayn, "Ni apocalípticos ni integrados," *Revista de Crítica Cultural*, no. 4, year 2 (1991): 32–34.

illusions of wealth on paper and not in production, which spiritually and materially dignifies the human being through work:

> Every day millions of doors are opened and closed in order to leap into opulence and to fall into bankruptcy. The most profitable strategy is to be syntonic with this phenomenon. Precise and superficial information is worth more than steel. This is so not only in matters of economic investment: in an analogous sense the new synchronic reason permeates politics, aesthetics, and even human relations. It is the age of the primacy of the bonfire of the vanities over poetry, of the opportune alliance over the strategic proposal, of the gallery over the museum. Only the ephemeral transcends. In order to progress, it is better to erase the one's footprints without nostalgia, or with a light and cheerful nostalgia.

The *Revista* honestly confesses that to contemplate all this misery with a " 'cool,' refrigerated" posture is a kind of "shamelessness." But "who can now throw themselves resolutely behind manifestos of anti-colonial, anti-imperialist, anti-bourgeois action, knowing that these models of 'consequent struggle' prove to be hardly more than cinematographic?" "What model of action do we appropriate, then, if we want to preserve the idea in which there is something in action which goes beyond its immanence and contingency?"

These doubts finally return to a postmodernist reaffirmation of a field of exploration exempt from ethical or utilitarian considerations: "Why not explore the gaps of politics, in esotericism and its proliferation of meanings, in symbolic action, in popular culture, in suggestive intuitions, in spasmodic revolt, in the economies of the displaced, in the hermeticism of vernacular and postmodern tribes, in the reasons of passion, in conversation?" In any case, any possibility of consolation is presided over by the guilt of knowing oneself to be impotently and irremediably placed between the irresponsibility of intellectual indifference and the unredeemed hell of the great dispossessed human masses:

> Urban marginality, rural deterioration, the regressive distribution of income, sustained [economic] informality, are categories which are in no way anachronistic, and which cohabit, without being diluted, with those of "stochastic complexity," "comparative advantages," virtuous and perverted discontinuities. Those ominous realities which gave force to the discourse of apocalypse are more important than

ever, paradoxically at a moment when the discourse which invokes them sounds out of date. . . . [O]ne thing seems irrefutable and symptomatic: while confusion is assumed with an increasingly cool indifference by the elites, the temperature of misery of the masses is rising.

The second strategy of micropolitics suggested by the posture of the *Revista* requires that the defeated dilute their presence in the everyday world and disguise themselves with the discourse of the conquerors in order to mock them at a distance so that no punishment can reach them. One variant of this is expressed in a now familiar reappraisal of the Latin American colonial baroque: The Indians who built the baroque churches disguised themselves in their sacred images, at the same time introjecting domination and ridiculing it. Already "excessive" in its metropolitan incarnation, the colonial baroque becomes the field of an unrestrained liberation of the imagination. The relation between baroque and defeat leads to imputing a neobaroquism to contemporary poetic texts in which there is allegedly a similar process of masquerade and dilution: "The city appears in this text as an allegory of a desire that is never fulfilled, submerged in continuous masks and displacements." [19] The everyday is changed into a symbolic field that materializes the attitudes of cool indifference: "The domestic icons only represent themselves. They are silent and indifferent and their twinklings of meaning are opaque (like a car's headlights on a foggy day)." [20] From this arises the neobaroque "hero," who coincides with the ideal personality of this neo–avant-garde: "Inserted in a system he hates, he extracts his fertility from the nutritious material of offers, and this bipolarity, this violence of finding himself negotiated by another who is none other than himself, is what gives him a coded character, ciphered in hieroglyphics, very different from the hero of epic and tragedy, and even more of the modern novel." [21]

The everyday becomes a "jungle of signs" extraordinarily overloaded with meanings, but these, paradoxically, may go undetected. This suggests yet another possibility of defeat for the neo–avant-garde, which quietly situates its products in the midst of "the obvious," "the same," aspiring to transform the mentality of the passerby with subversive practices that "are

19. Eugenia Brito, "La cita neobarroca: el crímen y el arte," *Revista de Crítica Cultural*, no. 1, year 1 (1990): 29–31.
20. Carlos Altamirano, on the cover of *Revista de Crítica Cultural*, no. 4, year 2 (1991).
21. Brito, "La cita neobarroca," 30.

irrecuperable by the logic of the market of cultural goods or the dominant sensibility: art-gesture, 'installations,' or 'happenings' in the daily skin and bone of cities. Fragments of a cryptic aesthetic, which almost tribally decides its own codes for interpreting itself, making itself indigestible for those who are not part of the tribe."[22] The danger of incomprehensible hermeticism, however, produces a compensatory intensification of the neo–avantgarde penchant for religiosity, now installed in the possibility of new forms of public perception (again, in this sense of the mystical and redemptive forces lodged in the everydayness of contemporary capitalism, Benjamin is a key point of reference).

Although it may be recognized that these objects of art are the product of "a not at all divine intelligence,"[23] to observe them in daily life requires that the interpreter create "a very special gaze," which lends these objects a feminine identification (because like women, they are "themselves mystic books") and leads to the supposition that "if the sacred texts have been dictated by the infinite intelligence of God, nothing in them can or should be attributed to chance: all that which is not understood is a riddle, which human patience and intelligence can, in the end, solve." This analogy, no matter how much it is meant only as an approximate notion, gives the hermeneutic act an aura of cabalistic ritual. The interpreter—the Benjaminian *flaneur*—is tacitly elevated to the hierarchy of those who possess the keys to an occult truth. He or she reveals to common mortals the "opaque meaning" of reality, introducing it "into a zone of more hidden meaning." In this way, a kind of synthesis of the religious (redemptive), the political, and the aesthetic is sketched over the fissure that modernity (in the Weberian sense) introduces between these spheres.

Redemocratization and Trauma

The strategies suggested by the *Revista* are post-political in the sense that they fuse the political and the aesthetic to the extreme that the latter completely replaces the former in its traditional sense—that is, as some form of organized pressure in the face of institutionalized hegemonic power according to a clearly defined agenda. The apparent novelty of this posture is diluted, however, when we consider that the neo–avantgarde constructs its identity along lines that are familiar from the abundant

22. Hopenhayn, "Ni apocalípticos," 34.
23. This quotation and those that follow are from Adriana Valdés, "Las licencias del entremedio," *Revista de Crítica Cultural*, no. 4, year 2 (1991): 41–45.

European and North American sociological literature about the so-called new social movements.[24] The similarities with the project of the *Revista* are obvious (to the extent that one could think of the *Revista* itself as a sort of new social movement): The new social movements are forms of radicalism of the middle sectors, whose aspirations are not stable in the long term, which do not have nation-states as a necessary referent, and which cannot be processed or "represented" by political organizations of a bureaucratic character, such as political parties, unions, or guilds. They agitate for a direct political participation of the social base, around very limited objectives related to the defense of human rights, the quality of life and the environment, and to the redefinition of sexual and gender identities. They prefer to fight within the framework of the state and the capitalist market, without aspiring to global and drastic reforms, communicating with similar groups through networks of unstable existence. The *Revista* affirms that "one does not aspire to overthrow the structures of the system, but rather to establish relative autonomies within them. The revolutionary ceases to be thought of as great changes in time in order to be recognized as small and significant changes in space."[25]

It is this same logic that leads the new social movements to move their demands to a more expressionistic level. They question and reinterpret the prevailing cultural models, the social norms and codes that establish the criteria of "normality" and "abnormality," "inclusion" and "exclusion." They create new symbolic meanings, challenging the delimitations of political action between the public and the private and fighting for the construction of autonomous sectoral spaces and identities in which sexual and cultural heterogeneities can be recognized, verbalized, and expressed. For this reason, they seek a strong sense of style and ritual expression.

If the political novelty of the *Revista* lies in the frank and open way in which it proposes a practice of new social movements in Chile, perhaps the fundamental unknown of its own activity, however, is related to its ambition to attain some degree of mass credibility for what is almost, by definition, an elitist or minority project. The roots of this ambition lie in the kind of political theatricality that has accompanied the democratic transition in Chile.

Since its installation in 1991, the government of the Reconciliation of

---

24. For a global vision, see, for example, *Social Research* 52, no. 4 (Winter 1985); *Teoría de los movimientos sociales*, ed. Jean L. Cohen (San José, Costa Rica: FLACSO, 1988); and Ron Eyerman and Andrew Jamison, *Social Movements: A Cognitive Approach* (University Park, Pa.: The Pennsylvania State University Press, 1991).
25. Hopenhayn, "Ni apocalípticos," 34.

Parties for Democracy, composed of the Christian Democrats and the so-called Renewed Socialists, has had to confront a triple dilemma in the process of reactivating democratic participation and representation: Coming from the social base, there is the urgent demand for a quick end to the high levels of unemployment and government disinvestment in social services and for an improvement of the impoverished conditions of life that befell at least one-third of the national population as a result of the neoliberal economic model imposed by the dictatorship; faced with the lack of an alternative, there is the economic imperative to continue with the neoliberal model, in spite of the fact that it reinforces social marginalization; coming from the military estates, there is the threat of new interventions if their immunity from prosecution for violations of human rights, their autonomy in the administration of their internal affairs, and the continuity of their constitutional power of political veto are not preserved. Confronted with these contradictions, the government has resorted to formulas already used by Christian Democracy before Allende, seeking the political deactivization of the social base by increasing social investment distributed according to patronage, at the same time that it projects the image of an extensive social and ideological pluralism and the democratic participation of all public sectors. This image has been constructed in part by the recruitment of intellectuals coming from different sectors active in the opposition to the dictatorship. Although these intellectuals may, in fact, be disconnected from, and unrepresentative of, the social base, the media can project them as proof of a politics of national integration and of a genuine debate and national consultation. In this context of pseudorepresentativity and consensus modulated by an apparatus of public relations, a publication such as the *Revista de Crítica Cultural* can take on a transcendence much greater than the small number of intellectuals involved in it would suggest.

The current political conjuncture in Chile is, in fact, highly favorable to the group and its strategy of deconstructive mimicry. As noted, however, in an arena of manipulated consensuses, this strategy runs the risk of going undetected and of completely diluting the critical identity of the group, which needs, at all costs, to conserve an "avant-garde" aggressiveness. Because of this, the *Revista* has had to refine its postmodernist image, distancing itself not only from the parties of the traditional Left, now in the opposition, but also from the Renewed Socialists and other forces in the government. (As in the case of new social movement theory, the affinities of the *Revista* with Renewed Socialism seem apparent at one level: As a revisionist current of the Chilean Left in the post-Allende, post-coup period, Renewed

Socialism rejected all forms of Leninism, opting, instead, for a strategy of strengthening the autonomy of groups of communal promotion and expression and denouncing the supposed political instrumentalization of them by the Marxist parties.)

At another level, however, the group postulates what it calls a "double rejection": on the one hand, of a "militancy of an ideological compromise that univocally subordinates work to the defense of a content of struggle, denunciation or accusation"—that is, of the traditional Left; on the other, of "the narcissistic dominant of a certain postmodernism that renders tribute to the system and to its forces of neo-conservatism by means of *skeptical relativism* (everything seen as of equal value, without motivational priority or counter-hegemonic urgency, after the failure of the utopias and the crisis of their political projects), and *conformist pluralism* (the passivization of differences called upon to coexist neutrally under a regime of reconciliation that deactivates their confrontational energies)."[26]

With this denunciation of the consensus represented by the government, the group proclaims an independence from bureaucratic structures that leans to a quasi-anarchist belief in social change based on individuals who naturally tend to the good when they are not coopted by state structures. Voluntarily deprived of a global program for society, the *Revista* adopts a strictly situational and spontaneist sense of political action, which should be undertaken without preconceptions. In the last instance, the only permanent political anchoring of this project is to reiterate the will to deconstruct the discourse of power, of all power.

The resurgence of what is, in effect, an anarchist project, after the monopolization of the Left by Communist and Socialist parties since the 1920s, is in itself highly significant. I believe that the historical importance of the postmodernist avant-garde represented by the *Revista* is to be found elsewhere, however, in what I call its "testimonial" function of assuming consciously in its theory and practice the consequences of the political defeat of the Left starting in 1973. Perhaps the greatest triumph of the military dictatorship was psychological, in that it was able to induce in large sectors of the population, in the name of a "realism," "pragmatism," or political "renewal," the conviction that many of its objectives were their own, thus depoliticizing civil society, weakening the influence of the political parties and the workers' unions, stimulating drastic ideological modifications like those

26. Nelly Richard, "De la rebeldía anarquizante al desmontaje ideológico," *Revista de Crítica Cultural*, no. 2, year 1 (1990): 6–8.

represented by "renewed" socialism, and imposing a reality principle that would accept capitalist modernization, the dominance of market mechanisms, and the limitation of all political expectations. This transformation of the Chilean cultural and political imaginary depended on the inculcation via terror in the population of what social psychologists call a posttraumatic stress disorder.

Posttraumatic stress disorder arises with the exposure to catastrophic events (such as those of the war in Chile), which entail the risk of death, destruction, and chaos for oneself or for those whom we recognize as role models or authorities.[27] These events generate an enormous overload of emotional energy in the cultural models of the self and its surroundings as spaces for "normal" and "safe" human behavior. The cognitive elaboration of the traumatic events is inadequate to produce personal and collective well being (in a clear parallel with the postmodernist rejection of the great narratives of human redemption), and alternative modes of thinking through them are not readily available. There is the simultaneous necessity of constantly assuming and reliving the episodes of utmost vulnerability, defenselessness, and victimization in the personal and collective histories, with an intense sensation of guilt and isolation, in a perpetual present marked by great closeness, confusion, contradiction, and emotional disorder. All of this results in rigid behaviors that refuse to (or cannot) overcome the past. The anger generated by these episodes is directed in a diffused way against the self or against the closest significant others. These are distrusted, imputed with the responsibility for the trauma, at the same time that the real origin of the subjugating force that caused the trauma is obscured.

The overcoming of posttraumatic stress comes about with an eventual capacity to integrate the catastrophic events into a narration that totalizes and consolidates them in a stable place of memory. In this way, positive aspects of the traumatic past are recuperated, and the real circumstances and true responsibilities are delimited, restructuring a cognitive capacity that erases unnecessary feelings of guilt. With this is attained a healthy questioning and a revitalization of the values that give meaning, style, and direction to life. This permits the reconstruction of identity around a new model of personal and social reality, together with the reconnection to a feeling of community.

27. Charles R. Figley, ed., *Trauma and Its Wake: The Study and Treatment of Post-Traumatic Stress Disorder* (New York: Brunner/Mazel Publishers, 1985), vols. 1 and 2.

The coincidence of this with the *Revista*'s ontology of frustration and marginality, of desperation and mental and physical exhaustion, should be immediately obvious. The cultural psychoanalysis it proposes, and its promotion of a politics of new social movements, could be understood as a therapeutic practice. However, the vehemence of its attack against the political institutions of the traditional Left (which recalls the tendency in posttraumatic stress to direct aggression against those closest to one), its inability to present real alternatives, and its exclusive fixation on aesthetic questions as the anchoring of all possible political action reveal that the group has not completely overcome the structure of denial and the rigidities imposed during the traumatic period. This involves its inability to transgress a taboo imposed by the military repression itself against speaking about its goals and nature.

Even though the military authorities have themselves often stressed that their takeover of the state, their intervention in civil society, and their handling of national politics should be understood as a war to neutralize international communism in Chile and to strengthen bourgeois institutionality against its assault, for a variety of reasons, some having to do with the understandable need to find ideological anchoring points for a mass opposition to the dictatorship, the majority of the political parties, the human rights organizations, and the Catholic church have denied the existence of a state of war in Chile in the years between 1973 and 1990 in favor of the concept of an illegitimate regime that violated human rights. The triumphalism about redemocratization flagrantly contrasts with the *permanent* effects of the military strategy in Chile, which have not been essentially modified. In this context, with a meaning foreign to its will, the assumption of posttraumatic stress by the postmodernist avant-garde takes on the character of a neurotic displacement: its vision of the recent national culture obscures the real origin of the violence that caused the social trauma in Chile and blurs and disorients the energies generated in it.

This neurotic displacement takes on a masochistic character in the sense that the group voluntarily abandons the great narratives of human redemption in order to restrict itself to micropolitical action without definite direction. This abandonment means to consciously decline civil and political rights that the human species fought great struggles to attain. It is inevitable, on the other hand, that the hegemonic institutionalized power will continue to use these macrodiscourses for social administration. Considering the ways in which power was exercised during the dictatorship in

Chile, this abandonment also implies a retreat caused by terror: a desire to ignore the reality of the violence in order to make peace with the power that inflicted it.

Even more, the fear hidden behind this attitude causes one to forget that the movement in defense of human rights in Chile was perhaps the most effective force in limiting state terror and in regrouping political heterogeneities into an opposition. It was this regrouping that created, in the long run, the conditions for the transition to democracy. Under the protection of the Catholic church, a bureaucratic institution such as the Vicarate of Solidarity made it possible for people from all ideological and political currents existing in Chile to unite around the fundamental goal of restoring a state of law that would protect the dignity of the human being. As a consequence of this common task, the rigidities that had been caused by the collapse of democracy in Chile were loosened. This bureaucracy of lawyers, social workers, and activists found support in international law, formulated and supervised by the United Nations, the principal institution guaranteeing the universal respect of human rights. In addition, there were the activities of many nongovernmental organizations, both national and international, concerned with the violation of human rights in Chile. These activities confirm the continued existence of a master narrative of human redemption that has not been exhausted and that is useful for the mobilization of a religious and secular faith that can transcend immediate ideological and political loyalties. Nevertheless, in the material published up to now by the *Revista de Crítica Cultural*, there are no references to the movement in defense of human rights in Chile. Instead, in the denunciation of all narratives of human redemption, there is a joy and ecstasy in romantic disillusion and in the theatrical gesture that this generates.

But I do not need to reiterate my discrepancy with the arguments of postmodernity. As I noted at the start, my study of the *Revista de Crítica Cultural* was intended, rather, to contribute to the critical understanding of one of the forms with which Chilean intellectuals assumed the pŏst-1973 trauma. It seems to me that this is more important than my discrepancy with their arguments. On the other hand, in relation to the present state of Latin American literary and cultural criticism, my study calls attention to the necessity of abandoning the macrotheoretical platforms on which it has been developing. This criticism finds itself in a crucial moment of its history: The tradition of canonizing and privileging certain texts of official high culture as fundamental instruments in the creation of national identities has no meaning before the effects of a transnational culture industry. Faced with this, the only road for a renewal is for criticism to constitute and to recognize itself as a criticism of culture—that is, as a Latin American cultural studies. This implies the elaboration of much more extensive problematics about symbolic production in general within a society. In turn, this requires the adoption of a decidedly anthropological and sociological perspective, which, in my opinion, should privilege the study of specific microexperiences above the grand macrotheoretical flight.

Reply to Vidal (from Chile)

Nelly Richard

I share Hernán Vidal's concern in his article for this collection with privileging concrete "microexperiences"[1] over theoretical abstractions. This seems to me a salutary way of reorienting Latin American academic criticism to deal with questions of immediate context, knowledge-in-use, local refunctionings, and differentiated modes of reception elicited by the dynamics of individual cultural settings. I believe, however, that his account of the *Revista de Crítica Cultural*, the journal for which I am responsible in Chile, betrays this concern: the microexperience the *Revista* is said to represent by him is captured by a hermeneutic macrodeterminism that subordinates texts that have appeared in it to the rigid armature of *programs*, instead of situating them in an open-ended play of critical discursivity.

Vidal's attempt to compose the conceptual logic of these texts by appropriating what he considers an eminently "postmodernist" device—the collage of transcribed passages he offers—contradicts what are usually understood as the principles of collage aesthetics (heterogeneity of tex-

1. Words or phrases in quotation marks here are cited from Vidal's article; those in italics are mine.

tures, dissimilarity of shapes and surfaces, etc.). His procedure erases obsessively from the scene of writing of the *Revista* everything that breaks, splits, or branches off: dead ends, provisional crossings, discordant trajectories, hybrid methodologies, and so on. A reading not so bound up with the self-ratification of its own presuppositions would have explored the *coming and going* of these texts, instead of congealing their movement into what is, in effect, a conceptual still life.

Vidal does seem to hesitate between two different ways of conceptualizing the relation of the *Revista* to what he calls the "ideological profile" of postmodernism. On the one hand, the practice of the journal, as a microexperience, enacts a peripheral postmodernity specific to Chile and its historical-political experience in the last twenty-five years, a postmodernity that then coexists with, but is not reducible to, metropolitan postmodernism; on the other, it seems yet another case of the importation of "intellectual fashions" billed as novelties in the periphery just as they are becoming obsolete in the metropolis.

I don't think, in any case, that postmodernism has a single face. The term associates—diffusely and confusedly—a series of discourses (and position-takings) that are not commensurate, that respond each in its own way to the symptomatology of the crisis. When one gets beyond the facile equation of postmodernism and market neoliberalism, it becomes readily apparent that some postmodernist texts activate (new) energies of resistance and critical opposition, while others deactivate them. Postmodernism lends itself to a multiplicity of significations, whose critical force depends on what, concretely, their theoretical-cultural articulations liberate or block. It seems to me all to the good that this evasive and polymorphous character of postmodernism escapes the ideological purism of wanting to continue controlling discursivity by imposing on it straight lines, homogenous blocks, smooth breaks, and uniform rationales.

None of the texts published in the *Revista*, moreover, claims postmodernism as a reference guide that one has to subscribe to or transcribe imitatively. Postmodernism signifies for us, instead, a *horizon of problems* in relation to which we can discuss local significations that are (unevenly) affected by the political, social, and cultural mutations of the contemporary world: for example, the transnationalization of capital and the globalization of information, the supersaturation of images and the hypermediatization of the real, the fragmentation of subjectivity and the pluralization of social identity, and the dissemination of power and the transversal character of lines of antagonism. The uses of the postmodernist register for critical debate in

Latin America lie, above all, in the appropriation-reconversion of certain figures (fragmentation, hybridism, de-centering, etc.) that are singled out for the concrete ways in which they bear on *local* problematics of our histories and societies: the role of racial-cultural *mestizaje* and other forms of transculturation in the formation of Latin America, the articulation of the center-periphery axis of colonial and neocolonial dependency in terms of model and copy, the multitemporal sedimentation of our peripheral modernity, the pluralism of difference as an expression of social heterogeneity in the context of processes of redemocratization, and so on. These Latin American problematics can be *reaccentuated* critically by certain of the new theoretical inflections of postmodernism, without this implying that Latin America *is* postmodernist—in the sense of copying or fitting exactly with what is understood as the international model of postmodernism.

The *Revista*, in other words, does not conceive of itself as part of a postmodernist International. Although it takes up a metropolitan knowledge-game in which the crisis of the center compels it to *re-center* its attention on its borders and periphery, it does so *from* the margins, borders, limits, periphery, interstices, in-between—*actual* liminal site-postures from which it can dialogue critically, in a process of both exchange and confrontation, with the *postmodernisms* and their metropolitan theorization as postmodern center-marginality.

The most highly charged aspect of Vidal's critique is undoubtedly its concern with the journal's relation to the political situation of Chile in the postcoup period. The loss of faith in the credo of radical militancy and the historical breakup of the revolutionary utopia define a trauma of absence and belonging that, in Vidal's own case, is sharpened by his exile in a North American university, a situation from which he has sought to maintain an organic contact with developments in Chile, even as it has prevented him from sharing the experience of the dictatorship on a daily and immediate basis. I find it impossible to read the extreme conflictivity of points of view that marks his essay without taking into account these fissures in his own personal history. I think, in particular, that he projects onto the *Revista* his own traumatic phantasmagoria of loss and suffering, his own obsession with *stigma*.

Vidal situates the project of the *Revista* in the crucible of the polarities and antagonisms that have traditionally divided the Left (for example, organized militancy and party coordination versus anarchism and avant-garde spontaneism). He wants to dramatize in this way the distinction between a "political-cultural front" and an "aesthetic neo–avant-garde" as it pertains

to questions of collective will and popular representativity in majority culture. It is true that the *Revista* does not have a "clearly defined agenda"
or global social "program" that it can oppose to the hegemony. In the absence of such enunciations, which would claim to speak for society as a
whole, we have consciously focused our project instead on the implementation of "limited objectives" in a highly differentiated and specific field: that
of Latin American cultural theory and criticism, in a situation in which this
field lacks notably the academic and editorial spaces and resources that
Vidal can rely on in his own work. In this sense, the *Revista* takes seriously
a function that Vidal seems to consider excessively modest on our part:
that of being an agent of the dynamic reactivation of cultural discussion and
critique. Modestly, the *Revista* directs itself primarily and specifically to the
cultural sphere, with its highly particular networks of discourses, practices,
and institutions. Its collaborators can express solidarity with human rights
issues and work on their behalf without necessarily obliging the journal to
become the bearer of "great narratives of human redemption"—especially
when these discourses (of totality, or of the Revolutionary Proletariat) are
themselves implicated in the repression of the critical potential of *localized
interventions* that no longer claim to speak for society as a whole or for the
general will, because they distrust ideological totalizations.

Declaration from the Lacandon Jungle

Zapatista National Liberation Army

TODAY WE SAY ENOUGH IS ENOUGH!
TO THE PEOPLE OF MEXICO:
MEXICAN BROTHERS AND SISTERS:

We are a product of 500 years of struggle: first against slavery, then during the War of Independence against Spain, then to avoid being absorbed by North American imperialism, then to promulgate our constitution and expel the French empire from our soil; later the dictatorship of Porfirio Díaz denied us the just application of the Reform laws and the people rebelled and leaders like Villa and Zapata emerged, poor men just like us. We have been denied by our rulers the most elemental conditions of life, so they can use us as cannon fodder and pillage the wealth of our country. They don't care that we have nothing, absolutely nothing, not even a roof over our heads, no land, no work, no health care, no food or education. Nor are we able to freely and democratically elect our political representatives, nor is there independence from foreigners, nor is there peace or justice for ourselves and our children.

But today we say ENOUGH IS ENOUGH. We are the inheritors of the true builders of our nation. The dispossessed, we are millions and we thereby call upon our brothers and sisters to join this struggle as the only path, so that we will not die of hunger due to the insatiable ambition of a seventy-year dictatorship led by a clique of traitors who represent the most conservative and sell-out groups. They are the same ones who opposed Hidalgo and Morelos, the same ones who betrayed Vicente Guerrero, the same ones who sold half our country to the foreign invader, the same ones who imported a European prince to rule our country, the same ones who formed the "scientific" Porfirista dictatorship, the same ones who opposed the Petroleum Expropriation, the same ones who massacred the railroad workers in 1958 and the students in 1968, the same ones who today take everything from us, absolutely everything.

To prevent the continuation of this injustice and as our last hope, after having tried to utilize all legal means provided in our Constitution, we go to our Constitution, to apply Article 39 which says: "National Sovereignty essentially and originally resides in the people. All political power emanates from the people and its purpose is to help the people. The people have, at all times, the inalienable right to alter or modify their form of government."

Therefore, according to our Constitution, we make this declaration to the Mexican federal army, the pillar of the Mexican dictatorship that we suffer from, monopolized by a one-party system and led by Carlos Salinas de Gotari, the illegitimate chief executive who today holds power.

According to this Declaration of War, we ask that other powers of the nation advocate restoring the legitimacy and the stability of the nation by overthrowing the dictator.

We also ask that international organizations and the International Red Cross watch over and regulate our combat, so that our efforts are carried out while still protecting our civilian population. We declare now and always that we are subject to the Geneva Accords. Forming the EZLN as our fighting arm of our liberation struggle, we have the Mexican people on our side, we have the beloved tri-colored flag, which is highly respected by our insurgent fighters. We use black and red in our uniform as our symbol of our working people on strike. Our flag carries the letters "EZLN," Zapatista National Liberation Army, and we always carry it into combat.

We reject in advance any effort to discredit our just cause by accusing us of being drug traffickers, drug guerrillas, thieves, or other names that might be used by our enemies. Our struggle follows the Constitution, which we esteem for its call for justice and equality.

Therefore, according to this Declaration of War, we give our military forces, the EZLN, the following orders:

First: Advance to the capital of the country, overcoming the Mexican federal army, protecting in our advance the civilian population and permitting the people in the liberated area the right to freely and democratically elect their own administrative authorities.

Second: Respect the lives of our prisoners and turn over all wounded to the International Red Cross.

Third: Initiate summary judgments against all soldiers of the Mexican federal army and political police who have received training or have been paid by foreigners who are accused of being traitors to our country, and against all those who have repressed and treated badly the civilian population and robbed or stolen from or attempted crimes against the good of the people.

Fourth: Form new armed forces with all those Mexicans who show their interest in joining our struggle, including those who, being enemy soldiers, turn themselves in without having fought against us, and promise to take orders from the General Command of the Zapatista National Liberation Army.

Fifth: Ask in advance for the unconditional surrender of the enemy's headquarters before we begin combat to avoid any loss of lives.

Sixth: Suspend the theft of our natural resources in the areas controlled by the EZLN.

To the People of Mexico: We, men and women, autonomous and free, are conscious that the war we have declared is our last resort, but also a just one. The dictators have been applying an undeclared genocidal war against our people for many years. Therefore we ask for your participation, and your willingness to support this plan, which struggles for work, land, housing, food, health care, education, independence, freedom, democracy, justice, and peace. We declare that we will not stop fighting until the basic demands of our people have been met by forming a government of our country that is free and democratic.

JOIN THE INSURGENT FORCES OF THE ZAPATISTA NATIONAL LIBERATION ARMY.

General Command of the EZLN

Contributors

Xavier Albó (Spain, Bolivia) is a researcher and activist at the Center for the Investigation and Promotion of the Peasantry (CIPCA) in La Paz, Bolivia. He has published more than thirty books on questions of Andean languages, cultures, and societies, including *Comunidad hoy* (1990). He is a member of the Jesuit order.

Michael Aronna (USA) completed a Ph.D. in Hispanic languages and literatures at the University of Pittsburgh with a dissertation on "Pueblo Enfermo": The Medicalization of the Discourse of the National in Turn-of-the-Century Spanish and Latin American Essay." He currently works as a translator and part-time lecturer in Spanish and Latin American literature in the New York City area.

John Beverley (USA) is professor of Spanish and Latin American literature at the University of Pittsburgh and an advisory editor of *boundary 2*. His publications include *Del Lazarillo al Sandinismo* (1987); *Literature and Politics in the Central American Revolutions,* with Marc Zimmerman (1990); and *Against Literature* (1993).

José Joaquín Brunner (Chile) is a sociologist at the Latin American Faculty for Social Sciences (FLACSO) in Santiago de Chile; he was director there between 1980 and 1988. He has published extensively on educational and cultural policy, recently *Un espejo trizado: Modernidad y cultura en América Latina* (1991).

Fernando Calderón (Bolivia) was, until 1991, the director of the Latin American Council of the Social Sciences (CLACSO) in Buenos Aires and has taught at various universities in the United States. His *Socialismo, autoritarismo y democracia* appeared in 1989.

Enrique Dussell (Argentina, Mexico) is one of the major philosophers associated with liberation theology in Latin America. The essay included here is adapted from his book *1492: El encubrimiento del otro (Hacia el origen del mito de la modernidad)* (1993).

Néstor García Canclini (Argentina, Mexico) directs the Institute for Graduate Studies of the Mexican National Institute of Anthropology and History and teaches sociology of art and communication at the Metropolitan University of Mexico City, Iztapalapa. His books include *Las culturas populares en el capitalismo* (1982) and *Culturas híbridas: Estrategías para entrar y salir de la modernidad* (1990).

Martín Hopenhayn (Chile) is a researcher at the Latin American Faculty for Social Sciences, specializing in political issues. His publications include *Escritos sin futuro* (1990).

Neil Larsen (USA) teaches Latin American and comparative literature at Northeastern University in Boston. His publications include *Modernism and Hegemony* (1990). His contribution here is part of a collection of his essays, forthcoming from the University of Minnesota Press, *Reading North by South*.

The Latin American Subaltern Studies Group invites the participation of other scholars working along the lines indicated in its Founding Statement. The current members and associates are Robert Carr, Ileana Rodríguez, Patricia Seed, Javier Sanjinés, John Beverley, José Rabasa, María Milagros López, Michael Clark, Norma Alarcón, Clara Lomas, Julio Ramos, and Walter Mignolo.

Norbert Lechner (Chile) is the current director of FLACSO. He is the editor of the important collection *Estado y política en América Latina* (1981) and *Cultura política y democratización* (1988). His own books include *La conflictiva y nunca acabada construcción del orden deseado* (1984) and *Patios interiores de la democracia* (1988).

María Milagros López (Puerto Rico) has been an activist in the Puerto Rican women's and welfare rights movements, as well as teaching social psychology and cultural studies at the University of Puerto Rico. Her essay here is adapted from a longer piece that appeared in *Social Text* and that forms the basis of a book on postwork society forthcoming from the University of Minnesota Press.

Raquel Olea (Chile) directs the Centro de Analisis y Difusión de la Condición de la Mujer in Santiago de Chile. Her essay here was originally published in the Latin American feminist journal *Mujeres en Acción*.

José Oviedo (Dominican Republic) is completing a dissertation in sociology and cultural studies at the University of Pittsburgh on the relations between postmodernist theory and democracy. He has previously published *Democracia y proyecto social demócrata en República Dominicana* (1986).

Aníbal Quijano (Peru) teaches sociology at the University of San Marcos in Lima and at SUNY-Binghamton. A prolific writer, his work in the 1960s and 1970s, for example his *Nationalism and Capitalism in Peru,* translated by Monthly Review Press in 1971, was influential in the elaboration of dependency theory.

Nelly Richard (Chile) is the editor of the *Revista de Crítica Cultural* in Santiago de Chile and perhaps the best-known theorist of postmodernism in Latin America. She was closely involved with the activity of the Chilean artistic avant-garde in opposition to the Pinochet dictatorship. Her books include *Márgenes y instituciones* (1986); *La estratificación de los márgenes* (1989); and *Masculino/femenino: Prácticas de la diferencia y cultura democrática* (1993).

Carlos Rincón (Colombia) directs the Latin America Institute of the Free University of Berlin. His *El cambio actual de la noción de la literatura* (1978) was a major revision of Latin American literary criticism in the direction suggested by reception theory. In the 1980s, he served as advisor to the Nicaraguan Ministry of Culture, in which capacity he produced, with Dieter Eich, the testimonial collection *Contras* (1985).

Silviano Santiago (Brazil) is one of Brazil's best-known writers and literary critics. He teaches at the Universidade Fluminense in Rio de Janeiro. His books include the novel *Stella Manhattan* (1985; an English translation is forthcoming) and several collections of criticism: *Uma literatura nos trópicos* (1978) and *Nas malhas da letra* (1989).

Beatriz Sarlo (Argentina) is the editor of the journal *Punto de Vista* in Buenos Aires. She teaches literary criticism and sociology of culture at the University of Buenos Aires, with a special interest in the development of the media and forms of popular and mass culture in Latin America. Her books include a study of Argentine journalism, *El imperio de los sentimientos* (1985); *Una modernidad periférica: Buenos Aires 1920–1930* (1988); and a collection on *Women's Writing in Latin America* (1991).

Roberto Schwarz (Brazil) is professor of literary theory at the University of Campinas, São Paulo. One of the most distinguished literary critics associated with the Brazilian Left, his publications include *Ao Vencedor as Batatas* (1977), *O Pai de Familia* (1978), and *Que Horas Sao?* (1987). His contribution here is taken from an English-language anthology of his essays, *Misplaced Ideas,* published by Verso in 1992.

Hernán Vidal (Chile) teaches in the Department of Spanish and Portuguese at the University of Minnesota. He was, for many years, one of the editors of the journal *Ideologies and Literature* and the monograph series connected with it, and he currently directs the Prisma Institute project on Literature and Human Rights. His numerous publications include *Literatura hispanoamericana e ideología liberal: Una problemática en torno al Boom* (1976); *Dar la vida por la vida* (1982); *Cultura nacional chilena, crítica literaria y derechos humanos* (1989); and *Dictadura militar, trauma social e inauguración de la sociología del teatro en Chile* (1991).

The Zapatista National Liberation Army (EZLN) coordinated and led an armed uprising in the southern Mexican state of Chiapas in early 1994. It takes its name from Emiliano Zapata, the most radical of the agrarian leaders of the Mexican Revolution of 1910–17. Its demands include, besides regional issues, the implementation of electoral reform in Mexico and opposition to the NAFTA.

Index

Permissions

Earlier versions of Neil Larsen's chapter were previously published in *Postmodern Culture* 1, 1 (1990) and *Nuevo Texto Crítico* 6 (1990). The version here will appear in a collection of Larsen's articles forthcoming from the University of Minnesota Press, and is included by permission of the press and the author.

Raquel Olea's chapter was previously published as "El Feminismo: ¿Moderno o Posmoderno?" in *Mujeres en Acción* (Winter 1991), and is included by permission.

Roberto Schwarz's chapter was previously published as "Brazilian Culture: Nationalism by Elimination," in his *Misplaced Ideas: Essays on Brazilian Culture,* ed. John Gledson (London: Verso/New Left Books, 1992), and is included by permission of Verso/New Left Books Ltd.

Library of Congress Cataloging-in-Publication Data
The postmodernism debate in Latin America / edited by John Beverley, José Oviedo, and Michael Aronna.
"A Boundary 2 book."
"The text of this book was originally published as volume 20, number 3 of
Boundary 2: an international journal of literature and culture, with the exception
of the following additional articles: Neil Larsen, Postmodernism and imperialism;
María Milagros López, Postwork society and postmodernism; Raquel Olea,
Feminism: modern or postmodern?; and Roberto Schwarz, National by elimination.
The declaration from the Lacandon Jungle by the Zapatista National Liberation Army
has also been added"—T.p. verso.
Includes bibliographical references and index.
ISBN 0-8223-1586-6. — ISBN 0-8223-1614-5 (pbk.)
1. Latin America—Civilization—20th century—Philosophy.2. Social sciences—
Latin America—Philosophy.3. Postmodernism—Latin America.I. Beverley, John.
II. Aronna, Michael.III. Oviedo, José.
F1414.2.P67   1995
980.03'3—dc20   94-23975 CIP